STORMING THE HEAVENS

Peasants and Revolution in China, 1925–1949
viewed through a Marxist lens

JENNY CLEGG

'Storming the Heavens
Peasants and Revolution in China, 1925–1949
viewed through a Marxist lens'
Jenny Clegg

First Published in 2025 by Manifesto Press

© Jenny Clegg

All rights reserved

MANIFESTO PRESS CO-OPERATIVE

Manifesto Press
Ruskin House
23 Coombe Road
Croydon CR0 1BD

TYPESET IN *DEGULAR* AND *BASKERVILLE*

DESIGNED BY **CORATA GROUP**

ISBN 978-1-907464-82-9

The moral rights of the author have been asserted

All rights reserved. Apart from fair dealing, e.g. for the purpose of private study or research, no part of the publication may be reproduced or transmitted, in any form or by any means, electronic, photocopying, recording or otherwise, without the prior permission of the owner.

studio@manifestopress.coop

manifestopress.coop

S*torming the Heavens* is a major accomplishment. It combines detailed historical analysis of China's agrarian social relations, prior to 1949 and beyond, with a keen sense of theory, integrating Western and Chinese sources, Marxist and non-Marxist alike, into a vibrant picture of struggle and transformation. The CPC's programs and practices are given detailed, and often admiring, attention, while still being carefully dissected with an eye to errors, misjudgments and shortcomings. The complexities of national versus agrarian movements, relations between poor and middle peasants, navigation of stages in social and political development, differences in class structure between north and south, and much more – all of this unfolds in a story that is both remarkably specific and deeply universal in its implications. All in all, a fine addition to our knowledge of modern China.

David Laibman, *Professor Emeritus, Economics, City University of New York; Editor Emeritus, Science & Society*

This monograph is a systematic study by a British Marxist economist of the situation in rural China during the Republican period. It presents an insightful analysis of the new democratic revolution in the countryside of China centred on the agrarian revolution led by Mao Zedong. This book is very important for any Chinese scholar who wishes to learn about the perspectives of research from experts outside China. It is extremely useful in all capitalist countries, especially those in the South, for understanding how to develop the countryside and truly safeguard the interests of the peasants through reforms, as well as for understanding the theories of Marxism-Leninism and its sinicization.

Cheng Enfu, *Member of the Chinese Academy of Social Sciences; President of the World Association for Political Economy*

For those who wish to understand the origins of the Chinese revolution, this book is an essential guide to negotiating the complex terrain of the agrarian class structure in pre-revolutionary China; the Marxist and alternative analyses of this structure; and the debates which underlay the eventual formulation by the CPC of the strategy that led to victory over both the Japanese and the Kuomintang. As well as discussion of the theoretical contribution of Mao Zedong to Marxism, as this guided CPC strategy, the book covers a range of debates over an extensive area of discourse.

Utsa Patnaik, *Professor Emerita at the Centre for Economic Studies and Planning, Jawaharlal Nehru University, New Delhi, India*

Jenny Clegg's *Storming the Heavens* offers a brilliantly enlightening Marxist understanding of socialist China. Based on forty years of research, it is focused on the dynamic and transforming relationship between the Communist Party of China and China's diverse peasant communities. Like the studies made by Lenin of Russia's peasantry, or Connolly's of Ireland's, both very different, it enables us to understand the specifically national characteristics of the Party's Marxist practice. It is essential reading for anyone wanting to understand China's role in the world today.

John Foster, *Professor Emeritus of Social Sciences, University of the West of Scotland; former International Secretary of the Communist Party of Britain*

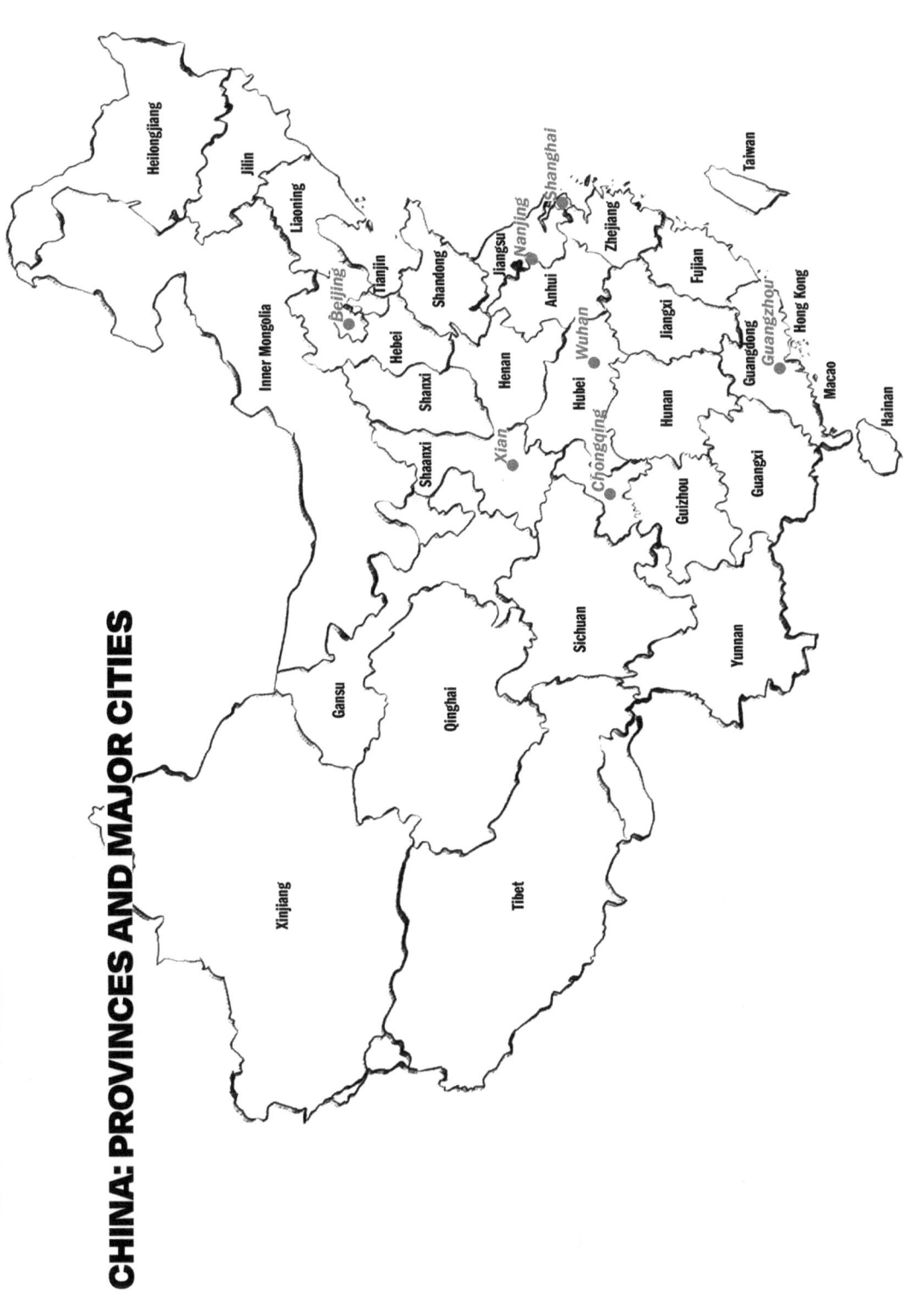

CONTENTS

ACKNOWLEDGMENTS		1
INTRODUCTION		2
PART 1	Landlord monopoly and peasant land hunger – the distinct characteristics of China's agrarian structure	31
Introduction		32
Chapter 1	Land ownership, rent and the condition of the peasantry	34
Chapter 2	Landlordism and commerce	47
Chapter 3	Landlord, state and village – the articulation of economic and political power in Chinese feudalism	60
Chapter 4	The impact of imperialism	78
PART 2	From stagnation to crisis: economic and political dimensions of agrarian China's decline	97
Introduction		98
Chapter 5	Market and technological constraints and the problem of monopoly rent	103
Chapter 6	Huang and the involuting peasant economy of North China – between Lenin and Chayanov	114
Chapter 7	The role of the state – for the common good or legitimising landlord power?	124
Chapter 8	The tenacity of Chinese feudalism	133
Chapter 9	Peasant rebellions and why they failed	143
Chapter 10	The failure of reforms	153
Chapter 11	The convoluted trajectory to revolution	161
PART 3	China's revolutionary experience from the First United Front to land revolution (1924-1937) and the evolution of Mao's strategy	167
Introduction		168

Chapter 12	Peasants and revolution – from Lenin to Mao	171
Chapter 13	China's first revolution and the CPC-KMT United Front (1924–1927)	181
Chapter 14	From the towns to the countryside: – rethinking revolutionary strategy	196
Chapter 15	The land revolution, soviet power and the dynamics of peasant class struggle	207
Chapter 16	Mao and the sinification of Marxism – class analysis and the mass line	219
Chapter 17	From agrarian to national revolution	230

PART 4 China's revolutionary experience from the Second United Front to land revolution (1937–1949) and the implementation of Mao's strategy — 243

Introduction		244
Chapter 18	The Anti-Japanese War and the United Front (1937–1945)	248
Chapter 19	Building the new democratic state	261
Chapter 20	The return to land revolution (1946–8)	274
Chapter 21	Mao's methods refined (1946–8)	287

PART 5 Peasants, revolution and the Communist Party of China — 303

Introduction		304
Chapter 22	From traditional rebellion to modern revolution	306
Chapter 23	Peasants as free trade familialists – Thaxton's contribution	320
Chapter 24	What difference did CPC leadership make?	330

CONCLUSION — 339

GLOSSARY — 363

BIBLIOGRAPHY — 364

INDEX — 376

ACKNOWLEDGEMENTS

First of all I would like to thank the following for their support and encouragement through the process of completing my Ph.D thesis: my supervisors, Paul Keleman and Hamza Alavi; fellow students, Zafar Ahmed and Leon Zamosc; also Paul Wingrove, Richard Baker, Brenda Howlett and Frances Bernstein. Most especially, my thanks go to my father for his constructive comments and constant encouragement which kept me going throughout.

To this I would add Kenny Coyle, for suggesting that, even after a 30-year-gap, my work should still be brought to light and published; Keith Bennett for helpful comments as I updated the work; and to Nick Wright and the team at Manifesto Press for delivering the book into print.

I also benefitted over the years from conversations with Isabel Crook, whose anthropologist's eye and deep empathy with the rural people of China have been a source of great inspiration, opening my mind in many different ways to understanding what revolution can mean to people's lives.

INTRODUCTION

When the Hunan peasantry began to join together in mass associations between 1926 and 1927, they moved onto the centre stage of modern Chinese, and indeed world, history. But what was the nature of this peasant movement? What were the peasants' goals and demands? In what way and how did their mobilisation come to take the central role in China's revolutionary process?

The conventional image of traditional China was of a static agrarian civilisation, a monolithic empire lacking any internal dynamic for development and progress. Chinese society was commonly viewed as one whose inertia was rooted at its base in self-contained village communities of peasant households engaging mainly in subsistence production, bound by patriarchal traditions of family and community, and cemented together at its apex by a bureaucratic and hierarchical state apparatus of scholar-officials serving the Emperor and legitimated by Confucian morality. Fundamental change, it was thought, could only be brought about by external forces. Marx, for example, expressed the view that:

> Complete isolation was the prime condition of the preservation of old China. That isolation having come to a violent end by the medium of England, dissolution must follow as surely as that of any mummy carefully preserved in a hermetically sealed coffin.[1]

However by the 1920s, the mounting struggles of the peasantry demonstrated a potential for reinvigorating Chinese society existing within the countryside. Mao Zedong's 1927 *Report on an Investigation into the Peasant Movement in Hunan* stands out for its insight in recognising the peasant movement as a source of revolutionary energy capable of shaking China's traditional society at its roots.

Peasant theories

Revolutionary theory, together with Western Peasant Studies, offer a number of different models for understanding the relationship between the peasantry and social change which may serve to guide analysis of the Chinese peasantry and their role in the Chinese revolution. Smallholder farming has commonly been conceived as a bastion of conservatism and traditionalism, resistant to social change. Marx was to famously rule on the French peasantry at the time of Louis Bonaparte that they were incapable of asserting their class interest in their own name: 'they cannot represent themselves, they must be represented'. Nevertheless, he saw the peasants as having two sides, contrasting the revolutionary, enlightened peasant to the conservative peasant bound by superstition; the peasant 'that sticks out beyond the condition of his own existence, the smallholding', and the one 'who wants to consolidate this holding': whereas the country folk who 'linked up with the towns, want to overthrow the old order through their own energies', those who exist 'in stupefied seclusion within this old order want to see themselves and their smallholdings saved....'[2]

Lenin was to consider Russia's traditional rural communities to be in dissolution under the impact of capitalism, with the peasantry differentiating into a rural bourgeoisie and proletariat. Taking revolutionary theory forward, he saw these newly emerging class forces as providing the impetus to challenge the dominant feudal system, capable of taking independent transformative action through alliance with the modern urban classes. In the long term however, faced with medieval patriarchal subsistence producers on the one hand, and conservative petty proprietors with a stake in protecting their private smallholding on the other, Lenin looked ultimately to the organisation of the poor peasantry as the main revolutionary force for socialism in the countryside.[3]

The perspectives of the Russian populists, the Narodniks, however, challenged Lenin's views on the development of capitalism in Russian agriculture and of peasant differentiation into two classes. They regarded the traditionalist peasantry as the revolutionary force both against capitalism, which undermined their traditional subsistence arrangements, and the Tsarist State, which promoted capitalist development by protecting urban industry whilst driving the peasants into the cash economy through the imposition of taxes, the taking of public lands, and the undermining of handicrafts.[4] Rather than relying on the revolutionary potential of the poor peasants, they perceived the traditional village communal system – the *mir* – as the embryo of socialism. Russian populism was to be developed further in the 1920s by the Soviet agrarian economist of the 1920s, A.V. Chayanov, who advocated the study of the peasant economy as a distinct field of economics, given its own logic of satisfying need rather than producing for profit.[5]

In the early years of the People's Republic of China (PRC), Western scholarship on China's agrarian revolution tended to focus on the ideology and organisation of the Communist Party of China's (CPC) revolutionary leadership, the peasants appearing rather as the objects of policy than as the subjects of change, as makers of their own history. From the 1970s, more empirical studies of the Chinese peasantry began to appear aimed at examining the issues affecting peasant lives, their behaviour, motives and goals within the context of the structure of pre-revolutionary rural society. These works were part of the growing field of Peasant Studies, emerging at this time to meet the challenge of understanding peasant participation in revolutions in the Third World, where, not least due to the impact of imperialism, class struggle and social change had taken on forms differing from the European experience upon which Marx, in the main, had based his theory.

Marxism offers the view of the peasant as an exploited member of a class-divided society, activated according to class solidarity and the needs of class struggle. But Peasant Studies also presented other models. Setting the academic frame, Hobsbawm placed peasants within a continuum of two ideal types: at one end, commodity producers operating within the framework of bourgeois institutions; at the other, traditional communalists. In doing so, he drew out a contrast between the individualism and passivity of the more commercialised small-scale cultivators, and the communalist peasantry's capacity for independent collective action.[6]

From the Marxist-Leninist perspective, agrarian revolution and the peasants' struggle against the landlords play a central role in the transition from feudalism to capitalism in eradicating feudal constraints on capital formation. In contrast, from the position of classical economics based on individualism, Popkin has viewed the peasant not as a revolutionary but as a rational entrepreneur, responding to the stimulus of market demand according to the motive of profit-maximisation for economic gain.[7] This orientation meant peasants sought reforms rather than radical change. The peasant-as-subsistence producer on the other hand acts, according to Scott, on the principle of 'safety first' to minimise risks and losses, bonding through crisis-averting institutional arrangements of reciprocity.[8] As traditional communalists, peasants are driven to rebel against state intervention and the expansion of capitalism.

Scott's influential study of the moral economy of the peasants of South East Asia connects peasant participation in revolution with their traditional defensive reactions to protect their pre-modern community structures against the challenge of capitalism and colonialism. Other analysts from within the Marxist spectrum have suggested that agrarian societies in Asia have been undergoing a distinctive capitalist transformation brought on by the combined forces of imperialism and the state and merchants, with a semi-proletarianising peasantry, dependent on both subsistence farming and wage labour to make a living, emerging as a revolutionary force.[9]

These varying conceptions then are bound up with conflicting perspectives on the process of agrarian change and development, and on how the peasants fit in with this. They offer not only a source of theoretical controversy and debate, but also, according to different understandings of peasant motives and goals, a basis for various strategies and programmes of development addressed very differently to the peasants as passive recipients of reform or active agents in revolutionary transformation.

Identifying the type of peasantry in China is crucial to an understanding of the potential for social change and of the revolutionary process itself as well as of the relation between the national and agrarian movements under the impact of imperialism. It is also clearly essential to the analysis of the relationship between the CPC and the peasantry, and of the appropriateness of the policies of land reform and the path of subsequent socio-economic development.

In such an investigation it is necessary to take into account the overall conditions of the peasantry in terms of land and labour, the degree and type of ownership, tenancy and labour services; their degree of homogeneity or differentiation; their involvement in subsistence or commodity production, that is, their insularity or social integration; in short, to find out whether their lives are affected primarily by market conditions, landlord domination and exploitation or the communal bonds of village organisation.

But the evidence of existing studies is contradictory. Skinner found China's peasant economy to be integrated in a network of local and national marketing systems operating throughout the countryside.[10] This contrasted with the anthropological literature in which peasants figure as traditional communalists bound by kinship and community ties.[11] Chinese Marxist scholars of the 1930s and 1940s on the other hand, seeing the vast majority of peasants farming inadequate plots with underemployed labour, sought to address the problem of agrarian stagnation and the lack of alternative means of survival. Pointing out that rents often exceeded 50 per cent of the crop, they viewed the tenant-peasants as heavily exploited members of a deeply class-divided society.[12]

Huang has suggested that such widely differing views of the Chinese peasantry may be accounted for by regional variation.[13] Broadly speaking, in the more commercialised South there were higher degrees of tenancy, village economies were more integrated with the local marketing system, and peasant households were more atomised, whilst in the less developed North, peasant landowners predominated, communities were more tightly knit and insular, and communal bonds were an important factor in peasant life.

Underlying different strands within Western Sinology, these three different views of the peasantry generate distinct perspectives on the overall structure of the pre-revolutionary society and the nature of landlordism and the state, the internal trends of development, the potential for change and obstacles to this. They then give rise to quite different views on the causes of revolution, the effects on agriculture of the expansion of commerce brought about by international capital, and the relationship of peasant organisation and lifestyle with the wider polity as well as with the revolutionary Party.

Skinner's view of a market-oriented peasantry is shared by Rawski[14] and Elvin[15], who trace China's history as a process of commercialisation free from the institutional barriers of feudal landlordism or a bureaucratic state, with potential to develop in positive relation to international markets. Myers on a similar basis has argued that revolution was caused not by systemic internal crisis but rather was the result of random disturbances.[16] From such perspectives, the collectivist goals of the CPC are seen to stand in conflict with the peasants' entrepreneurial individualism.[17]

Tawney however regarded the Chinese peasant as a subsistence-based familialist bound by the patriarchal communal and state institutions of an ancient civilisation. It is his description of the Chinese peasantry as standing up to their necks in water so that even a ripple would drown them that provides Scott with an opening for his account of the subsistence ethic of the 'moral economy' which, if violated by the overlords, the state or market forces, brings peasant rebellion to revolution.[18] Wolf, in a similar vein, singles out the expansion of capitalism, with the penetration of international capital undermining the traditional authority of the state and peasant community, as the underlying force behind peasant rebellion.[19]

Were the peasants essentially homogeneous or a partially differentiating strata with different sections pulling in different directions? Were they tradition-bound communalists struggling for survival in defence of subsistence practices against the combined pressures of the market and state under the weight of imperialist exploitation? Were they resistant to modern values and ideas, in opposition to modernising reforms, or were they inherently free-traders, active participants in the revolutionary struggle directed against feudal exploitation and oppression striving to reform the old order?[20] To what extent did the goals and organisational practices of the peasants and the CPC really correspond?

Different perspectives on the nature and motives of the Chinese peasants give rise to conflicting conceptions of the role of the CPC and the extent to which peasants adhered to its collectivist goals. Did the peasants need outside help to realise their demands with the CPC injecting a new political content and direction which the peasants' own spontaneous, localistic uprisings were unable to develop? Were they mere recipients of policies, indoctrinated and moulded by campaigns orchestrated by the CPC? Did the CPC build up a peasant following through its revolutionary political leadership or was it essentially a peasant party relying on a populist appeal to harness spontaneous peasant opposition?[21] Did it just recruit a clientele of followers using the age-old methods of offering peasant protection and a stable environment – for example through the provision of irrigation – just as the traditional benefactor state had done in the past?

Questions here give rise to consideration of the continuity or otherwise between the traditional struggles of the peasantry and a modern revolutionary transformation to establish a new socio-economic order. To what extent were pre-existing forms of peasant organisation and collective protest a basis from which the CPC were able to develop revolutionary class struggle in the countryside? Or were traditional rural customs and institutions in fact an obstacle to democratic transformation, whether as traditional methods of survival, patterns of village closure, or forms of feudal patronage binding peasants to the landlords and the state? How did peasant culture and beliefs influence the revolutionary process? To what extent did the Party itself absorb from the rural environment the traditional patterns of power and practices of elite leadership – as bandits or bureaucrats – using parochial loyalties and obedience to authority to its own ends?

From the Marxist perspective, the CPC, as a vanguard, served as a bridge between traditional rebellion and modern revolution. Lenin, considering that the outcome of the peasants' struggles depended on the influence of classes external to them, envisaged that the Party of the working class would provide leadership, imparting a new ideology and forms of organisation and consciousness into the countryside to articulate demands the peasants could not do for themselves. For Chesneaux, the ideas, the men and the organisation which set the Chinese peasants in motion came from the towns and cities, and it was the intervention of the CPC that allowed traditional peasant rebellion to develop into modern revolution.[22]

For Mao, the revolutionary nature of the peasants' struggles in the 1920s lay in the spontaneous formation of the peasant associations which replaced the traditional village organisations based on feudal-patriarchal power relations and dominated by the local landlord gentry. The significance of these embryonic organisations of mass power, in his view, was their direct challenge to the landlord-gentry, whose hold over the villages was the crucial condition of the whole system of feudal and imperialist exploitation and domination of the Chinese people.[23] Through experience, learning from mistakes, the CPC came to understand agrarian transformation as the main content of the democratic revolution, with the peasantry as its main force.

Any attempt to analyse China's peasant-centred path of revolution then has a wide range of issues to cover. There is more to these controversies than the matter of regional variation. The discussion in this study explores these themes of tradition and revolution, leadership and peasant agency –

the problems of elitism, pursuing questions about the nature of the peasants, their economy and attitudes to markets, their motives and goals and how these were expressed in different types of collective action, and considering the forms of peasant power and the problems of peasant divisions.

Aims and methods

In offering a new look at the Chinese revolution, the study aims to bring the peasant movement to the forefront, clarifying how it was organised by the CPC with a view to a socialist future. It focuses overall on three interconnected issues concerning the nature of the Chinese peasants, their goals and collective actions; the key characteristics and contradictions of China's pre-revolutionary society and its state of crisis; and the relationship between the CPC and the Chinese peasant movement.

The problem in analysing the nature of the Chinese peasantry and hence its role in the revolution and its relations with the revolutionary Party is related to the real difficulty of characterising the pre-revolutionary agrarian structure of economic and political power which was so unlike Europe given the absence of either a feudal pattern of manorial serfdom or a sector of large-scale capitalist farming. To begin to answer questions about the peasantry and the Party, it is in the first place necessary to clarify the objective socio-economic background to the revolution.

With its stagnating agriculture typified by the small-scale cultivation of uneconomic plots with traditional techniques, China's lack of development for many Western scholars is seen to be rooted in the persistence of subsistence farming as this inhibited the growth of the internal market. In the absence of large landed estates, it has been suggested that, although disparities of wealth and social conflicts over the distribution of resources did exist in pre-revolutionary rural China, they were not as severe and pervasive as portrayed by CPC leaders and the official ideology. In these ways, the urgent need in China for revolutionary transformation through land reform and the significance of the CPC's policies of peasant class organisation have been downplayed. With the distinctive features of traditional bureaucratic state and patriarchal village communities, focus has been rather on the state-peasant relationship and the need for reform.

This study aims to counter the charge that the CPC exaggerated the role of the landlords. Through an examination of land relations, it seeks to expose the common misconception of pre-revolutionary China as a society of owner-cultivators, whether shaped by bureaucratic and patriarchal traditions or by market relations, and to establish the landlord system as the main obstacle to China's development.

The analysis reveals the feudal nature of landlord-peasant relations which, despite the absence of manorial serfdom, dominated the structure of agrarian society through a system of land monopoly. It examines how the Asiatic features of the centralised bureaucratic state and patriarchal customs of family, community and patronage structured landlord power, and further considers the failure of capitalist development with agricultural production stagnating amidst the growth of commercial relations. It then explains the persistence of parcellised farming in terms of the conditions of exorbitant rent showing further how accelerated commercialisation under the impact of imperialism saw China reduced to a semi-feudal, semi-colonial society.

At the same time, the peculiar Chayanovian pattern of parcellised farming has tended to direct attention towards the middle peasants as the prime movers of revolutionary change in China as opposed to the poor peasants who from a Leninist perspective are the more likely allies of a revolutionary Party. The fact that, in contrast with the difficulties faced in organising the peasants in the South where class polarisation was more pronounced, the CPC had far greater success in developing roots among the peasants in the poorer, less fertile, owner-cultivator communities of the North, has reinforced this 'middle peasant thesis'.[24]

From a 'neo-Narodnik' perspective, it is taxation – and the state-village relationship, rather than rent – and the landlord-peasant relationship, that constitute the major form of exploitation. Peasant goals then are understood in terms of the establishment of a system of individual household production in contrast with the CPC's approach to peasant class organisation and the future socialist direction.

This challenge is taken up by showing how the dominant mode of production influenced other types of exploitation so shaping the conditions of different types of peasants beyond the direct rent relationship. In this way it reveals, in the land hunger of the great mass of owner-and tenant-peasants, their revolutionary potential against the conditions of monopoly ownership of land supported through tenacious links between the landlords and the rich peasants.

The particular nature and structure of landlordism then demonstrates both the objective potential as well as the political necessity of building an anti-feudal alliance involving the majority of peasants. Mass power against landlord domination was the central issue in a rural transformation that was aimed to benefit owner and tenant peasants alike but what conditions were then necessary for unleashing the full force of peasants, for the realisation of their revolutionary potential? How did the process of the agrarian revolution unfold?

The Chinese revolution overall was to follow an arduous path. From the failure of the first United Front with the Kuomintang (KMT) in the revolution of 1927, and the subsequent outbreak of civil war, the CPC retreated to the mountains to set up soviet 'Red' bases, carrying out a land revolution. Then, embarking on the Long March to escape KMT encirclement, it was to turn its focus to organising the anti-Japanese resistance forming a second United Front with the KMT. When this broke down again into civil war following the Japanese defeat, the Party stepped up for the final surge to eliminate feudal relations through thorough-going land reform, moving on to win victory with the establishment of the People's Republic of China in 1949.

As Li Lifeng has pointed out, in this long revolutionary process, the CPC always gave pre-eminence to mobilising the masses and winning mass support, whether it used the nation or class as the rallying call.[25] However, it was one thing to recognise the need for peasant mobilisation, it was quite another to organise the mass movement.

In reviewing the revolutionary process, tracing its zig-zag path within a shifting national context, the aim is to grasp the challenges faced as the CPC sought to adapt to the dynamics of a complex rural political environment. By identifying the steps in the evolution of its rural policies and Party organisation, it shows how the Party eventually overcame adversity.

China's conditions raised difficult questions for its revolutionaries: what was the relationship between imperialism and feudalism and how did these two aspects shape the country's class structure? What was the relationship between the national and social revolutions? And between the democratic capitalist and socialist revolutions? What was the revolutionary nature of the peasants and how was proletarian leadership of the peasant movement to be achieved? Indeed how could the working class lead a revolution when its own base was too small to maintain an independent political presence?

At first, the CPC only had the experience of the Russian revolution to learn from and, lacking a grounding in Marxist theories and principles itself, it tended to follow Comintern policy and advice. From Lenin came recognition of the importance of the working class alliance both with the peasants and with the national bourgeoisie against imperialism. Beyond this however, the theories of Lenin, Stalin and Trotsky regarding the revolutionary role of a vanguard Party in relation to the peasants, and of the relation between the national anti-imperialist and agrarian revolutions, did not match well the conditions of class struggle in China. The strategies then that brought the Bolsheviks to power in Russia failed to work for the CPC, their application having unexpected, even disastrous, results.

The particular difficulty in understanding agrarian revolution lay in identifying the roles of the various sections of the peasants. China lacked the newly emerging classes of rural bourgeoisie and proletariat that Lenin had identified as the revolutionary forces in the Russian countryside. However whilst the small producers appeared superficially homogeneous, conditions were such that a small amount of wealth made all the difference between life and death, dividing the mass of increasingly impoverished owners and tenants from the village rich of landlords and rich peasants who tended to draw together in the exercise of power and exploitation.

In the organisation of the anti-feudal struggle and the creation of the new democratic institutions of peasant mass power, the greatest challenge lay in transforming the political, social and economic relations within the villages. At grassroots level, rural conflict did not develop in a straightforward fashion with the persistent influence of the traditional elites and peasant dependence for survival on traditional bonds of patronage and patriarchalism cutting across class divisions, obstructing the development of class solidarities and complicating peasant action.

As it endeavoured to develop roots in village communities, the CPC not only faced obstruction from the local elites, but also confronted tendencies of parochialism as well as 'absolute egalitarianism' – excessive attacks on wealth and property – which drove peasants apart. It was to discover then that a peasantry not only differentiated by degrees of wealth and income, but also divided by factors other than class with kinship ties and territorial community bonds as well as traditional values and beliefs hindering the development of mass activism.

At the same time, traditional patterns of elite leadership – banditry, bureaucratism and benevolent protection – reappeared within the Party. In conditions of economic stagnation and isolation in remote villages, leaders of the new institutions and local organs of power, detached from the peasants, would tend to resort to commandism. Where they became absorbed into pre-existing networks of informal power, they would often find themselves embroiled in traditional factional strife. Peasant power also took its own shape in localism, personality cults and adventurism. All these kinds of difficulties presented further major obstacles to be overcome in the organisation of mass democratic power in the countryside.

This brings the discussion to its main purpose to explore Mao's analysis of the peasants, and rural classes as a whole, showing how, by applying the conceptual tools of Marxism, he was to develop and refine a strategy based on peasant mass mobilisation to eventually meet the challenges of the Chinese revolution.

Mao first made his mark during the first revolutionary upsurge of 1925–1927 with his *Report on an Investigation into the Peasant Movement in Hunan*.

This work, significant in its recognition of agrarian transformation as the main content of the Chinese revolution, moved beyond the view that the force behind the peasant struggle for land was that of a petty bourgeoisie seeking to utilise land for a profit – one adhered to by the Comintern and the existing CPC leadership. Instead it grasped the wider question of peasant livelihood.

Then as Mao came to understand how the revolution was in fact taking place in the armed struggles of the peasants against landlord power, he fundamentally shifted away from the focus on an urban-based nationwide movement to a rural-based long-term struggle, building independent soviet bases of peasant mass power to encircle the cities from the countryside.

With his grasp of the peasant movement as the main force of the Chinese revolution, Mao has been cast simplistically in the role of a peasant leader, with the Party he came to lead, cut off from an urban base and without roots in the working class, degenerating into a form of peasant power. According to Trotsky for one, the CPC never accepted proletarian leadership and was in effect captured by the peasants, rich peasants at that.[26]

But Mao's distinctive leadership methods were to develop through practice, learning from the hard experiences of defeat and disorganised struggle, the result of mistaken policies of the Comintern and urban-influenced leaders, as they endeavoured to break through the power domain of the rural elites. These efforts – first a Rightist 'rich peasant line' then a 'Leftist' 'anti-rich peasant line' as well as purges to root out 'alien class elements' – all foundered on the basis of misconceptions of the revolutionary nature of the peasants as petty bourgeois proprietors, or in contrast semi-proletarianised anti-capitalist poor, or simply a 'backward' mass in need of enlightenment.

Mao had followed Lenin in his grasp of peasant class power, however, observing the dynamics among the different sections of the peasants during the upsurge and ebb of revolution, he was led to draw his own conclusions as to the roles of the rural classes, marking a break with the formalistic adherence to Bolshevism.

Whilst he attributed the revolutionary energy in the countryside largely to the poor peasantry, it was his attitude towards the middle peasants that is often considered as distinguishing Mao's approach to rural revolution. It is a particular focus of this discussion to examine Mao's rationale for taking the middle peasants as central in the process of agrarian revolution, showing how this featured in his overall class analysis and how it played out in terms of strategy. Here, whilst rejecting Alavi's 'middle peasant thesis', the analysis draws on his approach in highlighting the importance of the dynamics among the different sections of the peasants.

It was not until he broke with the Soviet-style formula for a worker-peasant alliance that Mao was to finally find a strategy for organising the peasants as a democratic force to overturn landlord power. In this, the analysis of the classes in the countryside – a key step in the sinification of Marxism – was to prove essential. [27]

For Mao, class analysis encompassed both the material conditions of peasant production together with the behaviours and consciousness – of the revolutionary actors themselves. In this way, he grasped both the objective basis of class struggle and the subjective aspect of rural political dynamics.

In the first place, the application of Marxist conceptual tools enabled the CPC to identify different forms of wealth and exploitation, marking out a distinction from both neo-Narodnik homogeneity and a rigid misapplication of Leninist polarisation. It is this then that provided the key to disentangling feudal and capitalist elements in the rural economy. At the same time, it enabled the CPC to understand the behaviours which divided the peasants in terms of their differing conditions of production which was to prove essential to handling contradictions that arose amongst the peasants in the process of land reform.

It was by taking the differing peasant demands into consideration that the CPC was better able to adjust its policies, organisation and leadership styles to the complexities of rural conflict. Unfolding the peasant movement step by step, the Party was able to help create a sustained basis for peasant organisation to tackle the persistent influence of the traditional elites in a staged and targeted approach which ensured that the peasants, not the former elites, took the lead in a revolutionary transformation.

Mao was also to develop his own distinctive approach to the Party-mass relationship as the narrowly conceived mechanical application of Bolshevik methods of Party-building proved a hindrance to rural work. Maoist methods of the mass line and democratic centralism were to develop in the context of further debates within the Party over the meaning and practice of democracy and the ways to rectify cadre practice. Here again Mao's more positive view of the revolutionary potential of the peasants was the influential factor.

The ultimate challenge for the CPC however lay in handling the dynamics of the agrarian and national movements together as these unfolded independently yet in interaction with each other. The Party's failure in 1927, its inability to handle these dynamics as the peasant and national movements drew apart, was a reflection of the weakness of class analysis. A clearer understanding of the role of the national bourgeoisie was necessary for the CPC to be able to situate the agrarian revolution in the context of the overall national situation and it was only by grasping the interconnectedness of the two revolutionary movements in class terms that the CPC came to fully understand peasant dynamics.

The significance of the volume lies firstly in bringing into play in the analysis of the pre-revolutionary nature of Chinese society, the theories, highly underrated, of Chinese Marxist scholars such as Chen Boda and Chen Hanseng developed in the 1930s and 1940s. The application of Marxism opened the door to analysing how the semi-feudal and semi-colonial conditions influenced the role of Chinese classes in the revolution in ways quite different from the general European experience.

Also drawing on little-known debates among Chinese Marxist historians in the 1980s on the nature of Chinese feudalism and the failure of capitalist development, the study is able to combine class analysis with China's historical dynamics so as to understand the longer-term trends. On this material basis, the study is able to bring into focus CPC leadership in peasant organisation and how it eventually drew together the national and rural movements.

Taking as central the evolution of the 'mass line', the discussion reveals differences within the CPC on the question of rural work, Party building and democratic practice which further demonstrate what it was that set Mao Zedong's leadership apart. It shows how through a lengthy process of trial and error, Mao devised a strategy adapted to the dynamics of the rural struggle to break through the traditionalist loyalties of patronage and kinship which inhibited efforts to mobilise the mass of the peasants within the framework of class struggle. Setting his methods against the failings of Comintern-, Trotskyist-, and reformist-influenced policies and perspectives, the study highlights the lessons learned by the CPC from the Rightist underestimation of the peasants' revolutionary potential as well as Left Adventurism and excessive struggle.

Here, the study draws on CPC materials: primarily the works of Mao Zedong, but also those of other Communist leaders, namely Liu Shaoqi and Zhou Enlai, as well as a wider literature exploring the debates over Chinese communism.

However, in focusing here on the policies of the CPC, there is the danger of mistaking intentions for reality and a theoretical approach may also tend to over-generalise. In an effort to keep these limitations to a minimum, the discussion has endeavoured to take into consideration conflicting evidence in a range of empirical and case studies. At the same time, different perspectives and analytical approaches are brought under examination, drawing on the diversity of debates within Sinology and Peasant Studies, Western and Chinese Marxism.

In this way, the study seeks to enter into the revolutionary process, setting Mao's strategies and methods in the material context of rural politics to show how he finally came to meet the actual challenges of the agrarian revolution – the resistance of village elites; the traditional loyalties and peasant divisions which obscured the underlying class relations; the problems of bureaucratism and the shortcomings of the cadres – all within the shifting relations between the agrarian and national revolutions.[28]

As an effort to concretise those social, cultural, military, economic as well as political aspects that form the hallmarks of Maoism, the value of the study lies also in its contribution to understanding these distinctive methods, beyond their abstraction in general principles, as meaningful in practice in meeting the particular challenges of China's revolutionary struggle.

Set in the overlapping concerns of academic study of peasants and of China's history and transformation as well as debates within the Communist movement, the work sheds new light on controversies about reform and revolution, democracy and centralism, offering new ways of looking at the tensions between traditional peasant rebellion and modern revolution, and between the CPC goals and policies imposed from above and the spontaneous peasant actions from below.

The question of how a Leninist Party, interpreting and acting on the basis of historical materialism, is able to lead the masses, not automatically brought by themselves to socialist consciousness, is a much-contested conundrum. This study makes its contribution here, showing how the CPC's class-based policies enabled the peasants to transcend the limitations of their traditional dynamics of struggle, harmonising contradictions within the revolutionary forces in a staged process so as to maintain peasant leadership and prevent organisational subversion by taking a socialist direction.

Structure

Part 1 sets out to examine the characteristics of China's agrarian society and the deteriorating condition of the peasantry to reveal the nature and structure of feudal economic and political power with landlordism at the centre. These opening chapters, drawing on the works of the early Chinese Marxist scholars, Chen Boda and Chen Hanseng, present the objective conditions which frame the unfolding revolution. Critiquing the common notion of China as a society of small owner-cultivators, the discussion highlights the primacy of the struggle to eradicate the landlord system and carry out land reform motivated by the peasants' increasingly desperate battle for survival. At the same time, the study of production relations uncovers the differing conditions of poor, middle and rich peasant sectors.

Addressing the question of the distribution of land ownership, Chapter 1 looks at the evidence of surveys in the 1930s and subsequent investigations to reveal how the different perspectives on the extent of inequality have arisen as a result of using differing criteria to categorise the different types of peasants.

Analysis of rural relations is made all the more difficult by the increasing commercialisation of agriculture and the complexity of the forms of exploitation involving not only rent but also usury, wage labour as well as market-price manipulation. This takes the discussion of the landlord system beyond the extent of tenancy to more widespread problems of land insufficiency and underemployed labour, with deteriorating conditions affecting a majority of peasants as increasing rents and taxes cut into their necessary labour. This was to hasten the owner-cultivators' loss of land, driving the polarisation between landlord and peasant, and land ownership and cultivation.

Chapter 2 brings into play Chen Boda's study of land rent first published in 1947 focusing on the principal form of surplus labour.[29] This approach exposes the underlying contradiction between land monopoly in the hands of the few and the land hunger of the rural majority with the general trend towards the concentration of land ownership as opposed to its increasingly fragmented use as peasants competed to survive. In such conditions, Chen Boda shows that, despite the expansion of market relations and the weakening of traditional feudal bonds, a type of extra-economic power continued to prevail.

On the basis of this feudal land monopoly then, the landlord-peasant relationship was the determining factor of the agrarian system not only shaping rent relations but relations of production and exploitation as a whole. In this the peasants had a common interest as a class in the transformation of the land system despite their differing conditions of production.

Chapter 3 turns to an examination of the structures of political power. Noting the features of both the centralised bureaucratic state and the patriarchal kinship or clan system, it nevertheless challenges the Orientalist view of China as a system of elite power based on official rank rather than land ownership. Rather it shows how the landlords' subordination of the peasantry operated not only formally through the power of the state but also informally through the Confucian bonds of patron-client ties. This created a distinctive system in which influential families with roots in local hierarchies of kinship and community as well as land ownership were able to maintain predominance through the exercise of personalised power.

Chapter 4 moves on to address the controversy as to whether contact with the world market and foreign powers had a positive or negative effect on China's traditional state, society and economy. In examining the impact of imperialism in particular on the rural economy and society as well as on class structure, it argues that the interaction between world capitalism and feudal relations produced a number of contradictory trends which marked China's transformation into a semi-feudal and semi-colonial society.

The acceleration of commerce under the impact of foreign trade, banking and investment in fact saw both the intensification and gradual dissolution of the existing relations of exploitation. The combination of foreign and domestic exploitation hastened a crisis situation as investment and development were inhibited, land concentration increased and peasant impoverishment deepened. With the antagonism in landlord-peasant relations reaching a tipping point as the peasants' capacity for spontaneous rebellion was unleashed, new class forces also began to emerge in the cities. These however were too weak to grow independently. The encounter with world capitalism then brought with it a promise of change only to frustrate its realisation.

Part 2 considers the patterns of China's political economy through the lens of history to better understand the broader dynamics of class and state. Why was China's historical trajectory with the persistence of small-scale cultivation so different from Europe's? Why did the spread of market relations, instead of enhancing peasant independence and producing a class of entrepreneurial farmers, see landlord power grow and rural impoverishment increase? What was the role of the bureaucratic state? Chapters in Part 2 follow the key theme of the failure of capitalist development in China, examining and critiquing major works of Western writers and scholars on the question. In so doing, the line of argument takes issue with methodologies which concern themselves essentially with matters of distribution rather than directing analysis to the system of land tenure, to relations of production and surplus extraction, that is, the creation of wealth.

As Lenin was to argue, it is from the point of view of consumption that the peasants appeared undifferentiated, however differences between rich and poor concern the mode of surplus extraction and, whilst the former directs policy towards reforms to support the small farmers, when the economic relations of expropriation are revealed this 'leads inevitably to the theory of class struggle.'[30]

Chapter 5 examines the arguments of Tawney and Elvin in their contrasting explanations of China's agrarian stagnation as related to their views on the persistence of small-scale peasant farming. Whilst Tawney's explanation of the problem in terms of the impact of Western commerce on a society bound by tradition falls within Nurkse's notion of a 'low-level equilibrium trap', Elvin counters this with his own theory of 'high-level equilibrium trap', highlighting the constraints of traditional technologies to argue the positive potential of opening China's markets to the West. Both conceptions however take the question of the market as key.

Huang's study of the peasant economy of the North China plain, examined in Chapter 6, endeavours to steer a course between Chayanov and Lenin to find a semi-proletarianising peasant economy involuting under severe population pressure. This for him serves as the major constraint on capital formation and the expansion of farm size. His contribution is of value in drawing attention to the pattern of partial differentiation within the peasant economy, but overall, as with Tawney and Elvin, it lacks a systematic investigation of the unequal system of land distribution, treating rent as an added-on burden for the peasantry rather than the defining feature of the agrarian economic structure.

China's bureaucratic state and closed patriarchal community system are frequently regarded as chief factors in restricting private enterprise. With title and privilege gained through the open access exam system rather, apparently, than wealth, the Chinese state is often seen to have operated in its own sphere of power independent of landed property. Chinese history is then seen as driven by the to and fro of power shifts between centre and locality in the dynastic cycle rather than by class struggle.

Chapter 7 critically considers arguments of the separation of state and landlord articulated in the works of Perdue and of Huang for whom the Chinese bureaucratic system served as a benevolent protector of the people. Whilst Perdue highlights the tensions between landlord and state, private versus public interests, and Huang sets out the state-village axis as the central feature of Chinese social structure, both underrate the centrality of the landlord-peasant relationship.

Drawing on Chinese Marxist analyses of the enduring nature of feudal relations, Chapter 8 is pivotal in exploring the longer-term historical path which saw the landlord system adapt to the growth of market relations. Unlike in Europe where commerce confronted landlord power from urban bases, economic power in China accumulated in the hands of landlord-merchants closely linked with officialdom. How did the landlords gain control of commerce and what impact did this have on capitalist class formation? How did 'capitalist sprouts' become ensnared in feudal relations? Central to the explanation here is the distinctive structure of feudal power as the Asiatic features of bureaucratic state and patriarchal village community served to maintain social privilege, supporting the landlords' position from above and from below.

As China's agrarian economy stagnated under landlord power, peasant rebellions occurred on a massive scale. Why did these fail to bring about a fundamental change in the basis of the landlord class? Why did the efforts to modernise China both under the late Qing and the Republican period under the KMT fail to resolve the constraints on development?

Discussion in Chapter 9 of the role of dissident gentry and the traditional patterns of peasant protest raises key questions about problems of leadership and divisions among the peasants which provide vital clues as to the political challenges later faced by the CPC in its rural work. At the same time, it sets the scene for the confrontation to come with a revolutionary peasantry emerging to challenge the political and economic power of the landlords, a particular fusion of power at local levels that pointed to the need for social transformation through revolution from the grassroots.

Chapter 10 then addresses the various attempts at reform, including the KMT's village programmes aimed at supporting the small producers, noting the limited social basis for such efforts as the reason for their lack of success. Directed at change in the state-village relationship, the KMT's efforts failed to address power relations within the village. However, the problem of peasant impoverishment was not just a matter of wealth distribution but was rooted in the land ownership system, demanding not just reform but, as Mao was to recognise, a revolutionary social change. Chapter 11 draws the threads of Part 2 overall together to account for the process of refeudalisation and the emergence of a revolutionary peasantry.

Whilst analysis of China's agrarian society and the underlying class contradictions at the heart of the pre-revolutionary crisis reveal the objective conditions of agrarian struggle, to understand the revolutionary process as a whole requires consideration of the political conditions necessary for the underlying goals to be realised.

The next two parts offer a close examination of the twists and turns of China's revolutionary path as the CPC came to grips with the agrarian nature of the revolution and with the goals and political contents of the peasants' struggles, as it sought to analyse the potential for and obstacles to revolutionary organisation.

Part 3 covers the revolutionary period of 1925–1927 under the first CPC-KMT United Front, and the subsequent 10-year civil war, following the upsurge of the nationalist and peasant movements in the 1925 through to the devastating defeat for the CPC in 1927 and then their retreat to the Southern mountains to build Red base areas based on peasant mobilisation in land reform.

As it sought to come to terms with its failure in the 1927 revolution, the CPC faced the difficulty of how to build a Communist Party in the absence of a strong working-class base. The particular challenge was to understand the differences between the Chinese and Russian revolutionary processes.

Chapters in this section bring into focus the CPC's approach towards peasant organisation, Party building and proletarian leadership amidst changes in the national situation as Mao's distinctive methods of Party building and the mass line gradually took shape.

First setting out Lenin's understanding of the stages of democratic revolution and the role of the peasants, Chapter 12 then leads on to a discussion of Mao's earliest works in which he grasps Lenin's point about peasant class power whilst also seeking to capture the particular nature of the Chinese peasants. Both his first attempts to sketch out China's class structure and rural stratification, and his 1927 Hunan peasant report, are particularly significant in highlighting the different attitudes among the peasants towards revolution.

The analysis then follows the course of the 1925–7 revolution, considering the reasons why it ended in failure for the CPC. Whilst this first revolutionary period could be considered a victory for the KMT-led Northern Expedition, the CPC was to sustain serious damage under the White Terror launched by Chiang Kai-shek (Jiang Jieshi). Much previous discussion of the disaster has focused attention on the Stalin-Trotsky debate on the validity of the United Front approach. This, however, has overshadowed a further significant difference between Chen Duxiu, the CPC leader at the time, and Mao, about the problems and nature of the peasant struggle and the question of 'peasant excesses'. In examining both these debates, Chapter 13, whilst critiquing Trotsky's analysis of the Chinese revolution, also reappraises the views of Stalin and the Comintern, as it considers the 1927 failure from a new angle, that of the conflicting goals in the national and agrarian revolutions. At the same time it highlights the difficulties faced by the CPC in understanding proletarian leadership in China's conditions where the working class existed in only very small numbers.

Driven from city to countryside, the CPC was forced to change its strategic direction to get to grips with the new realities of its situation and face the challenges of rural class struggle. Chapter 14 considers how the Party endeavoured to come to terms with the 1927 defeat. A review of the 6th Party Congress shows how on the one hand its conclusions confirmed the democratic stage of revolution and the importance of mobilising peasants and workers, leaving questions however as to the nature and character of the revolution, and hence the matters of strategy, unclear. Whilst the CPC under Li Lisan's leadership then began to follow an adventurist direction seeking to re-establish links with the cities in line with its Comintern-influenced conception of the worker-peasant alliance, Mao began to develop an entirely new revolutionary strategy of long-term struggle to build peasant mass power against the landlords from independent soviet bases in the countryside.

Chapter 15 then goes on to examine the developments in Party organisation and land policy as now a new leadership group – the '28 Bolsheviks' – turned its attention to the problem of the 'rich peasant line' by rallying the poor peasants and 'bolshevising' the Party and the soviet organs of power. The discussion traces out in contrast the steps taken by Mao as, reflecting on his observations of the behaviour of different sections of the peasants during the upsurge and ebb of revolution, he began to reconsider the roles of the rural classes. His recognition of the importance of the middle peasants in the revolutionary process and his analysis of the interests of the rich peasants were pathbreaking, reaching beyond the 'Leftist' Leninist orthodoxy of the '28 Bolsheviks'. At the same time he also began to develop his own particular approaches towards Party building and peasant organisation through the mass line.

Chapter 16 is key in understanding the sinification of Marxism, showing how the CPC, by applying the Marxist method to distinguish different forms of wealth and exploitation, was able to unravel the complexities of the rural economy, with the incorporation of the rich peasants into the landlord system. At the same time, by this method, the CPC gained a better grasp of the different conditions of production among the peasants as a whole which influenced their different behaviours and attitudes to land confiscation. It was on this basis that Mao was able to devise a mass-based strategy, uniting poor and middle peasants, to bring the landlords under peasant control.

Returning to the question of the relationship between the agrarian and the national revolution, Chapter 17 follows through on Mao's critique of 'Leftist' errors, both his reassessment of the roles of the different peasant sectors in the agrarian transformation and the reconsideration of the role of the national bourgeoisie in the national revolution. The latter in particular casts a new light on the CPC's failure in the 1927 revolution as, lacking in class analysis, it was unable to bridge the two movements – the urban and the rural.

Based on these class reappraisals to grasp the link between the national and agrarian revolutions, Mao gained the leadership position to set the CPC on a course, independent from Comintern influence, towards a New Democracy based on a four-class bloc including the national bourgeoisie alongside the petty bourgeoisie, peasants and workers. This new orientation necessitated a readjustment from radical land distribution to more moderate land policies which then placed the Party in a position to forge a second United Front with the KMT to resist the Japanese invasion of 1937.

This period of New Democracy – in its first two phases of the Anti-Japanese War (1937–1945), and the Liberation War (1945–1949) – is then covered in Part 4. These years saw the CPC grow into a significant political force with control over large areas of North China, rising to take overall state power in 1949. As it recast its role in the context of war and occupation, the CPC under Mao's leadership, shifting from class struggle to a focus on national resistance, did not however abandon its approach of peasant mobilisation. Then, with the breakdown of the United Front in 1945 and the resumption of civil war with the KMT, the CPC transitioned once again from moderate land adjustments back to a radical land confiscation programme pursuing the complete eradication of feudal relations.

The contrast between the two periods brings into focus the critical importance of the national context with different land policies impacting on peasant organisation and the dynamics of the agrarian revolution in different ways. New Democracy now saw the CPC develop distinctive methods of handling class contradictions amidst intensified debates on democracy as practised within the Party as well as in relation to the wider society, the village and the peasantry.

By 1942, the severe circumstances of war and the challenge of holding together the various class interests that made up the patriotic New Democratic government in the base areas in the North, put CPC leadership to the test. With policies towards the landlords moderated, the Party had to find new ways to strengthen relations with the peasants and a Party rectification campaign was launched, focusing on the questions of leadership and Party-mass relations. It was to prove a major turning point in the establishment of Mao's mass line approach.

Chapter 18 opens the discussion by comparing the works of Mao and Liu Shaoqi on the question of Party rectification as they sought to tackle the problems of landlord influence and of commandism and bureaucratism within the organisational ranks. This reveals differences in their perceptions as to the root of the problems of rural work and the causes of Party degeneration. Whilst Liu's Confucian-influenced approach focused on the need for cadre self-education – self-cultivation – to serve as a force for enlightenment, Mao, adopting a more positive perspective on the revolutionary potential of the countryside, favoured 'opening the door' of the Party to mass interaction.

Chapter 19 turns to the seminal work, Selden's *The Yenan Way in Revolutionary China*. This sets out how Party rectification was to become the driving force against the bureaucratic stasis which arose out of economic stagnation in this barren and isolated Northern base area as the CPC turned to develop village economic programmes to boost production. For Selden, the CPC was to effect a new democratic transformation of state-village relations, transforming its mode of leadership and implanting a new politics to facilitate peasant participation from the bottom up. Others, on the contrary have argued it was an exercise in top-down authoritarianism as the CPC deepened and extended its control over rural society. Taking up these debates, the chapter explores further the challenges of maintaining class unity under United Front policies, widening the discussion to consider the combining of political with economic democracy in the New Democratic programme.

Following the breakdown in the CPC-KMT alliance in 1945, rural tensions over land began to explode. In a confused transition from moderate reform to radical land confiscation, with class contradictions sharpening in conditions of civil war, the Party once more faced not only obstruction from the remaining local elites but also 'Leftist' tendencies and dissatisfaction on the part of the poor peasants. With the help of detailed village studies by William Hinton and David and Isabel Crook, carried out at the time, it is possible to unravel the complexity of the events of 1947 and 1948 and to gain greater insight into the CPC-peasant relationship as the Party sought to overcome disorganisation and disunity within the peasant movement, making readjustments and rectifying errors in land policies.

Chapter 20 takes up the question of 'not-so-thorough' land reform with a detailed comparison of the various Party directives issued as it redirected policy to the eradication of feudal relations. Once again differences over the practice of democracy and Party rectification were to emerge within the CPC, the voluntarist approach of Liu Shaoqi towards free expression – 'doing everything the masses want' – contrasting with Mao's democratic centralism as the Party grappled with the difficulties of the 'poor peasant line' and the 'middle peasant line'.

Chapter 21 then turns to consider how the contradictions among the peasants and between the peasants and the cadres were finally resolved as the CPC's methods of mass mobilisation and Party rectification came to be refined. By once again applying class analysis, the CPC was able to focus on the targets of the anti-feudal strategy by sequence whilst calibrating peasant class dynamics to unfold momentum in a measured way according to local conditions. At the same time, the treatment of cadres' errors through education rather than punishment and an open-door approach enabled a two-way 'consciousness-raising' exchange between local Party leaders and villagers.

What made this fine-tuning of practice possible was a deeper understanding of Rightist and 'Leftist' errors as these arose amidst changes in the overall revolutionary situation. Understanding how these wider shifts impacted the different sections of peasants enabled a deeper analysis of peasant dynamics and the interaction between the agrarian and the national revolutions.

The last section, Part 5, provides a critical examination of some of the major works of scholarship on Chinese peasants in revolution from the field of Western Peasant Studies. Concerned to discover the roots of the success of the CPC's peasant mobilisation, these contributions, Marxist and non-Marxist, both by comparative and case study methods, offer rich detail and rewarding insights in their discussions of the nature of the Chinese peasants and the CPC-peasant relationship. These help in understanding the complexities of rural politics, opening up the subjective dimension of the revolutionary process to address the central question of how the peasants made the transition from the ties of tradition and clientelism to revolution and the part played by the CPC in this. However they tend to fall short on the central question of class analysis and class dynamics in the rural struggles, reaching different conclusions as to the nature of CPC-peasant relations on the basis of different views on the peasants as traditionalists or revolutionaries, subsistence- or market-oriented producers.

Chapter 22 starts with a critique of the 'middle peasant thesis' of Alavi and of Wolf, arguments drawn from their comparisons of peasant movements in different parts of the world. These foundational works in Peasant Studies drew attention to the hitherto much neglected role of the middle peasants, highlighting the political importance of patron-client ties which they saw as inhibiting the poorer peasants. Whilst Alavi from a Leninist perspective was concerned with the dynamics and stages of a peasant-driven revolution, Wolf set out the proposition that rural rebellions are essentially triggered in a fundamental collision between the subsistence-based world of the peasants and capitalism with the spread of international markets.

The two case studies of Perry and of Marks examine rural class conflict through a long-term historical lens to provide further examples of contrasting takes on the relationship between tradition and revolution. These authors open up discussion of the peasants' goals as expressed in the various types of traditional collective actions, as well as the forms of peasant power and questions of elite leadership. Perry offers particular insight on protectionism and predatory patterns of peasant behaviour in Northern Anhui, whilst Marks examines the rise and fall of the 1929 Haifeng Soviet, Guangdong province, and its 'cult of personality'. Whilst Perry sees the peasants as locked into a cycle of traditionalism, Marks on the other hand, from a Marxist perspective, sees peasants as collectively learning through the process of struggle.

Chapter 23 consists of an extended discussion of Thaxton's study of the Taihang peasants. The value of this particular work lies in its consideration of the influence of peasant culture and tradition on the revolutionary process, shedding new light on the question of peasant agency and of how the CPC came to harness this. However, Thaxton's proposition that market and moral economies were joined together in the consciousness and practices of the free-trading familialist villagers proves problematic with its assertion that the Yan'an village programmes 'made capitalism available to all'.

In fact, CPC success was far more than a matter of popular appeal: Party leadership was to prove itself in how it handled the different facets to traditionalism to overcome divisions among the peasants; how it sought to counter elitist and bureaucratic tendencies in its own organisation; and how it applied its understanding of the dynamic interactions between the national and agrarian revolution. Against the background of the above critiques, Chapter 24 brings into focus what difference the CPC actually made in the organisation of the peasant struggle for land and livelihood, connecting peasant agency and Party leadership in a two-way negotiated process.

It was by grasping the class issue that the CPC, developing policies designed to manage the rural dynamics and national contradictions, enabled the peasants to resolve their differences and transcend the limitations in their traditional dynamics of struggle so as to maintain their own leadership over the rural transformation process against degeneration from within. Through independent mass organisation, land reform in China was able to avoid unduly strengthening the forces of capitalism, preparing for the advance to socialism.

Finally, the conclusion reflects on the overall findings within a wider literature with some considerations of their relevance in the shifts and changes of rural policy as these unfolded in the decades after 1949.

Postscript

Just over one hundred years on from its foundation, it is timely to recall how the CPC came to power in 1949 as a result of its success in mobilising the peasants. The account of how the Party grew from its founding congress of just some dozen people held in secret on a boat on Shanghai's South Lake to become the world's largest political organisation with a membership of around 99 million and now leading the second largest economy in the world, is truly remarkable.

The authenticity of the CPC has been frequently called into question over the decades as a party of peasants rather than the working class. The Party in fact originally had its roots in the Chinese working class made up mostly of those employed in foreign enterprises which, although small, radicalised rapidly in the ferment which followed the betrayal of China's interests in the Treaty of Versailles at the end of the First World War. Mao, it should be recalled, began to develop his skills as an organiser among workers in the tin and coal mines of Anyuan, Hunan province. As secretary of the Hunan CPC branch between 1921 and 1923 he estimated he organised some 30,000 workers in unions, helping to establish more than 20 unions of mineworkers, railway workers municipal employees and printing press workers, and succeeding in improving the pay and conditions for over 22,000 workers.[31]

This discussion of the CPC's role in the peasant movement from 1925 to 1949 does not give a complete account of the CPC's rise to power but focusses instead on demonstrating the centrality of peasant activism to the Chinese revolution, detailing the steps made by the CPC in its rural work to bring the agrarian movement to its successful conclusion.

The work was originally presented as a PhD thesis, which was awarded by the University of Manchester in 1989. As a post-graduate student in the Department of Sociology, I attended seminars on the State and Peasants run by Professor Teodor Shanin and Hamza Alavi. There I was introduced to the central debates within Marxism on the peasants: Lenin and the Narodniks; Chayanov's notion of a peasant mode of production; and the 'middle peasant thesis' in particular Alavi's argument that Mao succeeded where the Bolsheviks had failed in grasping the role of the middle peasants in revolution; as well as the more contemporary debates on capitalism and the peasants. These controversies were to inform my work as I endeavoured to develop a Marxist perspective within the field of existing studies of the Chinese peasants in the pre-revolutionary era.

Addressing three key themes of China's agrarian crisis, the nature of the peasant revolution, and CPC-peasant relations, the study drew on a wide-ranging literature. The job of bringing such a broad-based work up-to-date has proved daunting and in the end only a few additional sources have been incorporated into the discussion. The publication of the work after 30 years is nevertheless considered worthwhile since the arguments remain both topical and valid whilst the principal resources used still provide the foundation for studies of the Chinese peasants of the period.

The significance of the volume as set out previously in its aims remains relevant: bringing into play the works of Chinese Marxist scholars of the period on feudal power and the feudal constraints on production as well as the later Chinese Marxist historians of the 1980s on how the process of refeudalisation overwhelmed emergent capitalist relations to provide a basis for analysing China's revolutionary process; to then show how the CPC succeeded in tackling the resilience of feudal power whilst handling the contradictions among the peasants, at the same time offering a distinctive appreciation of Mao's leadership in concrete context.

What now also stands out in the context of contemporary debate on the China model and Chinese style of governance, is the discussion of democracy and the Confucian state. Particularly in its examination of New Democracy and of the chaos that ensued in the land reform between 1946 and 1948 from the practice of 'doing everything the masses want', the study shows how through practice the CPC came to develop its own understandings of democracy. These were seen not simply in terms of universal suffrage with the introduction of local elections but as a matter of class organisation – the mass line – of the top-down bottom-up style of democratic centralism in Party-mass relations, and of economic democracy or sharing as a way of accommodating contradictory class forces to harmonise social tensions and conflicts by balancing different interests towards a common goal.

Although the New Democratic period ended with the transition to socialism in 1956, an understanding of its methods of building class consensus remain relevant to today's China in which the CPC continues to manage the growth of the private sector and the emergence of individual billionaires now within the integument of a far stronger state geared to achieving China's development and modernisation.

Authors such as Martin Jacques and leading Chinese intellectual, Zhang Weiwei, rejecting the applicability of the Western political system to China, highlight instead the positive features of the traditional meritocratic system in managing crises and maintaining stability with state legitimacy established through competence and efficiency rather than election.[32]

But rather than emphasising the continuity of the state, the discussion here demonstrates the revolutionary transformation of its class content through the anti-imperialist and anti-feudal struggle. The approach taken is far more critical of the patriarchal hierarchy of the Confucian state, its values of benevolence and virtue seen rather to cloak a highly exploitative feudal landlord system. The idea of the civilisational state advanced by the above authors presents the legitimacy of China's present system as rooted in its past in a way which seems to replicate an approach to theorising the Chinese centralised state as separate from class, an approach critiqued in this study.

Interestingly however, the methods identified by Zhang as key to China's approach to governance today such as establishing priorities and sequencing, learning from practice, adopting a long-term perspective, are very well illustrated in the discussion of the evolution of the CPC's political practice in organising the land revolution. These are valuable lessons from which the Western Left can learn much today.

The study has other implications for understanding China beyond 1949. It was originally undertaken at a time when China was undergoing a dramatic change in its rural policies from the early 1980s, with the break-up of the commune system and the adoption of reforms under Deng Xiaoping introducing the individual household responsibility system of farming. From the pursuit of class struggle aimed at restricting the emergence of 'spontaneous capitalist tendencies' during the 10 years of the Cultural Revolution, rural policy shifted to an emphasis on stability to increase production, opposing peasant self-sufficiency and promoting instead their participation in the market by encouraging aspirations to 'get rich'.[33]

For some, this radical shift demanded a fundamental critique of socialist China: the CPC was seen as having imposed policies of collectivism on a proprietorial peasantry, forcing them along the socialist path. Had the CPC in fact overestimated the revolutionary potential in the countryside? Was a complete re-examination of the peasants' role in the revolution and the nature of their goals in relation to the goals of the CPC called for?

The findings of this study point to the centrality of the peasants' struggle for land as a means of livelihood with proprietorship an issue for only a few, at the same time highlighting the importance of accommodating the different peasant interests according to concrete circumstances. This helps to put the transition under Deng Xiaoping in a different light. Rural China was set on its new course after 1979 when agricultural production had risen to such a level that China was basically able to feed and clothe its people. This was achieved as a result of collective efforts of the production teams in the commune system. The question of meeting subsistence needs was absolutely central to CPC policies after 1949 and the shift from the commune system to the household responsibility system, which saw peasants rewarded individually for labour, was only possible once these basic needs were met. Today, the people's livelihood remains at the core of CPC policy-making.

NOTES AND REFERENCES

1. See Schram and Carrere d'Encausse, 1969, p.120; see also Marx (1968).

2. K. Marx, 'The Eighteenth Brumaire of Louis Bonaparte', 1952, pp.303–304, in K. Marx and F. Engels, *Selected Works*, Vol. I, Lawrence and Wishart Ltd, London, 1950.

3. See, for example, Lenin, *Collected Works*, Vol. IX, p.100.

4. See 'The People and the State', one of the documents of the

People's Will in Shanin (ed.) 1983, pp.219–223.

5. Chayanov (1966).

6. Hobsbawm, 1973/4, pp.4–5.

7. Popkin (1979) uses the perspective of individual rationality to account for peasant participation in revolution in terms of individual economic incentives. See also Schultz (1964), especially Chapters 2 and 3.

8. Scott, 1976, p.5; pp.13–55.

9. See for example the concept of peasant subsumption under capitalism put forward by Alavi, 1982, pp.68–71; and Bernstein's discussion of the relationship between capital and the peasantry, 1977. For the Chinese context, see Huang, 1985, p.309; Li Yichou (1961) also argued that the semi-proletariat of the Chinese countryside, the poor peasants, were highly revolutionary.

10. Skinner (1964/5), especially Part I.

11. See Watson, 1984, pp.589–622, for a survey of the existing literature.

12. See, for example, Chen Boda, 1966a, p.38.

13. Huang, 1985, p.29.

14. Rawski (1972). This work is discussed further in Chapter 2.

15. Elvin (1973). This work is discussed further in Chapter 5.

16. Myers, 1970, pp.273–88. The random disturbances were natural disasters, wars, increased taxation and price fluctuations.

17. See, for example, Chen Yungfa, 1986, p.14.

18. Tawney, 1980, p.77.

19. Wolf, 1969, p.280.

20. This is the argument advanced by Thaxton (1983) and discussed in detail in Part 5.

21. For an interpretation of Mao's version of Marxist-Leninism as containing populist beliefs, see Meisner (1982), especially Chapter 3.

22. Chesneaux, 1973, pp.151–2.

23. Mao, *Selected Works*, Vol. I, p.25.

24. See Chang Liu, 2007, pp.187–192, for an argument which highlights these differences in the social structures. Chang makes the point that in the South, the highly stratified rural society of absentee landlords and their tenant-peasants gave rise to widespread and intense class conflicts which would surge up and subside, whereas in the North the solidary communities of owner-cultivators, in confrontation with the state over issues of tax and local corruption, offered a local political setting more conducive for CPC organisation over the long-term. The 'middle peasant thesis' of Alavi suggests from a Leninist perspective that the CPC succeeded where the Bolsheviks had failed in grasping the key role of these more independent peasants in the revolution. See discussion in Chapter 22.

25. Li Lifeng (2015).

26. See Gillin (1961); Isaacs, 1962, p.342.

27. Mao called for Marxism to be 'integrated with the specific characteristics of our country and given a national form' so as to be put into practice, and for it to be applied 'in accordance with Chinese characteristics'. *Selected Works*, Vol. II, p.260. For further discussion of the sinification of Marxism see Dirlik, 2005, pp.78–85.

28. Womack (1982) also places emphasis on the interaction of Mao's theory and practice, setting the evolution of Mao's political thought from the early years to the Long March *in vivo* in its practical context, using a wide range of documents to offer a detailed discussion. As distinct from this, by setting discussion within the conceptual frame of Marxism and Leninism in which the CPC debates were themselves conducted, as well as referencing scholarly works on Chinese Peasant Studies to engage with the rural political dynamics, this work aims to add greater explanatory value in showing how Mao responded to the problems within the revolutionary process.

29. Chen Hanseng (1936); Chen Boda (1966a). Chen Boda was a leading Marxist theoretician and Party activist who played a major role in the ideological debates in 1935–45 during the Yan'an period, and in the formulation of New Democracy. As Mao's political secretary from 1937, he edited the first volumes of Mao's works. He was later a major spokesman in the Cultural Revolution. For further biographical details see Wylie, 1980, pp.7–18; pp.59–66; pp.72–73; pp.291–8.

30. Lenin, *Collected Works*, Vol. I pp. 442–3; p.448.

31. Alavi, 1965, p.252.

32. Martin Jacques (2012); Zhang Weiwei (2012).

33. On the rationale for the people's communes see, for example, Editorial Departments of Renmin Ribao, Hongqi and Jiefangjun Bao (1968), also Yao Wenyuan (1975); on the rationale for the household responsibility system see, for example, Wang Guichin and others, 1985, p.7; also *Beijing Review Commentator*, 19 January 1981.

PART 1

Landlord monopoly and peasant land hunger – the distinct characteristics of China's agrarian structure

Introduction

The rationale of the CPC's policy to take peasant organisation in land reform as the central issue of the Chinese revolution was based on an analysis which focused on the political and economic centrality of landlordism and the landlord-peasant class conflict.

The assessment of the central role of the landlords in the structure of pre-revolutionary society was apparently challenged by surveys conducted by J. L. Buck in the early 1930s which suggested that the amount of land held by those who did not farm it themselves was too small to serve as an adequate base for a distinct and dominant landlord class.

Buck's claim was that almost three-quarters of privately-owned farmland was owned by the farmers themselves, with the owners comprising a little over half of the farmers; part-owners, less than one-third; and the rest, tenants.[1] This claim supports a view of China as a society of owner-cultivators. According to this perspective, land reform would have had only a marginal impact on economic growth.

R.H. Tawney similarly described Chinese agriculture as a system of '*la petite culture*'. According to him, China:

> possesses no landed aristocracy, no dominant class of junkers or squires… She is not afflicted by the complicated iniquities of feudal land laws; manorial estates worked by *corvées*, if they ever existed, have left few traces. Landlord and tenant are parties to a business contract, not members of different classes based on privilege and subordination.[2]

Apart from the question of the extent of tenancy, Tawney's suggestion of the business basis of tenancy arrangements raises a further issue as to the actual nature of the landlord-tenant relationship. The question here concerns the impact of the development of commerce on land relations, and whether in fact rural relations were determined by market conditions than rather than landlord power.

The centralised and hierarchical nature of the traditional Chinese state provides a further area of controversy concerning the centrality of landlordism since it appears that political power was in fact vested with the bureaucratic elite and not based upon the ownership of land.

To examine the question of the centrality of landlordism requires in the first place, an investigation of the overall conditions of land ownership and the peasantry, taking into account the different relations of exploitation which emerged with the development of commerce. Secondly, landlord-peasant relations must also be viewed in relation to other aspects of the rural power structure shaped by the bureaucratic state on the one hand and the patriarchal village community on the other. The examination here of the distinctive features of China's pre-revolutionary agrarian society reveals not only the dimensions of the crisis but also the contradictory effects of imperialism. In doing so it demonstrates the potential for revolutionary transformation given the semi-feudal and semi-colonial characteristics of Chinese society.

NOTES AND REFERENCES

1. Buck, 1964, p.9.
2. Tawney, 1980, p.63.

1

Land ownership, rent and the condition of the peasantry

How unequal was land ownership?

In pre-liberation China, the conditions and extent of land tenure, as well as productivity and population density, varied widely not only between different regions but between localities in the same region. Such variations make generalisations difficult, but whilst peasant ownership could vary from village to village, on the whole tenancy tended to increase with the development of commercialisation. Thus it is possible to draw a broad distinction between the more fertile, and commercially developed areas, easily accessible by transport, where rates of tenancy were higher given that higher productivity stimulated landlord interest in appropriating the surplus, and more remote, less fertile areas where owner-cultivated land was more widespread.

The basic contrast lies between the more commercially developed rice-growing South, with a greater population density, and the less developed North, given mainly to dry farming, especially wheat, where lack of water and transport made for a much less commercialised agrarian economy producing a low surplus. Whilst the Southern regions saw more absentee landlords, in the North there were more rich peasants and small landlords but with a preponderance of owner-cultivators farming with limited traditional techniques. The picture was nevertheless mixed since Northern China also had its more advanced areas in the lowland river valleys, whilst the mountainous areas in the South remained relatively underdeveloped.[1]

Despite the variations, and although wheat farming is not as intensive as rice cultivation, the outstanding characteristic of Chinese agriculture was that of small-scale cultivation: neither manorial estates nor large-scale capitalist farming were a particular feature. The parcellised nature of its agriculture gave China the appearance, as Buck's surveys reflected, of a society of relatively equal owner-cultivators. However, the CPC claimed that 10 per cent of the population held approximately 70–80 per cent of the land, whilst the remaining 90 per cent held only between 20 and 30 per cent, a claim which highlighted the extremes of wealth and poverty in the countryside as evidence of the condition of exploitation and oppression of the majority of peasants.[2] It is these broad figures that illuminated the background to the revolution.

Buck's surveys suggest that the inequalities in land ownership were not as extensive a problem as the CPC figures made out. Showing that peasant ownership was more prevalent in the North, his figures were 75 per cent owner-farmers and a only little over 12 per cent farm area rented, whereas for the South, less than 40 per cent were owner-farmers, 33 per cent part-owners, with tenants more prevalent at 25 per cent and 40 per cent farm area rented, rising to 47 per cent in Guangdong.[3] However, a subsequent review of a variety of surveys made in the 1920s and 1930s by Esherick finds that 41.7 per cent of cultivated land was rented, indicating that Buck's own figure of overall 28.7 per cent farm area rented was a considerable underestimation.[4]

Esherick points out the bias of Buck's surveys weighted towards wealthier, literate households. But at root the fundamental difference between Buck's figures and those used by the CPC is the matter of categorisation of rural classes. Whilst Buck figured that over half the peasantry were owner-cultivators, Mao estimated that these independent producers made up about one third of the rural population: here is a difference over which households counted in the independent peasant sector, indicating different criteria were being employed in analysing rural relations.[5]

Buck's simple distinction between owners and tenants in fact obscured the inequalities within the peasantry in terms of land, tools, and the yield and value of crops cultivated. Over time the CPC was to refine a class analysis which differentiated categories of rich, middle and poor peasants. Their methods found that the landholdings of rich peasants, in fact, formed a large proportion of the land owned by the peasants. Citing figures for the whole country, Jin Dequn states that whilst they constituted six per cent of the population, the rich peasants owned 18 per cent of the land.[6] Counting the rich peasants together with the landlords, he arrives at figures differing from Buck's, finding 10 per cent of the population owning 68 per cent of the land. Also taking the rich peasants and landlords together, Esherick puts this top 10 per cent of the population as owning 56 per cent of the land, with the landlords, forming about 3 to 4 per cent of the population, owning almost 39 per cent of the land, leaving the rich peasants at 6 to 7 per cent of the population owning 17 per cent of the land.[7] Whilst Esherick's estimates of the rich peasants are very close to those of Jin Dequn, his figure for the landlords' share of the land is considerably less than that suggested by the CPC. Nevertheless, Esherick's review still shows that a great deal of land was owned by the landlords, certainly providing a sufficient basis for a distinct class.

Chinese Marxists further estimated that the middle peasantry, making up 20 to 25 per cent of the population, owned about 15 per cent of the land, leaving the poor peasantry and rural proletariat at 65 to 70 per cent of the population holding only between 5 and 15 per cent of the land.[8]

Esherick's figure for the landless and the poor peasantry who owned less than 10 *mu*, is that they comprised 68 per cent of the population owning 14 per cent of the land.[9] This corresponds more closely with the CPC's estimates, highlighting the inadequacy of land ownership among the poorer majority in the countryside. On the other hand, his estimate for the middle peasantry, at 22 per cent of the population owning 30 per cent of the land, is quite at variance with the CPC figures. Esherick's suggestion that the CPC underestimated the land owned by the middle peasants and as a result exaggerated the holdings of the landlords is however only tentative.[10]

Esherick estimates that rented land totalled approximately 600 million *mu* but notes the figures for the total land redistributed in land reform at approximately 700 million *mu*, a discrepancy of some 100 million *mu*. This he suggests may have been confiscated from managerial farmers and rich peasants, whose holdings cultivated by hired labour were meant to be protected under land reform.[11] One possibility to be considered here is an increase in landlordism between the time of the surveys and the overthrow of the KMT, but this he rejects, citing Ash's argument that the extent of landlord holdings was declining in southern Jiangsu province in the 1930s, especially around Shanghai where the wealthy were turning away from landed property to investment in industry and commerce.[12]

As is to be discussed in the following chapter, Chen Boda considered that the general trend was towards the loss of land by the peasants and the greater concentration of land in the hands of the few with the intensification in the rate of exploitation through land rent. This concentration occurred within the landlord class itself as Chen Hanseng, writing in the mid-1930s, was to find, with the exorbitant surtaxes levied by the KMT government squeezing not only the peasantry but also the smaller landlords whose properties were bought out by those very large landowners better able to dodge taxes by various means. He notes that in southern Jiangsu only a small proportion, less than 10 per cent, of the large landlords were 'industrial men' investing in factories; other landlords were usurers and merchants who relied on income from rent for speculation.[13]

The number of landlords may have declined in the 1920s and 1930s with some seeking alternative sources of income since tenant peasants, hit by the depression in world trade, were unable to pay rent. But whilst the deteriorating economy also saw numbers of landlords driven into bankruptcy, there was the notable emergence of a new class of landlords who benefitted under KMT reforms, using links with the new police chiefs and tax farmers to enhance their position whilst taking advantage of trading opportunities and lending money at exorbitant rates.

Certainly after the Japanese invasion and the following years of civil war, because of the urgent need for food as well as the disruption of foreign trade and the loss of the big industrial and commercial cities, income from land rent became more and more a source of wealth for speculation.[14] Speculators often let land lie idle as ownership passed rapidly from hand to hand, and it is this that may well account for the discrepancy in the figures of rented lands and land redistributed. Esherick's figures are for rented lands under cultivation but an indication of the amount of land left idle is the decline in area of land under cultivation from 120 million hectares in 1936 to 98 million hectares in 1949.[15]

At any rate, it is not then regional variations alone that create problems in gaining understanding and assessing the conditions in the Chinese peasantry: it is also the general problem of categorising and distinguishing between the different rural classes that was made all the more difficult by the complexity of economic relations in the Chinese countryside. In fact, the widespread existence of exploitation through usury and hiring labour, as well as rent, rendered class analysis on the basis of ownership alone totally inadequate.

Inequalities among peasants and problems of insufficiency

Addressing the question of how to classify peasant families, Chen Hanseng argued:

> If we classify them according to the size of their landed property, then we shall miss other important aspects of the social and economic relations that affect production and consequently shall not be able to show the real economic status of the different types of families. If we classify them according to the relation of ownership and differentiate them as owners, part-owners and tenants, then we are again limited to a formal distinction which from the point of view of welfare may not be an important one. In reality a family here classified as owners if it has very little land of its own will be obliged to send out its members as hired labourers. To think of such a family primarily as a landowning one would give the wrong slant on its status. Such a family may be poorer than a tenant family which cultivates much land though owning little or none of it and hires a number of labourers.[16]

Whilst the simple distinction between tenant and owner peasant did not account for the fact that some tenants were rich peasants hiring labour or giving loans, more importantly it failed to reveal the extent of insufficiency which forced large numbers of peasants into debt or hiring out their labour.[17]

In order to identify classes among the peasants, Lenin, in his 1899 work *The Development of Capitalism in Russia*, used the criterion of sown area rather than ownership since he considered that inequalities in cultivated land indicated differences in the ability to command means of production. Measuring sown area would then reveal differences within the peasantry in relation to means of production. But in China, whilst classification according to ownership was inadequate in revealing the complexity of rural exploitation, neither was the criterion of sown area suitable since land was not a uniform unit.

Huge variations existed between regions: the rice bowls yielded four times as much as the poorer areas.[18] According to Chen Hanseng:

> Even if we classify the peasant families according to the area of the land they cultivate, trying to determine the economic position by the size of holding, such a classification would not be reliable as an indication of their economic status. The size of holding shows only the area of cultivation, and may not show the magnitude of the farm business. For example, it makes a good deal of difference whether a holding of, say, five *mou* is devoted to taro or rice; the money income from the one crop would be only a fraction of what the other brings in. On the other hand, the magnitude of the farm business by itself cannot furnish a reliable basis for a really revealing classification. There are some big landlord families managing small orchards... Judging from the size of the holding they cultivate, we should most likely mistake them for poor peasants; but nothing would be further from the truth, because most of their income comes from that part of their land which they lease out. Again to compare a family which cultivates all of its own land with that of a tenant, both cultivating the same number of *mou*, the size of their holdings would be exactly the same, but obviously because one has to pay rent and the other has not, they are in a very different economic position.[19]

The criterion of sown area did not reveal the full extent of the differences between those with adequate tools for cultivation and those without. The more well-to-do peasants could get more out of poor land through the application of fertiliser and only those with a surplus could undertake land improvements or afford the outlays in the cultivation of fruit and commercial crops, whilst poorer peasants had to rely on a good price or larger income from each unit of land. Otherwise, they had to grow less valuable crops for their own subsistence.[20] Furthermore a peasant with tools could get a better deal from the landlords than one without who fell victim to sharecropping.

Chen Hanseng's method of classification of the peasantry measured the livelihood of peasant households in terms of land and labour: the amount of land a family uses and the conditions under which it is used; and the labour which the family puts into the land or hires to use on the land:

> When a peasant family is barely capable of self-support from the land, and in its agricultural labour not directly exploited by, nor exploiting, others, we may say that such a family belongs to the class of 'middle peasants'. The status of the middle peasant helps us to determine that of the other two classes of peasantry. When a peasant family hires one or more agricultural labourers by the year, or hires a number of labourers by the day or by the season during busy times, to an extent exceeding in its total consumption of labour power that required by the average middle peasant family for self-support, or when the land which it cultivates surpasses in area the average of the land used by the middle peasant, we shall then classify this family as that of a 'rich peasant'... All the peasant families whose number of cultivated *mou* falls below that of the middle peasants, and whose members, besides living on the fruits of their own cultivation, have to rely upon a wage income or some income of an auxiliary nature, belong to the poor peasants in general.[21]

This method revealed that the vast majority of peasants had not enough land either in relation to their productive capacity or in relation to their needs.[22] It exposed the core problems of land hunger and underutilised labour. As Chen Hanseng found in the commercially developed province of Guangdong:

> Owing to the exorbitant charge of rent, the poor and middle peasants cannot secure adequate land to employ all their available labour power, and to make full use of even their antiquated implements.[23]

Indeed, the middle peasant holding, that is, the average holding of the peasantry, was below subsistence.[24]

A report on a rural investigation in the more backward province of Yunnan similarly found:

> ...a huge amount of potential labour power cannot be utilised under the present agrarian system in which the contradiction between land owning and land cultivation is so apparent. Those who own land have become parasitic and unproductive,

but those who actually produce and work in the fields cannot find adequate land…peasants with inadequate land or no land at all constitute an overwhelming majority of the peasants.[25]

Chen Hanseng reckoned that in all, in Guangdong province where tenancy rates were high, 72 per cent cultivated less than 10 *mu*, the minimum for subsistence. As a result there was a widespread problem of debt, affecting 60, and even 90 per cent of the households in some districts.[26]

Huang's study of the peasant economy of the North China plain finds that 43 per cent of rural households cultivated less than 10 *mu*, when 15 *mu* was the average minimum for sustaining a household.[27] Although the problem of debt was not as high in North China as in the South, Huang finds instances of debt affecting 37 per cent and 39 per cent of households in each of two sample villages.[28] However, wage labour was more prevalent in the North where according to Huang nearly 48 per cent of peasant households relied on selling their labour to meet their families' needs.[29]

The extent of debt and wage labour gives some indication of peasant insufficiency. However Buck's surveys did not reveal the scope of labour exploitation since they did not adequately account for the use of labour; neither did they demonstrate the problem of debt. In isolation from forms of exploitation other than rent, Buck's methods failed in the first place to distinguish the rich peasants who hired labour or practised usury, or even small landlords who cultivated orchards, from the other owner peasants who lived in the main by their own labour.

Secondly the surveys did not show the unequal distribution of land that existed within the peasantry. Chen Hanseng's study based in Southern China revealed further that both in terms of land owned and land cultivated, not only was there a high degree of concentration but there were also clear distinctions among the peasants. In terms of land cultivated, the rich peasants who made up less than one eighth of the peasant families, cultivated one third of the land, whilst the poor peasants, who accounted for two-thirds of peasant families, cultivated one third of the land.[30] The rich peasants owned most of the land owned by the peasantry, and most of this was of good quality; they leased in the least amount of land and cultivated twice the average holding. Poor peasants struggled desperately to survive: many of these families simply died out, since more than one in every 10 men in each generation could not afford to marry or raise a family.[31]

Rich peasants owned their own means of production and, with liquid capital above their own consumption needs, they were able to earn auxiliary income by diversifying their farm business, developing sidelines and hiring labour to cultivate commercial crops. They were thus commercially-minded, often owning small industrial or commercial undertakings – grain stores, flour mills, village shops.[32] On the other hand, Chen Hanseng observed that in general, in the 1930s, there was little improvement in the practice of agriculture in commercialised Guangdong since a decline in agricultural prices had caused rich peasants to cut their production costs by reducing wages and numbers of hired labourers and by putting less into land improvements such that yields fell.[33] Rather than extending cultivated acreage, increasing hired labour and raising yields, the rich peasants preferred to lease land out or engage in usury. The rich peasant sector was thus relatively weak in terms of production, accounting for less than one-fifth of the total agricultural output: it was, rather, closely tied up with the landlord classes, leasing land out for rent.[34]

Besides the struggle for survival on inadequate plots on the part of the poor peasants, and the reluctance of the rich peasants to improve agricultural practice, a further indication of agricultural stagnation and peasant impoverishment was the loss of land by the middle peasants. Chen Hanseng found that in areas of high tenancy, the middle peasants were losing land the fastest, whilst more than half the peasants were landless and forced into tenancy.[35] The fact that the middle peasants were losing out both in terms of land ownership and area cultivated, with land cultivation concentrating in the hands of the rich peasants, was a clear indication of the growing distress of the majority of the peasants.

Chen Hanseng's study of the agrarian problem in Southern China presents data which confirm the trend of higher rates of tenancy in the more fertile and commercialised areas, and higher degrees of peasant ownership in the less fertile districts. But although the less fertile areas exhibited less concentration of land ownership, land owned by the top 10 per cent still accounted for a considerable amount at over 40 per cent, and the number of peasants with land insufficient for their needs was no less than in the more developed areas.[36] What this highlights most of all is the fact that the best land was owned by the landlords and rich peasants, whilst the poor and middle peasants owned relatively poor infertile land.

As pointed out earlier, on the question of middle peasant holdings there is a difference between Esherick's findings and the CPC's own figures. This is of significance since the CPC, maintaining that the proportion of middle peasants in the population exceeded their landholdings as a proportion of total land, considered that these peasants stood to benefit from a more equal distribution of land. Esherick on the other hand maintains the reverse, that middle peasant holdings were greater in proportion to their numbers, suggesting they might lose out in the land reform process. However, he admits that his own use of 10 *mu* as a dividing line between poor and middle peasants is an arbitrary one which may well have underestimated the numbers of middle peasants and overestimated their holdings.

The point that needs to be clarified in fact is that whilst 10 *mu* may have been a reasonable average for minimum subsistence for the whole of China, in less fertile areas where the number of owner-cultivators was greater, the average was a good deal higher. Whereas Huang found that 15 *mu* was the minimum for subsistence in the North China plain, Chen Hanseng found that in some districts the land was so inferior that a family owning and cultivating a holding of 25 *mu* was still considered to be a poor family.[37] So since peasants owned the least fertile lands, Esherick's demarcation between poor and middle peasant holdings should perhaps be revised upwards.

The further important point to be made about the figures for middle peasant holdings, in considering the extent of inequality in land ownership, is that within the owner-peasants there was also a significant degree of polarity. Since these peasants on the whole owned the poorest lands, many in fact were in deficit. Buck's surveys do not reveal the extent of insufficiency among a substantial proportion of the owner-peasants, but it was the position of these peasants that Mao highlighted in his early work of 1926, *Analysis of the Classes in Chinese Society*, providing a further insight into inequalities in the countryside.

Mao here considered that the rural semi-proletariat – the semi-tenant and poor or tenant peasant could be subdivided into three sections: upper, middle and lower.[38] The upper section of the semi-tenant peasants owned part of their land and got the full crop on this: they were better off than tenant peasants but worse off than owner-peasants because they were short of part of the food they needed and, in order to make up their deficit, had to rent land, borrow at exorbitant interest rates, buy grain at high prices, sell part of their labour or engage in petty trading. The poor peasants without land were the worst off, surrendering half their crop or more in rent. Of these tenants, those who owned tools had funds to make up their deficit through sideline activities or would sell a part of their labour power, whilst those without adequate tools or funds had an even greater need to sell part of their labour power and borrow money. This lowest sector was the most hardest-pressed.

Mao further found that the owner-peasants, although on the whole able to invest more in production than the tenants, also fell into three distinct groups: the upper section with some surplus money and grain over and above what they needed for their own support; those who broke even more or less but who felt a squeeze on their living standards; and those who faced increasing deficits.[39] In Mao's estimation, those owner peasants who suffered some degree of insufficiency made up nearly half the total number.

Beyond the simple distinction between owner- and tenant peasants, Mao found deficit owner-peasants to be very close to the heavily exploited tenants and part-tenants and the rural proletariat in both economic position and political outlook. In his view, their difficulties in maintaining a livelihood against encroachment by the rural elites brought them into a common struggle. Taking the deficit owner-peasants together with the poor peasants and fairly large numbers of lumpen proletarians – peasants who had lost their land, and handicraftsmen who had lost all opportunity of employment – these constituted the majority of the rural population motivated through insufficiency to struggle for land.

Thus despite regional variations, with higher concentration of ownership, a higher degree of tenancy and a greater burden of debt in the Southern provinces, and more owner-peasants but a greater burden of rent in the less developed North, there were a number of revealing similarities. In the first place, whether in the North or South, a considerable majority of peasants farmed holdings insufficient both in relation to their needs and labour capacity. Even where a great deal of land in a village or locality was owned by the peasants, this was generally less fertile land insufficient for their needs. Secondly, a fairly general decrease in farm size indicated a widespread deterioration in agricultural production.[40] Finally, under very varying conditions, and even where tenancy was low, given the degree of polarisation within the peasantry, the numbers of middle peasants in proportion to the rural population tended to exceed their proportion of land owned, indicating that land redistribution could benefit not only the poor but a substantial number of middle peasants as well.[41]

One further area of discrepancy between Buck's figures and those used by the CPC concerns the area of clan lands. According to Buck, of the seven per cent of land which was publicly owned, including banner lands in the North East, lands held by schools, and temples, less than one per cent was clan land.[42] This is a very low figure which may be partly due to the fact that much of Buck's information came from the North, where large lineages were fewer than in the South. According to Chen Hanseng, clan land accounted for 35 per cent of cultivated land in Guangdong, rising to 70 per cent in some districts.[43] So whilst Buck's figures of 75 per cent owner-peasants in the North were enlarged by his inclusion of rich peasants, much of whose income came from exploitation, the discrepancy between his figures of 47 per cent farm area rented out in Guangdong in the South, and Chen Hanseng's figure for the same province of 75 per cent may in large part be accounted for by the fact that Chen Hanseng counted clan lands under the collective ownership of the landlords.[44]

Buck's findings, which appeared to provide evidence of China as a society of small owner-cultivators, have been found wanting in a number of respects. His surveys underestimated the amount of land owned by the landlords which was considerable and certainly provided a sufficient basis for a distinct class. Including the rich peasants in with the peasants as a whole, he did not take account of forms of exploitation other than rent, and so obscured the degree of polarisation within the peasantry. Above all, his surveys failed to reveal the extent of peasant insufficiency.

The CPC's estimates still provide a better reflection of the contrast between the wealth of the landlords and rich peasants, a minority of the population, and the worsening plight of the majority of the peasantry. This suggests that to understand the system of landlordism in China it is necessary to take into account not just the extent of tenancy but the conditions of the peasantry as a whole. Rather than a static measurement of peasant ownership such as Buck's, what is required is an analysis of the dynamics of the agrarian crisis which reveals the trend towards concentration of land ownership, the restriction of the rich peasant economy, and the increasing loss of the peasants' lands, with more and more becoming tenants paying exorbitant rents or clinging to tiny inadequate plots of land.

NOTES AND REFERENCES

1. Skinner depicts the Chinese Empire as consisting of nine micro-economic regions each with an inner core of fertile river valley lowlands, and an outer periphery of hilly or mountainous areas, marked by scarcity and environmental instability. 1977a, pp.214–5; 1977b, pp.284–5. See also Francesca Bray, 1984, pp.3–27, for an outline of the general characteristics of Chinese agriculture and the main agricultural regions.

2. For example, the *Basic Programme on the Chinese Agrarian Law*. Promulgated by the Central Committee of the Communist Party, October 10, 1947. See Selden, 1979, p.215 as reproduced from Hinton (1966).

3. Buck, 1964, pp.194–5.

4. Esherick, 1981, pp.394–400.

5. See Huang, 1975b, p.286.

6. Jin Dequn, 1981, p.63.

7. Esherick, 1981, p.405.

8. Jin Dequn, 1981, p.63; Du Jing, 1982, pp.107–8. The figure of 70 per cent poor peasants appears in Mao's 1927 'Report on an Investigation into the Peasant Movement in Hunan', *Selected Works*, Vol. I, pp.31–2. More detailed figures on the Chinese rural population were given in an article by Mao published in January 1926, 'An Analysis of

the various classes of the Chinese peasantry and their attitudes toward revolution', Schram, 1969a, pp.241–6. These were still clearly estimates. On the basis of this earlier article, Alavi (1965) argues that Mao would have included the section of deficit owner-peasants together with the semi-proletariat – semi-landholders, sharecroppers and poor peasants – to reach a total of 70 per cent (p.257). However, Mao clearly includes soldiers, beggars and hired labourers, referred to as elements déclassé in the 1926 essay, as well as handicraftsmen in his total in the Hunan Report.

9. One *mu* (also '*mou*') is approximately 1/15 hectare or 1/6 acre.

10. Esherick, 1981, p.405. He takes 10 *mu* as a dividing line between poor and middle peasant holdings, although he admits that this is somewhat arbitrary, (p.402; p.406). Middle peasant numbers and their holdings would also have been augmented under United Front land policies from 1937–1945, since some poor peasants were able to gain land, rising to new middle peasant status. See discussion in Chapters 20 and 21.

11. *Ibid.*, p.399.

12. Ash, 1976b, pp.12–3.

13. Chen Hanseng, 1933, pp.17–9.

14. See Thompson, 1990, pp.151–156, esp. p.154; Chen Boda, 1966, p.67.

15. See Croll, 1983, p.44. With one *mu* approximating 1/15 hectare this would have more than made up for the land rented-land redistributed discrepancy.

16. Chen Hanseng, 1936, pp.4–5.

17. For a detailed picture of patterns of ownership and tenancy in a single locality, see Crook and Gilmartin, 2013, pp.49–54. Observing that the categories of landlord, owner and renter were not always key determinants of socio-economic status, they found that, contrary to prevailing assumptions that landowners were more prosperous than renters, in fact 15 per cent of renters were more successful at their businesses, even after paying two-thirds of the harvest in rent, than the more numerous landowners at the bottom end of the spectrum.

18. Huang, 1975a, p.140.

19. Chen Hanseng, 1936, p.5.

20. *Ibid.*, p.7; p.12.

21. *Ibid.*, p.8.

22. According to estimates in 1928, about half the peasant families in China had land insufficient to provide them with food, let alone basic needs. See Croll, 1983, p.36.

23. Chen Hanseng, 1936, p.x.

24. *Ibid.*, pp.10–12.

25. Institute of Pacific Relations, 1939, p.56.

26. Chen Hanseng, 1936, pp.ix–x.

27. Huang, 1985, pp.293–4.

28. *Ibid.*, p.189.

29. *Ibid.*, p.83.
30. Chen Hanseng, 1936, p.11.
31. Moise, 1977, p.8.
32. Institute of Pacific Relations, 1939, p.204.
33. Chen Hanseng, 1936, p.98.
34. Chen Boda, 1966b, p.10.
35. Chen Hanseng, 1936, p10.
36. Chen Hanseng, 1933, pp.3–7.
37. Huang, 1985, pp.293–4; Chen Hanseng, 1933, p.5.
38. Mao, *Selected Works*, Vol. I, pp.17–8. In his early works, Mao categorised middle peasants as owner-cultivators distinct from tenants. However after carrying out more detailed researches in Xinwu County in 1930 he included both in the category of middle peasants defined as those having enough to eat and not dependent on loans. Later in 1933, in 'How to Analyse the Classes in the Rural Areas", *Selected Works*, Vol. I, pp.138–140, he took labour as the criteria distinguishing poor and middle peasants: whilst the former hired out their labour in part, the latter mainly relied on their own labour; those hiring in labour included landlords, rich peasants and well-to-do peasants. In other words, middle peasants may own their own land or be full tenants but do not hire out or hire in labour.
39. *Ibid.*, pp.15–6.
40. For figures on decreasing farm size and use of animals see Chen Hanseng, 1933, pp.24–8.
41. Jin Dequn, 1981, p.63–64; Du Jing, 1982, pp.107–8. pp.107–8.
42. Buck, 1964, p.9.
43. Chen Hanseng, 1936, p. ix; p.32.
44. *Ibid.*, p.3; p.6.

2
Landlordism and commerce

Commercialisation in China: promoting growth or stagnation?

In pre-liberation China then, a substantial proportion of the land was rented, with the concentration of ownership in the hands of the landlords and rich peasants contrasting with the inadequacy of the holdings of the majority of the peasants. However, even those who may agree that the amount of rented land was substantial and increasing, may differ over the nature of landlord-tenant relations. The CPC regarded the system of land tenure as a major constraint on economic growth; others have argued that a century or more earlier, tenancy was proving not to be detrimental to production but rather stimulated agricultural growth.[1]

From a study of commercialisation in 16th-century Fujian and 18th-century Hunan provinces, Rawski reaches the conclusion that there were no institutional barriers to agricultural growth, with production determined by market conditions, since as demand grew, prices rose, encouraging the producers to invest in production.[2] The development of commerce opened up new opportunities which provided an incentive for peasants to introduce new improved methods of intensive farming, using increased inputs of labour, fertiliser, and water as well as to diversify into new crops and handicrafts.

For Rawski, the changes in agrarian relations brought about by the development of commerce saw the emergence on the one hand of an independent, commercially-minded and market-oriented peasantry and, on the other hand, a new class of absentee landlords based on finance and trade, who lived in the towns and were no longer involved in production since they were more interested in the higher returns from commerce.[3]

Rawski finds that in commercialised areas, in contrast with less developed areas where problems of transport limited market development, tenure conditions were more favourable to the cultivator as tenants enjoyed greater security and the best rent conditions.[4] Commerce did not lead to a decline in the economic position of the tenant and rent was not a barrier to production. Rather, new tenure relations which took the place of the arrangements of sharecropping, such as share rent and fixed rent, permanent tenancy, rent deposits and cash rents, developed in recognition of the intensive labour effort put in by the cultivators, whilst the landlords settled for a stable fixed income from the land.

Share rent, a fixed percentage of the crop divided between landlord and tenant, and fixed rent, an amount of the crop pledged by the tenant to the landlord, differed from sharecropping in that the tenant owned their own tools and had a greater degree of independence.[5] Under fixed rents in particular, Rawski argued that tenants were in a position to gain from increasing production or switching to cash crops since any increases in yield or income would accrue to them.[6] Similarly, permanent tenancy – the 'two lords to a field system' – was an incentive to invest in land improvements since, under this system whereby the landlord owned the 'bottom soil' and the tenant held rights to the cultivation of the 'top soil', the responsibility for tax payment was shifted from the cultivator, whilst his tenure was secured with limits set to the landlord's prerogative to evict. In addition, rent deposits served as an economic guarantee for both parties to land tenure agreements, although small deposits were not returnable.[7] Cash rents also compared favourably with rent in kind for, whilst they were a commuted form of rent in kind, they invariably failed to keep abreast of rising rice prices, so falling short of the full value of the originally stipulated rice rent.[8]

Rawski's view is that whilst increasing demand stimulated production and also the demand for land, pushing up land prices and rent, the increase in land purchase and tenancy was by no means to the disadvantage of the cultivator as through these favourable tenure arrangements they were able to retain the benefits of increased production. Although rising land prices made it difficult to repurchase land once lost, and the increasing rents together with the introduction of rent deposits, were additional payments for the tenant to bear, these were more than compensated by increased income not only from higher yields but also from rising prices.[9]

But are these findings from case studies of the 16th and 18th centuries applicable to conditions in the first part of the 20th century? Can a continuous process of increasing commercialisation stimulating agricultural growth to the benefit of the peasants be assumed, as Rawski does, across the centuries?[10]

Commercialised agriculture certainly had continued to increase: it is estimated that in late Imperial China as a whole, peasants marketed from 20 to 30 per cent of their crops, rising to between 30 and 40 per cent in the 20th century.[11] But what is left out of Rawski's picture of the positive impact of market relations on agriculture and the peasantry is, in the first place, the differential impact of commercialisation on rich and poor households. Although rich and poor peasants alike marketed a considerable proportion of their product, Rawski's arguments are surely of limited applicability to only the most able and ambitious peasants: on the whole, only those better-off producers with sufficient resources for investment were in a position to take advantage of the increased marketing opportunities.

But secondly, what needs to be considered is that the new land relations, which might benefit the cultivator in a growing economy, could turn to their disadvantage under conditions of stagnation, instability and crisis, which were endemic in the first half of the 20th century.

Huang's study of the peasant economy of the North China plain, for example, finds the conditions of agricultural stagnation in the pre-revolutionary period as resulting from a long-term process of agrarian change dating back to the 16th and 17th centuries. Huang sees commercialisation and the spread of wage labour leading to the differentiation of owner peasants into managerial farmers operating wage labour-based farms, and a semi-proletarianised poor peasantry. He argues that whilst some were able to rise from the ranks of the peasantry to become managerial farmers by making a commercial success of the cultivation of cash crops, on the whole the greater investments required in cultivating commercial crops increased the risks for the small peasants, and those who lost out had to sell their labour in part to the managerial farmers.[12]

Huang distinguishes three patterns of agricultural commercialisation: firstly for upwardly mobile households which expanded their scale of production to become managerial farmers; secondly, for poor peasants who, under the pressures of subsistence were forced to take the risk of cash cropping, gambling on the possibility of higher short-term returns; and finally a dependent commercialisation artificially stimulated by foreign capital.[13] Here Huang's findings for North China in the 1930s contrast with those of Rawski for over a century earlier: land use was not alone determined by the free choice of the producers. In the case of the poor peasants, it was determined by the dictates of subsistence.[14] It was also shaped by a dependency relationship between peasants and foreign capital, as for example in the case of British American Tobacco, which offered subsidies to induce tobacco production but later withdrew them once the peasants had switched crops.[15]

Again, in contrast with Rawski's findings for the earlier period, Huang suggests that the combined workings of population pressure and the social stratification brought about by the development of commerce on a stagnant peasant economy without the outlet of relief provided by dynamic growth, resulted in a tenacious system that was particularly vicious in human terms as the semi-proletarianised poor peasantry were locked into a dual dependence on family farming and hired labour, compelled to accept below subsistence income from both.[16]

Huang's analysis finds the roots of this system in the period of the Ming-

Qing transition when servile relations between landlord and tenant, and employer and employee, gave way to freer relationships with the rise of managerial farming and the dissolution of the large serf-based estates which had originally been granted to landlords by the Imperial court.[17] Like Rawski, Huang notes that increasing commercialisation hastened the depersonalisation of agrarian relations. However, instead of promoting peasant security and permanent tenure, arrangements favourable to the cultivator, as Rawksi suggests, he takes a substantivist approach to focus on how the expansion of market relations in fact undermined the previous, more secure and stable arrangements as more personalised and relatively durable relationships were replaced by more and more impersonal and short-term arrangements.[18] By the 1930s, with land a more liquid asset, conditions were a far cry from the permanent tenure that characterised sharecropping, with landlords raising rents, increasing the turnover in land rentals by revoking agreements, and evicting tenants who refused to comply with their demands.[19]

Since, with the advance of commercialisation, permanent tenancy gave way to short-term leases, it does not seem in the long run to have been the incentive to production that Rawski claimed. In effect, permanent tenancy was a system of pre-capitalist mortgage whereby the owner-cultivator sold the bottom soil to a moneylender, who in return for paying taxes was entitled to collect rent, whilst the peasant retained the right to cultivate the top soil. The system did not really secure the rights of the cultivator: it remained open to the landlords to claim the topsoil if, for example, the tenant refused to pay rent increases, and tenants lost their surface rights if they defaulted on the rent.[20]

Huang further shows that the change to fixed rent appeared in a different light when seen against a background of instabilities affecting agricultural production. Although sharecropping was a disincentive to the tenant to improve the land, they shared with the landlords not only the gains but the losses in harvest. But under fixed rents, which were set regardless of whether the harvest was good or bad, the burden of risks and losses from natural or man-made disasters fell entirely on the peasants. Huang finds that the instabilities of the 20th century, at least in Northern China, saw a decline in total returns from the land, revealing that in this case the change to fixed rents was in fact the landlords' response to declining incomes due to increasing precariousness.[21] Contrary to conditions in the earlier centuries of Rawski's study, Huang then demonstrates that fixed rents proved harsher in an unstable environment. Rather than allowing tenants to benefit from improvements, fixed rents were favoured by the landlords to protect their own interests in the less fertile areas, whilst increasing peasant indebtedness. Furthermore, with both share- and fixed-rent arrangements, landlords were better able to avoid the traditional obligations of reducing rents in times of a bad harvest.[22]

Rather than stimulating production, commercialisation invariably provided the landlords with an excuse to raise rents and rent deposits. Huang finds that whilst the poor peasants' desperate need for land allowed the landlords to raise rents, they were also under great pressure to do so to keep up with rising prices, especially in the case of cash rents. Furthermore, the landlords did not return the rent deposits which accompanied the cash rental agreements on short-term leases.[23] The practice of rent deposits also became less of an economic guarantee and more a source of money income for the landlords. Since the large deposits could only be afforded by those better-off producers, they further provided a means whereby the landlords could appropriate the agricultural surplus. Rent deposits formed funds and a basis for the development of usury as poorer peasants would borrow to pay them. Developing with the monetisation of the rural economy, rent deposits protected the landlords from risk but drove the peasants into debt.[24]

Whilst Huang's thesis regarding managerial farming is discussed later, the point now is to note his findings regarding the detrimental effect of commerce on the peasants in promoting the spread of tenancy arrangements which were to their disadvantage, namely, the replacement of permanent tenancy in favour of short-term leases; an increase in the burden of rent with the shift away from the more personalised and secure sharecropping arrangements; and a rise in the rate of evictions as rent operated more according to the impersonal logic of the market. Although Huang's study of the 1930s and Rawski's study of the 16th and 18th centuries differ on the question of whether or not commerce developed to the detriment or advantage of the peasantry, both concur in the view that growth of commerce promoted freer, economic, and impersonal relations between landlord and tenant.

Chen Boda's analysis of rent and the question of land monopoly

Chen Boda's study of the system of land rent in pre-revolutionary China, originally written between 1945 and 1946 based on findings spanning the 1930s and early 1940s, focuses on the accelerating trends of peasant impoverishment and land concentration under the KMT government. His argument can be seen as levelled against 'Leftist' views that capitalism was developing under the impact of imperialism and of KMT reforms, showing that, at least in the first part of the 20th century, the monetisation and commoditisation of the rural economy in China was taking place to the detriment of agriculture and the producers, reinforcing instead a system of parasitic landlordism. His analysis of the underlying cause of the agrarian crisis also provides important insights into the relationship between the system of landlordism and the development of commerce in China, one not sufficiently taken into account by Western views on the liberalising impact of increasing marketisation.

Chen pointed out that the fundamental feature of China's lack of development was the low rate of surplus above necessary labour. He then found the existence of exorbitant rent, at 50 per cent of the crop and often more, as the main cause of agricultural stagnation and the peasants' declining income since, at such high levels of exploitation, the peasants struggled to maintain simple, let alone expanded reproduction, and had to rely on sidelines or borrowing for their living expenses. The fact that rent absorbed not only all the surplus but also cut into the necessary labour of the tenant demonstrated its extra-economic nature, and this is what made it such a burden on the peasantry especially in a stagnant economy.[25]

Equally, although it may be argued that taxation was not so high in China, Chen Boda showed that given the low rate of surplus labour, it also undermined the subsistence of owner-cultivators.[26] Under this burden of tax, owner-cultivators would fall into debt and lose their land, which was either bought by the landlords at low prices or simply taken in payment of debt. As land was concentrated in the hands of the landlords, this only affected the ownership, not the use of land: it remained advantageous to the landlords to lease the land in small parcels to collect the most rent, charging exorbitant levies on the grounds that they had to pay the taxes. The contradiction between the concentration of land ownership and its fragmented use, given an increasing demand on the part of the peasants for land to cultivate, formed the basis for monopoly rent which not only siphoned off the surplus but also cut into the consumption levels of the tenants.

The increase in the number of land-short peasants allowed the landlords to raise rents regardless of the fertility of the soil. As Chen pointed out, rent was levied on the poorest land and while the level of rent was generally lower in less fertile areas, the rate of rent in proportion to yield was in fact higher, indicating that the burden of rent was higher in the less developed regions.[27] Whereas under conditions of capitalist relations, rent reflects the fertility of the soil, that is in Marx's term, differential rent, this fact that in China on the whole the rate of rent was inverse to the quality of the land demonstrated that the poorest peasants on the worst land were subject to the highest degree of exploitation because their demand for land was greater.[28]

This exploitation of the poor peasants who bore the greatest burden of rent brings into sharp relief the contradiction in pre-revolutionary China between ownership and use of land which was the condition of monopoly rent. The peasants, driven by necessity into competition with each other, drove up the rate of rent on the least productive land. Landlord and tenant were hardly equal partners in a business contract in conditions where rent did not reflect the fertility of the soil, or where the increase in rent did not indicate land improvements but rather the demand of the land hungry peasants: the peasants rather were at the mercy of the monopoly conditions of the landlord system which also incorporated the rich peasants.

The key point in Chen's analysis, one that is fundamental to the Marxist approach, is that the predominant form of rent, whether levied at a fixed rate or as a proportion of the crop, was collected in kind. According to one source used by Chen, it was estimated that 80 per cent of rents were paid in kind in 1934.[29]

Both Rawski and Huang, for their different periods, found rent in kind to be the main form in the majority of their cases, but neither fully considers the implications of this for the development of commerce.[30] The predominance of rent in kind indicated the persistence of rent as a separate form of surplus labour, not simply an offshoot of profit. Commercialisation in China had produced no qualitative change in the predominant form of surplus labour into capital.

Commerce then developed not independently but under conditions of, and in fact on the basis of, the land monopoly as the collection of rent in kind gave the landlords control over the grain markets. Landlords engaging in commerce used rent in kind as a lever to accumulate vast fortunes through speculation. With their large reserves of grain, they could create gluts, forcing down the price at which the peasants sold their crops, then buying up large amounts at the forced down price, to be resold to the peasants at artificially inflated prices in times of shortage, which again the peasants were forced to accept since they had no reserves left themselves. The commoditisation of agricultural production only threw the peasants at the mercy of landlord-speculators who manipulated the prices at which the peasants were forced to sell or buy.

Chen argued that the peasants were compulsory sellers at low prices, the landlords and merchants, the buyers; but at high prices, the landlords and merchants were sellers, the impoverished peasants, the buyers. Whilst the rise in price of farm produce was usually tied up with the landlords' and merchants' price monopoly, the landlords viewed this as a justification for rent increase.[31] Similarly, the cultivation of cash crops was generally accompanied by an increase in rent.[32]

The landlords' dominance of commerce was reflected in the composition of the market towns which provided sites for their luxurious homes as, particularly from the 18th century, they increasingly became urban dwellers. Market towns essentially grew up on the basis of the periodic village fairs organised by the village gentry which served as a meeting point where merchants' agents purchased from the peasants and supplied them with goods. These developed into permanent sites as commerce grew, acting as a contact point between the surrounding villages and the nationwide markets controlled by the large merchants. The towns housed the gentry's rent-collecting agencies, pawn shops, grain stores, and tea-houses, and were parasitic on the surrounding countryside, catering for the luxuried consumption of the gentry whilst the villages remained partially self-sufficient.[33]

Through their dominant ownership, together with the rich peasants, of land and grain, the landlords controlled not only prices but also credit. Landlords would use the surplus collected through rent in kind to lend to the peasants at usurious rates to be repaid at the highest market prices.[34] In showing that, with the predominance of rent in kind, the landlords were able to exploit the peasants also through usurious loans and the manipulation of grain and other commodity prices, Chen's argument demonstrates how in China, merchant and usurer capital became closely interwoven with landed property. Since the merchants derived their wealth from a share in the feudal surplus, they joined with the landlords in swindling the peasants through speculation in commodities and land, driving them into dependence on costly loans which were supported by the peasants' demand for credit, not for production but for consumption needs. In this way peasants were forced to mortgage or sell their lands accounting for the increasing tenancy and land concentration. Through their control of commerce, the landlord-merchants were able to further squeeze the owner-cultivators into debt or pre-capitalist mortgage, so strengthening the conditions of land monopoly.

Chen argues further that since the monopoly of grain and control of its price was made possible through the extraction of rent in kind, the quest for grain for the purposes of speculation led to the quest for rent and land speculation. Wealth accumulated in rent or trade was used to buy more land in order to squeeze more rent from the peasants. The growth, then, of land ownership based on purchase rather than state grants or forcible annexation was a system that developed not on account of cultivation but of speculation. It was a system which arose from, and perpetuated, the concentration and monopoly ownership of land and exorbitant rents, aggravating the peasants' difficulties in obtaining land to cultivate. Land prices did not reflect land improvements but rose and fell through land speculation and the swindling of the peasants. The rate of increase in the price of poor land was faster than on good land as the more the peasants sank into poverty, the more they lost land and so were compelled to rent in poorer land at ever higher rates. Consequently poor land became more valuable: the poorer the land, the higher the rate of rent and the faster the increase in land price.[35]

A gradual trend towards money rent was taking place in cash crop areas around the Treaty Ports and in areas where large lineage organisations were strong and, in some places, cash payment constituted 25 per cent of the total rent collected.[36] Rawski suggested for the earlier period that money rent was less onerous, but Chen Boda argued that in general in the 1930s, in areas where industry, commerce and money relations were more developed, rent increased sharply. Observing the fact that in at least one county in Jiangsu province nearly all the big landlords had gone into business in Shanghai, Hunan and Hubei, Chen Hanseng comments:

> They wanted ready cash to invest in the commodity markets so they increased the rent-rate to get it. The average increase over ten years was 50 per cent. In cash crop areas…it nearly doubled and in some instances even trebled in ten years. The large sums of money which flowed into the pockets of the landlords through the increase in the rent-rate were diverted from the sphere of agriculture, and the money was turned into merchants' and usurers' capital.[37] The rise in rents forced up land prices. The landlords, taking advantage of the high price of land, induced the bankrupt peasants to sell their land which they had no hope of buying back at such inflated prices. The increase in the numbers of land-short peasants enabled the landlords to raise the rents even higher.

Chen Boda argued that despite the increased commercialisation of agriculture in the South and around the Treaty Ports, with the development of money rent and the rise in land prices, capitalist relations of production remained insignificant. Rent in kind predominated, and the amount and rate of money rent were essentially the same as rent in kind: the rate of money rent, like that of rent in kind, was highest on the poorest lands, and money rent was in general practically as high as rent in kind.[38]

In fact, money rent in China could not be calculated as a percentage of the amount of rent to investments put into the land as is the practice under conditions of capitalist relations. As noted earlier, money rent is normally calculated in relation to the price of land where this expresses capitalised rent as the purchase price of ground rent yielded by the land, rising as rent rises in reflection of land improvements. But as Chen Boda showed, on the whole in the monetised areas, the rise in money rent bore no relation to land improvements but reflected the demands of the impoverished peasants, expressing increased speculation on land yielding higher rents. The connection between the rise in rent and the rise in the price of land was related to the fact that speculation in grain inevitably led to speculation in land.

Money rent therefore represented not an excess over profit but a commuted form of rent in kind. In fact, the landlords would demand money rent or rent in kind, whichever was most advantageous to them at any particular time, sometimes switching from money rent back to rent in kind in order to gain from grain speculation as grain prices rose.[39] Rawski suggests that money rent was less onerous because it never caught up with the rising price of rice, but the situation was in fact different under conditions of market speculation and usury, when landlords accrued the gains, as well as in the case of falling rice prices. With cash rental agreements, peasants had to sell their produce at low prices during times of glut after a harvest to pay the landlords or, if rent was demanded in advance, they had to borrow at usurious rates.[40] Since monetisation further exposed the peasant to the exploitation of merchant capital, one commentator, referring to the situation of cash crop growers, remarked:

> The evils of money rent are as great, if not greater, than those of rent in kind.[41]

Monetisation further extended the practice of rent deposits and hence increased peasant indebtedness. Chen highlights the coercive nature of the practice in an example of one county near Shanghai in which rent deposits were demanded in the less developed part where land was the sole means of subsistence for the peasants, but not in the area near the city where the peasants did not rely entirely on the land for a living.[42]

An example of how the monetisation of the economy worked against the peasants is this account from the early 1940s of some tenants in Sichuan, who sold their crops to pay for rent deposits:

> They were compelled to sell their young growing crops to the wealthy landowners at half the price of harvested rice. In a few areas in this county, nearly all the tenants sold their young crops, some even their autumn crops, leaving only enough to pay rent. They themselves ate 'fairy rice' (a kind of fine earth), tightening their belt, saving their cattle and dreaming of reaping potatoes and sweet potatoes in winter and the first crops of the next spring to fill their empty stomachs.[43]

According to Chen Boda, then:

> ...the fertility of the soil, instead of being the condition for developing the peasants' own production, becomes one for the rich and influential to take the ownership of the land from the peasants. The development of commodity relations, money relations and capitalist relations, instead of pushing up agricultural production, hastens the loss of the peasants' own land. The landlords, compradores, officials and warlords grab all the fruits of the rise in land prices, resulting from economic expansion. To the peasants, the high price of land means the loss of their land and an indication of their worsening plight.[44]

What Chen's theory of monopoly rent shows is that, owing to the close connection of commerce and credit with rent, the economic benefits from increased production resulting from agricultural improvements would accrue to the landlords at the expense of the peasants. Commercialisation then, rather than promoting peasant independence, enabled the landlords to tighten their control in the economy.

The persisting predominance of rent in kind shows that, despite the changes in agrarian relations with the trend towards freer relationships developing from the Ming-Qing transition, there was no fundamental change in the form of surplus labour to capital, that is, although the landlords became more involved in trade and finance, there was no qualitative change in their class character and basis in landed property. Rather, since the landlords dominated the market and credit systems through rent in kind, in China, unlike Europe, merchant and usurer capital was based upon landed property.

Rawski's portrayal of commercial landlordism is not one that can be applied to the pre-revolutionary crisis period given the determining effect of the landlords' monopoly of grain on the economy and the operations of the market. Measuring rent as a percentage of the purchase price of land, Rawski came to the conclusion that commercial profits were higher and so of greater interest to the absentee landlords who regarded land as merely a stable and prestigious investment. But instead, in the conditions of pre-revolutionary China, their interest was precisely in rent for the purpose of commercial and financial speculation: the benefits of rent were to be measured not in relation to land prices, which were themselves determined by speculation, but rather by the economic power the collection of rent in kind gave over the marketing and credit systems.

As the landlords controlled the market and credit systems through rent in kind, the changes in agrarian relations – fixed rent, the shift from permanent ties to short-term tenancy, the increase in hired labour, rent deposits, land purchase and the cultivation of marketable produce, which all tended to dissolve servile ties – did not ultimately establish peasant independence. Instead, the development of commodity and money relations increased their exploitation, working in the interests of the landlords by reinforcing their monopoly position in the economy.

NOTES AND REFERENCES

1. Rawski (1972).
2. *Ibid.*, p.3; p.10.
3. *Ibid.*, p.29
4. *Ibid.*, p.147.
5. For further details on the different systems of rent, see Chen Boda, 1966a, pp.28–35; and Fried, 1956, p.102.
6. Rawski, 1972, p.18.
7. *Ibid.*, p.123.
8. *Ibid.*, p.155.
9. *Ibid.*, p.124.
10. *Ibid.*, pp.159–61. The debates here are explored further with reference to analyses by Chinese Marxist historians in Chapter 8.
11. See Lippitt, 1980, p.22.
12. Huang, 1985, p.108. Huang's discussion of managerial farming is critiqued in Chapter 6.
13. *Ibid.*, p.299.
14. *Ibid.*, p.162.
15. *Ibid.*, p.130.
16. *Ibid.*, p.201.
17. *Ibid.*, pp.85–103.
18. *Ibid.*, p.202.
19. *Ibid.*, pp.208–211
20. Perdue, 1987, p.153; Ash, 1976a, p.42.
21. Huang, 1985, pp.211–2.
22. Ash, 1976a, p.28.
23. Huang, 1985, pp.208–9; see also Perdue, 1987, p.154.
24. Perdue, 1987, p.156.
25. For a discussion of the rate of surplus labour in agriculture and the degree of landlords' exploitation of the peasantry, see Chen Boda, 1966a, pp.1–28.
26. See, for example, Huang, 1985, p.281.
27. Chen Boda, 1966a, pp.42–5.
28. See Marx's discussion of capitalist rent, *Capital* Vol. III, Part IV. Here he discussed two forms of capitalist rent – absolute rent and differential rent. Absolute rent was a monopoly rent related to a lower-than-average organic composition of capital in agriculture as compared with industry. Again this clearly did not apply in China where much of the land was used for subsistence farming.
29. Chen Boda, 1966a, p.31. Crook and Gilmartin (2013) suggest that in their area of study, rice replaced money as the main medium of exchange (p.47).
30. Rawski, 1972, p.148; p.152; Huang, 1985, p.208.
31. Chen Boda, 1966a, p.77.
32. *Ibid.*, pp.62–3.
33. For a detailed study of China's marketing system see Skinner, 1965, Part 1. For one example see the description in Crook and

Gilmartin (2013) of the market village of Prosperity where two teahouses in particular were used as the headquarters of the *Paoge*, a sworn brotherhood organisation dominated by the landlords and merchants (pp.27–30).

34. Perry, 1980, p.32.
35. Chen Boda, 1966a, p.87.
36. *Ibid.*, pp.30–3.
37. Chen Hanseng here is quoted in Chen Boda, 1966a, pp.62–3.
38. *Ibid.*, pp.48–51.
39. *Ibid.*, p.80.
40. Ash, 1976a, p.31.
41. Chen Boda, 1966a, p.51.
42. *Ibid.*, pp.52–4.
43. *Ibid.*, p.79.
44. *Ibid.*, p.88.

3

Landlord, state and village – the articulation of economic and political power in Chinese feudalism

Landlords and the state

A **further difficulty in understanding** the nature of the landlord system that existed in China lies in the evident difference in not only the economic but also the political structure as compared with European manorial serfdom. The unitary and centralised structure of power of the Chinese bureaucratic state, which showed a relative stability over two thousand years, contrasts with the political fragmentation experienced by feudal Europe.

European feudalism involved a system of hierarchical land rights with the absence of rights of the direct producers, the serfs, and administration in the hands of the enfeoffed barons. Political and economic power were fused at the base of society in the large landed estates. In contrast with this localised and decentralised structure of power, China exhibited the distinctive features of a bureaucratic state with, at its apex, the court of the Emperor, and a multitude of village clan-based communities structured by a patriarchal order as the social foundation. In the absence of a hereditary nobility based on large landed estates, administration was carried out not by a hierarchy of barons, but by a literate civil service, entry to which was via an examination system introduced during the Song dynasty (960–1271 AD). This civil service was responsible for the army, police, courts, education, welfare, irrigation and production, and formed a ranked structure from the Imperial court down to county-level magistrates.

The bureaucratic system in Chinese society is considered to have originated with the growth of hydraulics works which assumed importance not only in irrigation for both wet rice cultivation in Central and South China and the dry loess lands of the North, but also since water provided a major means of transport, and because of the need to control rivers against the dangers of floods.[1]

Given the distinctive features of the bureaucratic state and patriarchal clan system the question of whether the state or the landlords were the locus of power in Chinese society is a much-debated issue. The Marxist perspective takes the landlords' economic and political power as central: China is seen as a society ruled by an elite class based on land ownership which, through the medium of the state, is also the politically dominant class. Others have rather placed emphasis on the role of the bureaucracy, the state, in taking responsibility for the welfare of the people according to its own rationale independent of class. Instead of viewing Chinese society as structured by the relationship between the landlord and peasant classes, the focus is on the relationship between the bureaucracy and the closed and autonomous village communities, whether one of despotism or benevolence.

Wittfogel's conception of Oriental Despotism, taking the state solely as the product of the need for hydraulics, contradicts the Marxist perspective of the state's role in holding class antagonisms in check in the interests of the dominant class. The Orientalist lens views state and class as simultaneous, with class distinction decided by power and privilege not wealth.[2] Similarly Ho Ping-ti, seeing the power of the elite as invested solely by the state and not land ownership, provides a definition of the elite gentry as restricted to office-holders and potential office-holders, that is, those with the higher provincial or national degrees who were eligible to hold office.[3] Chang Chung-li, whilst also subscribing to the view that the elite was created by the state through the degree system with land holding of little importance, puts forward a broader definition to include the more numerous lower degree-holders, the *shengyuan* or scholar-gentry who were not necessarily office-holders but were distinguished by virtue of education. He makes the point that the Chinese elite was a highly cultured one whose power was not restricted to office-holding: social status and cultural standing were important aspects in establishing prestige and influence.[4]

Literacy was indeed a marker of the elite, enabling participation in the state systems of justice and taxation. However, against the view that office-holding served as the fundamental basis of power, it has been argued that with the development of land purchase, the landlords managed to secure an independent basis which in fact involved the separation of the economic power of the landlords from the political authority of the state. This argument rests on the view already touched on that, during the Ming-Qing transition, servile ties were replaced by more equal relations as commerce developed – in other words, relations of extra-economic coercion, which characterise the feudal combining of political and economic power, were dissolved.[5]

The problem in assessing the power of the gentry elite in the pre-revolutionary period, and whether or not this was based on officialdom or land ownership or reliant on economic or extra-economic means, is all the more difficult given the development of increasingly diversified types of landlords. At village level could be found small landlords ranging from enterprising farm managers to those relying on the traditional arrangements of sharecropping. Many village landlords were also grain merchants, pawn brokers, grocers, individual moneylenders and retired officials, as well as landowners. Whilst the village rich usually engaged in usury on a small scale, the larger landlords resident in the countryside with properties in different villages used the surplus from rent for commercial speculation.[6] Some very large landlords ruled over almost independent small kingdoms. Then there were also urban residents who combined landed property with investment in industry and urban development on a small scale, as well as large-scale land speculators, merchants and officials, with salaries far exceeding the profits from land.[7] All this marked a wide diversity in the extent and form of landlord power and influence, using force or persuasion, ranging from local tyrants and bullies to traditional paternalistic conservatives to those inclined towards modern reforms.

An investigation into land concentration in Jiangsu province in 1935, for example, contrasts two very different types of landlords:

> In the northernmost districts of the province, those landlords owning 10,000 to 20,000 *mou* each usually live in mud castles with armed guards, and their tenants are scattered in small villages within a two-mile radius, the castle acting as a trading centre for the whole community. Some of these big landlords maintain a rather large armed force...Against these armed forces of the landlords, the District Magistrates are politically impotent. Here, therefore...the economic strength of the landlord is closely identified with their political power.
>
> Whereas the cornerstone of the agrarian structure in Southern (Jiangsu) is the small landlord who usually owns less than 100 *mou*, that in the north is the big landlord of at least 1,000 *mou*. Whereas in the South, Chinese militarists and other nouveau riche including bureaucrats invest part of their money in factories, hotels and garages and sundry kinds of shops, these same people in Northern (Jiangsu) where trade and industry is backward, have to invest their money exclusively in land. This then is one of the apparent reasons for a much higher degree of land concentration in the north.[8]

However, this contrast between the landlords in Jiangsu with large-scale, virtually manorial holdings and small-scale commercial landlordism is only one example in a differentiated pattern of larger-scale landholding emerging with increasing numbers of large absentee landlords as commerce developed. A more typical contrast would be between the sophisticated, leisured, and by the 20th century, Westernised, urban dwelling landlord with considerable property, and the small village resident landlords like, for example, the managing landlord in Longbow village, featured in William Hinton's village study, *Fanshen*, who owned the largest holding in the village of a little over 100 *mu* which he managed himself.⁹ Despite the growing trend towards absentee landlordism, the village gentry, who rose from the rich peasants, or declined from the ranks of larger landlords and officials, remained an important presence in the countryside, controlling corporate properties and often owning the most fertile lands. Even in a highly commercialised province like Guangdong, as distinct from absentee landlords, those living in the village possessed 20 per cent of the land.¹⁰

Given such marked differences in wealth and lifestyle between the large absentee landlords and the small landlords residing in the village, it would appear that they did not belong to the same class. With the small landlords belonging to the village world as distinct from the upper tier of wealthy merchants and officials, they occupied separate strata in Chinese society.¹¹ But the differences between the village landlords and the peasantry should not be underestimated. Even in poor, less fertile areas, the landlords' houses were larger and more spacious than those of the peasants, and whilst they could afford to eat meat or fish throughout the year, most peasants only got a taste of these treats once or twice a year.¹² But above all landlords did not engage in production other than to supplement their income: they lived by exploitation and their non-involvement in manual labour marked a social and cultural gulf with other villagers whilst their education gave access to government offices denied to the illiterate poor.¹³

Although China was not ruled by a hereditary and permanent landed aristocracy there existed then, besides an upper tier of official gentry with formal state powers, a rural elite distinguished from the peasants by wealth and education with an independent status of its own deriving from local prestige and influence, an informal power which persisted even after the abolition of the exam system in 1904. The renowned Chinese anthropologist, Fei Xiaotong, set out two power structures, that of the bureaucracy at the top and of the gentry below. The latter were maintained economically by owning land, and politically by access to office, however their power derived not from government but from the organisation of the local community.¹⁴ Supporting this dualist view of the upper and lower tiers of power, Wakeman suggests as evidence of the existence of a class not ascribed by the state but with an independent status, that, as well as the degree-holding official and scholar-gentry, there existed eminent families or lineages of high social standing who were powerful and influential not by virtue of bureaucratic rank or degree but because of their local prestige associated with a social role of responsibility for the welfare of the community and for upholding Confucian moral values.¹⁵

The informal powers of the local landlords and gentry were vital given that, as far as the Imperial Court was concerned, control over the countryside was incomplete: a vacuum existed between the magistrates, who oversaw county affairs from their base in the walled towns, the *yamen*, and the surrounding villages. This vacuum was filled by the local gentry who became increasingly involved at an informal level in government and social service, as the state, with the abolition of *corvée* and the introduction of tax in cash, came to rely more on indirect than direct controls. By the early 19th century, the local gentry had assumed responsibility in local government for mediation in disputes, supervision of schools and irrigation works, the recruiting and training of local militia, and tax collection.

Wakeman considers that the fees and salaries gained from the performance of these duties provided new sources of wealth which replaced landed wealth as an essential ingredient of gentry status.[16] In contradiction with this, Beattie's study of the gentry in one locality finds that throughout the Ming (1368–1644 AD) and Qing (1644–1911 AD) dynasties there was in fact a continuity among the locally prominent families based on land ownership, despite the changes brought about by the massive peasant revolts of the 1630s and 1640s which hastened the dissolution of servile ties and reduced the tax privileges of the elite.[17] She argues that these families sustained themselves through intermarriage and lineage organisation. Such practices, she argues, were used deliberately by the elite to obtain corporate lands in order to finance schools to provide their male offspring with an education, essential to obtaining a degree and hence access to office. Thus land ownership, including the corporate lineage properties, provided an independent basis of wealth for the local elite families who remained influential through the association of their lineage with officialdom as well as through educational achievement, whether or not a family member actually held office at any given time.

Whilst the exam system gave the appearance of open access and mobility, underlying the non-hereditary civil service, Beattie thus uncovers the existence of a semi-permanent elite rooted in landed property. With the pillars of officialdom in place, land ownership as the route to degree-holding continued to serve as the crucial component of privilege, underpinning a strata of able, well-educated families, combining wealth, education and managerial functions, from which the state was able to recruit its officials. At local levels, these office holders, ex-officeholders and aspiring officials together formed an elite milieu congregating in the networks around temple societies, Confucian associations, and lineage organisations, which all provided a basis of support for the state.

Kinship, community and patron-client relations

Moving beyond this debate about the importance or not of land ownership for the Chinese elite, a wider account needs to be taken of the landlords' economic power. To measure the extent of tenancy, as has been seen in the previous section, does not fully reveal the influence of the landlords in the wider community. Where tenancy was lower and independent owner-peasants more numerous, it cannot be assumed that the landlords were less powerful and influential. In fact in areas of low tenancy not only was the burden of rent usually higher but land ownership was concentrated with a small percentage of the population owning a large proportion of the land.[18] For example, as just seen, whilst northern Jiangsu province had a relatively low rate of tenancy, every county had at least one or two very large landlords owning 10,000 *mu* or more, holding sway over the localities.[19]

However the important factor in determining the landlords' economic power was not simply the absolute size of the holdings, but that, in conditions in which the majority of peasant holdings were inadequate, the landlords' holdings in relation to others were larger. Even small landlords, owning a few acres more than the average in a locality were able to charge exorbitant rents on their extra lands. In this way, they accumulated a surplus which enabled them to lend or speculate in grain and other commodities, giving them substantial power and influence over other villagers.

The parcellised farming which predominated in China had developed from two roots: the bureaucratic state system which relied on taxing individual households and the patriarchal system which practised household division between sons. The economic base of landlordism in China then took the form, for the most part, not of large English manor-type estates with a concentration of fields, but a land monopoly which allowed the concentration of the surplus, collected mainly in rent in kind, whilst the land was split up into small inadequate sizes.[20] Rather than direct control over a large estate, this economic basis involved a different form of power since it allowed a small number of patrons with control over a few tenants to also acquire indirect control over the small peasants without directly owning their land. The inadequate holdings of the majority of peasants provided the basis for various forms of dependency relations developing between those with a surplus and those struggling to survive.

Since the landlords controlled the bulk of the surplus through the collection of rent in kind, as has been seen, as commerce developed, they also gained market dominance. Through usury and commercial speculation, they were able to draw not only tenants but also owner-peasants into their power domain. Relations of patronage and clientelism characterised not only the traditional sharecropping arrangements between landlord and tenant, but other forms of rent and exchange relations, including usury, trade in land and commodities, and wage labour. Despite the weakening of servile ties during the Ming-Qing transition, and the further development of commerce, what influenced exchange relations was not quite the impersonal logic of the market: in the Chinese countryside, where personal relations, contacts and influence remained important, patron-client ties of dependency were prevalent.

It was Morton Fried who noted the importance of cultivating friendly relations, *ganqing*, mutual feelings of obligation, even in a relatively commercialised environment.[21] He saw that with the development of commerce, peasants' lives and solutions to their subsistence extended beyond kin ties whilst the close relation between landlord and tenant in sharecropping gave way to looser arrangements as absentee landlordism grew. He then drew attention to the efforts of both landlords and tenants to cultivate good reciprocal relations. These longstanding relationships, as he saw it, involved mutual obligations in place of weakening kin ties. They were important for the peasants, due to their insecurity, as a means of obtaining in return for gifts and labour services, loans and favours from the landlords, as well as land to rent and reductions in times of bad harvest. For the landlords, although they could, if needed, rely on the backing of the courts and county magistrates, *ganqing* was an important protection against cheating in the payment of rent in kind, either in terms of its quality or the division of the crop.

The Chinese peasant was neither a tradition-bound subsistence producer nor a free independent farmer. What Fried revealed was that whilst the Chinese peasants lived beyond the orbit of kin relations in fact, as monetisation began to dissolve personal ties, the financial drain of rent and taxes from the village caused them to become more and more dependent upon non-kin factors. With all classes of peasants involved in market exchange, selling a proportion of their harvest, market conditions were such that *ganqing* relations of patronage assumed importance in the arrangements of renting land and hiring labour, given the competition among poorer peasants.

Fried explains that the reason why peasants paid exorbitant rents that threatened their very existence was that this bought favours and protection from the landlord.[22] The landlords justified their right to a portion of the harvest as benevolent protectors of the peasants in terms of relations of mutual obligation and of duties, responsibilities and rights. The cultivation of *ganqing* on the part of the landlords involved obligations to share risks and a commitment to the welfare of the community as demonstrated for example in granting gleaning rights as well as customary reductions in rent in times of crop failure.[23] Land tenure arrangements were thus simultaneously a system of exploitation and a means of providing protection or security, promoted by the landlords who granted reductions to gain supporters and extend their influence.

Despite the practices of wage labour and land purchase, land and labour were not then commodities free and unencumbered by personal ties. Huang argues that the spread of wage labour in the mid-18th century led to a fundamental redefinition of the legal status of agricultural workers and tenants from serfs to commoners.[24] But in fact, in place of servility, the early Qing State sought to foster instead these informal relations of benevolence and paternalism: the ideal relationship between landlord and tenant was considered to be like the friendship between 'master and guest'.[25] However such a 'friendship' in fact involved personal non-contractual obligations such as the payment of gifts and the performance of occasional services by tenants to their landlords.[26] Servile relations persisted and even in the large industrial and commercial centre of Shanghai, labour rent existed up to the 1940s.[27] Wage labour in the countryside remained on a small scale, as compared with Europe, mostly seasonal, frequently paid in kind and often representing a semi-feudal exchange of services for debt.[28]

Whilst the corporate ownership of land restricted its free disposability, limiting the development of the land market, the practices of pre-capitalist mortgage and the division of top and bottom soil allowed land purchase to develop without completely undermining customary ties to ancestral lands, since mortgagees and top soil cultivators retained rights to buy back their land. These arrangements saw market forces penetrate land relations without affecting a complete separation of the direct producers from the land.[29]

Commerce was then able to develop without the complete dissolution of extra-economic relations of exploitation and without the dispossession of the producers that would have paved the way for capitalist development. Extra-economic relations are in fact not restricted to serfdom or to the use of force: they also encompass the patron-client ties of dependency which, as in China, cloaked excessive exploitation in traditions of paternalism and benevolence. With the emergence of the system of land purchase which left patriarchal land relations intact, as commercial relations spread, nevertheless custom, patron-client ties and personalised power prevailed. Tied by obligations to lineage and family as well as non-kin relations of dependency and clientelism, the Chinese peasants, though not serfs or slaves, were not exactly free.

In order to understand the role of the local landlord-gentry, and the forms which the relations of patronage and dependency took, it is necessary to look both at the internal organisation of the village order and its external relations. It is in the various ways in which those with resources and connections were able to provide a link, acting as mediators between the rural communities and the wider society, in particular the state – in the person of the county-based magistrates – that the articulation of economic power into political dominance at the base of society is to be revealed.

Although production was household-based, village communities maintained a corporate existence both in terms of kinship and territorial organisation. Kinship and lineage organisation, as well as community organisations with responsibility for village welfare, provided a network of mutual support among peasant families. These played an important role in village life in managing corporate properties, granaries, and resources such as water and woodland, collecting taxes, settling disputes, offering facilities for borrowing, defraying burial expenses, organising house-building, supporting widows and orphans and organising social activities and village defence.[30]

But again, the varying conditions throughout China make it difficult to generalise about village organisation, and the question of whether villages were structured by class relations, lineage ties or community bonds has no easy answer. The most striking difference though is between villages in North and South China. In the South, where it is common to find villages of one surname, village and lineage organisation were usually congruent. The South was in fact noted for the existence of powerful and elaborate lineage organisations and, with higher degrees of tenancy and more elite members of a lineage, the organisation served as an important link between the urban-based gentry and the ordinary villagers.

However in the North, villages were more often multi-surname, and lineage organisation did not often cross the boundaries of the village. Instead, it has been argued that in these Northern, less commercialised and socially stratified communities of owner-cultivators, relations with the state had a greater influence than lineage on village organisation, with the fuller articulation of the village political role mainly to cope with the demands of taxation.[31] Nevertheless, kinship remained important as groups of close relatives would join together in the shared ownership of draught animals, in organising labour co-operation at harvest time, or in the exchange of tools and animals for labour.

The role of kinship and community organisation demonstrates that the village order was not simply structured around the landlord-peasant class relation: relations with the state and relations within and between lineages were also of importance. The degree of market integration was a further factor influencing the different ways villages might react to external changes or pressures. On the one hand, whilst kinship and territorial solidarity contributed towards community closure in the face of external demands of the market or state, on the other hand, increasing market penetration also accelerated the disintegration of community or kinship bonds as the numbers of tenants and semi-proletarians rose, so leaving villages even more vulnerable to outside interference.[32]

But despite the differences, there were some important similarities in lineage and community organisation in North and South China. Lineage unity is based on descent from a common founding ancestor, and recruitment is therefore closed; it is organised around corporate properties which provide for the maintenance of burial grounds, ancestral halls and schools, which in turn act as the focus of group belonging.[33] However, whilst most studies of lineage have concentrated on its emergence as a deliberate organisation of, and resource for, the gentry, these offer insufficient understanding of its roots at village level as a resource for the peasantry.

Faure suggests that lineage organisation, as it traces the line of descent, is a product of the rules of inheritance within the village. He argues then that the conscious reckoning of descent to establish claim to the inheritance of property makes lineage organisation important for the peasantry as a means to establish rights of settlement, and with these, the ability to impose restrictions on outsiders or newcomers in relation to a variety of customary rights such as gleaning rights or access to woodland, water or other resources.[33] This principle of exclusion becomes all the more important for the peasantry in conditions of scarcity and low surplus production.

As noted, a key regional difference in lineage organisation is that, unlike in the North China multi-surname village, in the South, where the community is organised by a single lineage, the links extend beyond settlement. However Faure considers that so long as rights of settlement are inheritable, common descent may coincide with local community without necessarily forming a single lineage village. In this regard, there were important similarities between lineage organisation in both North and South since lineage lines are no less important in a multi-surname village; nor is it possible to explain, within a single surname village, all relations with reference to lineage organisation alone.[35]

Nevertheless, in the South, lineage organisation developed the added dimension of an important political role. The spread of ancestral halls, serving as a symbol of official status and territorial domination is evidence of this but, for Faure, the gentry organisation of lineage was grafted onto its organisation at village level. The development of this political dimension in the South makes it possible to explain the persistence of kinship ties in a differentiating and increasingly commercialised society.

Whilst the right to settle embodied in descent from a founding ancestor divides villager from outsider, at the same time it establishes status within the village. Noting the ability of some families to dominate others, even when related by kin, Faure points out the importance of the establishing of property rights to the structure of a local community in terms of its relations of solidarity and power. With this, the ability to impose restrictions both outside and inside the village also makes for a hierarchical and patriarchal order. Relations of senior and junior, superior and inferior, were central not only to the Chinese family, they also established the relations between branches in the same lineage, and even in multi-surname villages in North China, fictive kinship existed by which every villager knew his or her precise generational standing relative to every other villager.[36]

What village organisation in North and South had in common was this patriarchal and hierarchical order based on property ownership, in which village affairs were in the hands of the male elders of the community or lineage. Selected on the basis of their property interests, outside contacts and literacy, leadership was drawn from the village rich, the most influential and respected branch of the lineage or, in the case of multi-surname villages, from those families within each lineage or surname group.[37]

Mao considered these forms of custom – clan organisation and the authority of the elders and temples; the patriarchal authority of the husband; the religious authority of local deities, together with the political authority of the state, reaching down to county level – as the backbone of a system of 'four ropes' binding the Chinese peasantry which provided a basis for landlord power.[38] The patriarchal clan system, with its hierarchical leadership and ancestral customs, may be seen to have formed a principal means of feudal exploitation and rule.[39]

The acceptance of an ordered hierarchy of superiority and inferiority within the village made it easier for landlords to influence village affairs, providing a basis to legitimise their superiority and thus facilitating the cultivation of patron-client ties. Landlords were able to take on the role of village benefactors, making charitable donations of land, supporting village granaries, caring for the underprivileged, taking on responsibility for village security, subsidising village ceremonies and entertainments, and mediating disputes.[40] Cultivating this role of benefactor had advantages for the gentry in gaining an image of worthiness to demonstrate their suitability for office. The landlords were able to influence village affairs, the management of corporate properties, granaries, water and other resources, to their own advantage through the village elders, often selected because of their good relations with the local elite.

On the other hand, as has been seen, these bonds of kinship and community were not merely tools used by the landlords to maintain their power and privileges, involving the peasants in arrangements of their own subjection. For the peasantry, kinship and community bonds provided access to land and resources; support in times of misfortune; and assistance in dealing with authorities. They were a resource in times of need, providing networks of mutual support, and to an extent levelling divisions of rich and poor. They also formed bonds of common solidarity in the face of external threat or oppressive demands, to protect peasant livelihood and way of life.

Faure's analysis of lineage as a peasant organisation, not merely a creation of the elite, is important in revealing that the peasantry could exercise a degree of independence, if limited. Not entirely subordinate to the landlords or the state, the peasants were potentially capable of opposing the system of dominance, having their own forms of organisation, their own leaders, their own ideas of social justice and equality, and traditions of collective action and support. Nevertheless, although the lineage and community organisations of the peasantry provided care for the needy, they were not egalitarian but hierarchical and dominated by the wealthiest families within the community with links into the wider field of feudal power.

Faure's analysis also reveals the limitations of these peasant organisations: as territorial organisations establishing hierarchical rights of settlement and property ownership, excluding outsiders, they were closed and segmented. These were communities divided not only along lines of loyalty to different lineages or factions but also according to distinction between property owners and the non-propertied poor tenants or labourers, and between established settlers and migrants. Some forms of customary arrangements sometimes expressly barred people without property.[41] Migrants and poor peasants, excluded from the security offered by these organisations, would then, given the scarcity of resources, form their own surrogate kinship groups or sworn brotherhoods for mutual support using legal or illegal methods including salt smuggling, theft and banditry.[42]

The internal structure of villages shaped their relations with society at large, as the territorial, exclusive nature of peasant organisation militated against villages establishing outside links. This also made village organisation liable to fall all the more under landlord influence and domination, since community closure facilitated the ability of the landlords and the village elite to control the channels of communication with the outside world. These powers became all the more important as market relations developed and the burden of taxation increased.

Landlords as mediators between state and village

The landlords' role as mediators between state and village took different forms, depending on the degree of village closure or integration by the market or state. It has already been seen that in the commercialised South, lineage provided an important link between the elite beyond the village and the peasantry. The large lineage organisations led by the gentry were a means for the peasants to gain access to land, protection and patronage, that is, membership of a powerful lineage entailed privileged access to leaders with personal contacts with officialdom who were thus able to exercise influence on behalf of the lineage members.[43] But for the gentry, kin ties were a resource to be exploited to enhance their powers. As well as providing the main route to office, lineage organisation also involved considerable economic powers associated in the South with the organisation of irrigation works and with the control of marketing areas.[44] Whilst paternalistic organisation based on loyalty to leaders cut across class lines to divide the peasants, gentry leaders of strong lineages would frequently foment local rivalries and feuds to annex the land of weaker lineages or to establish control over market towns. The economic gains helped to ameliorate conflicts between rich and poor within a large lineage whilst cementing solidarity against outsiders and rivals. But lineage feuding and bullying also provided a pretext for landlords to increase their exactions of protection money from the peasants.

In the North, where lineage organisation did not extend beyond the bounds of the village and where there were thus less elite members of a lineage, the link between village and local landlords and gentry was not so much through kinship but through common interests as property owners, defending their property against thieves and bandits. The landlords were active in organising crop-watching and village defence, and assumed a local influence by linking these through the local militia to the state's armed forces garrisoned in the county towns.[45]

The structure of power below county level was then shaped not only by corporate village and lineage organisations, but also by the landlords' own organisations. Temples as well as marketplaces provided ideal meeting grounds for the landlords and wealthy merchants who used their resources to make charitable donations and organise local defence, holding extravagant ceremonies and social events to attract newcomers. Membership of these various informal associations allowed the small village landlords to enhance their local influence and powers.[46] In the South local powerholders forged alliances with other lineage organisations to wield considerable influence over large areas of territory.[47] Even in those Northern villages where there was no resident member of the gentry, the influence of landlordism was felt through the social and political structure of religious and patriarchal clan authority whereby the village elders were as committed as the landlords in upholding relations of superiority and inferiority. Even if they did seek to represent the independent interests of their communities, the village elders still had to cultivate good relations with non-resident gentry, who remained influential in the organisation of militia and tax collection at the sub-county levels which served as a mid-point between the villages and the authorities.[48]

The local landlords were thus able to control the channels of communication between the state and local communities, either directly as village residents, or through their sub-county organisations. Acting as arbiters, they effectively filled the power vacuum between officialdom and village. The Qing State was to become more and more heavily reliant on their powers to maintain control over the villages both in peacetime, in the collection of taxes, and to repress peasant uprisings.[49] The importance of the gentry's role in village affairs lay in their connections with officialdom as a means to gain exemptions from tax on behalf of the local villagers. As wealthy members of the community with a recognised status as educated persons with official connections, the gentry then effectively dominated and led lineage and community organisations running village affairs through the cultivation of patron-client ties.

Under the Qing, the policing of the villages and the collection of taxes fell to the *baojia* who served as representatives of the state and agents of the county magistrates. Rather than forming an independent government administration within the village, these official village heads acted as little more than messengers between the community or lineage elders, the unofficial village heads, and the magistrates.[50] Orders would go from the magistrate, through the *baojia* to the elders. They would then call on the local influential families of the gentry who had contacts in the towns and could use their connections with officialdom to negotiate on the villagers' behalf.[51]

Using their prestige within local networks and their close links with the officialdom, the local landlords became intermediaries between state and village community. In this way, as Shue notes, they took on three separate roles: representing the state informally to the village communities; giving protection to the villages and acting as arbiters on their behalf over taxation; and also advancing their own interests.[52] These three aspects were in effect all part of the gentry's role in the articulation of power between the state and the patriarchal order of the village communities.

The *baojia* were to become increasingly susceptible to local landlord influence such that the latter became the mainstay of the system of taxation and social order, assuming not only responsibilities for these mechanisms of state control but also for ideological control through the village schools and ceremonies; famine control through the granaries; as well as control over irrigation.[53]

As tax collection came increasingly subject to landlord manipulation this led to greater corruption, bribery and embezzlement, whilst the village granaries, irrigation works were also exploited to the advantage of the landlords leading to increasing long-term ecological disasters. With the influence of the landlords and gentry eclipsing that of the state in the countryside, the state's servants – the magistrates and tax collectors – also fell under their command.

State power in the late Qing came to form an especially corrupt government.[54] The merging of powers at village level was matched at the higher tiers of Qing government which also saw the closer affiliation of large landlords, merchants and officials, with the landlords using rent in kind to trade and official connections to uphold their claims to exorbitant rent and evade taxes; the merchants using their commercial capital to buy land and gain office in state-run trading companies; and the officials using their salaries and embezzled funds to purchase land and engage in commodity speculation.

Although there were distinct layers in the political structure, the upper tier of officials and the lower tier of scholar-gentry and commoner landlords, the two were mutually interdependent and intertwined. Whilst it was their close connections with officialdom and their educated status that accounted for the importance of the local landholders in village affairs, allowing them to assume influence over the *baojia* and village institutions, at the same time, the centralised bureaucratic state administration itself relied upon the localised personal power of the landlords and gentry. This extended over both tenants and owner peasants given their control over surplus production, as well as their domination of the market and their control over the local militia. Whilst administrative responsibilities devolved onto the gentry, state power further came to depend on them to subvert and suppress peasant protest.

To focus only on the differences between Western manorial serfdom and the Chinese bureaucratic and patriarchal relations of power is to neglect the role of the landlord-gentry and their extra-economic powers to exploit the peasantry. Given the distinctive features of a bureaucratic state, originally based on state land ownership and the patriarchal village order, landlord power in China was not structured by a hierarchical system of hereditary land rights. Nevertheless, as in Europe, feudalism in China came to rest on the fusion of political and economic power at the base of society with the landlords assuming a central importance in the articulation of power as mediators, connected to official position in the bureaucracy and to patriarchal rule in the village. This system of personalised power set the frame for the appropriation of surplus production in the hands of the few whilst the majority struggled for their livelihood. As political and economic powers merged at the base of society, the conflict between the landlords and peasants became fundamental.

NOTES AND REFERENCES

1. Needham, 1969, p.181.
2. Wittfogel (1978), for example, pp.315–6. See also Wu Dakun, 1983a, pp.213–217.
3. Ho Ping-ti, 1962, pp.38–40.
4. Chang Chung-li, 1955, p.6ff. Chinese Marxist historians have made the distinction between the degree-holding gentry and the commoner landlords who mostly rose from the rich peasantry and who aspired to gentry status. See Li Wenzhi (1981); Fang Xing (1981).
5. See Huang, 1985, pp.97–103.
6. *Ibid.*, pp.175–9. Here Huang describes how a single landlord was able to dominate the economic life of a village, not only through rent, but also through the introduction of land pawning, a monopoly on money lending and manipulation of commodity markets.
7. *Ibid.*, p.178. Huang argues that wealth in the upper tier was of an entirely different order from that of the small village landlord, who in the 19th century might have had an income of a couple of hundred taels, whilst a county magistrate's salary was 30,000 *taels*, and that of a provincial governor, 180,000 *taels*.
8. Institute of Pacific Relations, 1939, pp.11–12.
9. Hinton, 1966, p.29. This example is further discussed in Chapter 6.
10. Chen Hanseng, 1936, p.21.
11. This is what Huang (1985) suggests, see pp.177–9.
12. Perry, 1980, pp.41–2; see also Yang, 1945, pp.32–3.
13. Mao regarded their non-participation in manual labour as the defining characteristic of a landlord. See *Selected Works*, Vol. I, p.138.
14. Fei Xiaotong, 1953, pp.83–4.
15. Wakeman, 1975, p.25.
16. *Ibid.*, p.31.
17. Beattie (1979), esp. pp.127–32.
18. Institute of Pacific Relations, 1939, p.3. The estimate here is that 20 to 30 per cent of the land in Northern China is rented out by landlords comprising three to four per cent of the population whilst the poor peasants who made up 60 to 70 per cent of the population do not own even 20 to 30 per cent of the land. See also Huang, 1975a, p.139.
19. Perry, 1980, p.27.
20. In his study of the PKI (Partai Kommunis Indonesia),

Olle Tornquist (1984) provides a similar analysis of the land question in certain parts of Central and Eastern Java where, given the existence of small peasant farms incapable of economic independence, a patron could centralise the surplus, through various ways – sharecropping, mortgages, usury, and commercial exchange – from a client, thereby acquiring, if not formal ownership, a considerable degree of control over their lands. See esp. pp.207-l0; p.249; pp.264–5.

21. Fried, 1956, pp.103–9.
22. *Ibid.*, p.193.
23. Thaxton, 1975, p.327.
24. Huang, 1985, pp.97–9.
25. Perdue, 1987, pp.150–1.
26. *Ibid.*, pp.152–3.
27. Chen Boda, 1966a, p.57.
28. See Institute of Pacific Relations, 1939, pp.69–73.
29. See Perdue, 1987, pp.137–9.
30. See Thaxton, 1983, pp.7–8; pp.60–65, on various forms of self-help.
31. Huang, 1985, p.29.
32. *Ibid.*, pp.259–274; pp.290–1.
33. Watson, J., 1982, p.594. In this article, Watson throws some light on the debate on lineage organisation in China by distinguishing between lineages, clans, higher-order lineages and surname associations.
34. Faure, 1988, p.179.
35. *Ibid.*, pp.170–2.
36. Huang, 1985, p.222; p.261.
37. *Ibid.*, pp.237–8.
38. Mao, *Selected Works*, Vol. I, pp.45–6. The differences here between Huang and Mao are discussed further in Chapter 7. For a discussion of the low status and lack of rights of women in the family and kinship system organised around men and male authority see Kay Ann Johnson, 1983, pp.8–18.
39. Wu Dakun, 1983a, p.223.
40. See Hsiao, K.C., 1960, pp.275–81, for an account of village activities initiated by the gentry.
41. Bianco, 1972, p.213.
42. Perry, 1980, p.59ff; Thaxton, 1983, pp.66–68.
43. Watson, 1982, pp.600–1.
44. See Perdue, 1987, p.170; Marks, 1984, pp.60–6.
45. Perry, 1980, pp.84–8.
46. Polachek, 1983, pp.812–3.
47. Watson, 1982, p.608.
48. Huang, 1985, p.231.
49. Hsiao, 1960, pp.294–5.
50. See *Ibid.*, pp.48–83, for an account of the *baojia* system; and pp.264–15, on the official and unofficial village heads. See also Shue, 1988, p.98.
51. Hsiao, 1960, p.317.
52. Shue, 1988, p.96.

53. There is a similarity between the role of the Chinese gentry and the *zamindars* in India, and the line of argument here draws on Alavi's discussion of the structure of feudalism in India, (Alavi, 1982, p.29; pp.33–36).

54. These points are drawn from Hsiao (1960), especially Part II. See also pp.133–9 for examples of corruption and connivance between the landlords and the officials.

4
The impact of imperialism

The Opium Wars, foreign imposition and uneven development

The **Opium Wars (1840–1842; 1856–1860)** marked the turning point in the transformation of China from an independent country into a semi-colonial society. Britain launched the wars to protect the lucrative opium trade on which it relied so as to eliminate the trade deficit between the goods imported from China and the cotton exports which failed to find a sufficient market in China. Whilst the opium trade drained the Qing state of silver reserves, weakening the currency and inducing a fiscal crisis, the wars resulted in China's loss of national sovereignty with the imposition of indemnities and unequal treaties which ceded territories and the regulation of tariffs to Britain.

Through the Treaty Ports, foreign powers were able to control China's foreign trade, lowering the prices of exports and dumping their own goods. Whilst the state passed on the burdens of indemnities in increased taxes, the effects of the unequal treaties were to squeeze domestic business, severely hitting substantial sectors of handicraft and subsidiary production and altering agriculture and rural relations to the detriment of the peasants.

Wider effects were felt as the opening up of the Treaty Ports caused disruption to traditional trade routes, contributing towards growing rural discontent. The Taiping rebellion, a peasant war of massive scale, lasted from 1850 to 1864 and spread throughout 16 provinces. At its core were unemployed boatmen, pedlars, porters and rural artisans, who were displaced when Guangzhou commerce was undermined with the opening of ports at Shanghai.[1] The rebellion struck a severe blow to state power, which had already devolved the responsibilities for ideological as well as famine and tax control to the gentry. Unable to contain the rebellion, the state had to rely on regional armies organised by the large landlords. This militarisation of the landlords led to the emergence of warlords with armies equipped by the Western powers, to whom military, together with political power, eventually passed. The rebellion was only finally suppressed by the joint forces of the Qing state and the imperialist powers.

Throughout the late 19th and early 20th centuries, the Chinese economy was continually debilitated by the payment of indemnities, the enforced reduction of customs revenue, the unequal terms of trade, and the payment of interest on loans.[2] Foreign loans were made to the

Chinese government at high rates of interest two or three per cent above European rates, and repayment was assured by the British control of customs revenue, and later, the salt tax. The proceeds of the loans were often wasted, notoriously on the Empress Dowager's marble boat in the Summer Palace. Railway loans were used to buy British goods, often at artificially high prices. Direct foreign investment then followed in coal mines, mining for other mineral resources, and other manufacturing industries, including textiles, tobacco and beer, whilst foreign banks financed foreign trade, controlled the exchange market and serviced debts. The fact that direct foreign investment was mainly concentrated in banking, transport and trade, suggests that it was geared towards the outflow of capital, adding to the drain on the Chinese economy, and inhibiting the development of national industry.

The impact of foreign trade and investment has been seen as the chief cause of China's underdevelopment as the economy was drained of any surplus for investment, whilst peasant production and handicrafts especially were ruined by exposure to the vagaries of the international markets, and Chinese industry was unable to compete against the privileges granted to foreign companies.

This view has not gone unchallenged, however. Foreign investment and trade were in fact only a small proportion of China's GNP: standing at one per cent and ten per cent respectively in the 1930s, their economic impact appeared very slight or only marginally detrimental.[3] It has been argued then that, rather than effecting a significant restructuring of the economy, foreign trade and investment in fact had some beneficial effects on economic growth. Foreign economic involvement was after all responsible for the introduction and development of a modern industry, with Chinese-owned firms growing alongside the foreign investment, and transport, especially railway construction, which opened up new areas for commercial and agricultural development.

For handicraft production, the opening to foreign trade has been seen as having mixed results: whilst some handicrafts were hard hit by competition from imports, increased demand stimulated the production of others. Furthermore the development of the Treaty Ports saw the spread of cash cropping, stimulating modern farming techniques, at the same time providing increased opportunities and alternative employment for the local peasantry. Beyond the Treaty Ports, for the most part, the predominantly self-sufficient peasant economy was considered to have been scarcely affected. From this perspective, it has been suggested that the main obstacles to China's development were internal – the restrictions of the bureaucratic state and a traditionalist subsistence peasant economy, with an inherent lack of demand inhibiting industrialisation, whether under Chinese or foreign ownership.

It is not possible to assess whether foreign economic involvement had beneficial or harmful effects on China without considering in the first place the question: for whom? The development of modern commerce and industry is not under dispute: they did develop, but the point is that they did so in a pattern of distorted and uneven growth which occurred at the expense of the peasantry whilst the opportunities for the rich to get richer without involvement in production grew. To understand how, it is necessary to appreciate that in China, commercial development was already taking place to the advantage of the landlords.

In fact, the impact of imperialism upon the economy and political order of the Qing and early Republican period was felt in the acceleration of existing trends with contradictory results which had major implications for social change. By intensifying commercialisation, it promoted the position of the merchant-landlords, who dominated the Chinese markets, whilst hastening rural decline. At the same time, whilst creating conditions for capitalism, it shaped a development which was fractured, dependent, and restricted, with its growth potential undermined as peasant impoverishment inhibited the expansion of a domestic market.

The effects on the rural economy

Under **the impact of imperialism**, a number of factors contributed to further peasant impoverishment, loss of land and increasing tenancy.

In the first place, the increasing frequency of natural disasters provided a particular dimension to the distressed condition of the rural population. Years of neglect in the maintenance of dykes had already led to a marked increase in floods and famine from the mid-19th century. But in the earlier part of the 20th century, as the central government, facing not only the depletion of its reserves as it paid out for indemnities but also a declining tax base as peasant impoverishment increased, cut back further on irrigation and public works, and drought, famine and floods became more widespread.[4]

As mounting taxes to pay the loans and indemnities passed to the peasants, this created considerable pressure on their low margins of production. The outflow of silver which accompanied the expansion of the opium trade contributed to a decline in the relation of copper currency to silver, and since the peasants paid their taxes in copper, the burden increased.

Meanwhile foreign goods, almost unlimited by taxes and customs duties, began to enter the Chinese markets on a growing scale. Many were competitive with Chinese products, and were especially damaging to peasant handicrafts. The impact of these imports was certainly mixed – they were never to replace peasant handicrafts and native products, many of which were resilient to competition, and the amount of the imports that did displace peasant industry may have been relatively small in terms of total GNP, nevertheless they were equivalent to a substantial proportion of Chinese handicraft production.[5]

The contradictory effects of foreign trade and investment were particularly evident in the case of cotton production with the splitting of the processes of spinning and weaving, originally combined in traditional household production. As imports of better quality machine-spun yarn flooded the market, this caused a drastic decline in household spinning, at the same time stimulating weaving with handicraft production surviving quite well against mechanised competition whilst new production centres emerged. So although some regions were hit hard, others apparently flourished.

Some have argued that the developments benefitted both peasants and the economy overall as world demand prompted an enormous increase in cotton production.[6] However, with foreign companies investing in plants processing raw materials such as cotton produced by the peasant farmers, handicrafts like weaving developed through a putting-out system. This involved merchants, under contract to supply the foreign companies, making capital advances to peasants too poor to otherwise afford the inputs required for commercial crops.[7] In this way control passed from the household weavers to the merchants. The expansion of the weaving industry then did not lead to reinvestment of the profits but to increased peasant indebtedness especially given the instability of world markets.

Away from the Treaty Ports, the traditional combination of agriculture and handicraft production that limited commercial development was reinforced as peasants burdened by taxes and rents, and farming land insufficient to their needs, made up for this by relying on sidelines and subsidiary activities rather than extending cultivation for the market.

Although some 60 to 70 per cent of agricultural production remained for subsistence, cash cropping developed unevenly as products such as tea, bamboo, silk, cotton, sugar, peanuts and soybeans became China's main exports. What drove the shift from subsistence farming was not only the need to pay rising taxes: especially in areas hit by declining handicrafts, peasants were under particular pressure to switch to cash crops.[8] As increased foreign demand stimulated production and commerce, some areas mostly around the Treaty Ports indeed saw the standard of living rising with ample opportunities for employment. However, as Chen Boda showed, the rate of exploitation rose. At the same time, with some 40 to 50 per cent of the land being turned over to cash cultivation in only two or three decades, this amounted to a substantial commitment of land to exports dependent on the conditions of the world market.[9] When the depression hit world trade after 1929, causing export prices to collapse,

Chinese produce along with a huge amount of labour, all flowed cheaply out of the country. Linked into the unstable world commodity markets through the putting-out system of peasant indebtedness, the cultivators of cash crops were particularly exposed and peasants had to sell their land to repay the capital advances.[10] The British American Tobacco Company provided a particular example: it had offered the peasants favourable terms to grow tobacco, but after they had signed the contracts, during the price wars of the 1920s and 1930s, the guarantees were withdrawn and prices cut to such levels that the peasants had barely enough to live on and could not afford to switch to another crop. In this way the peasants were locked into dependency whilst the surplus was extracted without reinvestment of profits.[11]

The collapse of world trade not only ended the temporary boom in the new handicraft centres, nor were its economic effects limited to the areas dependent on cash crops: the impact was felt throughout the economy, as foreign companies linked into the established national commercial networks through the agency of the large merchant-landlords.

Foreign competition, world crisis and the involvement of foreign companies did not then make agriculture profitable for domestic producers. Large-scale farms were broken up and, unable to find sufficient alternative occupations, peasants clung to diminishing plots of land as paupers.[12] The abundance of cheap labour in the countryside militated against investment in improved techniques, continuing reliance on traditional labour-intensive methods.

With agriculture skewed towards the needs of foreign markets, declining terms of trade, the undermining of handicrafts in many areas, together with increased taxes and currency instability, all hastened the peasants' loss of land and increased their indebtedness. The bankruptcy of the peasantry produced soaring rents and interest rates, making land purchase for the purpose of extracting rent, and usury, the most profitable of occupations whilst investment in national industry and agriculture was restricted. With world competition restricting domestic development, China's economic modernisation was also inhibited by the landlord system as merchants and officials used their fortunes to join the landlords in exploiting the peasants.[13]

The anarchic penetration of capital and commerce increased regional variations, promoting uneven and disjointed development. As Western enclaves grew at the expense of the rural hinterland and domestic business, cities exploited the countryside, twisting the pattern of growth. Whilst some new areas were opened up to commercial development, in other areas, hit by declining handicrafts, floods and famine, the economic system ran down.

In the more fertile South, where communications were easier and the economy and trade more developed, the increase in commercialisation intensified land concentration: tenancy rates were highest in the most fertile areas as peasants lost their good land the fastest.[14] Whilst the growth of specialised crops and food commodities for the towns increased, the landlords used rising prices as an excuse to raise rents, hampering development, although the rising prices of agricultural products were usually the result of the landlords' market monopoly.[15] As grain prices rose, everyone wanted to purchase land, and since land speculation proved more financially rewarding than returns on industrial investment especially during the war years after 1937, merchants and officials joined landlords in the scramble for land which turned into speculative gambling with lands left idle to force prices higher.[16] As has already been noted, the development of money rent in the areas of cash crop cultivation, and around the Treaty Ports, facilitated the landlords' manipulations to the detriment of the peasantry. The more the landlords came to possess, the more the peasants were squeezed for rent and the greater the commercial super-profits because the greater the amount of rent in kind to use for market speculation.

In the less fertile areas, farmed with the most basic techniques, where tenancy rates were lower, the economic system ran down and commerce and the population declined with land often left to waste. Famine hastened the dispossession of these bankrupted peasants, who, with no alternative opportunities, were driven to aimless migration. Land prices fell as peasants were forced to sell their plots and the landlords also sold up and moved away since the peasants were too impoverished to pay rent. Smaller landlords sold out to large absentee landlords, merchants and warlords who bought up huge tracts at rock-bottom prices to grow cash crops under contracts with foreign companies. To protect themselves from falling world prices, the remaining landlords raised rents, passing the burden of risk on to their tenants. So, while the volume of rent fell, the rate of exploitation increased. The decline in land prices whilst rents rose was, on the one hand, indicative of the landlords' swindling of the peasants, and on the other hand, a sign of peasant impoverishment in the famine-stricken areas, where, despite its low prices, sellers of land greatly outnumbered the buyers. Falling land prices did not reflect a decrease in exploitation through rent but rather the continuous calamities of famine and a decline in the agricultural economy brought about by low world commodity prices and exorbitant rents.[17]

Falling world commodity prices in the 1920s and 1930s, together with famine, increased the dispossession of the peasants: those areas hardest hit, with the additional pressures of high taxes and the destruction of handicrafts, were virtually cleared of owner-cultivators. Although it has been argued that some areas saw subsequent recovery during the war years that followed from 1937, inflation further increased the difficulties of the peasants as the landlords and other wealthy classes enriched themselves through speculation in commodities, land, government bonds and foreign exchange. Whether in the less developed or the more commercialised areas, whether prices were rising or falling, the conditions were detrimental to the peasants. With low land and commodity prices, the peasants sold up to the landlords and merchants; with rising commodity prices, the peasants bought whilst the landlords and merchants sold; and with rising land prices the peasants were unable to buy back their land whilst the landlords and merchants made windfalls from speculation.

Foreign trade and investment brought no change in the form of surplus labour with rent in kind remaining predominant. Since this allowed the landlords to monopolise the grain markets, which were key to other commodity markets, any reinforcement of the land monopoly also reinforced the landlords' dominance over commerce. The acceleration of commerce through integration into world markets therefore only strengthened the economic power of the landlords.

In this way, world capitalism tended to reinforce the monopoly land system, increasing land concentration and the land hunger which supported exorbitant rents, as commercial capital accelerated by foreign trade was used for land speculation rather than productive investment. Rather than promoting peasant independence, it marginalised and pauperised them, promoting their dependence on the landlords, so increasing opportunities for the rich to get richer without involvement in production, through exploitation and cheating.

The effects on class structure

The impact of foreign trade and investment was to accelerate the convergence of landlords, merchants, officials and militarists that had developed during the Qing dynasty.

Despite some efforts within the elite to introduce Western-influenced political and economic modernisation, neither the state, depleted of its reserves, nor the merchants, themselves under pressures of taxation and foreign competition, were able to promote reforms. At any rate, the foreign powers continually intervened to prop up the regressive social forces of the autocratic state, and later the warlords, to guarantee their advantage. Instead, as foreign capital sought links with merchants and officials to extend its role in China, these rich elites joined up with foreign companies and banks, and through these connections built themselves into powerful compradore and bureaucrat capitalist organisations. Acting as intermediate brokers for foreign capitalism, the compradore and bureaucrat bourgeoisie assisted in opening China up as a market for world trade, promoting the dependency of the Chinese economy on international capitalism.

Through the merchants, who took on the internal distribution of imports and the collection of goods for export, national markets were linked up with international markets, exposing the rural economy to the forces of world competition as described above. As Chinese merchants joined up with foreign trade, the cultivation of cash crops and the production of handicrafts under the putting-out system came under the control of foreign companies. Given the existing connection between commerce and landed property, as foreign companies developed their contacts with Chinese merchants, landlordism became interwoven with comprador capital: large landlords who also controlled the commodity markets became compradore capitalists, engaging in large-scale speculation. These compradore-landlords struck deals with foreign companies to make tenant-peasants grow cash crops, and then increased rents.[18] The fact that commercial farming was still carried out on small parcels and not large estates indicated that the landlords' main interest was the collection of rents rather than profitable investment.

Officials used their salaries to buy land and engage in commercial speculation, whilst merchants used their commercial super-profits to purchase land and also buy official positions in the state trading companies. These companies fused state and mercantile interests, linking bureaucrat with compradore capital. Through loans, the foreign powers established links between their banks and the Chinese state, promoting co-operation in the building of railways to facilitate trade. At the same time, improved transport permitted the easier movement of troops around the country.

Against the constant threat of rural unrest, a modern army was built up reliant on foreign military weapons. Foreign banks also worked with the Chinese state in the development of war industries. These ventures were instrumental in bringing together militarists, foreign companies, large merchants and government officials as the core of the bureaucrat capitalist strata.

A new type of landlord arose from the ranks of the militarists as army commanders used their salaries, bolstered by squeezes from the soldiers' payments, as well as embezzled taxes and loans, to engage in land purchase on a large scale. As a result of their massive transactions, land prices and consequently rent tended to rise generally causing a new wave of land concentration.[19] Whilst army commanders became large landowners, the increasing role of the local militia and the formation of regional armies saw the militarisation of the landlords at the various levels of society.

With Chinese trade and finance no longer limited to operation in the internal market but linked with international channels, opportunities for the wealthy increased. Merchants, landlords and officials alike used their funds to finance foreign trade and to speculate in commodities, land and exchange rates. To raise finance for their new endeavours, landlords intensified their exploitation of the peasantry. As they gravitated to residence in the Treaty Ports, these absentee landlords sought every means possible to increase their exploitation of the peasants – raising rents, demanding higher rent deposits, revoking permanent tenancies, shortening leases, abandoning traditional obligations and arrangements of shared risk, and undermining tenants' rights – to support their westernised luxuried lifestyles, to protect themselves from the vagaries of world prices and to cover increased taxation.

The impoverishment of the peasantry led not only to increased rates of tenancy but also created a labour market which opened up the possibilities of industrialisation and the emergence of new class forces. In this way, the impact of foreign trade and investment had contradictory effects. It simultaneously reinforced the landlords' control over land and commerce by undermining agriculture and restricting the internal market, whilst creating conditions which allowed the emergence of a national bourgeoisie and a working class. The latter, although it only numbered some three million, at most approximately one per cent of the population, was concentrated in the foreign-owned companies. Alongside these large-scale enterprises, smaller landlords, merchants and officials also began to invest in textiles and other light industries.

Foreign capital stimulated the development of a national capitalist class but at the same time restricted it to a limited and dependent growth. It provided an infrastructure of banking and transport which facilitated the emergence of a Chinese domestic industry alongside foreign investment, one that was apparently able to maintain a constant share of the market.[20] This however was the case only because Chinese and foreign-owned enterprises catered to different market sectors.[21] In the case of the Chinese cotton industry which saw an overall increase in output, traditional textile production was only able to withstand competition from the modern textile industry by payment of wages at less than subsistence. Even so the expansion of weaving did not match the losses of spinning.[22]

National industry surged during the First World War in a period of respite from international competition and continued to grow subsequently. According to Chang, from 1931 to 1936, industrial production in China grew at a remarkable annual rate of 9.3 per cent, at pace with overall economic growth.[23] Based on these figures, numbers of Western scholars, challenging the view that Republican China experienced economic stagnation, have called for a reappraisal of the 'Nanjing decade' from 1927

–1937.[24] The argument here is that the Nationalist government was in fact an early example of the East Asian developmental state, given its role in setting up new bureaucratic agencies aimed at launching industrialisation in areas such as steel, copper, machinery and electrical goods.

Chang's figures however do not account separately for the growth of foreign, bureaucrat and national enterprise during this period. At the heart of the KMT government's 'command economy' were the 'four big families' who ran the main national banks, extending their monopoly interests not only into the key industries but also commercial channels; at the same time, maintaining close links with foreign capital.[25] Foreign firms remained only a minority in terms of numbers, and foreign investment did not increase significantly during this period. Nevertheless foreign capital came to dominate the most dynamic sectors of the economy, in mining, railways, shipping, imports and exports, shipbuilding and textiles. Japanese investment grew at the expense of the British and although Chinese-owned enterprises did increase, producing much of China's industrial output, they only accounted for 25 per cent of total modern investment in 1936.[26]

Foreign companies not only had the advantages of superior techniques, but also had access to cheaper credit and favourable taxes from the Chinese state. Under-resourced, lacking in technical expertise and adequate banking, Chinese industry was unable to compete on an equal footing in obtaining raw materials and gaining markets, and stood little chance of independent development since foreign companies had greater financial support and dominated light industry through the supply of machinery and technology from their heavy industrial projects. National industries then grew in the shadow of foreign and bureaucrat capital. The fact that Chinese entrepreneurs invested mainly in the labour-intensive light industries but scarcely at all in heavy industry, is indicative of the impact foreign competition had on the structure of the Chinese industrialisation.

Whilst the interests of the warlords, compradores and bureaucrat capitalists were closely bound up with those of the foreign powers and the landlord system, the interests of the national bourgeoisie were essentially in conflict with feudal and imperialist interests. Foreign trade and investment inhibited the development of domestic industry precisely because it restricted the Chinese market, not just directly by competition but also indirectly by contributing to the impoverishment of the peasantry. Yet, national businesses remained dependent on foreign companies and banks whilst retaining links with landlordism, relying to varying degrees on revenues from rent to provide capital for their businesses. So, at the same time as imperialism created conditions for industrial development, it helped create a weak and dependent national bourgeoisie subject to the influence of the compradore bourgeoisie, the landlords and the foreign powers.

The effects on rural society

Although foreign trade constituted only a small percentage of GNP, to claim that the traditional agricultural sector was little affected is not to grasp the whole picture: the social as well as economic effects on the rural areas were immeasurably greater than simple figures reveal. The further weakening of the state and the increasing trend towards absentee landlordism, as landlords moved to the cities and merchants bought land, hit right at the heart of rural society. Commercialisation, instead of promoting peasant independence, drove the peasants all the more into dependency on the landlords, yet at the same time intensifying class tensions as traditional bonds disintegrated.

More interested in the money to be made from high rents and land speculation than in upholding traditional values, landlords increasingly abandoned their customary obligations of shared risk and shared commitment to community welfare, passing the burdens entirely on to the peasantry. They withdrew gleaning rights and, instead of reducing rent in times of bad harvest, they advanced loans at high rates of interest.[27] The customary reciprocity of the landlord-tenant arrangements thus became increasingly one-sided for, whilst the landlords refused to comply with their traditional obligations, they would use the courts to ensure that the peasants fulfilled theirs. The abandonment of even minimal traditional protections, or their manipulation to the landlords' advantage with the support of officials, drove the peasants further along the path, through debt, to loss of land and tenancy.

At the same time then that investment in modern agriculture was inhibited, the traditional ties and structure of Chinese society were further weakening as the state abandoned irrigation and public works and the increasing rate of tenancy and wage labour, driven by commercial development, undermined more and more the owner-cultivator communities bound by kinship and settlement rights. Corporate village properties were broken up with land speculation accelerating the sale of properties held in common. But despite the increase in absentee landlordism with the extension of land purchase, the slackening of the patron-client bond, and the alienation of land from social ties, peasants remained tied to the land by lack of alternative occupations and tied to the landlords because the land belonged to them.

The increase in commoditisation under the conditions of semi-colonialism had the effect then, if not of entirely dissolving, then transforming traditional relations as the landlords' powers over the peasants grew. In cash-cropping areas, powers shifted from village elders as new ruling groups of village landlords and rich peasants took over control of local processing, developing business and trade at the expense of peasant handicrafts.[28]

Landlord-tenant reciprocity was increasingly replaced by corruption, embezzlement and brute force as the rate of exploitation of the peasantry rose at the same time as their rent-paying capacities were undercut by the undermining of agriculture. The growing trend of absentee landlordism, and the increasing involvement of merchants and officials in land ownership, were by no means an indication of a fundamental change in the basis of landlord class shifting from land-holding to finance and institutional position. Although traditional personal bonds of kinship or benevolent patronage that tied the peasants to the landlords were on the wane, the absentee landlords relied more and more on the power and influence of the local landlords and wealthier members of the village communities to act as their middlemen in the collection of rent in kind and land transactions. Small landlords and rich peasants thus came under the patronage of wealthy officials, absentee landlords and merchants, benefitting from acting as their agents. Local gentry and absentee landlords would join together in rent collection agencies, and, especially after 1911, with the militia under the direct control of the landlords, they would organise armed bands to extort payments from the peasants.[29] The increasing number of poor peasants who were imprisoned for failure to pay rent demonstrates the collaboration between the magistrates' courts and the landlords.

With the increasing involvement of the landlords in politics and the military, and as the landlords and merchants joined with officials and militarists in the evasion of taxes, the merging of economic and political power was reinforced.[30] This fusion was reflected at local levels as the leading role of the rural elite was strengthened by their involvement in the system of taxation. The introduction of special levies in the late Qing and Republican periods to pay for policing and the armed forces saw the devolution of government fiscal power to the local elites in a system which was thus open to abuse with village headmen joining local officials in embezzlement. Especially where the solidarity of owner-cultivator communities had been undermined, with commercialisation increasing the numbers of tenants and wage labourers, villages were particularly vulnerable to bullying by 'local tyrants' who embezzled taxes.[31] Those quasi-officials operating at district or township levels, just below county government, presiding over districts of 10,000 to 60,000 in population, who were responsible for the local armed force, with control over tax collection and with judicial powers to arrest, put on trial and punish, these were, in Mao's words, 'virtually kings of the countryside'.[32]

Close links with the civilian administration allowed the gentry to assume influence over the official *baojia* heads and to dominate village organisations, subverting them from corporate institutions to a further means of surplus appropriation. With the acceleration of money relations, whilst in theory the income from the rent of corporate lands was to be used for the benefit of the lineage as a whole and corporate properties were not freely disposable, in practice this income was in the hands of officers who invariably came from the wealthier branches of the lineage. Chen Hanseng notes that, notwithstanding the inviolability of the corporate lineage properties, the manipulation of income in the possession of the few in effect transformed lineage land into a modified form of private property, with the elders acting as collective landlords.[33]

The important factor in the alienation of corporate assets and the dissolution of the traditional social fabric was the increase in luxury consumption of the village rich which saw a growing substitution of money for in-kind payments, accounting for the prevalence of money rent in areas under the control of large lineage organisations. This switch to money rent facilitated the free disposal of income by clan elders, who would raise rents and interest on loans, substitute cash crops for subsistence production, lease corporate land for a deposit to outsiders and sub-letting landlords, and use the income to purchase more land in order to increase the income from rent. Such developments, Chen points out, intensified the class division in village society with:

> ...the creation of a new exploiting class which is able to turn the common heritage, such as clan lands, to individual uses and, on the other hand, a peasant tenant class without status and eventually bereft even of the ability to question the actions of those who exercise power. Once a member of a self-governing corporation and taking part in those of its decisions which affected his own fortunes, the peasant has become a mere cog in a machine in the running of which he has no say and the performance of which he often does not understand.[34]

As Chen describes, tensions within the clans increased:

> The great majority of the peasant members are ignorant of what is taking place behind the doors where clan officials confer with politicians and businessmen. Those of the more prosperous peasants who do not belong to the favoured families often are indignant over some experience of 'squeeze' or injustice, but helpless, since those who control the clan funds also control all possible means of legal redress.[35]

Whilst the form of lineage organisation remained, its content was changed: no longer an organisation to protect the system of owner-cultivation, it became another means of peasant exploitation and lineage property another form of land monopoly. By usurping collective properties, the elders transformed the clan system into a part of the landlord system with the ordinary lineage members dependent on them for a livelihood in terms of access to land and loans.

Commercialisation then, instead of providing an impetus for wealthier members to break from the restraints of the community, instead allowed the village elites to pursue their own private interests within these corporate bodies, enhancing their position within their communities to increase their own personal wealth by sub-letting corporate lands, purchasing new lands and fomenting feuds to annex the lands of weaker lineages.

The acceleration of commerce then saw the landlords' power over the peasantry grow both economically and politically, in the South through their control over lineage organisations, and in the North, over the local militia. Even as lineages deteriorated with the acceleration of marketisation, their elite leaders still held prestige. However the breakdown in long-standing reciprocities also unleashed the peasants' capacity for independent action. At the same time as the landlords intensified their exploitation of the peasants, this reinforced the traditions of self-help and mutual support between peasant families to sustain themselves in times of crisis. Especially in the North, in areas where commerce was less developed and where no large lineage organisations existed to link the village communities to the wider elite strata, community bonds remained a strong basis of mutual support as peasants withdrew in angry opposition, closing their communities against the increasing demands of the state and market.[36]

The development of commerce too saw the peasant world developing beyond the confines of the village community. Army recruitment also served to widen their horizons. New bonds of mutuality, formed in the organisation of migration, banditry and salt-smuggling, further extended the ability of the peasantry to organise beyond their village communities. Along with the rising rents and interest rates, the demands of the warlords for more taxes and loans to finance the costly imports of military weapons so as to increase their powers, exacerbated peasant bankruptcy, and stoked rural unrest. Since peasant uprisings in turn were only suppressed by modern military weapons, the cycle of revolts-munitions-taxes and further revolts became more and more vicious.[37]

Semi-feudalism; semi-colonialism

In China, the distinctive features of a bureaucratic state, originally based on state land ownership and village communities, contrast with the European feudal pattern where landlord power was structured by a hierarchical system of land rights. Nevertheless, whilst pre-revolutionary agrarian China had the superficial appearance of a society of owner-cultivators at the base of the state hierarchy, in fact, the role of the landlords was central, both economically, given their predominant ownership of land, and in the articulation of power as mediators connected to official position in the bureaucracy and to patriarchal rule in the village where relations of superior-inferior or senior and junior in the kinship system prevailed. As in European feudalism, in the Chinese feudal system political and economic power became fused at the base of society.

To understand the landlords' hold on the peasantry it is necessary to look not only at the relations of land ownership, but also at debt, interest rates, mortgages, and control of markets and credit systems. A closer examination of the overall conditions of the majority of the peasantry revealed that the problem affecting both owner- and tenant-peasant was that of insufficient land, idle labour and, for those that had them, under-utilised means of production. This contrasted with the trend towards the concentration of land in the hands of the landlords and rich peasants.

Although the landlords had become increasingly involved in trade, finance and government, this did not indicate a shift from their economic basis in landed property and a corresponding shift in political power. Existing debates over whether the system of elite power was based on officialdom, degree-holding, local prestige, commercial or managerial functions, lineage organisation or land ownership, have failed to consider the fact that what characterised the agrarian system was that, despite the complexity of rural relations, rent in kind remained the predominant form of surplus appropriation, cutting into the necessary labour of the peasants. So despite the development of commerce, there was no fundamental change in the character of the landlord class and no transformation in the landlord-tenant relationship to a contractual commercial basis. On the contrary, through the collection of rent in kind, the landlords were in a position to gain control over the markets in grain, land and other commodities, thereby strengthening their grip over the economy and the peasantry as a whole.

The significant feature of the agrarian system in China was not so much the extent of tenancy nor the continuation of servile relations binding tenants to landlords, but the inadequacy of the plots of land, whether owned or rented, cultivated by the majority of the peasants. In these conditions, even those small landlords and rich peasants owning only a few acres had a considerable power and were able to charge exorbitant rents given the huge demand for land on the part of the impoverished peasants.

The land shortages of the majority of owner and tenant peasants shaped landlord-peasant relations in a distinctive way, as patronage and dependency framed a system of personalised power in which all landlords shared. Rather than servile relations binding tenant to landlord, unequal relations, cloaked in ties of mutual obligation between benefactor and client, affected not only the rental arrangements but other rural relations of exchange such as usury or wage labour. The combination of commerce and concentrated land ownership, together with the practices of patronage, meant that not only the tenant but also the owner peasants were encompassed within the power domain of the landlords.

Whilst the control of the surplus was articulated through the various forms of custom, at the same time in the complex web of relations that made up rural society, vertical ties tended to prevail over horizontal class solidarities. Lineage and communal bonds cut across class divisions shaping the village order with landlord power embedded in social networks and kinship groups in the countryside. Elite-led lineage and community defence organisations together with patron-client ties constituted an informal power structure below the county government administration. It was upon this localised power – the fusion of the landlords' economic and political powers – that the state and the absentee landlords increasingly relied. The political centrality of the local landlords was then demonstrated in their role as a lynchpin in the articulation of power between the state and the village communities based on their patriarchal influence over the peasantry.

The impact of foreign trade, banking and investment on China's feudal society was complex, contradictory and uneven.[38] Combining semi-colonialism with semi-feudalism, imperialist imposition was not alone responsible for China's economic deterioration. New openings for investment saw the emergence of a class of domestic industrialists whose growth was nevertheless thwarted as the acceleration of commerce aggravated the existing conditions of peasant land hunger and monopoly ownership of land. Overall the impact of imperialism saw the exploitation of the peasants increase and their competition for land intensify whilst land ownership became more and more concentrated.[39]

At the same time, China was to become more militarised under foreign intervention, with social tensions mounting. Due to the depredations of the warlords, world depression and the exactions of the imperialist powers, by the 1920s the peasants sank more and more into debt and tenancy. Whilst tenant peasants suffered from increasing rents, owner peasants were the victims of speculative swindling as well as bearing the heavy burden of taxes which supported the warlord armies that the landlords managed to evade. Increasing peasant impoverishment and the lack of development of the internal market exacerbated the conditions which made land purchase for the extraction of rent the dominant economic activity. The acceleration of commercial capital spurred speculation rather than investment, consolidating the links between the landlords, merchants, officials and warlords in their co-operation with foreign business.

Chinese agriculture was thus characterised by the landlords' dominant position in land ownership, the weakness of an independent rich peasant economy, and the marginalisation and impoverishment of the majority of peasants cultivating land insufficient for their needs. Whilst imperialism and the landlord system inhibited productive investment and the development of the market, the peasants were heavily exploited whether in commercialised or underdeveloped areas.

The pre-revolutionary agrarian crisis in China then saw the polarisation between the landlords and rich peasants with their control over land, and the increasingly land-hungry poorer tenant and owner peasants. But whilst the changes frayed the customary arrangements that bound the peasants to the landlords, this unleashed their capacity to organise independently, so leading to spontaneous protests and rebellions which met with an increasingly brutal response.

NOTES & REFERENCES

1. Chesneaux, 1973, p.23.
2. Between 1929 and 1934, it is estimated that loan and indemnity payments accounted for between 31.8 per cent and 40.5 per cent of national budget expenditures. See Lippitt, 1974, p.156.
3. This paragraph outlines the arguments of Feuerwerker (1983) and 1968, pp.73–15. Potter (1968) for example argues that Treaty Port industry was not detrimental to the peasants, p.5; p.174. Lasek (1983) summarises the debates on underdevelopment in China; Osinsky, 2010, pp.578–9, outlines the contrasting views.
4. See for example Perry, 1980, p.50; p.118–9.
5. See Riskin, 1980, p.123.
6. See Huang, 1985, p.126.
7. *Ibid.*, p.132–5.
8. See Feuerwerker, 1969, pp.125–132.
9. Feuerwerker, 1969, pp.127–8.
10. See the discussion of sugar growing in Marks, 1984, pp.100–108.
11. Huang, 1985, p.130; p.310. This demonstrates the lack of substance in the arguments of Potter (1968) who cites BAT's subsidies as an example of how modern industry helped to create a prosperous farming community instead of an impoverished peasantry: pp.182–3.
12. Chen Hanseng, 1936, p.64. He argues that the break-up of large farms run by rich peasants renting in land, and the decline in yields, was the result of high rents which made it impossible to hire the same amount of labour or put improvements into the soil.
13. Lippitt, 1980, p.64, argues that most of the surplus was wasted on the luxuried consumption of the gentry.
14. Chen Boda, 1966a, p.88.

15. *Ibid.*, p.77.
16. *Ibid.*, p.67; pp.96–7.
17. *Ibid.*, pp.100–2.
18. *Ibid.*, pp.65–6; 79–82.
19. Chen Hanseng, 1936, p. xiii–xiv.
20. Hou Chi-ming, 1965, pp.138–141.
21. Feuerwerker, 1983, p.201.
22. See Feuerwerker, 1969, pp17–31, and Huang, 1985, pp.132–5.
23. Chang, 1967, p.38, as cited in Osinsky (2010).
24. See discussion in Osinsky, 2010, pp.586–589.
25. Ho Kan-chih, 1977, pp 140–2. For an example of how the British-American Tobacco Company expanded its operations in China through the corruption of officials, see Institute of Pacific Relations, 1939, pp.175–9.
26. Hou Chi-ming, 1965, p.255.
27. See Thaxton, 1975, p.327.
28. For example, see the account of the expansion of peanut growing and the oil extraction industry in southern Hebei, Institute of Pacific Relations, 1939, pp.160–7.
29. Marks, 1984, p.147; Fei Xiaotong, 1939, p.188.
30. Chen Hanseng, 1933, pp.17–8.
31. See Huang, 1985, p.269; pp.273–4; pp.289–90.
32. Mao, *Selected Works*, Vol. I, pp.40–41.
33. Chen Hanseng, 1936, pp.40–1.
34. *Ibid.*, p.39.
35. *Ibid.*, p.39.
36. Huang, 1985, pp.259–264.
37. Chen Hanseng, 1936, pp. xiii–xiv.
38. Brandt (1997), who like Osinsky rejects the notion of Republican China as a period of economic deterioration, nevertheless similarly describes the growth process as 'spatially-differentiated and uneven'. p.283.
39. Huang (1985) similarly argues that the world market accelerated pre-existing trends in Chinese society, pointing to the limitations of both dualist and dependency theories, pp.21–3. I differ with Huang as to what these pre-existing trends were and hence the nature of the interaction between the internal social forces and imperialist intervention. See Part 2; Chapter 2.

PART 2

From stagnation to crisis: economic and political dimensions of agrarian China's decline

Introduction

At the start of the 19th century, China was the leading world civilisation: it had the largest population, an advanced system of administration, the largest trade, the greatest wealth and it had led the way in basic technologies. Yet Europe was to quickly catch up and overtake it. The question as to why China did not remain the pre-eminent power has preoccupied Western and Chinese scholars alike.

With this question in mind, Part 2 considers a range of explanations for China's economic stagnation – the limits of the market and technologies, the workings of the agricultural system, the nature of the state, and the failures of peasant rebellion as well as of reform efforts, both traditionalist and modernising. It does so primarily through critical examination of key arguments in Western sinology which focus on the distinctiveness of China's problems of development as compared with Europe. As identified in Part 1 these include: a stagnating agriculture typified by small-scale cultivation of uneconomic plots with traditional techniques; the fact that commercialisation in China, rather than strengthening the rights of the cultivator, led to increasing peasant impoverishment; and that, rather than a hierarchy of land rights and seigneurial privileges of manorial serfdom, power and status rested on official title and connections with the bureaucratic state on the one hand, and on patron-client ties and patriarchal authority within local communities on the other hand.

These generally acclaimed studies have called into question, either directly or implicitly, the nature of China's political economy as a system of feudal landlordism. Radical transformation of land ownership has been perceived to serve limited purpose – the solution instead to China's economic stagnation is thought to lie in reform. The following chapters however aim on the contrary to establish the political and economic centrality of landlord-peasant conflict by exploring the dynamics of class relations and the state to support a conclusion that reaches beyond the reform perspective to that of revolution.

China's long-term problems of stagnation and decline of the agrarian economy over time – the restrictions on investment and the limited development of the market – have frequently been seen in terms of the particularistic operation of the peasant economy. Various explanations have been put forward to account for the persistence of small family farming. Tawney, preoccupied with peasant impoverishment, sees the Chinese peasants as traditionalists unable to respond to market pressures; however for Elvin, they are rational farmers, and it is technological factors that explain China's 'investment trap'. Huang, meanwhile, finding the parcellised pattern of Chinese agriculture under extensive commercialisation shaped by the dual pressures of overpopulation and a partial social differentiation without relief of economic growth, focuses, from an essentially substantivist perspective, on the problem of the dissolution of traditional community solidarities.

Despite holding contrary views, these three key authors all take the small producer as the centre of analysis, sharing a view of the problems of investment in terms of relations between peasant producers and the market. In his *Theory of Peasant Economy* (1925), Chayanov, countering Lenin's argument that small production provided the basis for peasant differentiation with the emergence of a rural bourgeoisie and proletariat, presented instead an explanation for the lack of development of capitalism in agriculture and the persistence of family farming in Russia in terms of a peasant mode of production in which the application of labour was balanced to meet consumption needs rather than production for a profit.[1] For Chayanov, the smallholding of the 'middle peasant', who is neither capitalist nor proletarian but manages family labour according to its needs, is seen as key to rural development.

Lenin nevertheless was taking to task the Narodniks' view of the Russian peasantry as homogeneous small-scale producers, criticising their view of capitalism as a system of consumption not of investment. Following Marx's argument against Adam Smith, he made the point that the development of capitalism related to the sphere of production, and the creation of wealth, not to the sphere of circulation and exchange, and the distribution of wealth. From the point of view of consumption, income, the peasants appeared undifferentiated, however the differences existing between rich and poor concerned the mode of surplus extraction.[2] Whilst the Narodniks' called for reforms to address the problems of peasant impoverishment through aid to the small farmers, Lenin critiqued this 'viewpoint of the small producer' according to which '…his misfortunes are due to specific features of distribution, to mistakes in policy …' His concern was rather to reveal the economic relations of expropriation which 'leads inevitably to the theory of class struggle.'[3]

Lenin's arguments about the development of capitalism in agriculture and the emergence of new class forces in the countryside certainly have quite a different application in China's conditions, nevertheless his critical perspective on the 'viewpoint of the small producer' provides the underlying theme linking together the chapters that follow, insofar as these aim to move beyond issues of distribution and policy to direct focus on the study of production relations and the conditions of surplus creation. What is evidently absent from these key works of Western scholarship is any consideration of feudal rent as the major constraint on capitalist development in China, and the impact this had on peasant production and the peasant condition.

A further major controversy among Western scholars has been the nature of the Chinese state.[4] However, from Wittfogel's Orientalism to Marx's Asiatic mode of production, there is a certain acceptance that the problem of China's stagnation was associated with the suppression of private interests by the bureaucratic centralised state. The state's reliance on the patriarchal clan system and its individual household-based taxation system is seen to have perpetuated the closed nature of peasant farming with agriculture and handicrafts combined.

Landlord and state are considered to have had separate interests, forming two distinct power bases sustained by rent and tax respectively, with elite power and status deriving from official position in the bureaucratic hierarchy rather than landholdings as in the European feudal system. Tensions in Chinese society are then conceived in terms of conflicts between the interests of the state and the villages or between the upper and lower tiers of the power structure, that is, a dualist perspective.

From the Marxist perspective on the other hand, the state in a class-divided society serves to hold class antagonisms in check, enabling the economically dominant class to assume a politically dominant position. As such it is considered to act as an instrument in the subordination of the peasants' class struggle against the landlords.[5]

The common view of the separation of the political authority of the centralised state from the economic power of independent landlords is reflected in the key works of Perdue and Huang whose longitudinal studies consider developments over several centuries. Both scholars, questioning the CPC's analysis of the centrality of landlord-peasant relations, take the view that the state served peasant interests, acting as much in collision as in collusion with landlord interests.

These studies then are of particular interest in breaking with the view of Orientalist despotism, presenting a perspective on the traditional state as benevolent rather than totalitarian, a progressive force, protecting peasant welfare and promoting production. Perdue sets out a dichotomy between the public sphere of the bureaucratic state and the private interests of the landlords with the spread of commercialisation; Huang on the other hand conceives China's political economy as a three-cornered structure defined by the separate but interdependent axes linking state, village, and gentry. For him the pre-revolutionary crisis of the early decades of the 20th century was not so much the intensifying class struggle of landlord and peasant as the breakdown of the political authority of the state and the disintegration of state-village relations.

The question of the failure of capitalism to develop lies at the heart of debates among Chinese Marxist historians, who view the long-term trajectory in terms of the tenacity of feudal relations. Despite the emergence of 'capitalist sprouts' following the early Qing reforms, they ask how it was that the landlords were able to rebuild their power and position over the long run. The discussion among these historians opens up a further consideration as to how the Asiatic features of the bureaucratic state and patriarchal village communities served as a basis for refeudalisation with the landlords using officialdom and clientelism to restore their privileges and lay claim over the bulk of surplus production.

The tenacity of the landlord system also poses the further question of why periodic peasant uprisings, which occurred on a massive scale in China, failed to uproot feudal power. Were these rebellions no more than millenarian uprisings, aimed at restoring traditional equilibrium and security against the encroachment of market relations and an increasingly interventionist state? Why did peasant protest tend to fall under the influence of dissident gentry? In the Chinese village, kinship ties cut across class lines, greatly complicating peasant struggles, with different forms of rural conflict and a variety of local organisations forming a complex background. Vital to the discussion as to the revolutionary or traditionalist nature of the peasantry are considerations of divisions between those with and without resources. Also to be taken into account are changes in peasant consciousness as their conditions worsened in the early 20th century.

Finally, the question of the nature of the state and its relation to the landlord system also calls for an examination of the role of both traditional and modern reformers. From the efforts of enlightened Confucianists to settle owner-cultivators in the early Qing to the modernisers' programmes of the late Qing and Republican periods to address the problems of peasant impoverishment, reforms were directed at the small farmers. The viewpoint of the small producer presents social and economic problems in terms of imbalances in state-peasant relations and bureaucratic inadequacies. In fact the difficulties were ultimately more to do with the failure of a capitalist development to generate vigorous entrepreneurial classes in rural and urban areas in pursuit of their private interests against the restraints on economic development imposed by conditions of monopoly rent. It was this that made the revolutionary overthrow of the system of power rather than reform of the state the key issue, with peasants as the main motive force.

NOTES AND REFERENCES

1. Chayanov, 1966, pp.56–68; pp.88–9.

2. Lenin, *Collected Works*, Vol. I, pp.442–3.

3. Lenin, *Collected Works*, Vol. I, p.448.

4. See Perdue, 1987, pp.1–9, for discussion of the controversy between the theories of Oriental Despotism and the Confucian state.

5. See Engels, 1950 p.290, for the argument that, in a class-divided society, the state serves to hold class antagonisms in check, enabling the economically dominant class to assume a politically dominant position by acting as a vehicle of, in this case, the subordination of the peasants' class struggle against the landlords.

5
Market and technological constraints and the problem of monopoly rent

Tawney and the reformers: peasant traditions and the constraints of the internal market

Tawney's famous work of 1932, *Land and Labour in China*, presents the case for economic and political reforms to promote the internal market and democratise the state. Accepting Buck's conception of China as a society in which owner-cultivators predominated, he identified the traditions of the peasant household and the bureaucratic state as the main obstacles to progress and the major focus for reform. For him, the problems of peasant impoverishment were not rooted in landlord exploitation, rather, rural decline was the result of a particular interaction between commerce and a rural-based society whose rationale was subsistence production.

Noting the peculiarities of the market in which exorbitant rents and interest rates, and wildly fluctuating prices of land and commodities, resulted not in the stimulation of production but peasant impoverishment, he saw the peasants primarily as victims of merchants, forced through high interest rates and price manipulations on monopsonist markets to mortgage and sell their land. The inequalities in land ownership were seen then not as the cause but as an effect of rural decline.

Above all, Tawney considered that the chaos and social disintegration he witnessed in China resulted from the impact of commerce introduced by the West which upset the traditional arrangements of the state and peasant family as market forces and the influence of modern science dissolved the personal ties which bound the ancient civilisation together.

Tawney thought that Chinese peasants farmed not according to a profit-motivation but rather according to age-old household subsistence arrangements. Aimed to protect the individual against personal misfortune, these then weakened the force of economic incentive.[1] Similarly, the noted Chinese anthropologist, Fei Xiaotong, considered land to be valued for non-economic reasons, held for its security, arguing that land transactions were limited since to sell was to offend 'filial piety'.[2] This had a levelling effect through the practice of household division of property between sons, restricting the individual household's ability to seize economic opportunities. However, under conditions of population pressure, it appeared to be a good means of distributing limited and unexpanding resources amongst the largest possible number of human beings.³

The parcellised nature of cultivation in China, with its low productivity and backward technique, was then for Tawney and Fei Xiaotong to be explained in terms of production and property relations which did not conform with market principles but served rather as long-term reciprocal arrangements between family generations. Since the peasants were concerned not with production for profit but with subsistence and family survival, rather than rationalising production in response to market competition, they clung to uneconomic plots of land. Commercialisation increased their impoverishment and, corresponding with their decline, was the rise of parasitic classes of merchants, usurers and absentee landlords whose sole interest was the collection of rent, not production. The peculiarities of the market in terms of rent, interest rates and prices, reflected the ability of these classes to take advantage of the peasants' need through speculation.⁴

For Tawney then, the inequalities in land ownership and the imposition of exorbitant rents arose not from relations within the village but rather as a function of the financial relationship between town and countryside. Similarly, Fei Xiaotong's study of the destruction of silk handicraft production in competition with the influx of Japanese imports, showing how this led to the concentration of land in the hands of absentee landlords at the expense of peasant ownership, presents village decline as a function of the rural-urban market relationship. In his example, the decline in handicraft production led to shortages in family budgets so that peasants had to borrow from moneylenders. As villages depleted of reserves then sought financial help from the towns, these in turn absorbed the wealth of the villages through the system of pre-capitalist mortgage whereby rents collected were returned to the villages in the form of land purchases as further claims to rent.⁵

Seeing the rise in tenancy as working through credit and marketing systems which drained agricultural production, Tawney was to argue that the main problem for the peasants was not so much land tenure arrangements themselves but how to get a good price for their produce.⁶ Peasant insufficiency was a matter of distribution and consumption: China was caught in a vicious circle of poverty in which declining incomes and weak market demand inhibited industrialisation and opportunities for profitable investment.

To resolve the economic and political crisis brought about by the impact of foreign trade, Tawney advocated urgent reform in China to overcome the inadequacies of the market and channels of investment, especially to redirect the surplus dissipated by the merchants and usurers into productive investment. He proposed the setting up of credit and marketing co-operatives to by-pass the merchants, usurers and middlemen. These would facilitate the development of a stable peasant economy, promoting the internal market by increasing peasant purchasing power through the creation of opportunities for profitable investment and alternative occupations for under-employed labour in the villages in a programme of rural industrialisation based on handicraft production. The growth of industry alongside agriculture would provide a stimulus to increase agricultural demand for manufactured goods, transcending traditional techniques.[7]

Feuerwerker similarly saw China as caught in a vicious circle of underdevelopment, arguing that the weak demand of the peasantry accounted for the lack of development of industry which instead grew only on account of the requirements of the modern urban elite. This limited growth of manufacture then failed to create sufficient demand for raw materials to stimulate agricultural production.[8] The logic here is that of a low-level equilibrium trap described by Nurkse in terms of two interlinked vicious circles of poverty in which the lack of capital leads to low productivity, hence to low income, to a small capacity to save, and so to a lack of capital, whilst low productivity and hence low purchasing power leads to low inducement to invest as the second cause of the lack of capital leading to low productivity.[9]

Alternative explanations: Elvin and Myers

Countering the application of Nurkse's vicious circle to China, Elvin has advanced his own conception of a 'high-level equilibrium trap' whereby China's essentially small peasant economy operated within the framework of a highly efficient marketing and transport system.[10] Elvin rejects the notion of Chinese peasant society as self-sufficient, cellular and uncommercialised, arguing that from the 16th and 17th centuries onwards, with the development of commerce, fundamental changes occurred in China's economic structure. His view is rather that, following the break-up of manorial serfdom, the class system and political structure were transformed as landlords became more involved in trade and finance forming a new power structure not linked to land-holding but residing in the market towns and cities. This class of absentee landlords, Elvin considers, was based not on direct power within the villages but formed a sub-bureaucrat stratum in the towns as professional managers, directors and tax collectors exercised power over the villages through finance, commerce and institutional positions.[11] At the local level, the powers of the old village gentry were taken over by the *baojia* and the village headmen.

He sees power then as shifting from land ownership to trade, finance and institutional position, with the peasants gaining increasing independence.

Pointing to the development of large markets with large concentrations of capital in the hands of the merchants, Elvin goes on to explain the problem of economic growth in China in terms of technological constraints.[12] His argument is not to deny the assumption that inducement to invest is related to size of market, but rather to provide an alternative explanation for stagnation and the lack of investment in China to both the Nurkse view of the shortage of capital and restricted markets, and to the Marxist understanding of the constraints of a land monopoly.

Elvin's thesis is that those with savings chose to economise on capital and resources instead of investing in labour-saving machinery because resources, apart from labour that is, were short and increasingly expensive, whilst, with a falling agricultural surplus and falling *per capita* income, labour was cheapening. In conditions of stagnation given a diminishing surplus, Elvin argues that as Chinese agriculture intensified with population growth, the marginal productivity of labour declined, and with it, surplus above subsistence produced by the small peasant farm. The problem in his view was that the limits of agricultural productivity had been exhausted using traditional technology such that labour-intensive methods would not increase output, yet the abundance of cheap labour inhibited the use of improved methods to increase yields by raising labour productivity. Introducing the concept of the 'high-level equilibrium trap', he explains:

> With falling surplus in agriculture, and so falling *per capita* income and *per capita* demand, with cheapening labour but increasingly expensive resources and capital, with farming and transport technologies so good that no simple improvements could be made, rational strategy for peasant and merchant alike tended in the direction not so much of labour-saving machinery as of economising on resources and scarce capital. Huge but nearly static markets created no bottlenecks in the production system that might have prompted creativity. When temporary shortages arose, mercantile versatility, based on cheap transport, was a faster and surer remedy than the contrivance of machines.[13]

In contrast then with Tawney's view that saw the impact of foreign trade as undermining the traditional relations which bound Chinese society together so causing agriculture to decline, Elvin's analysis leads him to conclude that foreign trade would have a positive impact, as seen with the rapid commercial and industrial growth at the main points of contact around the Treaty Ports. He considered that opening to the West would provide China with the only opportunity of bringing about a sufficient change in the relative size of the market to at first ease and then break the 'high-level equilibrium trap'. Only a massive rise in demand as offered by Western markets could induce the investment in modern industrial-scientific inputs supplied by the West necessary to achieve greater yields per acre to cover the gap between the high costs of production and the low cost of labour replaced.[14]

Myers is another critic rejecting the applicability of Nurkse's vicious circle of low farm income and peasant purchasing power, limited markets and inhibited investment to China.[15] Claiming that households acted as economic units responsive to prices, he finds little evidence that merchants, absentee landlords and usurers blocked rural development and impoverished the peasants. Rather he employs the Chayanovian conception of a distinct peasant logic of production to argue that farm size depended on household labour and that, beyond a certain size supporting the households' consumption needs, peasants leased land out rather than investing in production, since this required a greater input in terms of livestock and fertiliser in order to make farming profitable. The optimum size of efficient farming was determined by the technical limits of traditional farming methods.

In Myers' view, the trend was away from inequalities in land ownership as large farms decreased whilst the number of landless peasants did not rise. He argues that in fact the land tenure system sustained rather than undermined the peasant economy since it served to equalise land use as peasants bought land in and leased it out according to the balance between the number of workers in a household and its consumption needs. In other words, land acted as a near-cash asset central to the credit system, without which farmers could not survive or reclaim land.[16]

A critical assessment

Tawney, Elvin and Myers all share in Buck's view of China as a world of small-holders. But where Tawney observed first-hand the impoverishment of the peasantry brought about by the impact of foreign trade, Myers and Elvin treat the peasant economy as stable and market-oriented with inequalities merely reflecting the rise and fall of family fortunes. Economic growth could be brought about through sustained inputs into the peasant household with no major change in the socio-economic framework necessary.

Tawney's analysis of the problems of income distribution and his proposals for reform have some similarity with those of the Narodniks who argued that capitalism could not develop because the impoverishment of the relatively homogeneous peasantry limited the home market. The arguments of Myers and Elvin also chime with the Chayanovian explanation of the persistence of a small peasant economy, namely, that farm size was determined by family size rather than by the use of capital, with a family farm expanding production not in order to make a profit but according to its own internal logic determined by its labour-consumer ratio. However, the fact that in China commercialisation did not significantly promote capitalist development and peasant differentiation but mass impoverishment requires further investigation into production relations and in particular the appropriation of surplus production.

Despite their contrary conclusions, Tawney, Elvin and Myers all share alike a central focus on the question of the market. However, from a Marxist perspective, the domestic market develops on account of the reproduction of constant capital, that is, it is the production of the means of production that provides the dynamic for the growth of the market in consumer goods. Notions, whether of a low-level or a high-level 'equilibrium trap', fail to appreciate the logic of capital in the development of the market and so overlook the conditions of productive investment, that is, the system of surplus creation. Tawney and Elvin both share the assumption that inducement to invest is a function of market size, with the mistaken implication that surplus derives from the sphere of circulation not the relations of production.

As has been seen, taking the question of surplus creation as the centre of his analysis, Chen Boda's study of land rent in pre-liberation China revealed, beneath the arrangements of commerce, the objective conditions of a high concentration of land ownership and a large demand for land by the peasants. As the condition for high levels of rent, it was this contradiction that served as the barrier to investment in China. The reason then for the persistence of parcellised production – the cultivation of uneconomic plots with traditional techniques – that characterised China's stagnating agricultural economy, lay in the existence of monopoly rent.

In the first place, excessive rent acted as a restraint on investment on tenant farms. Where Myers and Elvin argue the limits of traditional technology had been reached, Ash finds that the smaller-sized farms of the owner-peasants nevertheless undertook more investment in traditional technology, achieving higher yields than the larger tenant farms.[17] His explanation shows that the real factor inhibiting productive investment was not so much the high costs of available inputs but the burden of rent.

Where tenancy increased farm size above that of the owner-cultivators, the larger farms were not necessarily more economically viable than the smaller farms. Since rent cut into the necessary labour of the tenant, this affected their ability to undertake productive investment and improve cultivation, instead diverting resources from production to subsistence. Whilst tenants were driven to hire out labour or take out loans, the owner-cultivators on the other hand were able to invest more in animals, fertiliser, and traditional farming implements. Tenancy then did not appear to reduce inequalities between peasant households as Myers argues. Furthermore, the high prices of land resulting from monopoly ownership made it impossible for peasants to recover their land once lost. Whilst Myers argues that peasants would not have been able to survive without the opportunity to rent land, this did not mean as he suggests that the land tenure system was not exploitative.

Monopoly rent blocked investment to improve labour productivity not only by depriving tenant peasants of resources to invest even up to the level of the owner-cultivators. The point was also that investment in production yielded less income than pre-capitalist rent. Capitalist production can only emerge if the level of capitalist rent, that is, surplus profit over and above normal profit, is at least as high as pre-capitalist rent.[18] With land rent higher than the returns on investment in production, since high demand for land produced rents at 50 per cent of the crop on average, there was little incentive to extend cultivation. With exorbitant rents paid in kind, there was more potential to increase wealth without engaging in production, through rent, usury and commercial super-profits.

As commodity and land markets developed in conditions which supported such steep rents, the system of land purchase grew not on the basis of production for a profit, nor of sustaining the peasant household economy, but rather on that of speculation so that the landlords could get more rent. Since rent and prices were determined not by land improvements but by poor peasant need, development was hindered as land prices rose beyond the means of rich peasants cultivating for a profit, making it difficult for them to extend cultivation. Instead of surplus being reinvested in production, under this system of land purchase it was used to augment land ownership.

A further disincentive to investment in cultivation was then the fact that the landlords were able to accrue the benefits of increased productivity not only by raising rents but also by market manipulation, using rent in kind to swing prices about in their own favour. On the basis of monopoly rent, landlords were able to dominate commerce and so extend their control beyond their tenant farmers to owner-cultivators and rich peasant marketings, further inhibiting profitable investment by these farmers. Whilst rich peasants sought outlets other than investment in cultivation, owner-peasants, burdened by taxes and often farming land insufficient to their needs, had to make up for their insufficiency by relying on sidelines and subsidiary activities rather than extending cultivation for the market by renting in additional land given the exorbitant rates. The effect was to reinforce the traditional combination of agriculture and handicraft production that limited commercial development.

China's distinctive parcellised cultivation was then related to three factors. In the first place, it was advantageous to the landlords to lease land out to peasants in small plots to make the most rent. Secondly, since high rents undermined profits from agriculture and militated against extended cultivation and investment in production, whilst market manipulations and commercial speculation served as deterrents against increasing yields, rich peasants also preferred to lease land out rather than extend cultivation using hired labour to engage in large-scale cultivation for a profit. Thirdly, parcellisation resulted as poor peasants clung to inadequate plots of land for survival given that the lack of development limited alternative occupations. Although poor peasants often had to hire out their labour to meet the demands of excessive rents and taxes, on the whole they did so only on a part-time or temporary basis to supplement their income, continuing to cultivate marginal plots of land to maintain their subsistence rather than face complete dispossession in conditions of stagnation.

Whilst the development of a free market in land and labour was therefore restricted, the persistence of subsistence farming on small uneconomic plots, combined with subsidiary production and handicrafts, inhibited the development of the internal market. The high rates of interest and supply of cheap labour, both the results of the bankrupt peasant economy under the constraint of exorbitant rent, together with the restriction of the internal market in conditions of the lack of development of agriculture, were all further disincentives against investment in production, inhibiting the emergence of a rich peasant economy. On the other hand, the bankrupt small peasant economy offered alternative opportunities for those with wealth to take advantage of the inadequate conditions of others through usury, the employment of cheap labour and other forms of pre-capitalist exploitation.

The lack of capitalist development and the persistence of parcellisation were not then to be explained in terms of the subjective rationale of peasant traditions and conservatism in the face of commercial development. Rather, it was the stagnation of agriculture under conditions of exorbitant rent undermining incentives for productive investment and so limiting alternative opportunities, that reinforced the peasants' survival strategies.

Nor was parcellisation indicative of a highly efficient small peasant economy and the superiority of small-scale farming: what has been called the 'ingenuity' of the Chinese peasant lay in their ability to cut consumption to a minimum. According to Chayanov's logic of peasant production, the optimum size of a family farm, cultivating more intensively and applying more labour per unit of land according to consumption needs, is lower than that of a capitalist farm which hires labour and applies means of production for a return on investment. Operating consistently at 'break-even' or even at a loss to feed the family, the small peasant household farm persists given its greater capacity for survival in difficult conditions in which a capitalist farm would go out of business.[19]

The problem with the Chayanovian approach is that it ultimately fails to take into account the wider socio-economic framework determining the use of labour on the peasant family farm. If smaller farms were more efficient in terms of yield, this was not so much a demonstration of the superior logic of the peasant economy but rather an indication of how small peasants had to struggle so hard to survive through lack of alternative occupations, whilst, when hiring out labour they received only a part of what could be regarded as a living wage, barely covering their subsistence. Meanwhile, as has been argued, for the wealthier peasants it was simply not worthwhile to invest in production. Uneconomic parcels, low productivity and the struggle of the peasants to achieve simple let alone expanded reproduction were rather to be explained in terms of the wider social system, namely, the objective conditions of land monopoly and land hunger which produced the high levels of rent that blocked investment.

To explain the persistence of small-scale cultivation in China it has also been argued that an economy of smallholdings is ideal for rice growing. Rice requires more intensive cultivation than for example wheat, making it rational to maintain farming on a small scale. Chen Hanseng however, whilst accepting that in certain regions the net income per land unit of intensive agriculture is greater than that of extensive agriculture, makes the point that if the necessary productive costs and the necessary labour power per land unit are taken into account, larger-scale agriculture can be proved to be superior. In the case of the direct costs of animals and fertiliser, the larger the area of cultivation the greater the number of draught animals that can be supported and used, and the more the quantity of home-made fertiliser. Further, noting that in California, rice is sown over large acreages by plane, he argued that large-scale cultivation may result in lower yields but compensates by reducing production costs.[20]

How production costs would be reduced given a larger unit of cultivation is not something that Elvin or Myers appear to have considered in their argument that the costs of traditional technology, in terms of yield per land unit, had become prohibitive. If however efficiency in farming is considered not from the point of view of yield but taking costs of production and labour power into account, farm size is seen to be determined not so much by the balance between land and labour but by economic stagnation under the condition of monopoly rent.

Whilst Nurkse's vicious circle captures the constraints on the domestic market in terms of the lack of purchasing power and impoverishment of the peasantry, the approach does not get to the root of the problem of China's lack of investment. The major restrictions on capitalist development in China lay both in the feudal relations of exploitation with rent in kind as the predominant form of surplus labour, and in the ability of the imperialist powers to determine investment overall through their own banking and large-scale industries. Whilst the situation of peasant land hunger and the monopoly ownership of land was exacerbated under the impact of imperialism, economic growth in China was inhibited not only by the persistence of feudal relations but also by the lack of control over production conditions, in particular, the production of the means of production.

Although Tawney, unlike Buck, took into consideration the problems of debt and market pricing and so recognised the extent of peasant distress, he did not look beyond the relation between the peasants and the market to find the roots of their impoverishment. Nor did he take into account the landlords' domination of commerce through the collection of rent in kind. Market conditions, namely, the deviations in commodity prices and interest rates, and the fact that land prices and rent bore no relation to soil fertility, were to be explained not by the traditions of the peasantry but by the particular relations of commerce and production in China. Tawney further failed to make the fundamental distinction between commerce and the unequal trade imposed by the foreign powers.

Differing with Tawney as to the extent of commercial development in Chinese agriculture so as to posit a high-level rather than a low-level 'equilibrium trap', Elvin nevertheless shares the assumption that the problem of China's stagnation lay in the lack of inducement to invest in terms of market demand. A limited analysis of rural relations leads him to overestimate the degree to which commerce dissolved China's traditional institutions and feudal relations of production. What he then fails to grasp is that the development of commodity production did not bring about a fundamental change in the character of the landlord class and their mode of exploitation. At the same time, he overlooks the dependence of the absentee landlords on the local gentry and village elites in the extraction of the surplus from agriculture through extra-economic means. Whilst unlike Tawney, he considers the world market to have a positive potential for China, he too ignores the unequal relationship between China and the Imperialist powers which caused the latter to rely upon the feudal subordination of the majority of the Chinese peasant producers.

Elvin's 'high-level equilibrium trap' essentially denies any economic potential within China. However, this view of a lack of surplus capacity is challenged by Lippitt who has shown that the 'potential surplus' in pre-revolutionary China – extracted as rent, interest rates, taxes as well as unpaid labour services – might have totalled as much as 30 per cent of total agricultural output.[21] There was then further potential to increase production using traditional techniques through the mobilisation of under-employed labour to cultivate land left idle, as well as through co-operation in land improvements, raising the productivity of land if not the productivity of labour.

The constraint on productive investment in China was neither a tradition-bound nor highly efficient small peasant economy but the existence of monopoly rent. It was this that led to economic stagnation reinforcing the peasants' reliance on traditional survival strategies. The removal of this barrier meant the release of resources for investment and increased production, potentially unleashing a massive demand for manufactured goods among the peasants. The vast majority of peasants, not just tenants or part-tenants, who bore the burden of excessive rents, stood to gain from the eradication of such constraints.

NOTES AND REFERENCES

1. Tawney, 1980, p.21.
2. Fei Xiaotong, 1953, pp.182–3.
3. Tawney, 1980, p.47.
4. *Ibid.*, p.57; p.62.
5. Fei Xiaotong, 1953, p.186.
6. Tawney, 1980, p.67.
7. *Ibid.*, p.138.
8. Feuerwerker, 1968, p.27; see also 1983, p.197.
9. Nurkse, 1953, pp.5–6.
10. Elvin, 1973, p.269.
11. *Ibid.*, p.255; p.260.
12. *Ibid.*, p.286.
13. *Ibid.*, p.314.
14. *Ibid.*, p.319; p.314–5.
15. Myers, 1970, p.127. See Wiens, 1975, pp.279–88, who criticises Myers' lack of evidence for this assertion.
16. *Ibid.*, p.234.
17. Ash, 1976a, p.48.
18. This point is made by Patnaik, 1979, p.401. See Marx's discussion of capitalist rent, *Capital*, Vol. III, Part IV.
19. Chayanov, 1966, pp.56–68; pp.88–9.
20. Chen Hanseng, 1936, pp.12–13.
21. Lippitt, 1974; see also Huang, 1985, pp.19–20.

6

Huang and the involuting peasant economy of North China – between Lenin and Chayanov

Population pressure and the semi-proletarianisation of the Chinese peasantry

Huang's study of agricultural cultivation on the North China plain, based on surveys of a number of villages carried out by Japanese researchers in the 1930s, finds widespread commercialised cash cropping surviving, in combination with handicrafts, on the basis of family labour. Taking in the span of the two centuries preceding the Chinese revolution, he argues that this was an economy in long-term stagnation and decline in which, whilst commercialisation increasingly fragmented the homogeneous 'middle peasantry' into market winners and market losers, the process of peasant differentiation stopped short of producing a fully-fledged capitalist farming sector and a rural proletariat.

He describes this pattern of partial differentiation as one with a sector of profit-seeking, labour-employing but notably non-capitalising managerial farming emerging from the ranks of the most successful commercial cash-croppers, coexisting with smaller family farms who were losing out from the increased risks of marketing their produce but without being fully separated from the land. Rather, these formed a semi-proletariat struggling to survive on tiny plots of land whilst hiring out their labour to supplement their income for wages below subsistence levels.[1] Huang finds this to have been prevalent in the sample villages with nearly 48 per cent of peasant households reliant on selling their labour on a yearly or day-to-day basis to meet their families' needs. This was, he argues, a distinctive pattern of agrarian economic change in which commercialisation had failed to promote any significant development of the productive forces in an economy under the combined pressures of population growth and social stratification. His description of a commercialised agricultural economy with a bankrupt peasantry is in clear contrast with the views of Myers and Elvin of a viable and efficient small-scale family farming system.

Huang's analysis of economic stagnation focuses on the market-oriented yet non-investing managerial farmers who used hired workers alongside their own labour to cultivate between 100 to 200 *mu*. This sector accounted for only around 10 per cent of the cultivated area in the region, however, for Huang, they provide a concrete case study of key importance in the examination of the obstacles to capital formation in Chinese agriculture.

Finding that managerial farmers failed to invest in improved techniques to increase production for the market, Huang suggests that investigating why they did not do so would provide the key to understanding why capitalism did not develop in China.[2] Comparing the operation of managerial farms with that of family-based production, Huang finds the same use of land and technology with no evidence of higher yields. This lack of evidence of the productive advantage of managerial farming indicated that the reinvestment of the surplus to raise the rate of surplus labour was not taking place. However, where the two types of farms did differ was in the use of animals and labour: managerial farmers were able to obtain similar levels of output with substantially less labour; in comparison, family farms supported excess labour.[3]

Managerial farmers typically cultivated holdings of 100 to 200 *mu* but as farm size grew beyond this, landowners would abandon farming for the higher returns to be gained from officeholding and commerce. Whilst this path to financial reward and status might explain the trend towards leasing rather than farming holdings above 200 *mu*, Huang argues, it was not sufficient to explain the underdevelopment of the smaller managerial farms. So why did the managerial farmers not innovate on their considerable holdings? For an answer Huang looks to the excess labour generated within the peasant economy which drove down wages.

Noting how the growth of population from the early Qing outpaced the development of resources as cultivated area stopped expanding, so creating pressures to return to subsistence production, Huang sees small family farms continually adding more and more labour for less and less increase in production in order to survive. Here, Huang applies the notion of 'agricultural involution', a term developed by Geertz from a study of wet rice farming in Java where, similarly, in a context in which commercial and technological change had failed to drive forward agricultural capitalism, there was a marked tendency for farmers to respond to increased population through the intensification of labour.[4]

Following Geertz, Huang sees this increased absorption of labour on the land as rooted in the operation of the small peasant household which, as a unit of both production and consumption, would go on producing so long as the application of more labour produced higher yields, even if only marginally, increasing output per area even if not increasing output per head. In this way, the involuting small peasant households supported an excess of labour which drove down farm incomes creating a low wage economy. Huang then sees managerial farming as able to benefit from the more efficient use of this cheap labour, whilst poor peasants, drawing below subsistence income from the land and without opportunities for alternative occupations, were forced to accept below subsistence wages. Unable to support themselves through either farming or wage labour alone, they clung onto inadequate plots at the same time hiring out their labour on a temporary or daily basis as well as on longer-term or yearly contracts.

Huang points to the continual increase in the supply of cheap labour from the involuting peasant economy as a powerful disincentive to labour-saving investment, so explaining the non-capitalising character of the entrepreneurial managerial farmers. Instead of investing in cultivation, they relied on the margin of benefit they obtained, with the same use of land and technology as on family farms achieving similar yields, from their more efficient use of labour. In this way, as Huang sees it, the commercialising but stagnating agricultural economy of North China was patterned distinctively by partial differentiation with a profit-driven entrepreneurial sector failing to achieve any breakthroughs in farming technique to increase productivity, and a semi-proletarianised peasantry locked into simultaneous dependence on family farming and wage labour, or combining farming and handicrafts, none of which alone was sufficient to support subsistence. The reason why capitalism failed to develop in China, Huang then finds to lie in the particular response of family farms as a unit of production and consumption to population pressure.

In other words, it is to the semi-proletarianised poor peasant economy, involuting under population pressure, that Huang looks to provide an explanation for the problem of stagnation:

> ...to the extent that the poor-peasant economy shaped capital formation in the economy, we might see it as not only an effect, but a cause of under-development.[5]

It is the persistence then of family farming, with peasant households locked into a combination of wage labour, handicrafts and small farming, that restricted the full commoditisation of land and labour, containing investment and blocking class differentiation and the growth of the internal market.

However, for Huang, rather than demonstrating a Chayanovian logic of peasant economy, involution was a rational response by the peasants to economic stagnation. Examining the conditions of labour use, he reveals the extent of China's problem of under-utilised labour, exposing some of the limitations of the Chayanovian perspective: the fact that involuted family farms displayed yields comparable with, or in some cases even higher than, the larger managerial farms, showed not the superiority of small-scale farming but rather their inefficient use of labour, since their higher yields were achieved at the cost of greater than average labour time. He finds then in the parcellised pattern of the peasant economy of the North China plain less a balance between the drudgery of labour and the consumption needs of the family household than the pattern of poor peasants maximising their chances of survival and the rich peasants and managerial farmers optimising scarce resources.[6] Insofar as peasant production did not follow the logic of capitalism – employing labour regardless of its costs so long as its marginal productivity was above zero – involution for Huang was not the expression of a distinct peasant mode of production; it was rather a strategy for survival under severe pressures of the expanding population and a harsh economic environment.

This particularly tenacious pattern of involution and semi-proletarianisation was to become all the more vicious, Huang goes on to argue, as commercialisation accelerated in the 20th century under the impact of imperialism. As market risks increased, stable personalised relations between landlord and tenant were replaced by short-term impersonal arrangements to the detriment of the poor. As landlords escaped their traditional obligations, this made for an even harsher social environment for the small peasants who bore the brunt of population growth, social stratification and commercial risk.[7] By the 1930s, most small farms had been driven below subsistence levels.

Critical assessment

Huang's study is of value in highlighting the distinctive pattern of partial differentiation of the peasantry under the impact of commercialisation. His 'structure of semi-proletarianisation' forefronts a neglected aspect of China's stagnation, turning attention on to the question of wage labour, not only how widespread the hiring of labour was, but also bringing into focus the key problem of inadequate farm size and underemployed labour in China's overwhelmingly predominant sector of family farming.[8] His method of comparing the use of labour on managerial and family farms provides a way to measure the extent of under-utilised labour in the agrarian economy, that is, the land hunger of the peasants in relation to their productive capacity. Yet there are problems in generalising from a limited number of villages in a particular region: across China, social relations display a great diversity. With regard to population pressure in particular, the person-to-land ratio was highly variable from region to region with migration quite possibly easing pressure in one and increasing it in another.

Also problematic is the claim that population pressure was a cause rather than a symptom of China's lack of development: in this Huang essentially shares Elvin's argument of the persistence of subsistence production under the pressure of population growth. He does not on the other hand accept Elvin's explanation of stagnation in China in terms of a diminishing surplus, noting instead, from Lippitt, that the farming system did indeed overall produce above subsistence.[9] The point then is to examine how this surplus was produced and extracted so as to inhibit development, and from this to consider how a different mode of surplus production might have altered China's economic direction.

Whilst recognising rent as an extra-economic burden on poor peasant tenants and part tenants, Huang's analysis leaves aside questions of the structure of land ownership and the monopoly form of rent as a constraint on capital formation. He views rent only from the point of view of its impact on peasant income, as yet another burden borne by the poor peasants, and one which would not have been so great in a growing economy but which was all the heavier given the inadequate size of peasant farms.[10] The question he fails to ask is: had these rent demands been lifted and land redistributed according to subsistence need, would this not have alleviated the problem of involution? Such measures would surely have reduced the pressure on the poorer peasants to hire out their labour and may even have increased the demand for labour by the better-off family farms. Lacking in his analysis of excess labour then is a consideration of whether, under different and more proactive government policies to redirect labour, or with changes in production relations, the problem would have diminished.

Huang sees wages and rent as market-determined, yet Chen Boda, as has been seen, discovered the rate of rent to be inverse to the quality of the land.[11] This then was not a system of commercial rent which is determined by the profitability of the land. The vagaries of rent in China rather demonstrated the parasitic nature of the feudal landlord system. This was not simply a matter of the extent of tenancy: it was rather how the predominant form of surplus extraction, rent, influenced the other relations of production and exchange.

Rather than analysing the system as a whole, Huang takes wage labour and tenancy as two separate axes of social stratification, drawing an analytical distinction between managerial farming based on hired labour and landlordism based on renting out land. He then lends greater weight to labour hiring to explain the problem of stagnation since labour hiring was the main feature of the agrarian economy of the North China plain. Indeed it was the case that wage labour had become more widespread than tenancy, and managerial farmers far outnumbered leasing landlords, forming the majority of the resident village rich.[12] However, this weight in numbers by no means establishes managerial farming as the preponderant sector of the village economy in terms of surplus appropriation. According to Huang's own figures, whilst managerial farms worked around 10 per cent of the cultivated area, 18 per cent of the land was rented.[13]

Huang's analytical separation overall fails to reveal how the landlord system affected the environment in which the wage labour-based farms emerged, and how the predominant form of surplus modified the characteristics of other production relations, setting the conditions under which these developed. Huang finds the roots of managerial farming, as a distinct sector, to lie in the change in the legal status of agricultural workers and tenants from serfs to commoners brought about by the spread of wage labour in the mid-18th century, which saw freer and more equal employment practices within the labour-hiring entrepreneurial agricultural sector. What Huang does not take into account however is, as Li Wenzhi has pointed out, that different laws still remained in place for the gentry, accounting for the persistence of coercive employment practices.[14] In these circumstances, managerial farmers sought to adopt these extra-economic practices themselves: far from being an exemplar of non-coercive relations, working alongside their hired workers on terms of greater equality than those in the landlord sector, many managerial farmers were noted for their brutal treatment of hired labourers.

Huang does at least recognise managerial farming as being 'a part of a system in which landlordism was continually reproduced' in a system of upward mobility which saw the most successful farmers abandoning both farming and village residency to become absentee landlords.[15] China's flexible political structure with open access to the bureaucracy provided a path to financial reward and status other than through farming, fostering ambitions to seek entry to the higher tiers of society where wealth and power derived from connection with the Imperial state. In this way Huang understands the system was obstructive to managerial farming which he notes was also stifled from below as merchants and landlords monopolised land that might have been available for managerial farming, buttressing parcellisation and the supply of cheap labour, by renting out small unviable plots.[16] Although managerial farming produced better returns than land leasing through the efficient use of labour, for those with holdings above 200 mu, cultivation no longer paid since there were much greater financial opportunities open to the landholder, combining leasing out land with commerce and usury as well as education for a degree.[17]

Yet a further factor in explaining why managerial landlords sought to lease land out rather than continue farming, one not considered by Huang, was their exposure to the volatility of markets under the influence of the powerful merchant-landlords: given that the margins of the managerial farmers were so thin, land ownership offered a more stable option than extending cultivation. It was through the collection of rent in kind that landlords gained the power to manipulate markets, influencing conditions in the farming sector as a whole, whether rent-paying or not, shaping the way new production relations developed.

Finding managerial farmers neither a part of the landlord system, nor 'capitalist sprouts', Huang maintains they were part of the peasant economy since, although using labour more efficiently than family farms to achieve similar yields, they did not significantly differ from general farming practices in their use of land and technology.[18] Here Huang questions the CPC classification system according to which managerial farmers were members of the landlord class. The CPC took the mark of a landlord as someone who did not engage in production themselves, other than to supplement their income. Even those who merely hired labour on a long-term basis but did not practice exploitation in the form of land rent or usury were to be classed as landlords, including those who directed production or engaged in auxiliary labour, so long as they did not engage in productive labour themselves.[19] The non-involvement of China's elites in manual labour was taken by the CPC as the critical line of class division, signalling not just an economic but also the social and cultural gulf that existed between themselves and the peasantry.

Clearly the lines concerning direct engagement in labour were difficult to draw in practice, however Huang's claim is undermined by his own example of Sheng Ching-to, the biggest landholder in Longbow, the village at the centre of Hinton's famous 1940s village study, *Fanshen*.[20] Sheng was classed as a landlord even though he did not rent land out but rather farmed his holding with hired labour. Whilst not a leasing landlord, neither was he in fact, by Huang's criteria, a managerial farmer: he did not engage in production but ostentatiously grew long fingernails in a demonstration of superior status. His case was, rather, a prime example of how the village rich combined both commercial and feudal activities. Owning the most fertile lands in the village as well as a small distillery, Sheng used the surplus gained through a ruthless exploitation of wage labour, not to reinvest in agricultural production, but for usury, acquiring more land when his debtors defaulted. He managed the village corporate properties, as head of the local sub-county Confucian Association of 30 villages, and had also acted as village head, his cut of taxes forming the largest part of his income. In such a position, Sheng was not only able to enhance his economic strength and standing but also exert a political influence over the whole village in mediating with the outside world.

Longbow provides a good example of a North China village where the number of labourers far exceeded tenants as the village rich preferred to cultivate land using hired labour rather than lease it out. According to Hinton, the landlords, managerial farmers and rich peasants together owned only 18 per cent of the land but what they did have was a monopoly of the most fertile lands in the village and a considerable proportion of the farm animals.[21] Whilst the majority of families did not have enough to live on, this very small percentage of the village population drew a surplus far exceeding their own needs. This meant that the village rich had a considerable economic power over the peasants farming inadequate plots – a power based not on a large concentration of land but on the control of the surplus in conditions where surplus production was low overall. Essentially controlling credit and land transactions in the village, their influence extended beyond their hired labourers to take advantage of the other impoverished members of the community. Even if they engaged in productive labour and maintained an influence as successful farmers, so classed as rich peasants according to CPC criteria, they were not simply a part of the peasant economy but engaged in extra-economic exploitation – usury, land takeover, renting out draft animals, and commercial speculation as well as the ruthless exploitation of wage labour.

Hinton's Longbow study reveals the mixed character of resident village rich – leasing landlords reliant on rent, managerial landlords reliant on hiring labour or rich peasants. Although not idle but engaging in auxiliary or productive labour, managerial landlords and rich peasants lived to a greater or lesser extent by exploitation, with their income drawn from various sources of business and cultivation. In general, these resident village elites, rather than increasing hired labour to extend cultivated acreage under market conditions manipulated by the big merchant-landlords, preferred to combine production with some land leasing and usury.

As lineage leaders, they managed communal properties in the manner of collective landlords; as village chiefs, most of the taxes and requisitions passed through their hands, creating opportunities for embezzlement, and market dealings gave them openings for speculation.[22] Although some derived a certain influence as the most successful farmers, rather than developing as an independent class in opposition with feudal relations, they sought to take advantage of peasant impoverishment to enjoy the economic power which those with a surplus had over those with inadequate means. Often serving as agents and brokers for the larger landlords and merchants, they aimed to maintain their political and economic role in the villages through their connections with the gentry. Through these links, they gained the feudal protection and privileges of the landlords – the right to demand exorbitant rents and high rates of interest as well as exemptions from taxation and the rights of extra-economic exploitation of hired labourers as servants – essentially adopting the values of the Confucian system to claim superior status for themselves.

Overall then Huang's separation of the farming sector based on wage labour from the land leasing sector of China's rural economy does not hold up well: although he shows how an entrepreneurial sector within the peasantry with independent roots in commerce emerged, in his contention that managerial farmers were still part of the peasant economy, he masks their involvement in feudal relations of exploitation and traditional forms of power. Managerial farmers did not really form a separate sector but gained the benefit of extra-economic exploitation, maintaining a position both politically and economically under the overall system of landlord power. With commerce developing on the basis of a concentration of land ownership, and excessive rents acting as a restraint on investment, both wage labour and usury bore the stamp of pre-capitalist exploitation intertwined with the system of monopoly rent. The entrepreneurial agricultural sector that emerged under these conditions was weak and closely interwoven with the landlord economy.

Huang's view of managerial farming as a separate sector of the rural economy then takes insufficient account of the feudal constraints which inhibited the village rich from becoming fully fledged capitalist farmers. Rather than analysing the structure of land ownership, his explanation as to why capitalism failed to develop in China points to the particular workings of the peasant economy. But whilst the oversupply of cheap labour and demand for land from the bankrupt peasant economy undermined incentives to invest and innovate, what produced the Chayanovian effect of parcellised farming was not differentiation within a tenacious involuting peasant economy but stagnation under conditions of monopoly rent.

The peasants' struggle for subsistence within the vicious confines of involution and semi-proletarianisation was rooted in the contradiction between the concentrated ownership of land and its fragmented use. It was these conditions which gave rise to monopoly rent as the major block on economic growth. Rent then was not just an additional burden for a bankrupt peasantry: the landlord system was the key cause of their impoverishment. Huang however, arguing that the involuting peasant economy propped up not only a non-capitalising managerial farming sector but also a parasitic leasing landlordism as the needs of the peasants kept them tied to tiny plots of land to make up their income, turns effect into cause.[23]

These criticisms are not to detract from the importance of Huang's contribution but to point to the inadequacy of an analysis which limits the basic structural background of the stagnating rural economy to matters of population pressure with commercialisation producing only a partial peasant class differentiation.[24] What is lacking in fact is a comprehensive examination of how the system of surplus production under the tight control of landlordism not only limited the growth of managerial farming but also constrained the family farm sector; and further on how this system affected relations of exchange. Treating differentiation through commercial development as the main dimension in the peasants' loss of land, Huang does not consider how the manipulation of the market and credit systems by those who controlled the surplus conditioned the peasants' gains and losses. With the market power of merchant-landlords limiting opportunities for urban growth and diversified production, it was this system of control over land that stunted the process of peasant differentiation under commercialisation. The stagnating managerial farming sector and semi-proletarianised involuting peasant economy were together products of an economic environment under feudal constraint.

NOTES AND REFERENCES

1. Huang, 1985, pp.17–18;
2. *Ibid.*, pp.293–99; pp.301–10.
3. *Ibid.*, see Chapters 8 and 9 for a comparison of managerial and family farming methods.
4. *Ibid.*, pp.8–16; pp.155–6; p.298; Geertz, 1963, pp.32–71.
5. *Ibid.*, p.302.
6. *Ibid.*, p.295
7. *Ibid.*, see for example, p.271; p.284, for shifts in landlords' obligations. See Chapters 11 and 12 for deteriorating conditions of the peasants, and pp.293–304 for summary.
8. *Ibid.*, p.298.
9. On Elvin, see *ibid.*, p.11; p.18; on Lippitt, see pp.19–20; p.21.
10. *Ibid.*, for example, p.187; p.216; p.299.
11. As discussed in Part I, Chapter 2; Chen Boda, 1966a, p.57.
12. Huang, 1985, pp.72–74.
13. *Ibid.*, p.294.
14. Li Wenzi, 1981, pp.81–3, presents a different perspective on legal changes under the Qing to that of Huang, 1985, pp.97–103.
15. Huang, 1985, p.169.
16. *Ibid.*, p.177.
17. *Ibid.*, pp. 173–4.
18. *Ibid.*, p.294.
19. See *Decisions Concerning Some Problems Arising From Agrarian Reform* (1947); Selden, 1979, p.222; see also Li Lifeng (2015). For further discussion see Huang, 1985, p.71.
20. *Ibid.*, pp.82–3; Hinton, 1966, pp.29–33.
21. *Ibid.*, p.28.
22. Institute of Pacific Relations, 1939, p.204; also p.192; p.198.
23. Huang, p.201; pp.300–1.
24. *Ibid.*, p.17.

7
The role of the state – for the common good or legitimising landlord power?

Perdue and Huang on the separation of state and landlord

From the **Western perspective**, the Chinese bureaucratic state is frequently viewed as totalitarian and authoritarian, defined in terms of the unlimited power and arbitrary rule of the Emperor. Perpetuating the small peasant economy which served as its tax base, the state administration is seen to have inhibited progress. High taxes, corrupt officials, and restrictive practices which stifled individual initiative, tying up the market in bureaucratic controls, are identified as the reasons why the Chinese economy stagnated. Thus for example, Wittfogel's *Oriental Despotism* attributes the lack of capitalist development to the impositions of the state bureaucracy, and along similar lines Balazs argues that the despotic state would not tolerate any form of private enterprise.[1] Chinese scholar, Wu Dakun, however, raises concerns as to how such conceptions can be used by Western imperialists as a 'theoretical 'weapon' against 'backward' Asian nations.[2]

According to Marx's Asiatic mode of production, Chinese society formed a pyramid structure with the bureaucratic state resting atop a multitude of owner-cultivating communities. With neither hereditary nobility nor the emergence of free cities and a mercantile bourgeoisie, the economic system was distinguished by the absence of individual proprietary rights due to the sovereign being the sole proprietor, and to the organisation of self-sufficiency in the autonomous village communities.[3] Needham, drawing on the notion of the Asiatic mode of production, but rejecting Oriental Despotism, presents a view of the all-powerful mandarinate not as a totalitarian autocratic monolith, but as a rational and benevolent bureaucracy, responsible for the common good, taking an active role in promoting production and protecting the welfare of the people.[4]

As discussed in previous chapters, others have countered these views to argue that, given the development of commercial relations during the Ming and Qing dynasties, the Chinese state in fact presented no institutional barriers to the emergence of private interests as markets spread. Rather than arbitrary and interventionist, corrupt and inefficient, the state is seen as rational and laissez-faire, playing a passive role as a licensing authority and reacting to market trends rather than forestalling their fluctuations.[5]

All these conceptions hold in common the view that power and status in China, as distinct from European feudalism, were based not on landholdings but on officialdom, and gained through the exam system rather than the accumulation of economic power. The state then, with its own economic base of taxation, rather than serving any class interests, is seen to have been able to act independently, defining its own sphere of operation according to its own political imperatives.

The two works examined here, by Perdue and by Huang, both see the Qing state as acting as much to constrain as to unleash landlord interests. Arguing that social conflicts were more diversified beyond landlord-tenant relations, both challenge the Chinese Marxist analysis which takes landlords as, both politically and economically, the lynchpin in the semi-feudal agrarian system.

The idea of the state acting on behalf of the common good, protecting the peasants against corrupt officials and ruthless exploitation, has roots in the ideals of the state ethic of Confucianism, which held that the government ruled according to the 'mandate of heaven'. In his study of the Qing government, Perdue argues for the notion of the benevolent state: neither a despotic and conservative force, nor simply laissez-faire, he sees the state, with the tax-paying owner-cultivator communities providing an independent base, as capable of acting as a force for reform and progress with a commitment to developing production. This was driven by responsibilities to protect the welfare of society and to maintain the system of famine relief provided by irrigation and granaries.[6]

The Qing government, Perdue's argument goes, so as to stabilise its tax base, in its early years promoted the settlement of owner-cultivators with reforms bringing wasteland under cultivation, including tax exemptions for new settlers, the construction of irrigation works and the promotion of new seeds, tools and cropping patterns.[7] However, whilst these measures served to guarantee food supplies and protect peasant livelihood especially in times of disaster, they also unleashed private and commercial interests.

Perdue's analysis rests on making a fundamental distinction between long-term public interest represented by the state and private interests of the landlords seeking individual gain. Contrary to Marxist conceptions then, he sees relations between state and landlords in terms of this public-private dichotomy arguing that the state, in stimulating production, did not simply allow the landlords' private interests to develop freely but, as production revived, it would on occasion come into conflict with their efforts to seek individual gain as it sought to protect social welfare.

This restraint of private excesses did not, Perdue argues, make the state totalitarian: rather it lacked the power to direct social change or mould society according to its will since increasingly, with the development of commerce and the dissolution of traditional solidarities, individual interests prevailed over local communal mores.[8] As he sees it then the state had ultimately to accommodate the emerging private interests at the local levels and find ways of co-operating with them.[9] A key example of this was when, in order to reduce taxes for owner-cultivators as an incentive to increase production and improve social welfare, the Qing state introduced reforms to expose concealed lands, only to give way in the face of strong opposition from the landlords, who sought to preserve this means of tax avoidance. Giving in to the landlords' lobby, the state had to find another way of increasing production. It did so through the encouragement of private initiative – incentivising landlords to bring new land under cultivation and build waterworks, thus increasing production and keeping down food prices as a guarantee of peasant livelihood.[10] So whilst the state aimed to protect the interests of the people, and to promote greater social equality by reducing the tax privileges of the elite, when faced with opposition on the matter of land concealment, it responded to the conflict with concessions to the landlords.[11]

Perdue sets out the relationship between state and landlord, public and private interests, not only as separate but inverse since, with the development of market forces, a weakening state, increasingly less able to extend benevolent rule, gave way to the rise of powerful private interests. In an expanding economy, the state was able to fulfil the long-term aims of its public welfare role in co-operation with private interests in the development of production to increase food supply, but with commerce weakening the relationship of the peasants to their community and to the state, the long-term trend was one of declining state power and the growth of private interests.[12] This occurred as, with economic revival, population expanded eventually to exceed agricultural growth so resulting in a situation of scarcity in which short-term gain and long-term aims came into conflict. A weakened state then failed to maintain its long-term goals as it was unable to confront the powerful local private interests with which it competed.[13] It was this public-private contradiction then that produced crises, as for example when land clearance for private economic gain eventually endangered the ecological balance with widespread floods and droughts resulting as dyke and reservoir systems broke down.[14]

Although the state compromised with the landlords and protected and enforced their rights, since it relied on them not least for the collection of taxes, it nevertheless, as Perdue sees it, was not a mere tool of the landlord class given its independent base. Rather, it served as a force for the public good: as an arbiter in the conflict between landlord and peasant capable of eliminating the gentry's privileges, it sought to balance private gain with the public good, helping to protect peasant interests and peasant production.[15] It aimed to achieve a pattern of economic growth which harmonised welfare and economic gain through the provision of infrastructure and a fiscal framework within which individual initiative for private profit was allowed to drive economic development. The Qing government was however to become the victim of its own success, promoting growth only to undermine its own base by stimulating the market and the emergence of private interests so stoking competition and conflict instead of welfare and stability, the more so as population grew.

For Perdue, the Marxist perspective fails to account for the tensions between the public interests of the state and the private interests of society. The landlord-peasant conflict is for him only one, if an important one, amongst other forms of social contention.[16] Conflicts arise not simply out of class contradictions but as competition amongst various interests over scarce resources intensifies under population pressure. For Perdue then the crisis in the final years of the Qing was one in which the public-private conflict came to a head in the clash between the upper tier of state reformers looking to the long term and the local landlord-gentry interested only in short-term private gain.

Huang, like Perdue, sees state and landlord as fundamentally separate, with land ownership divorced from the powers of the administration, judiciary and military, such that the state served as a balancer between the interests of landlords and small farmers. However Huang, rejecting the standard centre-local dualism embraced by Perdue, seeks to bring in the village as an independent base of power: for Huang, the political economy of the Qing took the form of a three-cornered landlord-village-state structure.[17]

In his view, the major weakness in much of the scholarship on China, both dualist and Marxist, is that village organisation has generally been overlooked, conceived as integrated either under the totalitarian control of the state or the influence of the landlords or dissolved by market forces.[18] Instead he seeks to carve out a separate sphere of state-village relations distinguishing those less developed predominantly owner-cultivator communities where there was no resident landlord from those villages where market penetration had brought semi-proletarianisation.[19] As he sees it, whilst the latter were more easily dominated by 'local bullies and bad gentry' especially under KMT reforms, the former were more insulated from not only market but also landlord power given the absence of strong links to large lineage organisations which in the South crossed the divide between town and countryside. These in his view formed autonomous communities free from outside control with their own organisational structures and endogenous leaderships acting independently of the state and landlord influence.[20] Although the councils of elders were made up of the wealthiest families of middle peasant, rich peasant and managerial farmers, who formed a distinct self-perpetuating elite, as he sees it, these village leaders were also as farmers able to identify with the overall interests of community, representing these interests vis-à-vis the state not least over issues of taxation.

As the three corners or poles of Qing society – the Imperial state, the landlord-gentry and the autonomous village communities of small farmers – formed separate interests, Huang sees these interacting in cross-cutting ways with state-village, state-landlord and landlord-small farmer relations operating as separate axes of duality. Each axis contained both contradiction and interdependence, driven apart in tension and conflict, at the same time being pulled together through mutual dependence and reciprocity.

From this he goes on to argue that the state, whilst dependent both on the landlords from which it recruited its officials and on its peasant tax base, was at the same time capable of acting not only on behalf of the landlords but also in the peasants' interests as, for example, in the case of the early Qing reforms which protected the private property of the owner-cultivators so as to increase tax payments. Similarly, contradictions between landlord and peasant did not prevent them from taking joint action on occasion in the interests of preserving their private property against the excessive demands of the state.[21] Meanwhile traditional equilibrium was maintained as each pole set limits on, and balanced with, the others: state levies for example were limited by the willingness of local leaders to pay; the landlord-peasant contradiction was modified by their shared interest in protecting private property; and insofar as the landlords served as indispensable intermediaries, the state acted to protect their claims over tenants.

Like Perdue then, Huang considers that the CPC over-emphasised the landlord-peasant class contradiction. Instead, his analysis takes the state-village axis as central. As he sees it, stability, keeping the three corners of society in balance, turned crucially on the state's ability to manage and exercise control over the village communities. To do so, given the vast numbers of villages, demanded huge effort, a task on a scale far beyond the resources of the state which instead had to rely on the local gentry to mediate in securing the loyalty of the independent village elites.

With the state directly controlling the bureaucracy but only indirectly controlling the lower tier of society, Huang conceives the two tiers linked as if by rungs of a ladder, with the open access examination system serving as the mechanism to attract upwardly mobile members of the rural society from the small commoner landlords, rich peasants and managerial farmers. Giving commoners the prospect of gaining gentry status and the rewards of office, attached the village elite to the state bureaucracy in a way which lent the Qing system a particular flexibility and vitality. The ease of access from the lower to the higher, vastly more lucrative, echelons of the bureaucracy was key in enabling the state to maintain order in the villages so stabilising the system as a whole.

Huang's analysis essentially draws on a substantivist approach in seeing the root of China's revolutionary crisis to lie in the breakdown in the state-village relationship, brought about as the excessive demands of late Qing and then the Nationalist governments for tax and conscription bore down more and more heavily, alienating the village communities amidst an environment made harsher by the disintegration of traditional reciprocities under the demands of world markets.[22]

Critical assessment

Huang and Perdue then both offer a view of Chinese agrarian society as comprising diverse and separate interests, taking the conflict between landlord and peasant or landlord and tenant as only one among many different forms of social contestation. Their view of the Marxist class rationale as too limiting demonstrates a rather superficial understanding of the materialist method which in fact reveals how monopoly rent as the predominant form of surplus labour fettered production, so conditioning the development of other social relations.

In counterposing the long-term interests of society, the preserve of the state, and short-term private individual gain, Perdue fails to define private interest, that is, to distinguish different forms of surplus appropriation. Huang similarly obscures different forms of property: underlying the landlords' and peasants' joint actions to resist the depredations of the state, lay different even contradictory interests in terms of land ownership system – peasant-based and landlord-based.

Economics for Huang and Perdue is essentially about problems of scarcity, that is, the malfunctioning of market relations. However to penetrate beyond the level of appearance it is necessary to grasp, as Chen Boda did, the underlying differing determinants of feudal and capitalist land prices and rent. Failing to do so, their conceptions remain abstract with rural society appearing as a network of relationships between state, local community, and private individual rather than as structured by the contradictory relations of production that underlay the mechanisms of exchange and distribution.

Certainly, conditions of scarcity give rise to various forms of social conflict with different interest groups in competition over resources, but the centrality of the landlord-peasant struggle, as determinant of other social relations, rested on the landlords' ability overall to control the surplus product, extracted from the peasants through extra-economic means, and determine its allocation.

In fact both types of village identified by Huang were caught in conditions of economic stagnation as monopoly rent blocked development. The hold of landlordism on the one hand hastened the peasants' loss of land in more commercialised areas but stagnation under the overall system of monopoly ownership of land also reinforced rural isolation and village insularity in the more remote areas, increasing their dependence on influential families within the localities to deal with the outside world. Whilst Huang takes the importance of kinship and community organisation as demonstrating that the village order was not simply structured around the landlord-peasant class relation, as Mao saw it the political authority of the landlord system formed the backbone of the traditional hierarchical village order of clan, religious and patriarchal authority.[23]

The landlords then, through their domination of commerce and contacts with officialdom and with their influence permeating the villages through these traditional bonds, were able to control the channels of communication between town and countryside, state and village community, if not as village residents then through their sub-county organisations. At the same time, the stagnation and scarcity which fuelled conflict between the peasants and the state were conditioned by the limits on economic growth owing to monopoly rent.

For both Perdue and Huang, what defined the state's independence from the landlord system of exploitation was its ability to carry out reforms 'for the common good' and in the interests of the peasants. However, to argue from the Marxist perspective that the state in fact served landlord interests in preserving the system of surplus production is not to suggest that there was no tension in the relationship between landlords and the state. Nor is it to suggest that differences amongst the ruling elites were unimportant. What is in question rather is the assumption that the state acted for the long-term common good, for example in restraining excessive exploitation.[24]

Marxist analysis certainly does understand that disputes occur in any ruling class between different sections over how best to rule: the role of a central authority is to maintain stability, acting as arbiter between different factions, even against the short-term wishes of certain sections, with a view to preserving for the long term the system of exploitation. In balancing the overall long-term interests of a ruling class and the interests of different sections which may come into conflict especially in a crisis, the state may serve not simply as a tool of the ruling class, but with a measure of relative autonomy. Thus it is possible to recognise conflict and tension arising between the state and different factions of the ruling class without assuming the state exists independently of the landlords.

In China, contradictions then arose between reformers and conservatives, urban modernisers and traditionalist rural residents, localised patriarchal and centralised bureaucratic powerholders, in struggles over claims to the surplus. But essentially, they were all partners in the system of economic exploitation which kept peasants tied to the land: as the state mediated between their different interests, managing conflicts in the short-term among particular landlord factions, it did so in the interests of the system as a whole, preserving stability within a hierarchy of dominance and subservience.

The point here is illustrated by Wakeman: he suggests that when the upper-tier official gentry of the late Qing introduced measures to restrict privileges, they did so out of concern that corruption at the lower levels, where the lesser gentry had become more entrenched in local government, would jeopardise the entire system. Politically dependent on the state and with a commitment to office, the elite bureaucrats had a stake in the integrity of the empire; they acted then to defend their own positions of privilege. However, when faced with peasant armed uprisings, the upper and lower tiers would overcome their differences: the official literati then found the corrupt *shengyuan* a welcome ally in the construction of a new military infrastructure.[25] Similarly, Marks has pointed out how when protests mounted, the large rural-based landlords sought the military protection of the state, retreating to the comparative safety of the walled *yamen* to raise funds and organise an army whilst relying on the small landlords and village rich who had stayed behind to organise a militia in preparation for their return.[26] In this way, centre-local tensions were resolved as class contradictions sharpened.

The role of the state in the landlord system was then more than just a ladder to success: rather, the interests of state and landlord coalesced in reforms as well as in direct suppression of peasant rebellion, both different means to the same end of preserving the feudal system of surplus production and appropriation in the overall interest of the landlord class. Reforms, rather than serving the fundamental interests of the peasants, were measures of adjustment within the feudal system as a whole as it came under challenge from rural revolts. As such, they were an integral part of the political framework provided by the state which allowed the landlords to regain their economic dominance as they adapted to social changes brought about by the peasant rebellions and the development of commerce. A consideration in the next chapter of the discussion among Chinese Marxist historians of the long-term process of refeudalisation that took place through the Qing dynasty helps to clarify further the reciprocity between landlord and state.

NOTES AND REFERENCES

1. Balazs, 1964, p.78.
2. Wu Dakun, 1983b, p.74.
3. See Marx, 1978, pp.77–8; p.83. For further discussion of Marx's conception of the Asiatic Mode of Production see Anderson, 1974, pp.462–549; see also Wu Dakun, 1983, a&b.
4. Needham, 1969, pp.190–217.
5. e.g. Rawski, 1972, p.3; pp.162–3.
6. Perdue, 1987, p.59; p.135; pp.250–1.
7. *Ibid.*, pp.72–3; pp.113–4; pp.127–30.
8. *Ibid.*, e.g. p.59; p.135; p.250–1. 9. *Ibid.*, p.135; p.250.
9. *Ibid.*, pp.195–6.
10. *Ibid.*, p.79.
11. *Ibid.*, pp.74–5.
12. *Ibid.*, p.235.
13. *Ibid.*, p.198; p.233; p.236.
14. *Ibid.*, pp.224–33.
15. *Ibid.*, pp.161; pp.182.
16. *Ibid.*, pp.249–50.
17. Huang, 1985, pp.246–48.
18. *Ibid.*, pp.24–9.
19. *Ibid.*, pp.237–244.
20. See *Ibid.*, pp.237–40.
21. *Ibid.*, p.262. Huang draws on the argument of Perry (1980).
22. *Ibid.*, p.290; and Ch. 15.
23. Mao, *Selected Works*, Vol. I, pp.45–6. See earlier discussion in Chapter 3.
24. As Perdue (1987) argues, p.220; pp.223–4.
25. Wakeman, 1975, pp.34–5.
26. Marks, 1984, pp.276–7.

8
The tenacity of Chinese feudalism

From the 'sprouts of capitalism' to refeudalisation

From the late 16th century, China saw an unprecedented expansion of commodity production with the cultivation of new crops of tobacco, cotton, silk and sugar; rice too became commercialised and an entrepreneurial peasant economy developed, investing in new seeds, increased fertiliser, irrigation and new methods. Fu Yiling notes that the emergence of capitalist tenant farmers under the Qing in the 18th and 19th centuries involved in commercialised tobacco-growing whose use of hired labour indicated that not all the surplus of direct production was absorbed by rent. Apart from the capitalist character of their cash rents, their demands gave rise to competition for labour and the development of labour markets.[1]

Li Wenzhi also draws attention to the emergence of a rich peasant economy during the 18th century as both owner-cultivators and tenants applied their own and hired labour to cultivate cash or food crops and sidelines for marketing in the growing towns in exchange for articles for both production and consumption.[2] Into the 20th century, Chen Hanseng observed the existence of established large farms which were beginning to break up under the pressure of world competition; whilst Chen Boda found a differential element in cash rents though inhibited by conditions dictated by the operation of monopoly rent.[3]

Despite the increase in hired labour, the growth in commercialised farming, the development of labour markets and the land purchase system, capitalism failed to develop in China. With a view to analysing the roots of China's economic stagnation and decline, Chinese Marxist scholars have sought to explore how these emerging 'capitalist sprouts' were overtaken over the longer term in a process of refeudalisation, whereby, as production was restored, the landlords regained their political influence and laid claim to the bulk of the economic surplus.[4]

Li Wenzhi has attributed the 'slow and tortuous development of the sprouts of capitalism' to the 'oppression of feudal patriarchal forces'.[5] Whilst the successive peasant rebellions which brought about the downfall of the Song and Ming dynasties weakened the constraints of state, kinship and community bonds, the structure of feudal political power survived. These massive peasant rebellions compelled the state to carry out reforms: the powers of the Imperial Court over the people passed more and more from controls over the person and demand for unpaid labour or serfdom to the extraction of taxes, initiating the long-term shift from direct to indirect controls with the increasing role of commodities and money denoting a trend in the direction of capitalism. However, there was no fundamental change in the economic and political character or basis of the landlord class.[6]

After the downfall of the Ming during the early Qing period in the 17th century, the explosion of commercial activity stimulated changes in the distribution of land rights and the status of landlords with reforms in tenancy and labour hiring arrangements. By the 18th century, with investment from commerce and business flowing into the production and processing of cash crops, the scale of agricultural management increased and labour markets began to emerge. Serfdom started to give way, with hired workers beginning to break free of feudal bonds as managing landlords and farmers employed labour under contract on a more equal basis. Peasant rights in freer relations in land tenure and employment were being realised to a degree.[7]

Less dependent on direct control of land and more dependent on taxes, the early Qing state reduced the large-scale tax exemptions enjoyed by the elite of the Ming dynasty, and large landed estates began to break up whilst land rights became more dispersed as the state encouraged the settlement of smallholding owner-peasants. At the same time, the introduction of land purchase saw the number of commoner-non-gentry-landlords increase. Nevertheless, whilst these commoner landlords grew more numerous, those with gentry and official status remained considerable and by the mid Qing period, the trend in land rights began to change course from dispersal towards concentration.

For Fang Xing, the most important feature of China's landlord economy was that land could be bought and sold: this was the main difference between Chinese and European feudalism since land purchase allowed the landlord economy to adapt to the growth of a monetarised, commodity economy, strengthening its stability and endurance, and providing the means of reconstituting the official class.[8] Rather than maintaining a strict hierarchical structure of land rights, this flexibility made the Chinese feudal system particularly tenacious.

The significance of land purchase in Fang Xing's analysis lies in the way it drew merchants and moneylenders as well as officials into a trinity of landholders, appropriating and distributing the agricultural surplus. Commercial expansion and the development of national markets saw the growth of a class of large merchants and moneylenders involved in shipping grain from surplus to often newly settled deficit regions. As restrictions on land sales lifted, officials, gentry, merchants and usurers all used part of their wealth to buy land and absentee landlordism began to flourish. This trinity was the most strongly positioned in the land purchase system and so was able to establish a monopoly as commoner landholding diminished as a proportion.[9]

The wealthy bought land for security in their old age and to pass on to the future generations as well as for grain to market. Landed property was 'impervious to flood, fire, and brigands', but whilst commerce and usury were riskier, they earned a higher rate of return so landlords also looked to running businesses and money lending to accumulate wealth. For merchants, land was seen as a means to raise their standing above that of mere trade as they aimed to enter the leisured aristocracy as a route to gaining office in the state trading companies, and to acquiring gentry status with its cultural superiority and political privileges. The largest became merchants of the Imperial State *(huang shang)* running the salt industry, for example, whilst other merchants bought official titles or had their sons pass the examinations to become officials so gaining position in the bureaucratic hierarchy.[10] Later, opportunities for embezzlement also increased.

Wu Dakun on the other hand attaches particular significance to the Asiatic features of China's feudal society – the patriarchal clan system and the centralised state based on the taxing of individual households: it was the survival of these structures of feudal political power that enabled the landlord-gentry to restore their privileges and status, regaining political and economic dominance after peasant rebellion. Whereas in Europe, the decentralised state rested on independent feudal powers based on landholdings with economic, juridical, military and administrative power all combined together, in China the centralised state resisted fragmentation under local power-holders even as it increasingly depended on their patriarchal influence to maintain control in the countryside. These two aspects of the power structure formed the roots of the parcellised system of farming with the particular combination of agriculture and handicrafts, which Wu Dakun argues, caused China to develop at an especially slow speed.[11]

As can be seen, China's landlord system was held in place from above by the centralised state and from below by the patriarchal village order of clan and lineage.

Despite the early Qing reforms aimed at weakening landlord privileges, the bureaucratic state remained intact and the local landlord-gentry still retained the clear advantages of the cultural superiority which attached to office-holding. The Confucian ideology of the state, which upheld the division between mental and manual labour, continued to legitimise the power of the elite and their right to appropriate the surplus as the literate and luxuried class. At the same time, literacy allowed them to participate in, and influence the workings of the civilian administration of justice and taxation, and lobby effectively, whilst excluding the vast majority.

Feudal relations in China, as distinct from the European system of seigneurial rights and serfdom, now took the form of a looser system of benevolent patronage cultivated by the bureaucratic state. As Beattie has argued, rather than curtailing the elite, Qing reforms brought about a modification in their behaviour as they shifted their base from tax exemption to a greater reliance on corporate wealth and properties, lineage status and prestige. Rather than making blatant claims to privilege, they relied on more subtle ways of promoting their interests by ostensibly acting on behalf of others.[12]

The state promoted and supported this shift, placing value on *ganqing* as it took performance in the role of local benefactor as the marker of suitability of degree-holders for office-holding. Reforms made brutality and the worst excesses of extra-economic exploitation illegal, but in place of servility and direct coercion, an environment of informal extra-economic relations of benevolence and paternalism, of personalised power, evolved, knitting the influence of landlord and state into the village communities.

The state further reinforced landlord power at its roots in the kinship and social networks of the countryside by sustaining the local prestige and superior status of influential families through support of lineage organisation. Together with temple societies and Confucian associations, lineage organisations, with their support of schools through corporately-held village properties, provided an important means of state recruitment of officials. Even though lineage organisations formed a potential source of local power in opposition to central control, they were officially encouraged as a means to instil Confucian values of obedience and loyalty to superiors and to the state in the person of the Emperor so as to control 'deviant' behaviours.[13] Similarly the state supported other organisations such as community defence in which landlords could perform the role of patron-benefactor whilst helping to maintain social stability and order.[14] The territorial and hierarchical nature of these lineage and corporate organisations, based on relations of senior and junior in the kinship system, also served to legitimise the landlords' superior status.

Li Wenzhi's argument is that the main force that retarded capitalist development were the political measures adopted by the feudal centralised state machinery to sustain landlordism.[15] In a number of ways, Qing reforms were progressive in limiting landlord power through the restrictions on tax exemption and in the measures to free labour from the legal obligations of service, introducing a degree of equality for example with new regulations to forbid the beating of tenants.[16]

Nevertheless reforms remained limited and, as formal and informal powers intertwined, legal codes and the arbitration of disputes remained subject to landlord influence.

As seen previously, wage labour was to co-exist with conditions of semi-serfdom as feudal patriarchal relations between landlord and hired labour persisted. As Li Wenzhi points out, the new codes on improving the status of agricultural workers only applied to commoners; elsewhere legal codes stipulated the rights of the gentry to bonded labour reinforcing practices of personal subservience and coercion[17] Employment rights were not clearly fixed and often labour was employed without contract so landlords were often able to get away with ill-treatment of their hired labour. Whilst temporary hired labour received more equal treatment in the rich peasants' farms, those tenants who lived in the compounds of the bigger landlords remained at their beck and call providing unpaid labour services.[18] Such practices including payment in kind for labour services in the form of labour rent, persisted into the 1930s and 1940s.[19] This, as noted earlier, had an influence on the labour-hiring managerial farmers who aped these extra-economic exploitation practices.[20]

Legal codes governing property ownership were also limited with the Qing reforms essentially leaving systems of customary ties and obligations in place. Alongside the preservation of the system of corporate village properties, which were central to lineage organisation and support for schools, customary ties to ancestral lands were maintained through the practice of pre-capitalist mortgage. Both served to restrict the free disposability of land. In the case of the mortgage system, rather than securing the rights of the cultivator, as Perdue himself explained, since mortgagees retained rights to buy back their land, this blurred the distinction between the sale of land and pawning as security for a loan.[21] The renting out of land was usually kept within the kinship group and the landlord-tenant arrangements were also generally based on personal ties, practices which also tended to restrict land purchase. Permanent sales were very rare indicating that land was not solely a commodity to be bought and sold like any other. With peasants kept tied to the land by customary land rights and *ganqing* obligations, market forces penetrated into the agrarian economy without affecting a complete separation of the direct producers from the land, and landlords were able to monopolise land through purchase without peasant dispossession.[22]

Since customary practices remained prevalent, the state was heavily involved in resolving disputes, and arbitration was essentially subject to the exercise of personalised power and open to corruption and abuse.[23] Where laws did apply, the state, as Perdue himself acknowledges, was reluctant to enforce its codes beyond the point where this compromised the landlords' authority. Through their contacts with officialdom, landlords were in a position to influence the decisions of the magistrates to ensure that laws worked to their advantage, manipulating the changes in agrarian relations. Where peasant struggles managed to gain certain economic and legal rights, the landlords retaliated with countermeasures, developing, with state support, new forms of exploitation such as rent deposits which undermined even simple reproduction in the peasant economy so perpetuating their dependence. With the magistrates backing the landlords' claims in the courts, whilst upholding the peasants' obligations, the state in effect guaranteed the system of exorbitant rent.

Given their local influence and contacts with the local legal authorities, the gentry could simply place themselves above the law, resorting to means other than purchase to acquire land, annexing the peasants' holdings through bullying, extortion and plunder. Fomenting clan feuds was used as a means of imposing levies and protection money. Alongside the indirect extra-economic pressures of personal obligation and unequal reciprocities, direct coercion then remained a particular feature of feudal relations in China.

Finally, tax privileges were to remain a key factor in landlord survival. The state's household-based taxation of landowners effectively worked to the advantage of the wealthy who bore their equal share more lightly than the poor. But added to this, the landlords were able to use their personal influence as well as their institutional position to reclaim privileges of tax exemption and avoid payment altogether.

Feudal relations and class formation

Fang Xing finds the explanation for the lack of capitalist development in China in the pattern of class formation. Whilst in European feudal society, the moneyed power of merchants and usurers stood in basic opposition to landed power, this was not the case in China where merchants and usurers grew on the basis of feudal exploitation, distributing the surplus derived from the land produced under the tight control of the landlords.[24] The control of trade through rent in kind gave the landlord classes enormous political and economic power not only in the countryside, but also in the cities. Urban markets grew based on the consumption requirements of the elite of absentee landlords who used their income from rent to purchase luxury goods. Commodity exchange was then essentially a one-way flow of grain surpluses from the villages to the towns and cities to the benefit of the elite trinity, curtailing the development of capitalism in agriculture.

Cities in China, unlike in Europe, became centres of feudal political and military affairs as the merchants who made their wealth in commerce were not to challenge the existing social and political structure, seeking instead to adjust to the system of officialdom. Capital did not confront landed property as it did in Europe in the form of merchants, usurers and manufacturers seeking political freedoms and independence from their city bases. Instead the land-based moneyed classes aspired to office, adopting for themselves the values of the Confucian bureaucracy, adapting to the development of commerce through land purchase.[25]

With the gentry and bureaucrats holding sway over the urban areas, in the countryside the rich peasants, commoner landlords and managerial farmers followed suit in pursuing rank and privilege. Rather than developing into a class of capitalist farmers, these village elites then provided a constant source of regeneration of the landlord class as rich peasants strove to become landlords and commoner landlords sought gentry status.[26]

The support of feudal political power guaranteed the realisation of land rent for the landlord class, permitting them to raise rents higher and higher, increasing peasant impoverishment and inhibiting the emergence and development of a rich peasantry. Entrepreneurial farmers had little incentive to improve production since, owing to the close connection of commerce and credit with rent, the benefits of increased productivity accrued to the larger landlords not only directly through extra-economic rent but also through commodity exchange. Added to this, as speculation drove land prices up beyond their means, it was difficult for the rich peasants to extend cultivation. Those who did manage to derive a surplus from cultivation existed basically in conformity with the system of monopoly rent, employing cheap labour from a bankrupt small peasant economy whilst looking to acquire land for leasing in order to join the landlords' economic, political, social and cultural world. As well as the material benefits to be gained from tax avoidance and from feudal privileges to charge exorbitant rents and exercise extra-economic power over hired labour, gentry status offered a means to escape from the culturally demeaning involvement in production.

With accumulation in agriculture blocked by the landlords' manipulation of rent, property and market conditions, excessive rent and taxes hastened the owner-cultivators' loss of land. Lacking in alternative opportunities, however, the peasants remained tied to the land, clinging on to marginal plots rather than face complete dispossession, making do through household handicraft production or by hiring out their labour on a part-time basis. The reinforcement of these survival patterns then further limited the development of land and free labour markets, restricting internal demand to heighten the dependence of market towns on landlord consumption.

At the same time, the landlords' political privileges – their tax avoidance and the imposition of extra-economic means of coercion supported by the courts – were all factors in increasing the peasants' indebtedness leading to land usurpation. With the corresponding increase in the peasants' demand for land causing rents and land prices to increase further, this spurred land speculation and claims to a rising share of rent, so further hastening land concentration in the hands of the wealthy. For poor peasants, to commit themselves to the power domain of a benevolent protector, an arrangement of excessive exploitation cloaked in tradition, was virtually the only means of survival.

Clearly conditions under the Qing were very complex with the mixing of legal codes and extra-legal practices and with property relations and conditions of labour hiring subject to wide differences within and between regions. Regional differences reflected variations in the relative strengths of the feudal patriarchal relations and the new social forces: in newly opened-up regions for example, where the influence of feudal patriarchal forces was weaker, new relations of production emerged. But overall the development was uneven and elementary capitalistic enterprises, growing essentially in atypical locales, survived precariously in the interstices of the feudal system.

As Li Wenzhi points out, citing Marx, the extent to which commerce and the development of commodity and money relations bring about the dissolution of feudal relations of production depends on the solidity of the old mode of production and its internal structure.[27] Ultimately the old feudal ruling classes were too strong to be dislodged by new capitalist forces, and instead took advantage of the new economic developments to enhance their own powers.

Under the landlords' economic dominance, instead of unleashing development, commodity and money relations worked to the peasants' disadvantage, hastening their loss of land and resulting not in the stimulation of production but in agricultural decline. Peasant impoverishment increased with the perpetuation of conditions of low productivity, low surplus, poor equipment and high rates of exploitation.

Whilst the state relied on the masses of small peasants for tax payments, the owner-cultivators' loss of land meant a loss of revenue for the state.[28] As the position of the landlords grew with the continuing concentration of land ownership, the centralised state weakened as its tax base declined whilst the peasants fell more into dependency.[29] At the same time, the increased concentration of land ownership contrasted with its scattered use as landlords rented out small parcels to claim the greatest rent from peasants forced to cling on to land and patriarchal protections for lack of alternatives.

For Wu Dakun, it was the dual contradictions in the trend towards the concentration of land ownership and the fragmentation of its use alongside the strengthening of private interests at the expense of the public sphere, that caused the condition of the peasants to worsen despite the commercialisation trend. As the revenue of the state shrank, it could no longer finance public works and irrigation fell into disuse. Together with rising rents and peasants' loss of land, this then fuelled peasant protest and the state came to rely more on the growth of private landlords to fulfil its social and economic obligations in order to maintain stability. With power falling to the local landlords, their opportunities for embezzlement and evasion through collusion with the tax officials increased.

The officials, the gentry and the local powerholders, in control of town-countryside communications and state-village relations, then propped each other up in a most corrupt and oppressive regime. With the merging of political and economic power at the base of society, according to Wu Dakun:

> ...the intrinsic contradiction of the land system in the Chinese [feudal] society eventually developed into the contradiction between the landlord class...and the peasantry...[30]

As the relationship between the landlords who owned the land and the peasants who used the land became the fundamental axis of conflict, peasant revolution to overthrow feudal power was to be the main force in the transformation of Chinese society.

NOTES AND REFERENCES

1. Fu Yiling, 1980, p.313.
2. Li Wenzhi, 1981, p.86.
3. Chen Boda, 1966a, p.41; p.45.
4. See Grove and Esherick, 1980, pp.412–9, for an account of Japanese scholarship on refeudalisation in China in the 18th and 19th centuries.
5. Li Wenzhi, 1981, pp.87–9.
6. Wu Dakun, 1983b, pp.73–4.
7. Li Wenzhi, 1981, pp.68–71.
8. Fang Xing, 1981, p.123.
9. See Fang Xing, 1981, pp.123–132, on the close links between landlords, merchants and usurers in the Qing dynasty.
10. *Ibid.*, pp.131–2.
11. Wu Dakun, 1983b, pp.68–70.
12. Beattie, 1979, pp.98–9.
13. *Ibid.*, pp.93–4; pp.121–2.
14. Perry, 1980, p.85; p.122.
15. Li Wenzhi, 1981, p.88.
16. Perdue, 1987, p.151–2.
17. Li Wenzhi, 1981, p.88.
18. *Ibid.*, pp.81–3.
19. Chen Boda, 1966a, p.57.

20. Li Wenzhi, 1981, pp.81–3.

21. Perdue, 1987, pp.137–9; see also Institute of Pacific Relations, 1939, pp.7–9, which notes that a pre-capitalist mortgage was a disguised form of sale in repayment of debt, in other words, a stage in the loss of land. The mortgagee became only the nominal owner, making payments with little chance of redeeming the property, so the creditor in effect became the owner.

22. See Perdue, 1987, pp.137–9. Ch. 3; footnote 29. The discussion here also draws on Laclau's argument that under capitalism, as distinct from feudalism, economic relations penetrate the production process with the transformation of land and labour into commodities. See also Marx, *Capital*, Vol. III, 1970, pp.790–1.

There is a considerable body of debate on the nature of European feudalism and manorial serfdom, see Sweezy and others (1978). Dobb's discussion of the transition from feudalism to capitalism in Europe focusses on the crisis in the relationship between the feudal lords and the direct producers; Sweezy, arguing in favour of a wider definition of feudalism than that restricted to serfdom, focusses on the growth of the money economy as the solvent of feudal relations. Laclau (1979) in criticism of Sweezy, argues that in defining a mode of production, the ownership of the means of production and the form of surplus appropriation are the central issues.

23. Perdue, 1987, p.163.

24. Fang Xing, 1981, p.130; Wu Dakun, 1983b, p.68.

25. Fang Xing, 1981, p.132.

26. The argument in these two paragraphs demonstrates that neither of the two ways of capitalist development envisaged by Marx – when the producer becomes a merchant and capitalist, and when the merchant becomes a manufacturer – were developing in China. See Marx, *Capital*, Vol. III, 1970, p.334.

27. Li Wenzhi, 1981, p.87. See Marx, *Capital*, Vol. III, 1970, p.332. Fang Xing, 1981, pp.106–7 also refers to this.

28. Wu Dakun, 1983b, pp.71–72.

29. According to one estimate, from the beginning of the 18th century, government-owned and military colonised as well as clan lands occupied over 50 per cent of land, with less than 50 per cent in private ownership. However, by the time of the 1911 revolution, virtually all government land had been taken over by military and other corrupt officials, whilst after 1911 clan lands were essentially taken over as the private property of the village elites. Institute of Pacific Relations, 1939, p.2.

30. *Ibid.*, p.72.

9
Peasant rebellions and why they failed

A cycle of dynasties?

Viewed through the lens of Orientalism, the pattern of Chinese history is seen as an ever-repeating cycle of dynasties with power perpetually shifting between centre and locality, between the upper and the lower tiers of elite rule. But to focus on tensions between the different power holders is to reduce Chinese politics to factional struggles and to underestimate the impact of peasant rebellions against feudal oppression and the system of exploitation. Nevertheless, whilst rebellions mobilised peasants on a mass scale and compelled the ruling powers to readjust land and tax systems, they were never able to bring about fundamental social transformation. Instead, one dynasty followed another. Were these uprisings then really embryonic revolutionary movements, and if so, why did they fail?

On the one hand, since peasant rebellions tended to display the ephemeral and utopian characteristics of millenarianism, they have been seen not so much as transformative movements but rather as social valves functional to the system. The right to rebel against 'unjust rulers', claimed in the 3rd century BC by Mencius, was built into traditional Confucian rule under the 'mandate of heaven' as a means of legitimising the restoration of social equilibrium, with 'clean' officials pitted against corrupt tyrants in a struggle to transfer the balance of the surplus so as to provide the minimum of security for the cultivators.

However, peasant uprisings had a tendency to fall under the leadership of dissident gentry more interested in seizing the spoils of government than in changing its nature, such that, rather than overthrowing state power, they merely led to the renewal of its personnel.[1] This tendency to fall into a pattern of warring factions was displayed in the Taiping rebellion, the largest mass movement of the 19th century, which was to establish its Heavenly Kingdom across over 16 provinces. Initially rallying massive peasant support around a radical egalitarian land programme, it was only to degenerate, under an authoritarian, hierarchical and segmented structure, into power struggles over plunder.[2]

Marx, writing with some scepticism of the revolutionary nature of the Taipings, thought that:

> There is nothing extraordinary in this phenomenon, since oriental empires exhibit a permanent immobility in their social

foundation and a restless change in the persons and tribes who seize control of the political superstructure.³

The open exam system, seen as giving access to status and power, is generally regarded as serving to stabilise the system. But as the dynastic cycle entered its declining phase and opportunities for upward mobility became more limited, tensions between local and central power would intensify as the number of aspirant officeholders far exceeded the number of official positions. Since formal channels failed to offer enough openings for all to succeed, many sought to achieve office by organising armies and peasant revolts in order to seize power. At times, the 'upright' gentry and landholding peasants would need to defend the existing powerholders from attack by the dissident gentry and dispossessed peasants.⁴

The dynastic cycle with its shifts of power essentially followed the perpetual rise and fall of great and influential families. But what of the motives of the peasants themselves? To frame Chinese society in these Asiatic or Orientalist terms is to rule out any internal dynamic for change: to equate class with status and power, and class relations with hierarchical rungs of a ladder, is to reduce class struggle to factionalism. The simplistic counterposing of local and central power, benevolent and despotic government, 'clean' and 'unclean' officials discounts the fundamental reciprocity between the centralised state power and the local power of the landlord-gentry with their tensions ultimately resolving into concerted efforts to suppress and subvert peasant protest.

Countering the view of peasant rebellions as merely struggles between various elite factions, Mao emphasised the strong roots of the uprisings in peasant traditions, arguing that peasant movements were the motive force in Chinese history.⁵ Noting the phenomenon of enlightened gentry who involved themselves in the peasants' organisation, he distinguished between two lines intertwined in past peasant rebellions – that of the dissident gentry making a grab for power, and that of the peasantry with their revolutionary aspirations. Mao argued that the reason why the peasants had failed in the past to achieve their ends and overthrow state power was because the dissident gentry, who were more interested in seizing the spoils of government than in changing its nature, capitulated to the powerholders, causing rebellions to disintegrate from within.⁶ The question then is how the dissident gentry came to take the lead in peasant rebellion.

Patterns of collective action in the countryside

One of the main difficulties in assessing whether peasant rebellions were forms of revolutionary opposition to the state and the political power of the landlords or only a means of restoring traditional equilibrium is that collective protest and violence in the Chinese countryside took many different forms besides direct confrontation between peasant and landlord. These included banditry, tax resistance, food riots and the blocking of grain trade, as well as conflicts involving local or lineage rivalries and feuds over resources, territory and control of marketing systems.[7] Conflicts between established settlers and migrants, often from other provinces, could also be complicated by ethnic and religious divisions.[8] Competing groups often comprised both landlords and peasants, with landlords frequently involved as leaders of large-scale resistance and protest movements in the countryside. Perry's study of the Red Spears, a protectionist organisation of community defence, shows how landlords and peasants joined forces to protect their properties at first against the predations of local bandits, later developing into resistance against state taxes in the 1920s.[9] The different forms of rural protest, as has been seen in the discussion of Perdue and Huang, have been taken to suggest that causal factors other than class struggle are to be considered if rural tensions and conflicts are to be explained.

The different patterns of rural protest variously involved distinct types of rural organisation which intertwined in co-operation as well as conflict. Below county level, the Chinese countryside formed a complex web of vertical ties which often cut across class cleavages, binding the peasants to the rural elites whilst dividing peasant from peasant. Alongside the temple-based associations and Confucian societies of the wealthy merchants and gentry were the large lineages of the South and the closed, kinship-based corporate community organisations of the North. In addition there were the blood-oath fraternities of outsiders and immigrants, with few resources, which relied on egalitarian arrangements of mutual aid.[10]

As has been seen kinship and community relations were used by the peasants as a resource for survival: as the basis of various forms of self-help and mutual aid such as loan societies and crop-watching associations, they offered ways to minimise risk and protect against disaster. However many of these organisations also involved members of the traditional local elites, for example, in the management of corporate properties and the organisation of village self-defence, relief granaries and local irrigation works. Based on the control of settlement rights and protection of scarce resources, closed, corporatist communities were patriarchal, conservative and traditionalist. Conflicts between rich and poor were minimised for example by rotating the cultivation of corporate properties or when rich and poor members of a powerful lineage joined together in the exploitation of weaker lineages.[11] Similarly, rich and poor in village communities were united by their interests to protect property as those with resources assumed importance in organising community defence against bandit depredation.[12]

Some of these arrangements, including lineage, crop-watching and village self-defence, as well as begging, were supported by the state as means of preserving stability, managing conflict between rich and poor. Others like salt smuggling, which was closely connected with banditry and the secret societies, were illegal.[13] If the former organisations were particularly amenable to the landlords' political authority, the more loosely-knit secret societies were prepared to seize the property of the well-to-do in pursuit of their egalitarian ideals. These organisations of the dispossessed tended to draw support from newer migrants – poor peasants from other areas who, often receiving a poor reception from existing settlers, were only marginally integrated into village and clan.[14]

Capable of sustained opposition, these secret societies and brotherhoods played an important role in overthrowing dynasties. With bases in the towns but linked into rural society, as for example in the organisation of salt-smuggling, they brought the rural and the urban déclassé together.[15] It has been argued that, insofar as they served as a bridge between town and countryside whilst providing a training ground for armed struggle, the secret societies formed an embryonic revolutionary core within peasant rebellions mobilising an illegal petty bourgeoisie opposed to the state controls on commerce.[16]

On the other hand, the fact that revolts instigated by secret societies tended to degenerate, through lack of unity, into fratricidal gang warfare and capitulation has been seen as reflecting their nature as expressions of individual rebelliousness and reflexive defence rather than as organisations of class struggle. Providing a haven for the protection of dissidents from the Confucian orthodoxy, it is argued that they acted not so much as a progressive link between town and countryside but as a traditionalist political organisation rooted in, and conserving, the existing social networks of the countryside.[17]

Perry sees these two types of peasant organisation, the predatory and the protectionist, as both equally rooted in kinship and community networks. Whilst village crop-watching groups provided the basis of the Red Spears movement of tax resistance, families, clans and lineage settlements also were at the heart of the Nian rebellion of the 1850s and 1860s, formed from a coalition of bandits whose hard-core members were related by blood.[18] Predation and protectionism, she suggests, existed together in conditions of scarcity and stagnation, in a vicious cycle, dividing settlers against migrants, property owners against the dispossessed, in the organisation of community defence and crop-watching against pilferage and theft.[19]

Both types of organisations were liable to fall under landlord leadership since they operated across class lines: so long as peasants were in competition over scarce resources, reliant on close kin and community networks for survival and dependent on those with resources to organise local defence or bandit-style raids, it was difficult for them to form bonds of class solidarity outside these networks.[20]

Issues of leadership and division among the peasants

Dissident landlords and gentry who failed to get into office through the legitimate routes of gaining a degree or acting as a local benefactor were able to rely on lineage and community organisations as an alternative route to power. Since these networks involved both landlords and peasants, local chiefs bent on self-aggrandisement would use these to organise militia and build lineage alliances amassing large armies so as to seize territory and demand privilege and title from the state. Under such leadership, repeated peasant rebellions had then been unable to supplant feudal power, degenerating into cycles of factionalism over plunder and protectionism.

Huang has argued on the other hand that the elders who led the solidary owner-cultivator communities of the North were capable of independent action primarily to protect their community and property against bureaucratic intrusion.[21] These communities, where no large lineage organisations existed to tie peasants to the gentry and which were barely touched by market relations, were relatively insulated from the influence of landlord or state. As Huang sees it, the leaders of these villages, albeit drawn from the wealthiest farming households and forming a self-perpetuating elite, nevertheless, engaging in production themselves, were part of the farming community and genuinely represented its interests.

However, as previously discussed, Huang's analysis fails to take sufficient account of the incorporation of village elites into the system of feudal power through the hierarchy of senior and junior relations which structured social standing in single and multi-surname communities alike. The village rich, even where they engaged in productive labour, were not simply part and parcel of the peasant economy: they also took part in feudal exploitation and sought to gain prestige in the Confucian status system. These leading families, whether heading a village lineage or a village branch of a larger lineage, shared in the personalised power which subordinated the less important members within the community, whilst legitimising the system of gentry authority. Given their dual nature, on the one hand acting on behalf of the farming communities on matters of taxation and the state, yet with an interest in upholding the status hierarchy whilst drawing benefit from peasant impoverishment, their leadership failed to form an adequate opposition to the landlord system.

Dissident elites then gained leadership of peasant movements as their influence permeated local organisations not only directly but also indirectly. Even in those villages where there were no resident landlords, where the majority of owner peasants were not immediately under landlord protection or patronage, village organisation was still susceptible to elite influence through the social and political hierarchies of religious authority and kinship ties. As Huang himself admits, the villagers were nevertheless part and parcel of the larger power and trading systems.[22]

Whilst it was these peasant property owners whose organisations of self-defence formed the backbone of the traditionalist tax resistance uprisings of the early 20th century, the movements, as Perry found, also involved landlords and gentry. In the case of the Red Spears, a huge movement of possibly three million members, the overall leadership, at least according to Liu Shaoqi, reporting on the situation in the late 1930s as CPC organiser in North China, was mostly made up of 'tyrants or gentry'.[23]

The large-scale rural rebellions were then essentially traditionalist phenomena given that their organisation originated in the peasants' everyday kinship and community-based survival strategies. As Perry argues, the closed organisation of the villages, divided according to local and clientelist loyalties, provided the basis for autocratic and authoritarian leadership which welded together the semi-autonomous groups and gangs. Then in the face of the armed forces of the state and the landlord-officials, peasant movements would disintegrate from within, their elite commanders falling in with the existing powerholders to incorporate themselves into the feudal system of power and privilege.

But it was also the divisions among the peasants, between owner-cultivators and the dispossessed, between settlers and incomers, that go a long way in explaining the weakness of the peasants' traditional collective action. This was to be seen in the downfall of the Taiping rebellion which, whilst proclaiming a radically egalitarian land programme to win the support of the dispossessed, in practice introduced a policy of the purchase of land from farmers at liberal prices which favoured the interests of the well-to-do peasants producing a surplus. It was not possible to realise the demands of the poor for equal distribution and the elimination of differences in wealth whilst allowing the well-to-do freedom to trade. Without a policy to unite landless and landowning peasants, the Taiping regime resorted to requisition only to alienate their support in the countryside. Rather than developing a programme of investment, resources remained an object of plunder for the leadership which degenerated into fratricidal in-fighting.[24]

Mao was also struck by the divisions among the peasantry and how these led to the failure of their protests when, as a youth, he witnessed some rice riots in Changsha. He later observed:

> The Red and Green Gangs in the countryside also held meetings… They did not maintain good discipline, they took the rice of the middle peasants, and so isolated themselves. One of their leaders fled… finally taking refuge in the mountains, but he was caught there and executed.[25]

The Chinese peasants were then in many ways fatalistic, prone to vacillation between passivism and sporadic uprisings of blind violence. Peasant action for Perry, whether predatory or protectionist, was not a revolutionary but a parochial response to scarce resources.[26]

However scarcity itself was the result of the siphoning off of the bulk of the overall surplus by the wealthy elites using extra-economic means. Stagnation under conditions of monopoly rent meant rural isolation, reinforcing the protective order of kin and community in the system of personalised power. But whilst kinship and territory-based hierarchies made for a segmented peasantry, easily divided along localistic, lineage, religious and ethnic lines to become enmeshed in factionalised networks of elite personal power, it was landlord control of the channels of communication between state and village, town and countryside, either directly as village residents, or through their sub-county organisations, that trapped the peasants in relations of dependency.

The emergence of a revolutionary peasantry

To understand the tenacity of feudal power it is then necessary to grasp the limitations of rural protest: with peasants in isolation from urban areas and susceptible to landlord influence, their movements segmented into disparate kinship and territorial networks and lacking a unified base.

However the peasants' experience was also changing and developing particularly as the agrarian crisis deepened and the search for a livelihood grew harder. Under the impact of imperialism, which relied on the feudal extraction of the surplus, the exploitation of the peasants increased as landlords, abandoning the guise of benevolent protectors, resorted to brute force to obtain an increasing share of a diminishing surplus. At the same time, accelerated commercialisation undermined the stability of the state and village community, hastening the peasants' loss of land, which then allowed the landlords to strengthen their position further.

As political and economic power increasingly converged, the traditional legitimacy of landlord and state became tarnished in the peasants' eyes and the patron-client ties which kept the peasants divided tended to dissolve. For example, traditional lineages were weakened as the landlords bullied members to exact protection money, and their coercive armed measures made it all the more obvious to the peasants that these organisations were a means of landlord power not peasant security.[27]

Rural protest began to break through the vicious cycle of predation and protection. If peasants were susceptible to landlord influence, nevertheless, and here Huang has a point, village activities were not totally integrated under the totalitarian control of the state or absorbed into market relations or under landlord domination.

As Thaxton has argued, whilst they often shared in the same organisations, landlords and peasants did not necessarily share the same ideals. The peasants had in their own oral history, a rich folklore expressing egalitarian ideals of social justice and welfare. This popular culture supported an identity independent of the ideology of the Confucianist moral values of obedience and loyalty, shared and upheld by the state and landlords. In particular, by legitimising the division of mental and manual labour, the state ethic underwrote the role of officials and landlords and their patron-client ties.[28] The peasants' own anti-orthodox traditions on the other hand afforded a potential threat to the state, embodying in age-old practices of self-help and mutual exchange, different beliefs and values which informed distinct ideas about how things should be done, about the use of land and resources, and about the role of leaders and government.[29]

Thaxton then shows peasant rebellion to be not simply an expression of traditionalist conservatism under the leadership of patriarchal protectors: beyond patronage and clientelism, different moral standards influenced peasant relationships between themselves and with their leaders. If kinship and territorial bonds tended to obscure class alignments, there was nevertheless potential for divergence between the peasants and the dissident gentry within peasant uprisings as mobilisation on a mass scale extended beyond the control of the elite leadership.

Whilst Perry considers the peasants remained trapped in their struggles for survival, Thaxton sees them learning from bitter experience: peasant consciousness and solidarity began to grow and their goals and forms of organisation started to change as their collective actions and protests developed beyond traditional appeals to the landlords to fulfil their obligations as patrons into oppositionist forms of resistance.[30]

Not simply a conservative bastion of the bureaucratic state, nor caught in an aimless restiveness, the peasants expressed increasing opposition to the political and economic system of landlord exploitation as their plight worsened. As the agrarian crisis, brought on by the contradiction between the land monopoly and the land hunger, deepened, it saw in the increasing polarisation between the poor and middle peasants on the one hand and the landlords on the other, the fundamental condition of the coming revolution. The challenge was how to foster peasant unity.

NOTES AND REFERENCES

1. See Wolf, 1969, pp.113–6, for his description of the typical pattern of peasant revolts in China.

2. See Document 46: 'The Land System of the Heavenly Dynasty' in Michael, Vol. I, 1971, pp.309–20.

3. Marx is quoted here in Anderson, 1974, p.493.

4. Hsiao, K.C., 1960, p.513.

5. Mao, *Selected Works*, Vol. III, p.76.

6. See Schram, 1974a, pp.234–5.

7. For examples of lineage rivalries over marketing systems, see Marks, 1984, pp.60–75; on food riots, *Ibid.*, pp.76–86, and R. Bin Wong (1982); see Praznaik (1980) for an account of a tax protest in the early 20th century.

8. See Perdue (1986) for an account of an ethnic conflict between native Hunanese and immigrants from Jiangxi.

9. Perry, 1980, p.86.

10. Polachek, 1983, pp.809–814.

11. Watson, J., 1982, see footnote 10, p.614.

12. Perry, 1980, p.82.

13. For a discussion of the various legal and illegal survival strategies of the peasants see Perry, 1980, Chapter 3; and Thaxton, 1983, pp.60–8.

14. See Polachek, 1983, p.814.

15. Chesneaux, 1972, pp.17–19.

16. *Ibid.*, p.21.

17. This paragraph outlines the argument of Bianco (1972).

18. Perry, 1980, p.128.

19. *Ibid.*, pp.58–95.

20. *Ibid.*, p.252.

21. Huang, 1985, pp.237–240.

22. *Ibid.*, p.244.

23. cited in *ibid.*, p.245.

24. Hsiao, K.C., 1960, p.447; p.485; see also Wang Qingcheng, 1980, p.163. He argues that the egalitarian ideals of the Taiping's land system could not possibly have gained the support of the well-to-do peasants since it obstructed the development of a commodity economy. Taiping policy then changed in 1853 to the promotion of commerce and industry.

25. See Schram, 1974, p.220.

26. Perry, 1980, pp.148–50.

27. Marks, 1984, p.147.

28. Thaxton, 1983, pp.19–27.

29. For further descriptions of traditional forms of mutual aid see Fried, 1956, pp.117–20; Thaxton, 1975, pp.33–40.

30. See Thaxton, 1983, pp.68–78. The works of Perry, Thaxton and Marks are discussed in greater detail in Part 5, Chapter 22.

10
The failure of reforms

Reform efforts from the Qing to the Republican era

Traditions of reformism had strong roots in the history of the dynastic cycle. As dynasties fell through corruption and decline, enlightened officials, stepping forward with reforms to renew 'the mandate of heaven', were seen as a major force of progress acting to defend the peasants' interests.[1]

Later Qing reforms, aimed at strengthening the tax collection system, sought to involve the gentry in local government only to see corruption increase. Further efforts followed to formalise local government and modernise the bureaucracy, however the expansion of schools, railways and the police only increased the tax burden on the peasants and rural protests escalated.[2] In 1909 and 1910, Central China experienced mounting tax resistance movements together with widespread food riots in which the rural gentry also took part. In the 1911 revolution, 'People's Armies' recruited among the peasantry amassed virtually overnight and seized some cities. As peasant troops took control of the shops and markets, sometimes looting, the urban reformers turned against them as an 'unruly rabble'.[3] With peasant armies lining up with feudal militarists, the violence was seen by the growing urban population in the Treaty Ports as a resurgence of rural traditionalism against modernisation. Whilst the new policies failed to benefit the countryside, the peasants for their part blamed the reforming officials for the increased levies which worsened their economic difficulties.

By the 1930s, the KMT government, under increasing pressure from its more left-wing members, adopted more far-reaching reforms to improve the rural economy with better access to markets and credit. In order for reform policies to penetrate more deeply into the rural areas, a modern infrastructure of communication and scientific, legal and technical services was needed. Where reform efforts from the 1890s saw the devolution of state power to the informal sphere of landlord-gentry influence, the KMT sought to formalise sub-county and village government into an effective administrative apparatus in order to deliver these services to the peasant households. But again, reform efforts were to prove no more successful than previous attempts.

The crisis in state-village relations

To explain the failure of the modernising reforms of the late Qing and Nationalist governments, Huang, as previously noted, turns attention to the breakdown of village order under the increasing impositions of a bureaucratic state which strained relations with society to breaking point.[4] His argument frames modernising reforms in the context of the dislocation of traditional equilibrium with the acceleration of commerce under imperialism upsetting the balance of state-landlord-village axes. Landlord-tenant relations became more impersonal and exploitative; the solidary bonds of the village communities were dissolving; and a weakening state came to rely more on the local landlords to squeeze taxes from an increasingly impoverished peasantry.

For Huang, the critical point of tension was to be located in the state-village axis as an increasingly intrusive state, reaching down into villages, found the traditional social order in decline and its tax base shrinking further as owner-cultivator communities disintegrated into semi-proletarianisation under the forces of commercialisation. Where Qing reforms devolved state power to the informal powers of the gentry, KMT reforms, seeking to replace the inadequate old fiscal apparatus, extended bureaucratisation down to the level of village administration, drawing the lesser landlords and village elites into official positions. This effort to introduce a new decentralised machinery of tax collection, Huang argues, is what altered the relationship between state and village.

On the one hand, increasing state impositions were met by tax resistance on a mass scale. Forming the backbone of these movements for Huang, as has been seen, were the relatively autonomous villages of owner-cultivators where community organisations remained intact and where village leaders had real powers to represent the interests of the community, so they were able to resist the intrusive demands of the state.[5]

Elsewhere, those more atomised communities, where market penetration had led to a greater semi-proletarianisation, were more exposed to the outside influences of the state and landlords and became open to political abuse.[6] Where tax resistance movements saw landlords and peasants unite, in the atomised communities increased taxation divided villagers: as the burden fell heavily on the dwindling number of owner-cultivators, these were to demand taxation by head rather than landholding such that the semi-proletarianised tenant households would also have to pay a share.[7] So as Huang sees it, the breakdown of traditional community consensus took its toll on village elders: without sufficient financial inducement and amidst divisions among the peasants over the tax share-out, they refused to serve as village leaders in the new rural bureaucracy. This left a power vacuum to be filled by 'local bullies and tyrants' from the smaller landlords and lower gentry as well as from new elite beneficiaries of the reform programmes.[8]

For Huang then, the major dimension of the pre-revolutionary situation was the crisis of the political authority of the state over the village, as reforms devolving state power and politicising the local elites took place just as traditional village leadership was in disintegration. Clearly bureaucratic state intervention and peasant disaffection over increased levies were an integral part of the pre-revolutionary crisis. However, as Keating has commented, Huang's substantivist view of social change at village level in terms of the 'dissolution' of old solidarities and cohesiveness takes no account of any class conflict that might have acted as a 'motive force of historical development'.[9] Whilst his focus takes the state-village dynamic as independent of landlord-peasant class struggle, it was in fact the overall constraint on development under monopoly rent which saw conditions of scarcity fuel conflict between the peasants and the state over taxation.

The decline in the political authority of the state over the village should rather be situated within the intensifying crisis in class relations between landlord and peasant with the landlords' increasing brutality undermining the customs of benevolence which legitimised equally their claim to the surplus and the state's role as protector of the people. Huang's overall analysis is problematic in that it sees the state, the landlords, and the village rich, as separate spheres. However, as Chinese Marxists have pointed out the acceleration of commercialisation under the impact of imperialism in fact hastened the convergence of landlords, merchants, officials and militarists, with land increasingly concentrated in the hands of a few as peasant bankruptcy and loss of land deepened. With the polarisation of landlord-peasant relations and mounting rural protests, the state raised taxes to finance a coercive apparatus, protecting the landlords as they engaged increasingly in land speculation, rent hikes, tax embezzlement and other corrupt practices.

By taking tax resistance as the main content of peasant protest, Huang's analysis puts emphasis on the one hand on the commonality of landlords and peasants as landowners and taxpayers, and on the other on the increasing divisions among the owner-cultivator and semi-proletarianised peasants. But where Huang sees only the weakness of a divided peasantry, Mao saw the potential power of unity between the middle and poor peasants in opposition to the converging forces of the landlords, merchants and officials, as not only tenant farmers but also the owner-cultivator households confronted the landlords in their roles of merchant, usurer and magistrate. Burdened by taxes, exploited by market speculation, suffering loss of handicrafts and victims of wildly fluctuating land prices, these owner-peasants were increasingly marginalised as impoverishment through debt and through the subversion of the clan hastened their loss of land driving them into the power domain of the landlords.

Where Huang's analysis ends with a power vacuum at the local level, Mao's analysis then begins with the Hunan peasant movement seizing control from the local bullies and bad gentry.

From reform to revolution

The rural reforms rolled out by the Nationalist government in the 1930s were aimed at realising a system of peasant ownership, introducing arrangements for permanent tenancy and rent reductions to a level fixed to the value of land rather than as a share of the crop, so that peasants would be better able to buy back land from the landlords. At the same time credit and marketing, as well as processing co-operatives were set up to strengthen the market position of the small producers along the lines Tawney had envisaged.

The reform of village administration, merging the *baojia* with the village heads, was an attempt to introduce rural self-government and local autonomy. The problem was that behind the village heads stood the clan and lineage leaders and the local gentry. In practice, the transfer of power only created a new ruling group of landlords, rich peasants, scholars and clan elders, boosting the position of those who already dominated the economic, social and juridicial life of the village communities.

Chen Hanseng described this fusion of economic and political controls in the village administration as follows:

> In this twilight of responsibilities, many chances for graft and exploitation of the weak make their shameless appearance, evils for which there is no remedy in the system itself… It might be contended that such a strengthening of clan managers… represents the fulfilment of an ancient dream of patriarchal rule. But actually these elders who are intriguing with others who exercise political and economic power are not strengthening the clan. Even where they do not deliberately line their own pockets…they permit the clan to lose in inner cohesion, in social usefulness, and in prestige, while their own status in society rises…[10]

With local administration in their hands, the landlords also took over the co-operatives to obtain loans for themselves as they took control of processing and marketing.[11] The majority of peasants on the other hand were too poor to buy back land or to compete with the landlords and merchants in obtaining loans, and could not afford improvements in farming technique. The KMT's village programmes were in effect hijacked by the same parasitic classes they aimed to obstruct. Any reforms which the local powerholders could not use to their advantage, such as rent reductions and the strengthening of tenants' rights, they opposed.[12] With their heavily militarised budgets growing, rather than lose the support of the landlords who were the mainstay of the tax system and social order, the KMT abandoned reforms, leaving the resident landlords and rich peasants in control of village power, free to engage in embezzlement, speculation and usury.

The reform perspective, failing to address the roots of landlord influence over the village communities, was unable to explain this degeneration. To establish adequate administrative roots in the villages to carry out reforms so as to promote the internal market, it was necessary to address the question of alliance with the peasantry. Policies such as those initiated by the KMT and advocated by Tawney to support the small producer were not possible in China: there was no adequate social basis.

In the absence of independent capitalist elements capable of opposing feudal power, landlords, merchants and rich peasants, rather than transforming into investing classes, existed primarily through peasant exploitation: business was dependent upon, and secondary to land rent. Nascent capitalism was intertwined with feudalism and could not destroy it without destroying its own roots. Reforming elements among the gentry and merchants were ultimately tied to traditional forms of exploitation, reliant on the power of the local elites over the peasantry. Nor could rich peasants and artisans provide a basis for social reform: they generally served as agents of the landlords and merchants, and under their domination, were incapable of acting as an independent revolutionary force to unite town and countryside against feudal ties and to set free economic forces for the development of capitalism.

The weakness of the class basis for reform in the face of feudal power was to be seen in the failure of the Taiping rebellion. On the other hand this movement of impoverished peasantry proved to be of such strength that it had only been possible to suppress it through the combined forces of feudalism and imperialism. The gentry had only been able to retain their positions by subverting the peasants' struggles from within, not by actually carrying out thoroughgoing reforms.

Between a mass peasant mobilisation against feudalism which was seen to threaten the roots of business, and the impossibility of reforms to promote a rich peasant economy independent of the gentry, the KMT were left with no alternative other than to rely on the feudal classes to undermine the struggles of the dispossessed in an attempt to preserve the tax system. In their efforts to modernise the country, then, the KMT, as it came up against the system of landlord power, was to end up in its service, at the same time relying on loans from imperialist powers, since it failed to organise the peasant movement. Without identifying the social forces capable of producing change, reforms only ended up as functional to the existing system.

This is essentially the conclusion drawn by Crook and Gilmartin whose study of one community, Prosperity village, during the KMT period, offers an analysis of the government and church organisation initiatives to improve the local social conditions. They point to the failure of these reform efforts to identify the power structure and vested interests in the community opposed to the reform agenda and similarly their failure to develop allies for their projects.[13] Villages rather were seen simply as the recipients of policy but it was landlord domination at the local level which made the redistribution of income through the channels of credit and marketing impossible. In handing over power to the village heads and focusing on delivering benefits to the more well-to-do peasants, the KMT in effect underestimated the semi-feudal ties of the rich peasants to the landlords. At the local levels, the new administration simply operated within the power domain of the local gentry, and fell under their control because the reforms did not address their central role in the political and social organisation of the village.

To see traditional China as a homogeneous society of small producers engaged in subsistence production, interested in family survival not profit, as Tawney and the reformers did, was to fail to recognise the potential for change from within. Analysis remained at the superficial level of the peasant household and its relation to the market not the underlying production relations and classes; it focused on exchange between town and countryside not the structure of power and economic relations within the village. This was Lenin's point to the Narodniks: the fundamental issue to be addressed was that of wealth creation not its distribution. In failing to do so, the reformist view of China as a system of small production underestimated the landlord system, both economically and politically, questioning neither the structure of village power nor the nature of the state which rested upon this.

Despite the limitations of his overall analysis, Huang is right to pinpoint the importance of the breakdown of village governance in the pre-revolutionary crisis. The CPC itself took the village as the main unit in organising rural transformation, for the reason, however, that the traditional village order provided the basis for the continuing economic and political regeneration of landlord power. A change of government by reform in the upper tier was not sufficient to resolve China's problems. With the towns dependent upon land revenue extracted from the countryside and dominated by the landlords, merchants and officials, the forces for social transformation lay in the countryside in the peasant mobilisation to break the power of the landlords and gentry, opening the door to the revolutionary alliance of urban and rural classes.

Breaking with China's traditions of enlightened reformism, Mao saw rural discontent not in terms of opposition to corruption and the degeneration of the state but as a struggle for a new form of class power. Perceiving this essence of peasant protests as a force of potential opposition to the power of the gentry, he turned to the organisation of the peasant movement as the essential condition of social, political and economic change in the countryside. In his *Report of an Investigation into the Peasant Movement in Hunan*, he made the point that the question of 'clean' or corrupt officials depended upon whether a county was dominated by local bullies and bad gentry, or whether the peasants had risen.[14] The fundamental question as to whether peasant rebellions were functional to the existing system, modified by reforms, or whether they were revolutionary against the state which upheld the interests of the landlord class, was for Mao a question of leadership of the class struggle – by the dissident gentry or by the peasant masses.

Beyond the tensions between centre and locality, Mao sought to address the problem of the fusion of economic and political power at the base of society. Against the reformists, he saw effective village administration not as a vehicle but as a product of change, created out of class struggle through the organisation of a peasant mass movement. Mao then looked to the peasantry not as mere objects of policy but as an active force for change. Arguing that the peasants were the main force in the revolution, he sought to tackle the class struggle within the villages to transform relations of power, relying on the mass movement as the source of new policies and forms of organisation.

NOTES & REFERENCES

1. One such reformer was Wang Mang (45 BC–23 AD) who during the Han dynasty carried out successive reforms of the system of officialdom, currency, land tenure, taxation and state monopolies of commodities; another was Hai Rui, a magistrate during the Ming dynasty from 1558–1562 AD, who criticised the Emperor's abuse of power and opposed state encroachment of peasants' land.

2. Huang, 1985, p.276.

3. Marks, 1984, pp.133–9; p.144.

4. Huang, 1985, pp.276–7.

5. *Ibid.*, p.290.

6. *Ibid.*, p.285.

7. *Ibid.*, p.306.

8. *Ibid.*, pp.289–90.

9. Keating, 1987, p.193
10. Institute of Pacific Relations, 1939, p.216.
11. Crook and Gilmartin (2015), esp. pp.261–9 on how the salt co-operative in Prosperity village became a battlefield in an ongoing contention between rival power factions in the community.
12. See Institute of Pacific Relations, 1939, pp.144–149.
13. Crook and Gilmartin, 2015, p.269.
14. Mao, *Selected Works*, Vol. I, pp.42–3.

11
The convoluted trajectory to revolution

The question as to why capitalism failed to develop in China as in Europe has been a theme throughout the discussion in this part. Clearly there is more empirical work that needs to be done on the historical conditions of capital formation in the Chinese agrarian economy but at the heart of the matter here has been a question of methodology. Whether focusing on peasant impoverishment and involution, economic stagnation and the lack of investment, the role of the state, or social conflict and peasant protest, the key works of Western scholarship under discussion have failed to take analysis beyond the general context of population pressure and resource scarcity.

Differing as to whether commerce developed to the detriment or advantage of the peasantry, these scholars have tended to take the expansion of commerce and its impact in promoting freer and more impersonal economic relations at face value, without enquiring into the different forms of property. Landlordism and rent relations are treated superficially as just part of an economic whole. Without applying the distinction between feudal and capitalist forms of rent, without penetrating the system of land ownership, China's problems of economic stagnation appear only as matters of market operation and peasant household behaviour.

To understand the peasant condition on the other hand requires a comprehensive analysis of patterns of land tenure and surplus extraction through rent, wage and usury, and the conditions of commercial speculation. In this way, through the study of production relations, the roots of underdevelopment in China are discovered in the landlords' overall control over the creation, appropriation, distribution and use of the surplus. Applying this method reveals how the conditions of land and labour markets, of employment as well as tenancy, were shaped by the wider economy of the landlord system, with land ownership patterns constraining investment and so restricting industrialisation and the creation of an internal market. This then uncovers the inherent potential for the development of the productive forces once constraints on investment were released, identifying the class contradictions arising from these conditions and thereby pointing to the solution to the agrarian crisis through class struggle.

The distinctive nature of agrarian China over the centuries is to be seen in the tenacity and flexibility of the feudal system with the particular intertwining of feudal and embryonic capitalist relations in agriculture. Following the peasant rebellion which overthrew the Ming dynasty, the development of commerce from the mid-18th century saw a certain commoditisation of land and labour. However, whilst landlord powers of direct compulsion over tenants and labourers were reduced, the spread of commodity and money relations failed to fully penetrate the production process to effect a qualitative change in the dominant form of surplus appropriation. Even in Huang's village case studies in cash cropping areas, the feudal forms of rent in kind and share cropping arrangements were common, indicating the limited development of the cash economy.

Despite the social upheavals, the bureaucratic state hierarchy and kinship-based village order remained essentially in place providing the means for the landlords to restore their power and positions of privilege as benevolent patrons in a process of refeudalisation. As obligation in the guise of reciprocity took the place of the weakening servile ties of direct control over persons, a form of indirect coercion remained integral within this system of personalised power. Although the elite was not a landed aristocracy, it was nevertheless feudal: rank, title and privilege were not tied directly to land ownership but to office, exam, and local prestige in a system which was to lend legitimacy to the landlords' claims to an extra-economic share of the surplus derived from the land. With state backing, lineage and kinship relations came to form one of the principal vehicles of feudal exploitation and rule as, cutting across class contradictions, the village patriarchy served to link the village communities into the field of landlord power.

The pattern of commercial expansion then was to be moulded within traditional arrangements of clan, territorial rights, and patriarchal communalism which kept peasants tied to the land and to the landlords. The buying and selling of land saw market forces enter land relations, however the absolute rights of individual ownership accompanied by total alienability were never fully established in China as in Europe.

Whilst peasants had gained certain rights, their conditions of subservience were never completely eradicated. Bound by customary obligations on the one hand and kept to the payment of tax and rent by the ideological and police controls of the state on the other, surviving by the close combination of agriculture and handicrafts production, the peasants were then unable to completely break free from feudal and patriarchal ties and further increase their independence through free trade. Instead, as illiterates, they remained excluded from the networks of personalised power upheld by the bureaucratic hierarchy to which access was to be gained only by education.

Feudal relations, on the other hand, were to prove accommodative to the changing circumstances as the landlords gained control over land through land purchase. The looser arrangements of land purchase saw the rise of a class of private landlords whose economic power was not entirely separated from the political authority of the centralised state.[1] Official salaries, commercial super-profits, as well as rent were all used for the purpose of buying land in order to accrue wealth, and, with the increasing interchange of wealth between land buying, commerce and money-lending, land became more and more concentrated in the hands of absentee landlords, leading the economy into stagnation.[2] With the competition among peasants for land intensifying, cultivation then was to further fragment under parcellisation for rent, whilst the poorer peasants relied increasingly on kinship and clientelism as a resource for protection and survival.

As the spread of market relations weakened the traditional state and village communities, the private powers of the landlords grew at the expense of owner-cultivation at the base of the state. However, 'capitalist sprouts' or managerial farmers proved unable to establish themselves, remaining confined within the interstices of feudalism as commerce, dominated by landed interests, intertwined with feudal relations. Those entrepreneurial farmers who benefitted from commercialisation became closely tied to the landlord economy and landlord power, the village rich and landlord-gentry entangling together in the informal networks that linked, through status and privilege, with the formal power of the Confucian state.

At the lower levels, these elites, deriving influence from lineage position and land ownership, ran local affairs on an informal basis. Assuming importance as mediators in the state-village hierarchy in matters of taxation, jurisprudence, and local defence, these local powerholders were in control of the social, political and economic interchange between town and countryside.

Development across China was clearly uneven with variations in the strength of feudal relations and forces, however to understand the failure of capitalism to develop, as Li Wenzhi pointed out, it is necessary to keep the landlord system as a whole in view.[3] As political economy overall under the Qing came to display the particular pattern of commercialisation which hastened peasant impoverishment rather than promoting peasant independence, fragmenting owner-cultivator communities, class differentiation remained trapped within feudal arrangements. Involution in the peasant economy therefore developed as the contradiction between land ownership and its use gave rise to monopoly rent which served as the major block on development.

The landlord-peasant class struggle was to follow a convoluted course through both reforms and rebellions as ties of kinship and notions of paternalist benevolence masked class contradictions and obstructed the development of class solidarities. Widespread rebellions fuelled by impoverishment were never to succeed in inflicting a thorough defeat on the system of political power as dissident gentry, who joined the rural protests, used kinship loyalties and territorial bonds to advance their own interests, subverting the movements from within.

Reforms equally fell short of achieving any fundamental social transformation, with concessions made only to restore temporarily the balance in the distribution of surplus between rulers and owner-cultivators, leaving the dominant form of surplus labour unaltered.[5] As such, these adjustments were an essential part of the political framework of the state, serving as a safety valve to defuse peasant rebellion.

The Orientalist view of Chinese history sees only a perpetual cycle of dynasties, rising and falling as power shifts between centre and locality, upper and lower tiers of society, in the struggle between 'just' and unjust' rulers. But for Mao, peasant struggles against landlord power were the motive force of Chinese history. As he saw it, reforms such as reductions in taxes were not to protect the peasants' interests, rather they were introduced only because there was nothing to take from the peasants since they were so poor.[4] If the peasants did win some concessions, this was to hold class antagonisms in check for the sake of preserving social stability so as to revive production.

Whilst the role of reformers was to neutralise or subvert peasants' struggle, elite-led rebellions against corrupt officials were ultimately essentially a means of strengthening the state by getting rid of unpopular figures since, once in power, the new office holders did not so much make concessions as counterattack and seek reprisals against the peasants' organisations. Mao himself had witnessed as a youth the execution of a number of poor peasants after a riot in Changsha.[5] From this he realised there were no 'clean' officials because in reality the state served the overall interests of the landlord class as an instrument of peasant subordination whether by coercive or benevolent means.

The looser arrangements of the Confucian system gave the appearance of an independent benevolent state but this was an illusion: with peasants kept tied to the land, state and landlord were co-conspirators in peasant oppression. Tensions and conflicts existed between the Imperial state and the local powerholders, however these tended to resolve into joint action against peasant revolt.

The landlords' grip over a stagnating economy and their control over urban-rural exchange as well as state-village links kept the peasants trapped, in conditions of scarcity, in conflicts over subsistence, polarising between those with and those without access to resources. The clientelist system of personalised power with its inherent factionalism separated peasants from each other whilst kinship hierarchies saw the wealthiest members of the rural communities hold on to positions as local powerholders. Although not totally integrated under landlord power, the peasants, divided amongst themselves, were particularly susceptible to elite leadership as they rose in protest.

Change in China then was not simply a matter of seizing state power: the fundamental issue was the transformation of the village order, overturning the very basis of the landlords' political and economic power through the radical redistribution of land. The reforms of the Nationalist government, which were aimed at supporting the small farmers as commodity producers, failed to address the land tenure system and the roots of landlord power in the village order. Whilst the viewpoint of the small producer sees problems as located in state-peasant relations, the root of China's predicament was a matter of class – the absence of vigorous and independent private interests strong enough to carry through reforms to release the constraint on investment so as to open up an internal market serving the peasants' needs in production and consumption.

As the conflict between the landlords and peasants intensified into a revolutionary situation what was lacking was a strategy to unite the disparate anti-feudal forces at the same time guarding against leadership degeneration to achieve the fundamental transformation of Chinese agrarian society.

NOTES AND REFERENCES

1. See Huang, 1985, p.12, footnote re Hu Rulei.

2. Fang Xing, 1981, p.130.

3. Li Wenzhi, 1981, p.87.

4. Cited in Schram, 1974a, pp.234–5.

5. See *Ibid.*, p.220.

PART 3

China's revolutionary experience from the First
United Front to land revolution (1924–1937)
and the evolution of Mao's strategy

Introduction

With land ownership concentrated in the hands of a few leaving the majority of the peasants in conditions of land hunger and dependence exacerbated by the debilitating effects of foreign trade and investment, the main obstacles to economic growth, democracy, and social progress in China were the feudal structure of power and land ownership, and the imperialist powers which exploited and supported this. The national and the agrarian questions then – the issues of peasant and nation – were the two defining issues of the Chinese revolution.

The struggle for national liberation and the agrarian revolution however developed according to their independent dynamics, impacting on each other in both positive and negative ways. As the CPC came to grasp, in fact, the one could not succeed without the other: only a mass mobilisation of the Chinese people, in the main the peasants, could resist the weight of the colonial powers and the Chinese landlord system, and such a mobilisation was only possible through the struggle against the feudal forces which denied democratic rights and land to the peasants. In the combined struggles for land and national independence, the organisation of the peasants held the key to China's future.

This section covers the early period of China's revolutionary process: the first Chinese revolution and the first CPC-KMT United Front from 1924–7, as well as the following 10-year civil war from 1927–1937. It follows the advance and defeat of the revolutionary forces, examining the dynamics between the national and the agrarian movements, then considering the class dynamics and policies of the land revolution carried out by the CPC in its mountain bases in the South.

In understanding the nature of the revolution, the CPC only had the Russian experience and Lenin's analysis to draw on. Undoubtedly, China had lessons to learn from those experiences and in particular from Lenin's understanding of the revolutionary role of the peasantry. Nevertheless, in less developed China, with capitalist development restricted by feudalism and imperialism, the conditions of the peasantry differed from those in Europe. The agrarian revolution, and the roles of the rich, middle and poor peasants within it, had their own distinctive features.

In the earlier phases of the revolution, the CPC's understanding of the distinctive behaviours of the different Chinese classes as the struggles unfolded was inhibited by the tendency, under Comintern influence, to follow too closely the Russian model. The CPC struggled to grasp the meaning of proletarian leadership in a country with such a small working class, but it was the issue of the role of the peasantry in the democratic stage of the revolution that was to prove its key challenge.

With the national and agrarian revolutions pulling apart, the revolutionary upsurge of 1926 was to end in a devastating defeat for the CPC in 1927. Adherence to United Front politics accounted for an initial hesitance and over-dependence on the KMT on the part of the Party, and the lack of an effective peasant mobilisation under limited land policies was to prove a major factor in its failure. Sustaining serious damage under KMT purges and suppression, the CPC was forced into retreat into the mountain areas in the South. There followed some 10 years of isolation as, harassed and encircled by KMT forces, the Party endeavoured to establish bases of independent soviet power through policies of land confiscation.

In these early years, the CPC was exposed to the arguments of Trotsky as well as Stalin.[1] Despite their differences over the revolutionary stages, what both leaders shared was an essentially European perspective on Chinese class structure and class struggle. Both, drawing on the Russian experience, looked to the urban centres and working class organisation in China as the core element of revolutionary strategy.

In line with the Leninist understanding of revolutionary stages, the CPC under Comintern guidance came to the view that the national bourgeoisie had defected from the revolution and that therefore the task should turn to building the worker-peasant alliance. But now cut off from any working-class organisation in the cities, the CPC confronted huge challenges in setting up soviet-style governments in the rural areas given resistance from traditional elites and clannish closure of rural communities against outsiders. At the same time, egalitarian excesses and radical land confiscations saw potential allies driven into a corner, making the opposition to land reform all the more determined.

Not unlike the experience of the KMT government at local levels, the organs of the Party and soviet power in the villages were exposed to infiltration by the traditional elites, at the same time suffering problems of bureaucratic degeneration and entanglement in factional feuds. The role of the rich peasants was to become a particular preoccupation as the CPC leadership, vacillating between pro-rich peasant policy and anti-rich peasant campaigns, constantly shifted its approach to land reform in its endeavour to bring the peasant population under its proletarian leadership.

Whilst both the Comintern and the CPC leaders continued to insist that the Party's most important social base remained in the cities, Mao during this period began to formulate an entirely different strategy for a popular mass-based democratic revolution which was to take the landlord-peasant conflict and the agrarian revolution as central. This recognition of the peasant movement as the main content of the revolution was to provide the basis of a revolutionary strategy of protracted war, encircling the cities from the independent bases of peasant democratic power in the countryside, in which a new-style Red Army played a key role.

Dealing in practice with the issues of peasant organisation and agrarian reform, Mao was able to draw concrete lessons from the limitations of policy during the early period of alliance with the KMT whilst also learning from the mistakes of extremism in land reform in the 10 years that followed. Step by step, through trial and error, he was to develop policies and methods of land confiscation and redistribution with the organisation of the peasant ranks as a class. In this, two methods of analysis come into play: firstly the close observation of the changing behaviours of the different types of peasants in the upsurge and ebb of revolution, and secondly, helping to explain this, the application of Marxist concepts of exploitation setting out clear criteria of peasant classification.

In this way, Mao came to break with the dogma of the 1905 soviets as he began to recognise on the one hand the role of rich peasants not only as exploiting elements but also, insofar as they carried out farming, as a positive part of the peasant economy, and on the other hand, the role of middle peasants, who also experienced some exploitation, as a reliable ally of the proletariat, that is, not so much a marginal force but an important part of the motive forces of the revolution.[2] Only by doing so was he able to steer a path out of the mire of clan factionalism and intrigue which constantly entangled the CPC at local levels, developing distinctive methods of Party organisation and Party building together with the institutionalisation of the mass line fostering a new democratic power through organising the peasants in land reform.

NOTES AND REFERENCES

1. Saich considers that Trotskyists generally enjoyed little sustained influence within the CPC or among the Chinese working class. Saich, academia.edu, accessed: 27/4/2020.

2. Mao Zedong, 'The Chinese Revolution and the Chinese Communist Party', 1939, *Selected Works*, Vol. III, pp.92–3.

12
Peasants and revolution – from Lenin to Mao

Lenin's revolutionary stages

Against views which looked exclusively to the industrial centres as the source of revolutionary forces in Russia, Lenin, in *The Development of Capitalism in Russia* (1899), pointed to the growth of agrarian capitalism as a revolutionary force against feudalism. In the emergence of the new classes of rural bourgeoisie and proletariat Lenin saw a powerful impulse for bourgeois democratic advance which would open the door to socialist revolution. His argument contradicted the views of both Plekhanov and the Narodniks who equally saw the Russian peasantry as essentially homogeneous. Plekhanov regarded the peasants, in their political indifference and intellectual 'backwardness', as a 'bulwark of absolutism' and, giving up hope of revolution developing in the countryside, favoured reliance on the liberal bourgeoisie. The Narodniks, on the contrary, saw the peasants' own organisation, the *mir*, as the focus of popular resistance against both the Tsar and large-scale capitalism.

Lenin argued that capitalism was developing in agriculture with the polarisation between the rich peasants, who cultivated substantial farms using hired labour and applying capital, and the majority of the peasants with insufficient land, who had to rely on hiring out their labour. Whilst the Narodniks only talked about exploitation in general, Lenin distinguished between feudal and capitalist modes of appropriation and identified three different sectors of agricultural production: the landlord-tenant sector; the sector of independent or middle peasants, who remained largely self-sufficient; and the capitalist sector.

Initially, Lenin regarded the middle peasants as a social force in dissolution as the development of capitalism in agriculture promoted peasant differentiation. Thus he considered that the *mir*, far from providing a vehicle for the transformation of Russian society, was lacking in revolutionary content and in fact constituted a part of the old feudal order to be swept away in the democratic revolution. Nevertheless, the success of the revolution depended on forging links between town and countryside through the alliance between the working class and the new agrarian classes. As well as the rural labourers, Lenin also regarded the rich peasants, as emergent capitalist farmers, to be allies against feudalism. He thus sought to develop the links between town and countryside through a limited agrarian programme aimed at uniting the rural proletariat with the rich peasants in a struggle against the surviving feudal relations which inhibited agrarian capitalism. However a wider agrarian programme, Lenin thought, would benefit the rural bourgeoisie more than was necessary, creating obstacles for the continuation of the revolution to the socialist stage.[1]

In Lenin's view, the reforms proposed by the Narodniks adopted the viewpoint of the small producer against exploitation in general, and ignored the class differences emerging within the peasantry.[2] Such reforms would in effect redistribute wealth from the feudal to the capitalist sector, strengthening the rich peasants. Rather than looking only at the differences between rich and poor, that is, exploitation in general, Lenin, distinguishing capitalist from feudal exploitation, was then able not only to clearly identify the targets of the bourgeois democratic revolution but also to organise the peasants' struggles in such a way as to avoid strengthening the forces of capitalism more than was necessary so creating conditions favourable for the development of socialist revolution.

However, Lenin did alter his perspective on the peasant movement as a whole, and the middle peasants in particular, following the 1905 revolution. The extent of peasant involvement in the revolution and the scale of their actions demonstrated the independence of their movement and exposed the inadequacy of the limited agrarian programme. Lenin realised that he had overestimated the degree of capitalist development in Russia, and this had caused him to underestimate the feudal burden on the peasantry and hence their capacity for revolution.[3]

Where previously he had looked to the new classes in the countryside as the main revolutionary force, Lenin came to recognise the central role of the peasant movement as a whole, including the middle peasants, in a revolution against the Tsarist state order. This became clear as he realised that there were two different possible outcomes of the 1905 revolution: an alliance between the Tsar and the liberal bourgeoisie which would maintain the peasants' subordination to the landlords and preserve their large estates, or a worker-peasant alliance which would break up the estates, completely undermining the basis of landlord power and promoting an independent peasantry.[4]

This meant that the issue at the point of agrarian transformation was a class struggle between the landlords and peasants over the direction of the agrarian revolution: the preservation of the old order based on peasant subordination or the creation of a new order through the development of the peasants as an independent political force in alliance with the proletariat. Lenin favoured an alliance with the peasants as a whole arguing that, whilst they were petty bourgeois and may lack class consciousness and have reactionary sentiments, the common feature of all peasant strata was their involvement in a movement that was democratic and that expressed their interests not so much in the absolute preservation of private property as in the confiscation of the landed estates, the principal form of private property.[5]

Lenin then included the confiscation of landed estates in an extensive agrarian programme which aimed at land nationalisation as the quickest route to socialism under a Worker-Peasant Republic, conceding that there was some substance in the Narodniks' argument of the contradiction between small-scale and large-scale production.[6]

The revolutionary task was to forge an alliance between the proletariat and the peasantry to achieve a decisive victory over Tsarism. The key question here was how to realise working-class leadership in the democratic revolution. Since the issue at the heart of the struggle was that of peasant subordination or independence, Lenin argued that proletarian leadership would encourage the revolutionary activity of the peasants and foster their political consciousness and organisation so as to destroy the old order, not by legal or peaceful means, but by armed uprisings to establish a new order.[7]

Lenin recognised the peasants as an independent force involved in a social war distinct from the workers with their own organisations, the revolutionary peasant committees, which forged the link between the spontaneous struggles for land and the political struggle for democracy. Nevertheless, the democratic revolution would only succeed as a nationwide upsurge of workers and peasants engaged in simultaneous, if independent, strikes in which the towns led the countryside. Although the Narodniks had recognised the progressive aspect of the peasant movement, they had neglected its bourgeois content and had identified capitalism with the landlord path only. They had therefore overlooked the crucial question of how the working class would lead the peasants.

Taking a staged approach, Lenin considered that, whilst the proletariat aimed to forge an alliance with the peasants as a whole against feudalism, power had to pass in the continuing revolution to an alliance with the poorest strata of the rural population in order to secure, through land nationalisation and the soviets, a transition to the socialist stage. Lenin thought that after winning land there would be a strong tendency among the peasants to develop a stake in this private property and resist further changes: only the poor peasants, out of economic interest, would support socialist transformation. Thus he looked to the poor peasantry as the most reliable ally of the urban working class.[8]

As the final outcome of the 1905 revolution produced an alliance between the liberal bourgeoisie and the landlords, Lenin envisaged that the new regime would adopt reforms to promote capitalist agriculture, transferring the basis of Tsarist power from the traditionalist middle peasantry to the rich peasants. Only the proletariat could realise all the peasants' demands for land but, with the defection of the liberal bourgeoisie and the vacillation of the petty bourgeoisie, it was considered that the stakes of struggle in the rural areas involved, as it were, a race between the bourgeoisie and the proletariat for influence over the peasants – a struggle for or against their proprietary instincts. In these conditions, Lenin focused on strengthening the Party and consolidating class organisation, in particular, the organisation of the poor peasants, in order to isolate the influence of the bourgeoisie in the countryside.[9]

Thus whilst conceding to the Narodniks that the middle peasants had a role in the democratic revolution against Tsarist autocracy and the landlords, Lenin, in distinguishing the two possible outcomes of an alliance between Tsarism and the liberal bourgeoisie or a Worker-Peasant Republic, focussed on the class issue within the peasants' struggles against the landlords, that is, the question of bourgeois or proletarian leadership.

It has been suggested however that despite Lenin's repeated calls to organise the poor peasants, it was the middle peasants who were the most militant in the Russian revolution, and further, that the Bolsheviks underestimated the importance of the middle peasants and their own organisation, the *mir*. It was this, together with a failure to come to terms with the difficulties in organising the poor peasants and rural proletarians that is taken by some analysts to account for the weakness of Bolshevik organisation in the countryside, proving most telling in the socialist stage.[10]

What then was the relevance of Russia's experience to China? The Comintern was to play a major role in shaping CPC strategy in the early stages of the Chinese revolution, and Lenin's understanding of the peasant movement and its changing role in the different stages of the revolutionary process was taken as the fundamental guideline.

But were the Chinese peasantry essentially homogeneous small producers or was a polarisation process underway? Agricultural production in China did not divide easily into the three sectors that Lenin had outlined: the absence of a clearly distinguished sector of capitalist farming made it particularly hard to identify potential class groupings within the peasantry. What types of peasants, if any, would serve as revolutionary allies of the proletariat? The weak development of capitalism suggested a tradition-bound undifferentiated peasantry lacking in revolutionary potential as a bastion of the autocratic state. On the other hand, the increasing polarisation between the impoverished masses of peasants and the landlords and rich peasants with their monopoly ownership of land suggested that the middle peasants were a social force in disintegration.

At first, China's revolutionaries were sceptical of any transformative potential existing among the peasants. Largely drawn from the anti-imperialist intelligentsia themselves, they shared the city-based view of the peasantry as traditionalists: ignorant and superstitious, subservient yet also unruly. The peasants were criticised for not acting – not participating in anti-imperialist activities – but then also condemned when they did act. Sun Yat-sen praised the Boxers for their spirit of resistance, but at the same time deplored their excesses as shameful, the acts of bandits.[11] In the view of the CPC's first leader, Chen Duxiu, the peasants had little to contribute to the revolution being too scattered and difficult to organise.[12] However, the views of the CPC started to shift after 1925 as peasants began to organise in associations demanding rent and interest reductions.[13]

Mao and peasant mass power

Mao's *Report on an Investigation into the Peasant Movement in Hunan* issued in early 1927 stood out as a powerful call to recognise the revolutionary energy that existed in the Chinese countryside. It was a challenge both to those in the CPC and on the Left who dismissed the peasantry for their petty bourgeois conservatism, and to those on the other hand who condemned peasant activism as barbaric, excessive and terrifying. Anticipating the likely defection of the KMT leadership, it insisted on the need to unleash the agrarian revolution by mobilising the vast force of impoverished peasants to break the political authority of the landlord gentry. The heart of the matter for Mao, as for Lenin, was the attitude towards mass power.

As Mao saw it, the agrarian revolution was taking place in the peasants' struggle against the landlord system as a whole. Rural discontent expressed not only opposition to government corruption: in the formation of the peasant associations, Mao saw a source of opposition not just to the warlords and bad gentry but to the domination of the villages by landlords through the traditional structures of rural order.

A few months earlier in 1926, he had witnessed an outbreak of violence in a district in Zhejiang province in East China where the peasants caused an insurrection because the landlords had refused to reduce rents when the crops had failed. The peasants burned the police station, distributed the arms, and turned to go to the homes of the village landlord gentry to 'eat up the powerful families'.[14]

On the actions of the Hunan peasants, Mao noted that:

> After the peasants are organised, the first thing they do is to smash the political prestige and power of the landlord class,

especially of the local bullies and bad gentry. i.e. to overthrow the power of the landlords so far as their social position in the countryside is concerned, and to foster the growth of the power of the peasants.[15]

The peasant associations pressed the landlords to fulfil their traditional obligations, for example, in the customary reduction of rent in times of bad harvest. They assumed judicial powers in presiding over disputes, undermining the powers of the magistrates, and organised self-defence, taking over the armed militia of the bad gentry. Under the peasant association even the clan elders dared not embezzle funds which were redirected to finance village schools and defray the expenses of the peasant association.[16] As they took over village organisation and the activities of the clan, the peasant associations reintroduced in their own administrative methods the aspects of self-help that the elders had abandoned. The organised peasantry, so Mao argued, thus challenged both the gentry and the patriarchal traditional order of the village community, breaking the links between the clan and the gentry.

For Mao, then, the essence of the peasants' opposition to the social, political and economic power of the gentry was a struggle for a new form of class power. At this early phase of the movement under the CPC-KMT alliance, Mao was not advocating any particular economic programme either of rent and interest rate reduction or more radical land confiscation: the point was rather that for any economic change in the countryside to succeed, the organisation of the peasants' class power was essential.[17]

The Hunan Report represented the distinct break between reform and revolution in China. In focusing the struggle against the warlords, 'local bullies' and 'bad gentry', the KMT took up the traditional stance of reforming officials acting in the interests of the peasants against corrupt government. For Mao, the question of whether officials were 'clean' or not was a matter of class, depending on whether the peasants had risen to overturn a corrupt administration.[18]

The point was that central and local power, the warlords and the local landlords, were not separate: with economic and political power fused at the social base, the success of the struggle against the warlords and corrupt government depended on the success of the peasants' struggle at the base of society to transform the structure of village power dominated by the local landlords.

Past peasant rebellions had seen dissident gentry manoeuvre to subvert peasant protest, undermining their organisations from within, and subsequently carrying out reprisals against peasant activists. The tenacious influence of the local elites and their political intrigues were to present the CPC with an exceptionally difficult challenge in organising the rural revolution. In Russia, the *kulaks* were a force of opposition against feudalism but, based on China's historical experience, Mao was opposed to drawing the village rich into the revolutionary ranks of the peasants. Rather he noted with approval how, as the peasants became more organised, the small and middle landlords and rich peasants applied to join their associations in vain.[19]

But how was the revolutionary potential of the independent peasant movement identified in the Hunan Report to be explained? Mao also made a point of rejecting any suggestion of a Chinese Narodnik view of a 'backward' peasantry in protest against the encroachment of capitalism. Refuting the notion of the peasants as traditionalists, Mao set out to examine the restrictions placed by the peasant associations on the export of grain from the villages, on the raising of pigs, chickens and ducks, and on sumptuous feasts, which he considered were:

> ...a form of peasants' self-protection against exploitation by the city merchants...As the prices of industrial goods are extremely high and those of farm products extremely low, the peasants are impoverished by the ruthless exploitation of the merchants; thus they cultivate frugality as a means of self-protection. As to the peasants' ban on sending grain outside the area, this was imposed because the poor peasants, not having enough grain to feed themselves, had to buy grain on the market and consequently prevent the price from going up. All these are due to the impoverishment of the peasants and the contradiction between town and country; the peasants are certainly not practising the so-called doctrine of Oriental Culture by rejecting industrial goods or trade between town and country.[20]

This then was not a tradition-bound reactionary 'ignorant' peasantry: rather Mao was to note elsewhere in his report how the villagers were actively breaking through the bonds of feudal patriarchal traditions of clan and temple.

Critical to understanding the revolutionary situation in the countryside was the question of peasant classification. Given that peasant differentiation was less clear-cut than in Russia, analysing the distinct roles of the different sections of the peasants in the agrarian revolution was not so simple. In his earliest work on the *Analysis of the Classes in Chinese Society* (1926), Mao, following Lenin, classified owner peasants among the petty bourgeoisie separate from the semi-proletariat of part owners or semi-tenants and poor tenant peasants. Later he was to drop the owner-tenant demarcation, subsuming issues of tenancy and owner-cultivation under the classifications of rich, middle and poor.

Nonetheless, even at this early stage, as discussed in Chapter 1, Mao was to note gradations between the upper, middle and lower sections of both tenants and owner-cultivators.[21] Differentiating between peasants with a surplus, those struggling to break even and those with a deficit, Mao drew attention to the issue of peasant land insufficiency showing that the owner- and part-owner peasants, far from forming a stable strata or bastion of conservatism, were gradually declining into the marginalised and pauperised section of the rural economy, closer in conditions to those of the poor peasant tenants and semi-tenants.

The revolutionary condition of the Chinese peasantry was to be defined by the agrarian structure – the contradiction between the concentration of land ownership and its fragmented use. It was the deficiency of the small producers whether as part-tenants or marginalised producers that, as Mao was to grasp, was the main cause of their discontent, providing the motive for agrarian revolution.

The Chinese anti-feudal struggle was then of a quite different character from the European movements. Its main forces were not those of emergent capitalist farmers – rich peasants were not an incipient rural bourgeoisie, rather they remained tied to the landlords politically and economically whilst the poorest of the rural population were not so much becoming proletarianised as pauperised on small parcels of land. With the vast majority of peasants losing out both in terms of land ownership and area cultivated, this was not so much a system of owner-cultivation in dissolution under the pressures of capitalist polarisation, as one which was seeing the increasing marginalisation of the middle sector of the peasants.

To follow Lenin in viewing tenants and owner-cultivators as separate sectors of the agrarian economy was essentially to obscure the revolutionary potential of the peasantry as a whole, of the independent as well as tenant peasants. Mao's 1926 analysis of classes pointed more to the similarities than the differences in the positions of the majority of tenants and deficit owner-cultivators, seeing that the latter were most receptive to revolutionary agitation and had a particularly important role to play in the revolution. Not only was there potential for unity between the poorer sections of both the owner peasants and tenants against feudal monopoly interests, but Mao also considered that the middle section of the owner peasants could be drawn into the movement such that even the upper section would be influenced, so uniting the overwhelming majority of the rural population against the feudal and semi-feudal classes.[22]

More so than Lenin, Mao then appreciated the important revolutionary potential of the owner peasants as determined by the distinctive features of the agrarian crisis in China of monopoly land ownership and the peasants' land hunger. But whilst these conditions provided the objective basis for uniting poor and middle peasants, the greatest challenge that the CPC faced in leading the peasant movement was that of framing a land policy that worked to benefit the majority in both the landlord-tenant and the owner-cultivator sectors of the rural economy. Without uniting the poor and middle peasants as the driving force of rural transformation, it would prove impossible to break the power of the traditional local elites over the village order.

Mao's investigations in Hunan had found the poor peasants to be the most prepared to challenge the political authority of the landlord gentry, taking on leading positions in the peasant associations. However, as he came to include the middle peasants among the motive forces of the revolution and a reliable ally of the proletariat, Mao, whilst looking to the poor peasants to take the initiative, came to make unity with the middle peasants the central principle of the anti-feudal struggle.[23]

In fact it was only by applying Marxist methods, using the criteria of exploitation, that Mao was able to mark out the distinct positions of the rich, middle and poor peasants amidst the complex web of rural economic relationships. Combined with his observations of their differing attitudes amidst the shifting dynamics of the revolution, this formed his major contribution to peasant theory in China, providing in practice the means to conduct the anti-feudal struggle on a principled basis targeted against the landlords to bring about revolutionary success.

The process of developing land policy as the basis for peasant organisation was not to be straightforward: it was rather one of painful trial and error. A formulaic application of Lenin's analysis and the Russian example was to prove a hindrance not least in underestimating the role of the middle peasants. The sinification of Marxism was to develop the leading role of the CPC as an independent political force hand in hand with the organisation of an independent peasant movement in a step-by-step process, as Mao refined, through both theory and practice, the analysis and understanding of classes in the Chinese countryside and in the wider revolution.

NOTES AND REFERENCES

1. Lenin, *Collected Works*, Vol.6, pp.444–5.

2. For a further discussion of Lenin's critique of the Narodniks see Ennew, Hirst and Tribe, 1977, especially pp.296–306.

3. See Lenin, *Collected Works*, Vol. 10, p.177; Vol.13, p.291. See also Hussain and Tribe, 1981, esp. Chapter 2: Russian Marxism and the Agrarian Question, pp.55–84, for a discussion of Lenin's change in policy.

4. See Lenin, *Collected Works*, Vol.9, pp.55–8; Vol.13, p.239.

5. Lenin, *Collected Works*, Vol.9, p.98.

6. Lenin, *Collected Works*, Vol.13, pp.229–30.

7. Lenin, *Collected Works*, Vol.9, p.56.

8. Lenin, *Collected Works*, Vol.13, pp.323–4; Vol.9, p.100.

9. Lenin, *Collected Works*, Vol.15, pp.349–50.

10. See Alavi, 1973, p.303; and Shanin, 1972, p.199.

11. Han Xiaorong, 2005, p.20.

12. *Ibid.*, p.21.

13. *Ibid.*, p.52.

14. See Schram, 1969a, pp.248–9.

15. Mao, *Selected Works*, Vol. I, p.35.

16. *Ibid.*, pp.45–6.

17. *Ibid.*, p.35.

18. *Ibid.*, pp.42–3.

19. *Ibid.*, p.24.

20. *Ibid.*, p.54.

21. *Ibid.*, pp.15–6.

22. *Ibid.*, pp.15–18.

23. Mao, *Selected Works*, Vol. III, p.92–3.

13
China's first revolution and the CPC-KMT United Front (1924–1927)

From revolutionary upsurge to defeat

The CPC was formed in 1921 amidst the intellectual ferment that followed the betrayal of China's interests in 1919 at the Versailles Peace Conference following World War 1, at a time when a more politically conscious urban proletariat was beginning to emerge onto the political stage. A massive Hong Kong seamen's strike in 1922, in which both the CPC and KMT were involved, saw an influx of workers into both parties. Meanwhile the politicisation of the intelligentsia was to spread to the national bourgeoisie who in 1925 responded to the call for a boycott of Japanese goods not least since buying national products instead was to their own benefit.[1] As the national revolution surged forward under the leadership of the KMT and Sun Yat-sen, it split with the warlords and became a mass party in 1924, increasing worker and peasant membership and clarifying its aims to drive out the militarists, reduce rents and extend democratic rights. CPC members were allowed to join as individuals and be elected to all positions and, in line with the advice of the Comintern, the Party adopted a strategy of cooperation with the KMT. This United Front was seen as the realisation of the anti-imperialist alliance of the workers, peasants, petty bourgeoisie and national bourgeoisie.

In May 1925, huge student demonstrations in support of striking workers ended in violence with the death of a number of Chinese at the hands of foreign police under British command. Following the incident, the KMT, supported by the CPC and the Soviet Union, prepared to launch their Northern Expedition sending its armies northwards to overturn the warlords and unite the country. At this time, peasant protests against the landlords began to rise. The CPC saw the Northern Expedition as an opportunity to mobilise workers and peasants on a mass scale. Organisers, Mao amongst them, were sent to the rural areas in advance of the KMT army to assist the peasant associations. With the KMT troops beginning their northward march in July 1926, millions of workers and peasants were organising, but ultimately the CPC was to suffer a massive defeat by the autumn of 1927 as the leadership of the KMT turned to crush the social revolution.

The main questions for the Communist movement in the Chinese revolution throughout this period concerned the role of the national bourgeoisie and the relationship between the anti-imperialist national struggle and the agrarian revolution. The CPC at this time tended to attach greater importance to the alliance with the KMT than to organising the peasants' struggles. However, there were differing perspectives on the issues not only between Stalin and Trotsky but also among the Chinese communists from the CPC leader, Chen Duxiu, to Mao Zedong. Underlying these differences, but obscured by the focus on the rights and wrongs of the KMT alliance, were quite different attitudes towards the peasants.

For Stalin, the main difference in the character of the Chinese revolution from that of the Russian revolution was that the former was anti-imperialist. Since China was an oppressed nation, this meant that the national bourgeoisie could play a progressive, even revolutionary, role unlike the liberal bourgeoisie in Russia, an oppressing nation.[2] Stalin then advocated CPC cooperation with the KMT to realise an anti-imperialist 'bloc of four classes', the logic being that, given the small size of the working class, only by joining up with the forces of the national bourgeoisie did a Party, which stood for the organised workers, stand a chance. Secondly, based on the assumption that the peasantry formed a rural petty bourgeoisie interested in private property, it was thought that the rural producers would follow the leadership of the KMT nationalists.

The Comintern was instrumental in negotiating the United Front agreement in 1924 according to which the KMT 'should be the central force of the national revolution and should assume its leadership', a condition whereby the CPC became an integral part of the KMT.[3] Chen Duxiu, accepting that the working class as too weak to lead, was in favour of the arrangement of reliance on the national bourgeoisie in the democratic stage of the revolution, arguing that this would promote capitalism and hence the growth of the working class. The struggle for socialism would then have to await this development.[4]

Whilst promoting the CPC-KMT alliance, Stalin also understood that the national bourgeoisie had tendencies to compromise and that Communists would of necessity have to pass from the United Front bloc of four classes to a revolutionary bloc of two classes, the working class and the peasants, as the revolution progressed. This transition might nevertheless be accomplished under the banner of the KMT as this transformed through mass mobilisation from a party of the revolutionary petty bourgeoisie.[5]

However when Chiang Kai-shek seized the leadership of the KMT in March 1926, imposing restrictions on CPC organising within its ranks, the Party was faced with a dilemma. Nevertheless, it was decided to remain within the KMT and pursue efforts to build up the strength of worker and peasant organisation within the four-class bloc.

With peasant organisation going from strength to strength, the Executive Committee of the Comintern, at its 7th plenum in November 1926 declared the movement was entering a period of revolutionary action. As with the Russian revolution, it was seen to have reached that critical juncture of transition between the choice of alliance with the bourgeoisie or with the peasantry.[6] Stalin now emphasised the need for an agrarian programme to draw the peasants into the revolution and admonished the CPC leadership for Right Opportunism: in his opinion, what had allowed Chiang's March coup to succeed and to subsequently consolidate his position was insufficient effort by the CPC to intensify the agrarian and labour movements. But at the same time, Stalin was against withdrawal from the KMT, calling for mass mobilisation in both cities and countryside to push the Nationalist party towards more radical policies in opposition to Chiang's efforts to turn it into a party of the bourgeoisie alone. In rural areas, just as in Russia, the focus was to become the struggle over class leadership of the peasant movement.

By January 1927, according to Mao's Hunan Report, the peasants were ready to rise 'like a tornado'. At the centre of the movement was the challenge of the poorer peasants – 70 per cent of the rural population – to the political authority of the local landlords, a challenge capable of breaking China's semi-feudal semi-colonial condition at its very base. In this way, the peasants would provide the main force of resistance against counter-revolution as their associations took over the armed forces of the local landlords and formed their own militia. Even where small landlords and rich peasants were allowed into the peasant associations, it was the poor peasants who took the leading roles, paving the way for revolutionary rural government.

The KMT's advance to the Yangtze River set off a further wave of strikes in the cities of Central China, and Wuhan came under the control of 'Leftists' in the KMT. However, the national and agrarian movements were beginning to diverge. On the one hand, the mounting revolution in the countryside exposed the failure of the urban-based KMT to develop a genuine agrarian programme to meet the peasants' demands. Leading KMT officials and many of its army officers had landed connections, holdings which came under threat as the peasant movement escalated. Increasingly, the CPC found itself caught between the pressure of the mass revolutionary actions and the effort to maintain the KMT alliance.

Reaction came with Chiang Kai-shek's massacre of communists in Shanghai in April 1927. The communist forces experienced a massive blow. However, the situation in Wuhan became more and more radicalised as the 'Left' KMT split with Chiang's right-wing leadership, consolidating its position amidst a wave of mass strikes which swept the city. Stalin took Chiang's move as a sign that the national bourgeoisie had defected to the counter-revolution leaving the petty-bourgeoisie at the head of the revolution. He then called on the CPC to continue to cooperate with the 'Left' KMT in Wuhan now seen to be the revolutionary centre of a three-class bloc with continuing opportunities for the CPC to push for radical policies of social revolution, organising the peasants in preparation for armed struggle.

The peasant movement in the surrounding Hunan province was rising to the ascendancy: with some nine million members joining peasant associations nationally, and peasants stepping forward in the wake of the KMT armies' advance to disarm landlord militia, the agrarian revolution, now recognised as the central component of the revolutionary struggle, was to be intensified.[7] To resist the counter-revolution and break the power of the local gentry, Stalin called for the movement to advance systematically under the slogan of land confiscation, with peasant associations to take over the government in the rural areas. At the same time, he was to warn against excesses in the mass movement.[8] However within the CPC a debate broke out over whether to extend the revolution, advancing further against the warlords, or to deepen revolutionary action at village level with Chen Duxiu opting for the former, a choice which meant a greater reliance on the Wuhan army rather than the mobilisation of the peasants. Seeing this choice as incompatible with land reform, he proposed to postpone the intensification of the agrarian revolution to a later stage. Instead, he adopted a moderate agrarian programme focusing the peasants' struggle against warlords and 'bad' gentry by limiting land confiscation to large estates only.[9] But even this was to prove too much for the 'Leftists' of the Wuhan government who preferred to remain reliant on its army rather than arm the peasants: whilst prepared to advance a programme of radical rent reduction, they were reluctant to support land confiscations which would alienate the landowning officers.[10]

As peasants began taking matters into their own hands in land takeovers, the Wuhan government criticised the peasant associations for 'going too far' and further blamed the CPC for the 'excesses' of the mass movements.[11] Then in June, the Wuhan leadership turned against the labour and peasant organisations and by July the last links between the CPC and KMT were ruptured. Only a small section of the 'Left' KMT continued to resist the reactionary trend against revolutionary advance.

Taking this now as the betrayal of the revolution by the petty bourgeoisie, the CPC attempted to seize the leadership of the revolutionary movements of the workers and peasants, shifting to a strategy of rebellions and uprisings aimed at coordinating strikes in town and countryside. The Nanchang uprising led by Zhou Enlai in August took the first step of armed resistance to KMT reaction. In September, Mao led the Autumn

Harvest Uprising, replacing the banner of the KMT now with an independent political programme of armed struggle for land.[12] Stalin meanwhile, still reluctant to finally abandon the KMT, was to criticise the uprisings as 'putschist'. It was not until November 1927 that he was prepared to call for the shift in the revolution to a new stage, only then advising the CPC to take up arms for the establishment of soviets with a programme of land nationalisation.[13]

The uprisings met limited response in the towns but the peasants were extremely radicalised, carrying out complete confiscation of land and eliminating private ownership, burning leases, cancelling debts, pulling down land boundaries and gathering together all oxen, ploughs and pigs for public use, pooling not only land but tools, animals and personal possessions so as to practice 'farming together and eating together'.[14] However, these attempts at insurrection, the CPC's first step towards leadership of a nationwide revolution, ended in failure by December 1927, and the CPC's already decimated forces suffered further damage.

The CPC's defeat was clearly the result of serious political errors. But what exactly were these errors? Stalin and the Comintern blamed Chen Duxiu's leadership for carrying out Right opportunist policies against their instructions – not sufficiently criticising the KMT and at times acting as a brake on the mass movements.[15] In particular, Chen had failed to unleash the agrarian revolution following the defection of the KMT leadership. This verdict was supported at the 6th Congress of the CPC in 1928 as it set out the path for the way forward.

Others, most notably Trotsky, criticised Stalin himself for insisting that the CPC maintain its alliance with the KMT even after Chiang's Shanghai massacre in April 1927. But it was also clear that the CPC leadership, very dependent on the advice of the Comintern, was lacking in both policy and experience. Neither the Comintern nor the CPC were up to the challenge of handling the dynamics and divergences that emerged within and between the national and the agrarian revolutions.

Trotsky's critique of the Comintern's United Front strategy

Trotsky had opposed the policy of collaboration with the KMT which in his eyes was essentially the party of the Chinese bourgeoisie. As he saw it, the CPC's slavish adherence to Stalin's policies had 'strangled' the revolution: the bourgeoisie had gained a victory precisely because the Chinese proletariat had been prohibited by the policies and instructions of the Comintern which held to the alliance with the KMT even when it was attacking the working class.[16]

Trotsky argued that the impact of foreign capital and the development of commerce had brought about a fundamental change in the landowning classes with the convergence of landlords, merchants and officials linked with the city bourgeoisie and increasingly integrated with the world capitalist system. In his view then, the alliance with the bourgeoisie in carrying out the national revolution against imperialism was fundamentally misconceived; in fact, the struggle against the remaining feudal elements was fundamentally bound up with a struggle against capitalism. He therefore rejected Stalin's formula of the 'four class bloc' since it enabled the national bourgeoisie to destroy the workers' revolutionary movement in preparation for achieving a bloc between the national bourgeoisie and imperialism. In such a bloc, Trotsky claimed:

> ... the big bourgeoisie leads the petty bourgeois democrats, the phrasemongers of the national united front, behind it, and the latter, in turn, confuse the workers and drag them along behind the bourgeoisie. When the proletarian 'tail', despite the efforts of the petty bourgeois phrasemongers, begins to stir too violently, the bourgeoisie orders its generals to stamp on it. Then the opportunists observe with an air of profundity that the bourgeoisie had 'betrayed' the national cause.[17]

As Trotsky saw it, the policy of alliance with the KMT converted the CPC to its appendage and acted as a brake on worker and peasant organisation. He believed Stalin was completely mistaken in his view of the KMT as a bloc inclusive of workers and revolutionary peasants, and was further mistaken in assuming that the national bourgeoisie could play a progressive role when it was, as he, Trotsky, argued, intrinsically tied to foreign capitalism and opposed to the working class.[18]

Following the Shanghai massacre, Trotsky further maintained that the CPC should have foreseen the desertion of the 'Left' KMT to the side of counter-revolution. Again Stalin was mistaken in his assessment of the Wuhan government as a 'prototype worker-peasant democratic dictatorship'.[19] Instead of supporting the 'Left' KMT, Trotsky argued, the CPC should have called for soviets, organising the armed struggles of the workers and peasants.[20] Failure to do so for fear of provoking the KMT implied a reliance on the national bourgeoisie and a restriction and sacrifice of the revolution.

For Trotsky, Stalin's assessment in 1927 that, despite the betrayal of the national bourgeoisie, the mass movement remained in a directly revolutionary situation on a nationwide scale with the initiative in the hands of the CPC was an illusion: the national bourgeoisie had never supported the revolution so had not 'betrayed' it. In fact, as Trotsky saw it, the revolution had been defeated and was in decline with the decimation of the working class base of the CPC, so Stalin's notion of the possible emergence of a democratic dictatorship of workers and peasants was a total fallacy. There could be no intermediate stage in China: the only choice was between a bourgeois or proletarian dictatorship. Writing in October 1928, he stated:

> ... if the revolutionary policy had been correct, if the Communist Party had been completely independent of the Kuo Min Tang, if the Soviets had been established in 1925–1927, the revolutionary development could have already led China today to the dictatorship of the proletariat by passing beyond the democratic stage.[21]

A worker-peasant democratic dictatorship based on an alliance with the peasantry as a whole was an impossibility since, for Trotsky, there were only two choices for China: an alliance of the proletariat with the poor peasants or an alliance of the bourgeoisie with the rich peasants. To oppose the dictatorship of the proletariat then with the formula of democratic dictatorship was to drag the revolution backwards.

This view was confirmed for Trotsky by what he saw as the seeds of socialism in the Canton Uprising of December 1927 which, though untimely, saw the soviet government proclaiming 'workers' control of production through factory committees, the nationalisation of big industry, transportation and the banks,' and even the confiscation of the dwellings and property of the bourgeoisie for the benefit of the nation.[22] Through its socialist acts and proletarian methods, the Canton government had proved for Trotsky the irrelevance of the democratic programme, pointing the way forward to the next stage of socialist revolution and proletarian dictatorship. Evidently taking the peasant excesses as a struggle against capitalist exploitation, he urged that the proletariat be directed towards the task of organising the poor peasants against the rich peasants and bourgeoisie in preparation for a socialist victory. Trotsky blamed Stalin's failure to recognise the defeat of the revolution as entirely responsible for the subsequent 'putschism' and weak leadership of the three uprisings, which only facilitated the destruction of what remained of the proletarian organisation by the already victorious enemy.[23] On the other hand he maintained that, had the CPC organised the soviets beforehand, there might have been more chance of success.

Disputing Stalin's analysis of the national bourgeoisie, Trotsky also took a different position on rural capitalism to claim that the task of the proletariat was to win leadership of the poor peasants' movement:

> Large and middle-scale land ownership [as it exists in China] is most closely intertwined with urban, including foreign, capitalism. The most widespread, generally hated exploiter in the village is the usurious wealthy peasant, the agent of urban

> banking capital. The agrarian revolution has therefore as much of an anti-feudal as it has of an anti-bourgeois character in China. The first stage of our October revolution, in which the wealthy peasant marched hand in hand with the middle and poor peasant, and frequently at their head, against the landlord, will not, or as much as will not, take place in China. The agrarian revolution there will be from the very beginning, and also later on, an uprising not only against the few landlords and bureaucrats, but also against the wealthy peasants and usurers…The breaking up of the rich peasants will be the first and not the second step in the Chinese October.[24]

His view of the revolution in the countryside was one which essentially dismissed the middle peasants as virtually non-existent:

> In China, every peasant uprising is, from the start, a civil war of the poor against the rich, that is, against the village bourgeoisie. The middle peasantry in China is insignificant. Almost 80 per cent of the peasants are poor. They and they alone play a revolutionary role. The problem is not to unite the workers with the peasants as a whole but with the village poor. They have a common enemy: the bourgeoisie. No one but the workers can lead the poor peasants to victory. Their mutual victory can lead to no other regime but the dictatorship of the proletariat[25]

In effect Trotsky ruled out any role for an independent peasant movement. He saw the increasing differences of wealth among the rural population, exacerbated by the spread of commoditisation and the monetarisation of the economy with its involvement in world capitalist markets, in terms of the polarisation between the bourgeoisie and the proletariat. But it is here that the error of his analysis is exposed. Integration with the world capitalist market had not brought about a fundamental change in the predominant form of surplus labour in China. Money rent existed only on a small scale and was primarily a transmuted form of rent in kind, taking all the surplus and cutting into the necessary labour of the tenant, arising not like differential rent from differences in land productivity but from the private monopoly of land.[26]

Trotsky's assessment of the national bourgeoisie as a reactionary rather than a progressive force, intent on attacking the working class, was also incorrect. Insofar as the industries owned by the national bourgeoisie catered for the domestic market, which was restricted by feudal relations and disrupted by the wars between warlords, whilst imperialist ascendancy prevented any possibility of its expansion, these Chinese capitalists were capable of supporting revolution for the sake of national unity to allow economic growth. This stance was to be witnessed by the funds contributed by Chinese industrialists to the Hong Kong strikers in 1925.

Chen Duxiu's hesitancy

Chen stood accused by Stalin and the 6th Congress of the CPC of adhering to the line of the United Front and KMT leadership of the national revolution at the expense of mobilising the peasants. But was this a fair critique? Did Chen hold back the peasant revolution and was he mistaken to do so?

Critics have drawn attention to his widely quoted view that the peasants were too scattered and difficult to organise, making it hard to bring them into the revolution. Nevertheless, as Guo has pointed out, Chen went on to say that they were capable of becoming 'a mighty force in the national revolution….one day, if organisation were to be provided…'[27]

In pushing the blame for the failure of the revolution in 1927 onto the CPC, the Comintern's criticisms of the leaders' failure to organise the peasants were not entirely accurate. Chen certainly encouraged work among the peasants from 1925 and the CPC's programme to establish peasant associations built a powerful movement involving millions in the months that followed. But it was during the Wuhan period after Chiang's massacre had polarised the situation among the nationalists, that Chen's main error occurred as he failed to go on the offensive to win the leadership of the KMT.[28]

Stalin and the Comintern at this time had urged the CPC to advance the agrarian movement further under the slogan of land confiscation, calling for peasant associations to win leadership in local government in order to gain political power in the countryside and to organise a peasant army. The aim was to exercise leadership within the KMT rather than splitting with it by drawing in large numbers of workers and peasants so as to transform the class character of the party from within. Chen on the other hand had opposed more radical proposals to confiscate all landlord land, postponing the question of land reform, and instead prioritising the United Front against the warlords and imperialism. His limited reforms were deemed to slow down the revolution, leaving the local gentry in control in the rural areas where they maintained a base for the counter-revolution.

It was not that Chen did not recognise the links in the overall system of feudal and imperialist exploitation. As their understanding of the peasants' role in the revolution deepened, the CPC, and not just Mao, shifted from seeing imperialism, the warlords and the local landlords and gentry all as independent factors, gaining an appreciation of how the political power of the landlords at local levels, with its roots in feudal exploitation, served as the main base of imperialism and warlordism.[29]

Chen's limited programme of land confiscation aimed to neutralise the small proprietors, both urban and rural.[30] In this, it apparently drew on the moderation of the Russian Bolsheviks who had sought to promote unity with the rich peasants as emergent capitalist farmers in a bourgeois democratic revolution directed against feudalism. But limiting land confiscation to the large landlords only was not enough to satisfy the demands of the peasants. Acceding to the complaints of the Wuhan 'Left' KMT leadership as spontaneous land confiscations spread, Chen criticised egalitarian tendencies among the poor peasants, pointing out how 'an exaggerated policy of attack' had emerged in the peasant upsurge. This attitude of 'overturn everything and do as you want', he thought, had brought conditions of terror to the villages'.[31]

A few months earlier, in his Hunan report, Mao had taken quite a different point of view: responding to criticisms of the peasants as 'going too far' in parading the gentry through the streets wearing tall paper hats, Mao argued that 'to right a wrong' it was necessary to 'exceed the limits', and even 'to impose a brief reign of terror in every rural area' in order to break the counter-revolutionaries and overthrow the authority of the gentry.[32] Schram has claimed, on grounds such as these, that Mao's practice was characterised by an extreme voluntarism.[33] However Lenin too, it should be noted, following the defection of the liberal bourgeoisie recognised the necessity of unleashing the full force of the peasants as a whole against landlord power despite their limitations in class consciousness and even reactionary views.

Chen had sought to restrain the actions of the poor peasants in order to protect and neutralise the rich peasants, but for Mao the poor peasants formed the backbone of the agrarian revolution. Whilst they might commit mistakes, their enthusiasm should not be dampened by restricting their activities. On the peasants' efforts to ban the export of grains from localities, Chen and Mao took a very different position. Chen, whilst noting that these bans had been introduced to serve the interests of those who suffered from food shortages, pointed out that the practice 'severed the economic artery of urban-rural trade': the important issue for him was that, in focusing against feudalism, protection should be afforded to the urban-rural capitalist economy.[34] Mao, on the other hand, as has been seen, made a particular point to reject the portrayal of such bans as an expression of an anti-industry 'Oriental Culture': they were the actions of impoverished peasants against unequal exchange between town and countryside.

With regard to mistakes on the part of poor peasant leaders, Mao favoured education not condemnation, opposing the sending of soldiers to make arrests lest this undermine the prestige of peasants.[35] However, whilst Chen recognised that the problem of 'excesses' should not be used against the worker-peasant movement, he evidently saw such tendencies as obstacles in the bourgeois democratic revolution, noting that the peasant bans on grain deprived the army of supplies. In a telegram of June 15, 1927, to the Comintern, highlighting the difficulties of mobilising the peasant movement without upsetting cooperation with the 'Left' KMT, he pointed out that the officer corps of the Wuhan government's armed forces:

> ...comes mostly from the small and middle land-holding class; thus their sentiments are averse to land reform. What the soldiers talk about among themselves is not so much confiscation of land as the 'excesses' committed by the peasant movement....
>
> Such "excesses" have prompted the soldiers who are of small or middle property-holding background to combine with the village gentry and other exploiters into an anti-communist, anti-peasant front.[36]

Criticisms that Chen held back the revolution, relying on the KMT armies rather than the peasant movement to protect and extend the gains of the revolution, therefore have some legitimacy. Mao on the other hand had emphasised the necessity of arming the peasants since March 1927. But was it actually possible to follow Stalin's advice to take control of the social revolution without a split with the KMT under the circumstances at the time?

Stalin reassessed: a question of conflicting goals?

Saich has argued that the Comintern's instruction to the CPC to promote the national revolution in cooperation with the KMT ran counter to its other instruction to pursue the social revolution since this brought it into conflict with powerful elements within the KMT.[37] He therefore claims that Chen's mistake was in fact Stalin's mistake in underestimating the difficulties in balancing between the nationalist movement and the movements of workers and peasants. But were the demands of the national and agrarian revolution fundamentally incompatible?

The CPC's task to bridge the urban and the rural and forge a new relationship between town and countryside as the basis of the revolutionary class alliances presented enormous challenges. The cities and the countryside had their own political dynamics, at times running counter to each other. There were tensions within the CPC itself between urban and rural organisers. The Northern Expedition, for example, confronted resistance from territorial peasant organisations and, whilst the CPC decided to support the Nationalist march against the warlords, there was opposition among some of its pro-peasant activists.[38] Those working in the countryside found greatest success when their activities were integrated into existing rural practices and forms of organisation, such as crop-watching and village defence. But from an urban perspective, these organisations were feudal and protected the landlords. The factionalism, anarchism and parochialism that characterised peasant protest, the individualistic and charismatic styles of the rural leadership cliques, the tendencies of banditry, plunder and violent extremism which emerged within peasant movements, all these clashed with the urban aspirations for democracy which motivated the national movement.[39]

The spontaneous seizures of land by the peasants made Stalin's advice to adhere to the KMT alliance more and more difficult to follow during the Wuhan period. The problem was, on the other hand, that moderate land reform favoured by the 'Left' KMT fell well short of satisfying the peasants' land hunger. Zhou Enlai was to maintain that Chen's approach to revolution remained within the frame of bourgeois legality.[40] However it was not so much that peasant radicalism jeopardised the United Front against imperialism: there were tensions between the national and agrarian revolutions and these could only be resolved through proletarian leadership uniting the peasants in mass mobilisation to break the hold of feudal forces at the local levels which served as the power base for the warlords and imperialist forces.

Confined within bourgeois legality, there was virtually no discussion in the CPC of concrete methods and policies of land confiscation. Whilst Stalin had suggested that the peasants' excesses should be dealt with by their own organisations rather than with the help of troops, no guidelines had been established as to how these were to be handled.[41] Observing the chaotic conditions, Chen noted that any distinctions between independent self-cultivator peasants, small property-holders who rented out land, and 'local bullies', had become completely blurred, resulting in a 'widening of targets'.[42] His criticism of 'Leftist excesses' in particular drew attention to the divisions that emerged among the peasants as their movement surged. Noting the egalitarian practices of the unemployed and landless wanderers who wanted 'not only to divide up the land equally but to share all kinds of property' he argued that these 'could not but lead to conflict with the tenant farmers and independent peasants.' Similarly, the ban on the export of grain from the localities 'prevented the broad mass of the independent peasants who possessed a surplus from exchanging it for the necessities of daily life'.[43] Such contradictions of interest among the peasants were essentially a matter for proletarian leadership to resolve.

Chen evidently had misgivings about unleashing the peasant movement under these conditions despite Stalin's urging. But this failure to rely on the mass mobilisation of the peasantry as the force against the counter-revolutionary turn of the KMT at this critical point of struggle between the bourgeoisie and proletariat for leadership of the peasant movement left the direction of the revolution to a national bourgeoisie too weak to lead.

Zhou Enlai suggests that the reason why Chen hesitated to promote mass activism when it became necessary for the CPC to take the lead lay in the difficulties the CPC had in understanding how the proletariat could lead a bourgeois democratic revolution. Rather they saw their role as assisting the bourgeoisie to lead in the first stage, only stepping up to the forefront to take the socialist direction at a later stage. This, as Zhou confirms, was contrary to the advice of Stalin and the Comintern, for whom the purpose of the United Front was not to support the leadership of the bourgeoisie but to strengthen the position and influence of workers and peasants in the KMT.[44]

Although Saich tends to absolve Chen as he attempts to push the blame back onto Stalin and the Comintern, he raises a key point in highlighting the resistance of powerful elements in the KMT to the CPC's social mobilisation. Stalin's United Front strategy rested on the assumption that the Chinese bourgeoisie, like the Western bourgeoisie, would support agrarian reforms against feudalism to expand the internal market.[45] But this proved to be mistaken: Chiang and other KMT leaders had certain nationalist sympathies but nevertheless turned to sabotage the CPC's work in organising the workers' and peasants' struggles as the revolution progressed. Even the 'Left' KMT leadership at Wuhan was not in favour of the confiscation of the landlords' land.[46]

Where Stalin and the Comintern erred was in underestimating the influence of the compradore bourgeoisie and large landlords on the nationalist movement as well as the links of the KMT to the countryside: although less so than the big bourgeoisie, the urban-based national bourgeoisie still retained roots in the countryside as landowners. As a result, they tended to vacillate over the question of land reform. With the nationalist leaders in the KMT susceptible to the influence of the reactionary classes, it was not so straightforward as Stalin thought for the CPC to 'push the KMT to the left' by organising the workers and peasants without a struggle for leadership.

It would be true to say that under Chen's leadership the CPC had not taken the opportunities that had existed, however the failure of the 1927 revolution was primarily due to the overwhelming predominance of the counter-revolutionary forces and the lack of a revolutionary army.[47] The nationalist and peasant movement had pulled apart as the KMT right strengthened the militarist elements whilst the 'Leftist' excesses of rural poor exacerbated contradictions among the peasants, complicating mass organisation. The CPC lacked the political maturity and the practical organisational strength to tackle the contradictions that arose.

Overall, this was a failure of class analysis: at this stage neither the Comintern nor the CPC had a grasp of the distinctive features of China's national democratic revolution and how it differed from the European path, with China's semi-feudal and semi-colonial conditions restricting the development of capitalism so creating a weak and vacillating national bourgeoise reluctant to meet the peasants' demand for land, together with a semi-feudal, semi-capitalist rich peasantry also prone to side with the counter-revolution.

It was only through further experience in peasant organisation and land reform that the CPC learnt how to handle the particular class contradictions, to unify the peasant movement and to find the balance between the national and the agrarian revolutions, thereby taking charge of the revolutionary situation overall. The national revolution against feudalism and imperialism could only succeed backed by the strength of mass mobilisation of the peasants, through the overthrow of the landlords' rule in a transformation of the land system. The key to revolutionary success then lay in the development of policies and methods to unite the peasant movement in carrying out the agrarian revolution.

NOTES AND REFERENCES

1. Chesneaux and others, 1977, pp.118–9.
2. Stalin, 1940, p.205.
3. See Claudin, 1975, p.276–7; p.227.
4. Wang Hongmo, 1985, pp.17–8.
5. Stalin, 1940, p.189.
6. See Mavrakis, 1976, p.136.
7. Ho Kan-chih, 1977, p.78.
8. Stalin, 1940, p.213; p.218.
9. See Ho Kan-chih, 1977, pp.78–80
10. *Ibid.*, p.83.
11. *Ibid.*, p.82.
12. See Schram, 1969a, pp.56–7.
13. See Zhou Enlai, 1981, p.196; Guo Dehong, 1981, pp.19–21. In August 1927, Stalin was prepared to amend his view of a two-stage transition from a four-class bloc passing to a two-class bloc into a three-stage view: unlike the Russian revolution, the Chinese revolution would pass from the United Front of four classes with the national bourgeoisie supporting the revolution against imperialism to a second stage of agrarian revolution against feudalism, with the growth of the peasant movement and the defection of the national bourgeoisie, and then thirdly reaching the stage of the Chinese

14. Guo Dehong, 1981, pp.21–2.
15. See Schram and Carrere d'Encausse, 1969, pp.232–3.
16. Trotsky, 1967, pp.39–40.
17. *Ibid.*, p.31.
18. *Ibid.*, p.21.
19. *Ibid.*, p.274.
20. *Ibid.*, p.42.
21. *Ibid.*, p.189.
22. *Ibid.*, p.124.
23. *Ibid.*, p.160; p.213.
24. *Ibid.*, p.125.
25. Trotsky, 1973, p.21.
26. As discussed in Chapter 2.
27. Guo Xuyin, 1984, p.60.
28. Zhou Enlai, 1981, p.190.
29. Guo Xuyin, 1984, p.54.
30. Guo Dehong, 1981, p.18–19.
31. Guo Xuyin, 1984, p.60.
32. Mao, *Selected Works*, Vol. I, p.27. The differences between Chen Duxiu and Mao on the revolutionary nature of the peasants, including the issue of 'peasant excesses', are also discussed by Womack, 1982, esp. pp.63–73.
33. Schram, 1969a, p.79; p.125.
34. Guo Xuyin, 1984, pp.60–1.
35. Mao, *Selected Works*, Vol. I, p.33.
36. Cited in GuoXuyin, 1984, p.62.

soviet revolution. Stalin, 1940, p.207.

37. Saich, academia.edu, accessed: 27/4/2020.
38. See Chao Kuo-chun, 1960, p.16; Ho Kan-chih, 1977, pp.61–2. According to Marks, 1984, p.219, Peng Pai was vehemently opposed to the Northern Expedition.
39. See Marks, 1984, pp.215–7, for the example of Peng Pai's methods in organising a peasants' union: rather than attacking traditional beliefs, he endeavoured to infuse them with a new content. See also Perry, 1980, pp.215–7 for references to debates within the CPC at this time over whether rural oppositionist organisations were revolutionary or feudal.
40. Zhou Enlai, 1981, p.179.
41. Stalin, 1940, p.218; Guo Dehong, 1981, p.17.
42. Guo Xuyin, 1984, p.59.
43. *Ibid.*, pp.60–61.
44. Zhou Enlai, 1981, pp.178–9; p.190.
45. Swarup, 1966, p.58.
46. Zhou Enlai, 1981, pp.186–8.
47. *Ibid.*, p.183.

14

From the towns to the countryside – rethinking revolutionary strategy

On the nature and character of the revolution

Following the defeat of 1927, the CPC had to face up to the future prospects for the revolution. Since in Trotsky's eyes, the Comintern and CPC had allowed the national bourgeoisie to win the democratic revolution, he envisaged that there would now follow a relatively long period of counter-revolution with the political consolidation of the ruling classes, including the national bourgeoisie, with imperialism.[1] Policies of economic stabilisation and the introduction of Stolypin-type reforms would foster the rural bourgeoisie.[2] With the likelihood of a new upsurge rather remote, he thought that the CPC should focus on rebuilding its bases in the cities, concentrating on legal struggles, in preparation for the sharpening of class contradictions over time as economic revival saw the regeneration of the working class and consequently a new build-up to socialist revolution.[3]

For Stalin, what Trotsky took as a revolutionary decline in the face of bourgeois victory was, in fact, a temporary low ebb, a trough between two waves, given that in fact none of the democratic aims of the revolution had been fulfilled: imperialism and feudalism remained the main obstacles making reforms in agriculture impossible. It was therefore in the hands of the CPC to resolve both the national and the agrarian question. With urban protests at a low ebb but peasant actions continuing, Stalin saw the nature of the Chinese revolution as uneven, the ripples or waves of rural uprisings an indication that a new upsurge in the form of peasant revolution was imminent. He then called on the CPC to prepare for a new nationwide upsurge of workers and peasants.[4] The Comintern at the same time warned against 'Left putschism' and the adventurism of the three uprisings, advising the Chinese communist activists to combat the trend towards scattered, spontaneous and unconnected partisan peasant uprisings: these could only become a starting point for a national upsurge on the condition that they were linked and co-ordinated through the struggles of the proletarian centres.[5]

The 6th Congress of the CPC which met in 1928 attempted, under Comintern guidance, to correct the past mistakes of Right Opportunism and 'Left Adventurism', emphasising on the one hand reliance on methods of mass mobilisation, at the same time criticising 'putschism'.[6] Prior to the Congress, according to Zhou Enlai, Stalin had clarified the issue of proletarian leadership by pointing to the role of the proletariat in the 1905 revolution in Russia.[7] This helped to explain the importance of developing an independent peasant movement. It had also helped to clear up the influence of Trotskyist adventurism which had conceived the Wuhan period in terms of the Russian transition between February and October 1917, and had then called to accelerate the revolution. This was seen to have exerted an influence on the subsequent excesses of the three uprisings – 'burning towns and killing landlords' – in a struggle mistakenly directed against the bourgeoisie, petty bourgeoisie and rich peasants.

The Congress confirmed the bourgeois democratic nature of the revolution, endorsing Stalin's general strategy for the United Front period of transitioning to agrarian revolution, pushing the KMT to the Left under proletarian leadership through the organisation of the mass struggles in the cities and the countryside. But with the national bourgeoisie seen now to be collaborating with imperialism and feudalism, leaving the petty bourgeoisie vacillating, the Congress resolved to take the workers and peasants as the main forces of the revolution and to focus on the organisation of trade unions and peasant associations to build soviets in preparation for the nationwide upsurge.

Countering Trotskyist influence, the Congress rejected the conception of permanent revolution and instead highlighted the uneven nature of the struggle. This helped in identifying the adventurist weakness of the three uprisings in their failure to distinguish between ebb and upsurge in the tide of revolution. Against 'Leftism', the Congress resolved not to intensify the struggle against the rich peasants, but to focus on feudal relations in accordance with the democratic aims of the revolution. It was further resolved to drop the programme of land nationalisation: agrarian reform was to be directed at the confiscation of landlords' land, establishing peasants' private ownership in the soviet bases. Despite these correctives, some ambiguity on the role of the rich peasants pointed to a persisting controversy as to the actual nature of the agrarian revolution.[8]

However, the conclusion of the Congress that the responsibility for the failure of the revolution lay with leadership's policies of restraining the mass movement, as has been seen, was not entirely correct. Mao for one had taken the opportunity to organise the peasants in preparation for the Northern Expedition's advance. Criticised by Stalin for adventurism in the Autumn Harvest Uprising, he was however not a delegate at the 6th Congress and, according to Zhou Enlai, this made it difficult to draw on the lessons of the 1927 revolution in an all-round way, that is, including the experiences in peasant organisation.[9] It meant that, whilst resolving to take the agrarian question as the central issue of the revolution, the Congress nevertheless still looked to the recapture of its proletarian base in the urban areas as of paramount importance, and, following the Russian example, continued to prioritise workers' struggles.

With its working-class bases all but wiped out by Chiang's White Terror, the CPC focussed on the need to develop working-class activists to lead the whole revolutionary movement as a matter of urgency. Leaders of working-class origin, rather than those with experience of peasant organisation, were promoted, with the Comintern advising that the dangers of Right Opportunism and 'Left Adventurism' were to be overcome by strengthening the proletarian base of the Party and proletarian leadership over the peasantry.[10] Conditions in China however differed from those in Russia given the overwhelming predominance of the peasantry and the relatively small working class, and given the weakness of the CPC itself as the political organisation of the working class in relation to the rising peasant movement. The failure to sum up the experiences of the peasant movement was to lead to further Rightist, but also mainly 'Leftist', errors in the subsequent period of the second revolutionary civil war from 1927 to 1937.

Over these 10 years, as the CPC confronted the challenge of building bases in the countryside cut off from the cities, it came to realise that the source of independent strength, which it had lacked in its subordination to the KMT in the United Front, lay in the organised peasant movement. To make this political breakthrough, however, it was to prove necessary to abandon the 1905 conception of a city-based nationwide insurrection involving simultaneous strikes in town and countryside with the peasants following the lead of the working class actions. This took a lengthy process with different policies and practices being implemented in the different base areas, as those areas under Mao's leadership, learning from mistakes, began to develop strategies to deal with the resistance of the traditional local elites to a radical programme of village transformation.

Stalin, Li Lisan and the question of a nationwide revolution

After 1927, whilst the workers' organisations in the cities had been decimated, in the rural areas the Red Army and the soviet bases continued to grow, providing dynamic new forces for the revolutionary movement. With such a weak base in the cities amongst working-class activists, the question facing the CPC was how to sustain its organisation so as to exercise proletarian leadership over the peasant upsurge and advance the democratic revolution as a whole.

Now under the leadership of Li Lisan, the CPC organised a number of insurrections between June and September 1930, mobilising the Red

Army from the rural bases to which it had retreated, in an attempt to capture a number of towns and cities. Li saw the rising peasant movement as a means to regain an urban-based influence: his expectation was that the insurrections would spread rapidly and spontaneously, unleashing an outbreak of workers' struggles in a few key cities and that, following victories in one or two provinces, this would bring about a countrywide revolutionary socialist upsurge.[11] With this end in mind, Li sought to apply a land policy in the base areas which contained certain socialist measures including the establishment of collective farms.

When Li's attempts at insurrection met with defeat, the Comintern criticised him for adventurism: following a line of permanent revolution, he had, it said, abandoned the organisation of the peasants to concentrate on revolution in the cities. But was Li in fact following Comintern instructions which, pointing to signs of a new revolutionary wave developing in 1929, had advised him to overcome 'petty bourgeois waverings' and take the initiative?[12]

In defence of Li it has been suggested that he was in effect scapegoated for mistakes which emanated from Stalin: from a Trotskyist perspective, it was Stalin's positive view that a revolutionary upsurge was on the horizon that encouraged what was in effect a partisan army without working class leadership.[13] However, Stalin and Li differed over whether the revolutionary situation was one of 'low ebb' or 'high tide': whilst Li thought that uprisings would spread rapidly and spontaneously, developing through victories from province to province into a revolutionary escalation across China as a whole, Comintern leaders were opposed to this notion of bringing about an 'immediate nationwide revolution.'[14]

For the Comintern however the role of peasant war gave the revolution both a wave-like and uneven character, making it necessary to distinguish between the peasant upsurge and the overall revolutionary situation in the country as a whole. Li had made the mistake of equating an upsurge in the peasant movement with an immediate revolutionary situation when in fact the waves of peasant protest could lead to a nationwide revolutionary situation only if the overall conditions were favourable. Failing to appreciate the uneven character of the revolution, and not understanding that the objective situation was one of a low ebb, Li had led insurrections which were impulsive and 'putschist'. At the same time, he had overlooked the actual subjective weakness of the revolutionary forces and so had failed to develop the political organisation of the democratic revolution, instead adopting socialist measures prematurely.[15]

It should be noted that Li's city-seizure strategy had roots in the traditions of China's 'roving bandit' groups and armies which plundered towns and cities.[16]. Retreating to the mountainous regions, the CPC initially found in these least developed areas its most willing supporters among other outcast groups – secret society chiefs, leaders of local brotherhoods were all recruited into the guerrilla units. To account for this Polachek has pointed out that the main difficulty confronting the CPC in carrying out the agrarian revolution through land reform in the soviet bases after 1928 was the traditional closure of local communities against outsiders. He highlights how in his area of study, between 1929 to 1933, the CPC, unable to gain a foothold in the localistic, territorial lineage organisations of the native settlers, relied instead on Hakka immigrant communities who were more open to outside influence.[17]

Perry discovers a similar situation: finding the traditional local defence organisation of the Red Spears resistant to outside interference of any sort, the CPC cadres turned their attention instead to the rival predatory 'Bare Egg Society'.[18] Marks' study of the short-lived Haifeng Soviet in 1927 also reveals the millenarian characteristics of peasant rebellion with a personality cult around the leader Peng Pai, drawing into the CPC a large influx of new members with no training or experience. As Marks points out, this form of peasant power based on individualistic leadership was prone to impetuous action.[19]

These case studies point to a wider problem – soviet power in the rural bases was often a far cry from the realisation of democratic power based on the worker-peasant alliance. Peasant power instead expressed itself on the one hand in bandit-style adventurism and on the other in traditional parochialism and antipathy to outsiders, with leaders setting up 'independent kingdoms', a tendency known as 'mountaintopism', using their high personal status to gather a mass following. Party organisation tended to absorb the localist patterns of closure, with branches formed by members of the same surname group where branch meetings were in effect clan gatherings.[20] Power often remained in the hands of elite-led coalitions and cliques, whether with territorial local defence or bandit and secret society connections, which maintained their hold over the peasantry on the basis of territorial, lineage and blood brother loyalties, and the CPC would find itself embroiled in factional struggles as between the 'Bare Eggs' and the Red Spears.

No doubt it was then a scepticism of peasant power that caused the Communist leaders – both Li Lisan and the Comintern – to look to the towns and cities to generate new forms of mass democracy, new activists and a new leadership for the agrarian revolution: in their view, only by linking with workers' organisations in the urban centres would the peasant revolution be victorious.

Whilst criticising the 'Li Lisan line' of capturing the cities, the Comintern still adhered to the view that the movement of real significance was that of the workers' strikes in the towns. Although it considered peasant war as revolutionary due to its mass nature, and called on the CPC to pay attention to peasant organisation, the Comintern held that, in a nationwide revolution under proletarian hegemony, the movement in the towns would play the central and leading role. It then consistently urged the CPC to focus on proletarian organisation and to develop its base from working-class cells in the cities. Whilst coming to recognise the successes of the Red Army, the Comintern nevertheless considered its weaknesses in organisation and social composition as liable to 'putschism', directing that it become a workers' as well as a peasants' army.[21]

After the failure of Li's insurrections, Stalin was prepared to give greater recognition to the independent regimes in the rural base areas and accepted the role of the Red Army. Nevertheless the Comintern was still warning the CPC in 1931 that the predominance of peasant membership in the organs of revolution made these prone to conservatism or adventurism, stating:

> The hegemony of the proletariat and the victorious development of the revolution can be assured on the condition that the Chinese Communist Party become a proletarian party not only as regards political line, but also as regards its composition and the role of the workers in all its leading organs.[22]

The peasants were essentially conceived as a subordinate ally of the working class: the need to link peasant organisation in the soviet rural bases with workers' organisation in the urban centres was seen as the fundamental condition for proletarian leadership.

Li Lisan's policies then, whilst caught up in traditional forms of protest, in fact were also influenced by the Comintern. Despite the differences, both shared in common the strategy of an urban-centred nationwide revolution based on coordinated uprisings in the towns and countryside. However, a completely different perspective on the Chinese revolution was to be developed in the CPC base in the Jinggang mountains under the leadership of Mao Zedong.

Revolution from the independent bases of peasant democratic power

The **Autumn Harvest Uprising** of 1927 had marked a turning point for Mao as, seeing how the peasants persisted in their struggle, taking up arms against the landlords' counter-offensive, he grasped that only a revolutionary army could lead the agrarian struggle, which stood at the centre of the Chinese revolution, to victory.

Following the defeat of the uprising, Mao retreated with his forces to set up the first rural revolutionary base area in the Jinggang mountains.

From there he, with Zhu De, developed an innovatory military strategy using guerrilla warfare in the countryside to surround the cities. This was to change the whole form of the revolution as it concluded that the strategy of first attracting the masses on a nationwide scale and then establishing political power did not correspond to the actual situation in China. The democratic revolution instead was in essence a peasant revolution with a protracted as well as uneven nature.

The Comintern had recognised the uneven character of the revolution in the waves of upsurge and ebb on the part of the mass movements, but Mao was to point out in addition the uneven nature of the counter-revolutionary forces. He maintained that whilst the counter-revolutionary forces were strong in the cities, making mass organisation difficult, in the economically less developed areas of the countryside, least integrated into the market and beyond government control, the opposite conditions prevailed. Here, the revolutionary forces of the peasants were stronger relative to the counter-revolution, and whilst the warlords, backed by the different imperialist powers, struggled for influence over China, it was possible, amidst the rivalries in the counter-revolutionary camp, for bases of independent political power to be established in these small remote areas.[23]

This meant that, different from the Russian experience, it was not necessary for the CPC to go through a long period of legal struggle or political agitation to win the support of the people on a mass scale before launching insurrection and war. Nor was it necessary to seize the cities first and then occupy the countryside. In China, the situation was the reverse since the imperialist question resolved itself into the peasant question such that the revolution was already being carried out in the armed struggle of the peasants against the armed counter-revolution.[24]

According to Mao, it was this possibility of building bases in the countryside independent from the urban centres that gave the revolution its protracted nature. Through the implementation of land reform policies to develop a mass peasant movement, the establishment of these bases would be vital in bringing about a new upsurge with the growth of the agrarian revolution contributing to the development of a revolutionary situation nationwide.[25]

For Trotsky, the perspective of national revolution based on the prior establishment of bases of independent political power, opened up by the 'isolated Chinese communists' organising peasant armed struggle, was 'the perspective of a terrific debacle and of adventurist degeneration of the remnants of the Communist Party.'[26] With the liquidation of the working class bases of the CPC, he saw its increasing peasant membership as a 'menacing process', the persistence of peasant uprisings no more than a 'mere echo' of the city battles of 1927.[27] It was impossible in his view for the peasants to create soviets independently: under no circumstances, he stated baldly, could peasant war be substituted for the dictatorship of the proletariat.[28]

As has been seen, Trotsky considered conditions in China were such that only a struggle for socialism was capable of mobilising the masses and, since working class organisations had been decimated, this was still a long way off from realisation. Stalin, on the other hand, maintaining that the revolution was still in its democratic stage with the establishment of a worker-peasant democratic dictatorship an imminent possibility, attached far greater importance to the role of the peasantry and to their organisation. No mere reflection of the workers' battles, the persisting struggles of the peasants were rather indications of a new revolutionary situation on the horizon. Nevertheless, the peasants were still essentially a junior partner to the proletariat.

Stalin's understanding was that the Chinese revolution differed from the Russian revolution only because of the national question and insofar as the national question resolved itself into the peasant question. Holding to the conception of the revolution based on the Russian experience as a nationwide simultaneous upsurge of workers and peasants, Stalin did not recognise that the uneven situation also gave the Chinese revolution a protracted character. This allowed for the creation of new regimes of independent political power based on peasant organisation forming a new democratic social order against landlordism in isolated bases in the countryside. Thus Stalin essentially underestimated the significance of peasant war, the Red Army, and the establishment of regimes of independent power as the cornerstones of revolutionary strategy.

In contrast with Trotsky's negativity, Mao shared Stalin's greater optimism that the subjective conditions of peasants' traditional consciousness could be developed and transformed through struggle, and that the peasant movement would develop through the political organisation of the democratic revolution. He also agreed with the Comintern criticism that Li Lisan, in advancing to a socialist programme, had neglected the subjective factor. However he saw the Comintern's criticisms of Li's policies being premature as unduly pessimistic, downplaying the role of the Red Army and the rural soviets because it saw the important factor as the strength of the CPC's working-class base.

For the Comintern, the transformative factor in raising peasant consciousness and forms of protest was to be the link with the working class: the organisation of the peasant movement in the soviet bases was essentially preparatory to the revolutionary stage of taking the cities. Mao's strategy on the other hand was to rely on the peasants' political and military organisation. For him, the establishment of bases of independent political power was not merely a preparation for the revolution – it meant that the revolution was actually taking place as part of a protracted process in the countryside with the creation of a new political and social order. The weakness of Li's 'putschism' from Mao's perspective was its failure to grasp the importance both of work among the masses of peasants in connection with land reform as well as the armed struggle prior to, and in the process creating, a revolutionary situation: he should not have tried to spread the revolution without having established independent bases and, through the process of peasant organisation, creating in these areas a new form of political power.

Stalin had criticised Li's insurrectionist tactics on the grounds that these disregarded the uneven development of the objective situation, but Mao in fact was to question the whole strategy directed at the conquest of the cities. Li's tactics were a reflection of the distinctive Chinese bandit style, but the perceived urgent need for a working-class base to provide proletarian leadership over the peasant movement also exerted pressure for the premature use of armed forces to conquer the towns.

As Zhou Enlai was to argue later, Li's mistakes found their origin in the strategy adopted at the 6th CPC Congress with the approval of the Comintern which, in failing to highlight the central problem of peasant land, peasant armed struggle and the need to establish independent regimes, was essentially urban-oriented.[29] Without recognition of the subjective importance of these factors in contributing towards the development of revolution through the organisation of the peasant mass movement, the CPC's search for a working class base only gave rise to 'putschism'.

Zhou attributed these weaknesses in part to the impact of the Comintern's criticisms of the CPC in the aftermath of 1927 which had identified the errors of the CPC leaders in terms of their class origin. This then led to mistakes at the 6th Congress as just mentioned which gave status to delegates of working-class origin instead of learning from the experiences of people like Mao in organising the peasants' armed struggle to carry through the land revolution.[30]

Rather than focusing on proletarian leadership in relation to the workers' movement in the cities, Mao was to take the countryside as the centre of operations so prioritising the need to address the problems of organising and guiding the peasant movement as the main content of the democratic revolution. The CPC leadership had sought to tackle the problems of the 'mountaintopism' – the tendency for elite-led bandit-style coalitions setting up 'independent kingdoms' in the various revolutionary base areas – through the centralisation of power; however Mao, whilst supporting centralisation, also sought to tackle traditions of militarism by creating a different type of army in the Jinggang mountain base. Peasant war was to be fought by a new style of army involved not only in warfare but in political and productive work, with equal treatment of officers and men, and with discipline established on the basis of training and education not physical coercion.[31]

Mao's revolutionary strategy of guerrilla struggle, using bases in the countryside to surround the cities in a protracted war, changed the perspective on the relationship between the proletariat and the peasantry. Contrary to the views of the Comintern and CPC leadership, Mao saw the organisation of the struggles in the countryside and the expansion of the Red Army as a necessity in assisting the struggle in the cities and accelerating the revolutionary upsurge. Whilst it would be a mistake to abandon the struggle in the cities:

> ...it is also a mistake for any of our Party members to fear the development of the power of the peasants lest it become stronger than the workers and hence detrimental to the revolution. For the revolution in semi-colonial China will fail only if the peasant struggle is deprived of the leadership of the workers, and it will never suffer just because the peasants, through their struggle, become more powerful than the workers.[32]

From subordinate allies of the proletariat, the peasants and their independent struggles were brought by Mao to the centre stage. His focus was then to shift to problems of leadership and peasant mobilisation, finding new methods and approaches in land reform and revolutionary democratic organisation at village level in order to develop the mass movement and consolidate independent soviet political power in the rural areas. These were to be based on a clearer analysis of the rural classes and a closer understanding of their behaviours.

NOTES AND REFERENCES

1. Trotsky, 1967, p.176.
2. *Ibid.*, p.209. Stolypin issued an agrarian law in 1906 to break up the peasant commune which Lenin argued would promote the development of *kulak* farms.
3. *Ibid.*, pp.183–4.
4. See Zhou Enlai, 1981, p.198.
5. Schram and Carrere d'Encausse, 1969, p.243; see also Swarup, 1966, p.206.
6. Zhou Trotsky, 1967, pp.177–210, for an account of the conference.
7. *Ibid.*, p.188.
8. Swarup, 1966, p.121; Guo Dehong, 1981, pp.27–8.
9. Zhou Enlai, 1981, p.194; pp.209–10.
10. *Ibid.*, pp.206–8.
11. See Mao, *Selected Works*, Vol. IV, 1967, pp.178–9.

12. See Saich, academia.edu, accessed: 27/4/2020.
13. Isaacs, 1962, p.330; see also Schwartz, 1968, pp.156–63.
14. Hsiao T-L, 1961, pp.25–6; Zhou Enlai, 1981, pp.197–8.
15. See Ho Kan-chih, 1977, p.105.
16. Huang, 1978, p.11.
17. Polachek, 1983, p.825.
18. Perry, 1980, pp.218–224; see also Huang, 1978, p.8, on the fusion between the CPC and the local Triad lodge at Xingguo county.
19. See Marks, 1984, pp.184–9; pp.224–9, on the cult of Peng Pai.
20. Mao, *Selected Works*, Vol. I, p.94.
21. See Schram and Carrere d'Encausse, 1969, p.244.
22. In Schram and Carrere d'Encausse, 1969, p.246. See also Zhou Enlai, 1981, p.201. Zhou notes that when he attended the Comintern International in 1940, all the leading comrades were still worried that the CPC was too far separated from the working class: 'I said that after we had been tempered through protracted struggles in the villages, it was entirely possible for us to become proletarianised…some comrades of the Comintern were quite shocked when they heard this view and took exception to it.' (1981), p.201.
23. See Mao 'Why Can China's Red Political Power Exist?' (1928); 'The Struggle in the Ching Kang (Jinggang) Mountains' (1928); 'A Single Spark Can Start a Prairie Fire' (1930), all in *Selected Works*, Vol. I. See also Womack, 1982, pp.96–101, on the early development of Mao's ideas of protracted, rural-centred revolution from 1929. Womack highlights what he calls Mao's interstitial tactics in the context of China's semi-colonial conditions which opened the possibility of exploiting hostilities among warlords backed by rival imperialist powers.
24. Mao, *Selected Works*, Vol. II, p.267.
25. Huang, 1978, pp.18–20.
26. Trotsky, 1967, p.229.
27. *Ibid.*, pp.154–5.
28. *Ibid.*, p.299; p.233.
29. Zhou, 1981, p.204.
30. *Ibid.*, pp.182–3; pp.198–9; pp.209–10 for Zhou's summary of the mistakes of the Congress; and pp.209-l0 for a discussion of the impact of the Comintern's criticisms on the CPC.
31. Mao, *Selected Works*, Vol. I, pp.80–2.
32. *Ibid.*, pp.122–3.

15

The land revolution, soviet power and the dynamics of peasant class struggle

Li Lisan, the '28 Bolsheviks' and the rich peasant question

The major challenge faced by the CPC in carrying out land reform in the remote mountain areas in the South was the tenacity of the traditional local elites. Patron-client ties and lineage organisations were especially strong in these regions where factionalised alliances of large landlords encompassing wide areas took the opportunity to exploit divisions among the peasantry at grassroots levels. The lower strata of the elite, the village-based small landlords and rich peasants who served as lineage heads, village patrons and elders, would remain in the countryside after the large landlords had retreated to the towns, continuing to seek to influence the peasants in order to limit their struggles. This 'intermediate class' would resist land redistribution by obfuscation and foot-dragging. Alternatively they would sabotage reforms from within, directing the changes in such a way as to protect their own position and properties. If the agrarian movement began to advance against them, they would defect to the counter-revolution; however, so long as they remained a presence in the soviet areas this kept open the possibility for the large landlord and KMT forces to return and re-establish their positions.[1]

The 6th Congress had taken the CPC's land programme forward, rejecting the limited reforms of Chen Duxiu in favour of a policy of confiscation of all landlord land. At the same time, the radical approach of the complete confiscation and equal distribution of land followed during the three uprisings was criticised as 'an illusion of petty bourgeois socialism'. These extreme measures, it was observed, met considerable obstruction from the 'intermediate' class, who, having suffered blows during the revolutionary upsurge, had been driven into opposition. It was also seen to have threatened the excess properties of the middle peasants, encroaching on their interests.[2]

However, the 6th Congress failed to agree more precise guidelines on methods of land confiscation and land distribution and, whilst it set out the general line of taking the poor peasants as the 'main force of the proletariat in the countryside' to unite with the middle peasants, policy regarding the rich peasants was left unclear.[3]

The *Resolution on the Peasant Question* viewed rich peasants as allies in the democratic revolution against the landlords, exempting their land from confiscation, and it resolved not to intensify the struggle against them or oppose them unconditionally, noting how they would quickly turn to the counter-revolutionary camp. However, the *Resolution on the Land Question* did not appear to include the rich peasants as a revolutionary force. Contrasting the European struggle for land as that of petty proprietors asserting rights to ownership against the entrenched landed system with the struggle in China against land monopoly, it stated:

> The force behind the peasant struggle for land is not the struggle of the petty bourgeoisie for utilising land for a profit, but of completely impoverished and landless peasants…and those who have not yet completely suffered confiscation (and in addition) of those self-cultivating farmers who have little land and who mightily strive for independence of business to cast off or escape the exploitation and oppression of the feudal system.[4]

The 'rich peasant question' was to preoccupy the CPC leadership for the following years until 1935, with policy shifting under a series of leadership changes from Li Lisan to the group of '28 Bolsheviks' and finally to Mao.

Li Lisan had adopted a two-staged approach, exercising leniency towards the rich peasants in the early phases of the movement according to the line of the *Resolution on the Peasant Question*, whilst later applying certain socialist measures to consolidate the soviet bases. However, when he was removed from power in September 1931, the '28 Bolsheviks' who took over the key positions in the central organs of the CPC criticised his 'rich peasant line' as Rightist. This new leading group, recently returned from studying in Moscow where they had sided with Stalin against Trotsky, followed the Comintern view that the difficulties in leadership in the soviet bases had stemmed from the 6th CPC Congress resolution not to intensify the struggle against the rich peasants. According to this view, Li, in making concessions to the rich peasants in the initial stages of the agrarian movement, had allowed them to infiltrate the peasant organisations.

The '28 Bolsheviks' reverted then to a more radical policy towards the rich peasants. Whereas Lenin had seen the possibility of the *kulaks* playing a positive role in struggles against feudal property relations in the Russian revolution, the new CPC leadership did not consider this to be the case in China: as they saw it, the strong ties of the rich peasants with the landlords gave them a feudalistic character. Rich peasants then were not to be treated as allies in the democratic revolution: Li had failed in initially adopting a lenient approach rather than struggling against them from the start.[5]

At the same time the new leadership rejected Li's second stage socialist land law which aimed to annihilate the rich peasants in the soviet bases, as premature. Whilst Li saw the class struggle as continuous with an immediate transition to socialist revolution and the elimination of private property, the '28 Bolsheviks' considered that the prospects for a nationwide revolution were long-term rather than immediate and that therefore, in the democratic stage of the revolution, soviet power had to guarantee the system of peasants' private land ownership.

The '28 Bolsheviks' turned their attention instead to breaking up the elite-led coalitions seen to have gained entry into many CPC branches and the village soviets under Li's policies of leniency. The cliques of bandit leaders, gamblers, and secret society elements which had joined the revolutionary forces as the CPC linked up with outcast groups were thought to be not only adventurist but also quick to compromise with the counter-revolutionary forces. The new leadership was to adopt a centralised approach, pursuing an anti-rich peasant line within the frame of top-down political and military structures to control localistic tendencies, at the same time bolshevising the Party and soviet organs of power by recruiting members from a working-class background and by setting up poor peasant leagues.

Land confiscation and land redistribution

During both Li Lisan's and the '28 Bolsheviks' leadership periods, Mao was to develop his own policies of land confiscation and land distribution in the Jinggang mountain base and later in the Jiangxi Soviet. Swarup has argued that the roots of Mao's different approach may be found in the line of the *Resolution on the Land Question* which, by not explicitly including the rich peasants as a revolutionary force, marked a new departure from the European model of agrarian revolution emphasising peasant land hunger instead.[6]

Rather than following Li Lisan's 'rich peasant' line, Mao had in 1928 continued to pursue a radical programme of complete confiscation of both rich peasants' and landlords' land in an effort to eradicate the traditional village elites and carry out a more thorough land reform.[7] Nevertheless, in line with the analysis of the 6th CPC Congress, he had noted how the programme of land nationalisation under the Canton Soviet attacked not only the big and middle landlords but also the smaller landlords and rich peasants with the effect that 'the intermediate class' − the small village based landlords and rich peasants − 'deserts to the enemy as soon as the White Terror struck'.[8] He noted:

> In the early period of the revolution, the intermediate class apparently capitulated to the poor peasantry, but in reality they took advantage of the former social position of the poor peasants, as well as of their clannishness, in order to threaten them and delay land redistribution...In this period the poor peasants, having been long ill-treated and feeling uncertain about the victory of the revolution, often accepted the proposals of the intermediate class and dared not take positive action. Positive action is taken in the villages against the intermediate class only at a time of real revolutionary upsurge...[9]

Observing the strength of clan sentiment over class consciousness in the villages, Mao saw how the local elites were able to maintain control over the peasants and obstruct land reform, so providing opportunities for the large landlords to restore their influence. He further observed:

> When the revolution in the country as a whole is at a low ebb, the most difficult problem in the areas under the independent regime is our lack of firm hold on the intermediate class. The intermediate class turns traitor to the revolution mainly because it has received too heavy a blow. But when the country as a whole is in revolutionary upsurge, the poor peasantry gains courage because it has something to rely upon while the intermediate class dares not get out of hand because it has something to fear.[10]

When the revolutionary movement was on the rise, the small landlords and rich peasants would placate the peasants and send them gifts, but in a 'low ebb' the intermediate class would attach itself to the big landlords, leaving the poor peasants an isolated force. Organising peasant struggles then presented a dual and interlinked challenge: averting the landlords' subversion of the peasants' organisations as well as avoiding the dangers of extremism.

From the experiences of peasant upsurge and revolutionary defeat in 1927 and 1928, Mao then drew lessons as to the errors of both Rightism and 'Leftism'. Having rejected Li Lisan's approach of leniency to the rich peasants in 1928, from 1929 he also then began to shift away from the policies of complete confiscation to focus on the takeover of the land of the landlord classes only, including the small landlords' as well as public or clan land.[11] In doing so, in July 1929 he introduced the stipulation that land owned by the peasants was not to be touched.[12]

Aimed at correcting Li Lisan's 'rich peasant line', the Land Law of February 1930, drawn up with Mao's sponsorship, adopted an egalitarian approach to land redistribution set out in the principle to 'draw on the plentiful to make up for the scarce, and draw on the fat to make up for the lean'. Nevertheless, allowances were to be made for rich peasants to retain some of their holdings as Mao observed that, whilst engaging partly in feudal exploitation, they became dissatisfied if land redistribution left them with idle capital.[13]

In 1929 and 1930, Mao was learning lessons about the importance of protecting the interests of the middle peasants as well as taking account of the dual characteristics of the rich peasants who, whilst engaged in feudal exploitation, were also tied in to the peasant economy in terms of farming and land use, and were concerned with the utilisation of their capital.

However, Mao differed with Li Lisan not only on the question of land confiscation but more significantly on the criterion of its redistribution: whether this should be on a *per capita* basis or according to labour power.[14] At the heart of the issue here was the further question of uniting the poor and middle peasants.

Li Lisan's Land Law distributed land according to labour power, a method which was essentially generous to the rich peasants, benefitting the better-off families with greater numbers of able-bodied members whilst providing no solution to a considerable proportion of the peasant population – those poorest families whose members were too young or too old to work, or were incapacitated.[15] As a preventive measure against the perpetuation of dependency relations within villages, Li called for the takeover of public or corporate land by the soviets to be run as collective farms worked by hired hands, supporting a welfare system of relief for the very poor who lacked labour power.[16] In practice however, cliques of the village elites were able to use collective farms as a means to retain control of public lands and take advantage of joint productive efforts, using these deceptive means to slow down the peasants' efforts to distribute the land.[17]

Mao on the other hand adopted the practice of redistributing land on a *per capita* basis. Evidence from surveys revealed that despite the variations in land utilisation, land ownership and forms of rent and tenancy from village to village, in fertile and infertile districts alike, the number of middle peasants in general exceeded the proportion of land owned by them.[18] The significance of this fact meant that the majority of middle – owner or part-owner – peasants thus stood to gain from *per capita* land distribution: it meant that the opportunity to make up their land deficiency provided owner peasants with a motive for opposing the feudal land monopoly and supporting land confiscation.

Per capita land distribution catered for families without labour who could gain an independent income by renting out their land to rich peasants with excess means of production.[19] Mao favoured the break-up of public lands for redistribution; he also proposed the allocation of land to hired hands, that is, their re-peasantisation, as well as the allocation of land to be farmed by the landlords for a living.[20] Whilst Li placed socialist-type restrictions on the purchase, sale and leasing of land in the soviet areas to prevent the re-emergence of a landlord class, Mao's *per capita* land distribution confirmed the peasants' right to private property in line with the bourgeois democratic stage of the revolution.[21] The *per capita* criterion was then seen as the main means of increasing the peasants' enthusiasm for land reform, effecting a unity between poor and middle, owner and tenant peasants, against the efforts of the traditional village power-holders to foment division.

When the '28 Bolsheviks' took over the CPC leadership, Mao initially supported their policies. He was in agreement on the need to establish democratic not socialist power, and on preventing the small landlords and rich peasantry from retaining their leading roles in the village communities. He supported the efforts to centralise Party and soviet organisation as a means to break up the traditional leadership cliques.[22] Where he differed was in their approach of rich peasant 'annihilation' and 'eliminating the landlords physically and the rich peasants economically'.

Aimed at undermining the local elites, radical land laws had been adopted to confiscate the land not only of landlords but also of rich peasants.[23] Measures included depriving landlords from owning any land to make a living, even sending them to labour camps, and allotting rich peasants infertile land only.[24] But where the '28 Bolsheviks had criticised Li Lisan as a Rightist, Mao was also concerned with his 'Leftist' errors, linking these with the tendency to over-estimate the development of capitalism in the countryside. Li's view that the agrarian struggle would pass quickly on to the socialist stage appeared, like Trotsky's, to misinterpret peasant extremism against all forms of wealth and private property as a struggle of the rural poor against capitalism.

Mao's initial support of the radical land laws of the '28 Bolsheviks' was, Lotviet suggests, reluctant: he did not wish to openly defy the CPC leadership.[25] In fact he had already begun to move away from the egalitarian principles of the February 1930 Land Law as he observed that it turned middle peasants with excess holdings hostile to the revolution.[26] Following the foundation of the Jiangxi Soviet in November 1931 under his leadership, he was to adopt a more moderate policy to avoid alienating the middle and rich peasants. It was this, as Mao came to understand from his observations of peasant dynamics in the upsurge and ebb of the agrarian movement, that was to be the crucial factor to the success of the CPC and of the revolution.

The '28 Bolsheviks': bolshevising the Party, the poor peasant leagues and the middle peasant question

The struggle of the '28 Bolsheviks' against Right opportunism and the 'rich peasant line' took on a new direction in 1933 as a land investigation drive turned its focus onto the soviet officials and the Party members themselves.

In a number of areas where the traditional local elites had gained positions in the soviets under Li's policies of leniency, the results of land reforms had been uneven with some benefitting more than others. As the CPC saw it, these elements had put on 'revolutionary masks' changing from open to underground resistance to obstruct the process and, relying on their traditional superiority, had taken the opportunity to 'snatch the fruits' of the revolution. Consequently the activism of the masses had been hindered and the majority remained poor.[27] A second round of land confiscation and redistribution was then to be carried out, whilst the cadres were to be put under investigation to uncover any clan and localistic ties.

The particular concern of the CPC leadership was that the persistence of landlord and rich peasant influence had left poor peasants with only a minor role in village affairs. The failure to counter rich peasant leadership was seen to be rooted in 'peasant conservatism' and the 'lack of class consciousness among the middle peasants'. The small peasants were considered not only to be amenable as producers to proletarian leadership but also as private proprietors they were equally susceptible to bourgeois influence. The CPC leadership considered the difficulties in establishing soviet power among the peasantry in the light of what they saw as the revolutionary betrayal by the national bourgeoisie which had its influence on the rich peasants who also turned traitor in the heat of the struggle. Proletarian leadership was seen to face a dual task of intensifying the struggle against the rich peasants to curb their political influence in the initial stages of the agrarian movement, and then of containing the vacillations of the small peasants by countering the influence of the bourgeois betrayal whilst confirming the democratic nature of the soviet regimes.

From the point of view of the '28 Bolsheviks', since the middle peasants were a vacillating element, the role of poor peasants as the only reliable ally of the proletariat had to be emphasised in the struggle against rich peasant leadership.[28] In line with the recommendation of the Comintern, priority was to be given to the organisation of the farm workers' unions and poor peasant leagues in order to bolshevise the leadership and ranks of the Party and consolidate soviet power.[29] The aim was to sharpen the class consciousness of the wavering small producers to counter the political influence of the rich peasants and to expose and eliminate counter-revolutionaries, 'comb[ing] out all the secret agents of the landlords and rich peasants who have sneaked into the Party and the soviet organisations'.[30]

Poor peasant leagues were to be initiated by committees of hired hands founded with the primary purpose of opposing the rich peasants.[31] Following the purge on local leadership, these were to lead the new round of land reform mobilising the poor peasants in a redistribution of the 'fruits' which had been misappropriated by the landlords and rich peasants.[32] The overriding priority then of land reform was to meet the demands of the poor peasants: their interests were not to be sacrificed nor was it correct to give in to the middle peasants for the sake of consolidating an alliance with them.[33]

The conduct of the new campaign in fact varied from place to place across the different base areas with land policies undergoing constant revision.[33] As it developed, differences began to emerge between the central soviet government, which was under Mao's leadership, and the Central Committee of the CPC under the '28 Bolsheviks' over the second land redistribution measures and methods of bolshevising of the Party and mass mobilisation.

Mao became concerned that, as the CPC leadership turned its attention to address Right Opportunism, its renewed radicalism and emphasis on class organisation was driving the landlords and rich peasants into an impasse whilst inhibiting the middle peasants.[35] It was at this point that he made significant policy breakthroughs in prioritising unity with the middle peasants and also in exercising a certain leniency in economic rather than political terms to neutralise the role of the rich peasants rather than mobilising the poor peasants to intensify the struggle against them.

Whilst the Central Committee of the CPC looked to the class organisation of the poor peasants to deal with the landlords and rich peasants, Mao was to develop a different focus:

> We must concentrate all our efforts [especially our alliance with the middle peasants] in coping with the resistance of the landlords and rich peasants. At the present time, there must not be any confusion in the ranks of the peasants themselves.[36]

The limited success in agrarian reform indeed reflected the efforts on the part of the landlords and rich peasants to hinder the struggle, but equally, as Mao saw it, there were weaknesses in the organisation of the revolutionary forces. A second land redistribution risked targeting those peasants who had gained land under reforms already carried out, causing disorganisation and division among the peasants. These conditions could only play into the hands of the former power-holders who, even when they were excluded from the new power organs, would still attempt to manipulate village politics using the new village leaders as their agents in their efforts to restore their position through their patriarchal influence. The danger in the land investigation drive was that the CPC would get increasingly drawn into the factionalism and competitive strategies of the traditional elites rather than building a new social order of soviet power.[37]

The methods of the '28 Bolsheviks' emphasising poor peasant class sentiment and reasserting radical land policies, were problematic for Mao in that these tended to endanger the middle peasant alliance, and it was precisely when the peasants were divided that the traditional elite intrigued to preserve their influence. Giving priority to the demands of the poor peasants risked widening land confiscation to target middle peasant holdings.[38] Organising the rural proletariat together with the semi-proletariat separately also risked directing the struggle not just against the rich peasants but also the well-to-do middle peasants since they also hired labour. Such an approach would be particularly disruptive in the areas where many former poor peasants had gained from land redistribution to attain middle peasant status: these now had a stake in their new properties and often hired labourers on a daily basis.[39]

In practice, in fact, the organisation of poor peasant leagues and farm workers unions proved to be very difficult. Given the lack of capitalist development, the rural proletariat in China was very small and easily isolated. On the other hand, the economic circumstances of land hunger amongst owner as well as tenant peasants created a huge force of potential opposition against the feudal land monopoly and feudal power.

Whilst objective conditions provided the basis for unity between poor and middle peasants, Mao warned of the danger of egalitarian excesses rousing fears which would cause the middle peasants to panic.[40] As the previous experience of the three uprisings had shown, the pursuit of absolute equality in living standards had led to attacks on those middle peasants whose production, either through high yields or surplus land, exceeded their consumption.[41] It was these 'Leftist' excesses which, in overstepping the boundaries of the anti-feudal struggle, had caused middle peasants more generally to waver, disorganising the peasant movement whilst strengthening opposition among the rich and middle peasants, and increasing the landlords' will to resist.

Based on his observations of the dynamics of agrarian movement, Mao had come to the view that the attitude of the middle peasants on whether or not to side with the poor peasants was critical in determining the fate of the agrarian revolution: the feudal power of the village landlords could not be eradicated without their support.[42] When in an upsurge, poor peasant extremism drove the intermediate class to the side of counter-revolution this also impacted on the middle peasants, creating antagonisms among the peasants; then when the situation ebbed in favour of the counter-revolution the poor peasants were left exposed to landlord blandishments or reprisals. The poor peasants could only succeed against the traditional village elites if they gained the support of the middle peasants; together they had the power to control the intermediate class in the independent base areas. But without this unity, the situation would be exposed to intrigue, opening the way for the return of the large landlords and the revival of the old patriarchal influences.

Tackling the problem of clannishness and 'rich peasant leadership' then went hand in hand with the need to restrain the peasants' egalitarian and extremist tendencies. Involving the middle peasants early on in a mobilisation campaign would help to moderate the egalitarian demands of the poor peasants. Their role then in the revolutionary movement was not so much as a conservative influence, as the '28 Bolsheviks' maintained, but as a guard against reprisals and the revival of clannishness and patron-client ties of dependency in a low ebb. Unity with the middle peasants then was the key both to limiting extremism in an upsurge and to maintaining a firm hold over the intermediate class in a low ebb.

The anti-rich peasant line and radical land laws were influenced by the leadership priorities of both the Comintern and the '28 Bolsheviks' which saw bolshevising the Party and consolidating the organs of soviet power against the influence of the rich peasants and the traditional elites in terms of bolstering working class composition and organisation. For Mao however, bolshevisation was the art of leading the masses.[43]

What this involved in fact was the development of techniques to unite the different sections of the peasants so as to mobilise them on a mass scale, guiding their struggles through the phases of upsurge and ebb, of egalitarianism and clannishness, to focus on the feudal targets. Land reform had to address the contradictions between the desire of the better-off households to 'get rich', the poor peasants' tendencies to demand the pooling and sharing of all resources, as well as the protectionism among the owner-cultivator communities.

Mao's land policies continued to edge away from the radical measures of the '28 Bolsheviks' towards a more moderate framework with a view in particular to protecting middle peasant interests as he gained a better understanding of their central role in the agrarian revolution. At the same time, Mao was to find new ways not only of countering the problems of traditional power, of community closure and factionalism that saw the landlords and rich peasants remain dominant at village level, but also of dealing with workerist tendencies which, as he came to see, led to the bureaucratic degeneration of the Party and the soviet organs of power. These new ways took shape in innovative forms and relations of political organisation aimed to develop the power of mass democracy.

NOTES AND REFERENCES

1. Averill, 1987, p.294.

2. Guo Dehong, 1981, pp.28–9; see also T-L Hsiao, 1969, p.20.

3. Swarup, 1966, p.121; Guo Dehong, 1981, pp.27–8.

4. cited in Swarup, 1966, p.120.

5. See Guo Dehong, 1981, pp.33–4; Chao Kuo-chun, 1960, p.23.

6. Swarup, 1966, p.121.

7. See Guo Dehong, 1981, pp.23–4.

8. *Ibid.*, p.22. For Mao's definition of the intermediate class, see *Selected Works*, Vol. I, p.87.

9. Mao, *Selected Works*, Vol. I, p.88.

10. *Ibid.*, p.89. See also Womack, 1982, p, 135.

11. *Ibid.*, p.307; see also Rue, 1966, p.187.

12. Guo Dehong, 1981, p.29.

13. Mao, *Selected Works*, Vol. I, pp.90–1.

14. Rue, 1966, pp.200–3.

15. See Jin Dequn, 1981, p.60.

16. See T-L. Hsiao, 1969, pp.127–30 for Li Lisan's 'Provisional Land Law; and see Guo Dehong, 1981, p.34, for further comment. Li's chief leniency in relation to the rich peasants was his advocation of land distribution according to labour power, see Jin Dequn, 1981, p.56, and the following discussion.

17. For further details of how Li's land law strengthened the position of the rich peasants see Huang, 1978, p.14; Averill, 1987, p.294. According to Kim, 1969, p.82, both Li's and Mao's land laws of 1930 followed the 'rich peasant line' in restricting land confiscations to leased properties thus allowing the rich peasants to retain land cultivated by hired labour. However, according to Huang, in Xingguo County in 1931, Mao was carrying out a policy of confiscating all the surplus properties of the rich peasants. Mao then erred from Right to 'Left' in his evolving approach. The main difference between Mao and Li regarding the rich peasants was in fact over the criterion of land distribution.

18. See Jin Dequn, 1981, p.59; p.63.

19. See Du Jing, 1982, p.136.

20. See Rue, 1966, p.201; T-L Hsiao, 1969, p.21, notes a certain ambiguity in Mao's position before 1931.

21. See Du Jing, 1982, p.132; and Guo Dehong, 1981, pp.35–6.

22. Hsiao T-L, 1961, pp.98–113.

23. *Ibid.*, p.187.

24. See Guo Dehong, 1981, pp.37–8; Lotveit, 1978, pp.151–2; p.170.
25. Lotveit, 1978, pp.183–4; Kim (1969) rejects the suggestion made by Hsiao, Rue and Swarup that the 'rich peasant line' was part of a factional struggle for leadership, arguing that in fact Mao and the '28 Bolsheviks' collaborated in implementing this policy, p.94.
26. See Huang, 1978, p.17.
27. See Hsiao T-L, 1969, pp.203–4; p.231; Lotveit, 1978, p.156.
28. See Rue, 1966, p.259.
29. Hsiao T-L, 1961, pp.170–5; Swarup, 1966, p.128; p.133.
30. See Guo Dehong, 1981, pp.41–3; Rue, 1966, p.246.
31. Kim, 1969, pp.88–91.
32. Hsiao T-L, 1969, p.231.
33. See Guo Dehong, 1981, p.38. Rue, 1966, p.247, also mentions that Mao's land law was criticised as following a 'rich peasant line'.
34. See Saich, academia.edu, accessed: 27/4/2020, for the constant shifts in classifications in 1933 and 1934 with middle peasants reclassified as landlords and then demoted back to the ranks of the middle peasants.
35. Hsiao T-L, 1969, p.286; see also Guo Dehong, 1981, pp.43–44.
36. See Hsiao T-L, 1969, p.219.
37. Polachek, 1983, p.825.
38. See Du Jing, 1982, p.121.
39. This point is made by Swarup, 1966, pp.131–2; see also Isaacs, 1962, p.346.
40. Lotveit, 1978, p.172, notes Mao's critical attitude towards the extremist measures. See also T-L Hsiao, 1969, pp.80–1.
41. See Guo Dehong, 1981, p.40. Mao had recognised the possibility of winning these well-to-do farmers, the 'right wing' of the peasant movement, to the side of the revolution in 1926 in his essay of 'Analysis of the Classes in Chinese Society, Selected Works', Vol. 1, p.16.
42. See Du Jing, 1982, pp.118–9; Kim, 1969, p.97.
43. Hsiao T-L, 1969, p.250. Kim, 1969, p.94, argues that the land investigation drive was part of the anti-rich peasant policy which aimed to consolidate the leadership of the '28 Bolsheviks'; Womack (1982) points out that the CPC's turn against the rich peasants coincided with Stalin's decision to liquidate the *kulaks* in 1929–1930, p.136. Mao first began to criticise 'absolute egalitarianism' as practised in the Red Army in December 1929. See *Selected Works*, Vol. I, p.111.

16
Mao and the sinification of Marxism – class analysis and the mass line

How to analyse the classes in the rural areas

As the CPC leadership's land investigation drive proceeded, Mao was to observe a series of problems occurring with Party and soviet cadres protecting landlords and rich peasants from their own clan or village; cadres accepting false accusations of landlords and rich peasants against other peasant activists; wrong analysis of class status, mistaking middle peasants for rich peasants and harming their interests; and a misconception of the rich peasant problem in the failure to appreciate their involvement in production as distinct from the landlords.[1]

The campaign drive was leading to confusion with the widening of the targets of confiscation: rich peasants were identified as landlords and subject to excessive struggle, and better-off peasants were mistaken for rich peasants. On the other hand, rich peasants and landlords would not be recognised as such, whilst clan and localistic attachments made it difficult to organise the poor and middle peasants against landlord and rich peasant leaders of the same lineage.

When extreme measures were taken against rich peasants, this also aroused fears among middle peasants who had gained land in the first stages of the reform that they would now be identified as rich peasants. In addition, restrictions applied to the better-off peasants engaging in trade were damaging to the economy of the base areas.[2]

The difficulties as Mao saw it arose because there were no criteria set out for the cadres to use in developing the campaign: they had no means on the one hand to distinguish class from lineage and clan divisions, nor was there any way of dealing with egalitarian tendencies which based confiscation and distribution on differences in income or on exploitation in general, generating conflicts between the poor and the relatively better-off producers.

To effectively destroy the economic and political foundations of the landlord gentry and village bosses, oppose rich peasant leadership, and deal with the subversive activities in the soviet bases, struggle had to be conducted on a principled basis. This required a clear method of identifying the different classes to distinguish revolutionary forces and the potential allies from the main feudal targets.

The distinction between landlord and rich peasant was vital, particularly when it came to dealing with the village elites, but given the complexity of the rural relations of exploitation which included wage labour and usury as well as rent, this was not an easy task. On the one hand, the close ties between the rich peasants and the village landlords socially, economically and politically made it difficult to distinguish between them, yet, whilst they did not constitute an independent *kulak* class, the rich peasants' interests were nevertheless partially as commercial producers. As Mao recognised in relation to the land investigation drive, how the rich peasants were treated was of particular significance in shaping the attitudes of the middle peasants, and it was especially when middle peasant interests were encroached upon that problems of disorganisation within the peasant movement arose.

Mao saw that cadres had particular difficulties in grasping the criterion of exploitation, often confusing capitalist and feudal exploitation, and wealth derived from labour with wealth derived from exploitation.[3] In 1933 he wrote *How to Analyse the Classes in the Rural Areas* as a document to guide and direct the campaign against feudal exploitation. Its purpose was to clear up any confusion over the nature of the surplus to be confiscated in land reform and so to clarify the distinctions between landlords and rich peasants as well as between rich and middle peasants.[4]

The distinction Mao drew between landlords and rich peasants turned on the question of their involvement in production. Landlords lived by exploitation principally in the form of land rent although they had other lesser forms of income from usury, hiring labour and engaging in commercial and industrial undertakings. They did not engage in production themselves other than to supplement their income. Rich peasants, however, did take part in production: although they might lease out land, lend money and engage in industrial and commercial undertakings, they did so only as a subsidiary activity, relying at least partially on their own labour for a living. The principal form of exploitation on which they relied for the other or major part of their income was hiring labour.

Middle peasants were to be distinguished from poor peasants in their ability to survive by relying mainly or wholly on their own labour. Since the middle peasants owned adequate means of production, they had a greater relative independence. With sufficient funds for sidelines, they did not as a rule need to sell their labour power. Poor peasants with less than adequate tools had to sell a small part of their labour power in order to survive, particularly since they had to lease in more land than the middle peasants.

As in his earlier works, Mao importantly highlighted the differences within the middle peasant sector: whilst lower middle peasants with insufficient land were close to the poor peasants, the comparatively well-to-do tended to have good land and high yields, engaging in sideline production but also using hired labour and lending money. This made the dividing line between rich and middle peasant particularly difficult.[5] If having surplus food and clothing or having higher than average yields or above average land holdings were taken as the criteria for identifying a rich peasant, then many middle peasants would be considered rich.[6]

Lenin had used the criterion of sown area to distinguish classes within the small farming sector, against the Narodniks who, from the point of view of income, regarded the peasants as relatively homogenous. For him, the issue was not income distribution but relations of production. However the criterion of sown area was not suitable in China where land fertility varied enormously even within a locality. To avoid confusion in identifying class status, it was necessary to distinguish between surplus land with yields over and above staple food for self-consumption, surplus land exceeding the local average *per capita* holding, and surplus land used for feudal exploitation.[7] The complexity of the situation in the Chinese countryside was further compounded by the existence of a web of traditional exchanges between peasant households, both tenants and owner-peasants, who joined together to form loan societies, buy draught animals, and exchange labour in return for the use of means of production.

Lenin's classification of the peasantry into rich, middle and poor, identified potential or actual classes. Chayanov on the other hand considered inequalities between peasant households as indicative not of a distinct class polarisation but rather reflecting different stages in the generational life-cycle of the family. As he argued, the size of a family farm was determined by its labour-consumer ratio not the logic of capitalist production.[8] Given the complexity of labour exchanges in the Chinese countryside, it was certainly difficult to ascertain whether the expropriation of surplus labour was a precondition for the development of class differentiation or whether it was balanced out in the long run in the various exchanges between peasant households who might support each other in times of crisis or of need.[9]

In defining more precise methods of identifying classes, Mao settled for one which considered budgetary data from each household. His method of distinguishing between traditional exchanges between peasant households on a mutual basis, and exchanges involving exploitation, that is, distinguishing between rich and middle peasants, was to examine the degree and duration of the arrangements for the hiring of labour and the proportion of own to hired labour.[10] Mao then distinguished between middle peasants who lived mainly by their own labour, hiring labour to supplement their income, and the rich peasants who relied mainly on outside labour, drawing a regular income from the exploitation of labour which exceeded income from their own labour. Distinction was made between the long-term and more permanent hiring of labour by the rich peasants, which often took a semi-feudal form in the performance of labour services, and the short-term and seasonal hiring of labour by the upper middle peasants, who contracted labour during the busy seasons at fixed rates by the hour or by quota. Those households which relied on their own labour and did not hire any workers but derived most of their income from collecting rent or usury were classed as rich peasant households, whilst those which lent money but relied principally on their own labour for a livelihood were classed as middle peasants.

Controlling the landlords

Mao's class analysis provided the key to tackling the problems considered by the '28 Bolsheviks' as the 'rich peasant line'. It did so because it made the realisation of an anti-feudal alliance in the countryside possible, laying out the basis for an agrarian programme which, following the general line of relying on the poor peasants, brought together all the different kinds of peasants with their different and often conflicting demands. It enabled class struggle to be carried out according to clear criteria, dealing with contradictions among the peasants so as to develop a movement of peasant class power to transform the village order. It did so by equipping the grassroots cadres and the peasants alike with the tools to tackle the problems of clannishness and extremism which created divisions and cleavages open to landlord manipulations.

By differentiating feudal wealth from capital, identifying the principal form of exploitation and the degree and duration of these forms, whilst also taking own labour into account, cadres would be able to mark out the different classes amongst the village populations. Distinguishing between the surplus land under feudal rent and the surplus lands of the peasants cultivated by their own labour, the struggle could be directed against feudal exploitation rather than all wealth in general. On this basis it became possible to gain the support of the middle peasants whilst neutralising the rich peasants. At the same time, *per capita* land redistribution aimed to draw the poor and middle peasants together, enabling poor peasants to establish themselves on a more independent basis whilst also involving owner-cultivators as an active force in, and not merely bypassed by, agrarian reform, bringing benefit to those with insufficient land.

By driving a wedge between the rich peasants and the village landlords, at the same time engaging the middle peasants, it became possible to tackle the tenacity of clan ties and the persistent influence of the landlords, isolating them on the one hand and at the same time creating a united force of poor and middle peasants to exercise control over them.

Mao maintained that the rich peasants were to be treated neither as targets, like landlords, in the anti-feudal struggle, nor, like the middle peasants, as allies. As leaders of lineage branches, they were closely tied to the landlords: with the weak development of capitalism these wealthier members of the farming community, engaging in feudal exploitation themselves to a degree, tended to take the landlords' side. However, unlike the policies of the '28 Bolsheviks' of allotting only poor land to the rich peasants, Mao took note of their demands for their capital to be taken into consideration in agrarian reform: his focus was on their feudal holdings not their capital. Whilst he was not in favour of rich peasants participating in the peasants' associations and power organs of the soviets, he saw that once landlord power was eliminated and soviet power established, it would be possible to develop a progressive relationship with them in a democratic economy, emphasising the development of production rather than intensifying class struggle. By offering rich peasants a way out in promoting commercial farming, it was possible to diminish their support for the landlords.

At the same time treating rich peasants fairly was important in building unity with the middle peasants: it helped to strengthen support among the better-off middle peasants by showing that getting rich through private enterprise and hard work had a role to play in a new regime which abolished feudal exploitation not wealth.[11]

The confiscation and redistribution of public land alongside the landlords' individual holdings also undermined the landlords' power since it broke up the economic basis of lineage organisation. However, it was at this point of breaking up of village collective properties that complications in local politics intensified, with intrigues instigated by the village corporate organisations. CPC branches would get caught up on the side of oppositionist groups of immigrants, identifying their rivals, the conservative clans, as 'counter-revolutionary'. To deal with such factionalism, Mao recommended that when corporate lands were broken up, the clan members should be given land which was to be redistributed among both the native settlers and immigrants on a *per capita* basis.[12] At the same time, policies of economic development encouraged the rich peasants to abandon their traditional roles as managers of village properties and concentrate on their private interests as capitalist farmers. Meanwhile, the dependency ties rooted in the reliance of the impoverished on welfare from public granaries run by the village elites were undermined as the redistributed property helped to establish their individual household independence.

However, Mao's methods were at first dismissed by CPC's Comintern adherents as following petty bourgeois politics.[13] He was to be criticised as a Rightist for making allowances for rich peasant economic interests, and his policies of *per capita* land distribution were seen as an example of peasant mentality:

> This in fact has taken the middle peasants as the centre and created conditions in which the poor peasants and hired hands cannot possibly develop equally. This is a departure from the class viewpoint of the proletarian political party.[14]

Mao was then accused of failing to carry out the policy of 'turning the petty bourgeoisie into proletarians and then forcing them into the revolution'.[15] His 'non-class' approach which benefited the middle peasants and left the landlords and rich peasants with land to cultivate to meet their needs was seen to represent a 'petty bourgeois device to consolidate private ownership which confused class consciousness and hindered class struggle'.[16]

But *per capita* land distribution was in fact quite distinct from the 'non class' egalitarian approach which made no distinction between different forms of wealth and exploitation, and thus failed to protect the interests of well-to-do middle peasants cultivating land surplus to subsistence whilst also alienating the rich peasants. For Mao 'absolute egalitarianism' was an illusion of the small producers: *per capita* distribution of land was the means to realise the goals of the democratic revolution to establish a system of peasants' individual production.[17]

Tackling bureaucratism

To counter the problems of factionalism, parochialism, clannishness and localistic power under highly personalised styles of leadership, traditions which the CPC tended to absorb into their organisation at local levels as they established their rural bases, the Party as has been noted had sought to centralise military and political structures whilst introducing democratic elections, at the same time pursuing radical land laws and the establishment of the poor peasant leagues.

However, during the period of the land investigation drive, Mao also began to develop new approaches to Party organisation and Party-building, reshaping styles of leadership around the 'mass line', fostering democratic power through the organisation of peasants in land reform, to create a new type of social and political order within the villages. His concern was not only to address the problem of traditional elite influence in peasant organisation but also the tendency towards bureaucratic degeneration in the organs of the Party and soviet government at grassroots level.

Marks' study of the downfall of the short-lived Haifeng Soviet in 1927 sheds light on the problems here. Weakened by internal conflicts as well as by increased military pressure from KMT troops and the severance of trade, the CPC struggled to impose leadership in the Soviet, resorting to commandism and bureaucratism. Conflicts had arisen between the pro-peasant policies and the charismatic leadership style of Peng Pai and the workerist trends within the CPC leadership clique. With no mass base of support from below among the peasants who followed Peng, the CPC's 'soviet power' was essentially only the executive committee of the Party branch under another name, bureaucratically imposed from the outside.[18] Marks observes in particular that since Peng was regarded by his followers as an all-powerful, infallible leader, this made it hard for the CPC to conduct criticism and self-criticism to resolve the difficulties within the soviet.

The methods of the '28 Bolsheviks' in centralising power to control the landlords and rich peasants only tended to reproduce the hierarchical 'top-down' traditions of the bureaucratic state as well as elite-led lineage organisation, without the development of peasant mass power. Whilst Mao supported centralisation, he was concerned that the workerist approach of relying primarily on the rural proletariat and semi-proletariat for support was leading to bureaucratic degeneration in the organs of soviet power with the creation of leadership cliques divorced from the wider village population. To break up the personalised cliques of traditional power and at the same time tackle bureaucratism in the Party and soviets required transformation from below. Thus Mao conceived the land investigation drive as a mass mobilisation not merely against the traditional power-holders but also against bureaucratic practices of commandism and formalism in the exercise of soviet power.[19]

Where the CPC leadership directed criticisms at the peasants as unreliable and difficult to organise, Mao turned attention towards mistakes in Party practices, finding fault with careerism and opportunism as well as localism.[20] He criticised the tendencies of committees to work over the heads of the masses, achieving results by imposition and not by persuasion and education to win them over.[21] For Mao, it was the Party's estrangement from the masses that created a vacuum which the landlords and rich peasants were able to exploit to maintain their influence over village politics. To overcome the inadequacies in the exercise of soviet power and to counter traditional influences required the creation of new forms and institutions of democratic power and leadership styles, transforming the traditional relations between the peasants and their leaders and local government.

To avoid confusion in the peasants' ranks and between the peasants and cadres when confronting the landlords and rich peasants, the land investigation carried out in the areas under Mao's control was organised as a mass movement to investigate class status, favouring a wider participation. Implementing his classification scheme as a mass participatory method, Mao was to begin a new process of self- and mutual education by both peasants and cadres.

Class analysis was to be used to transform traditional peasant consciousness.[22] Peasants and cadres alike initially judged inequalities spontaneously according to wealth or income and not exploitation. Without guidelines, they tended to act on the basis of traditional loyalties. But through the investigation of class status, the peasants came to understand the class structure of their social environment. Rather than degenerating into the settling of old scores and clan factionalism manipulated by the traditional power-holders, struggle against the local gentry and village bosses was to be carried out by objective measures, transforming village politics through the exercise of mass power.

Using the land investigation drive in this way to mobilise the peasants, Mao aimed to foster unity between the poor and middle peasants as the best means of dealing with the subversive and divisive activities of the traditional elite. He criticised the 'closed door' approach of the poor peasant leagues and warned against the dangers of taking arbitrary actions if the investigations were left up to a few.[23] Instead he attached great importance to open village mass meetings to discuss decisions especially about taking actions against class enemies: whilst clan and localistic loyalties prevented the transformation of traditional patterns of leadership, village mass meetings were seen to be a means of developing education against the strong bonds of clan sentiment.[24] It would not do to rely on poor peasant leagues alone: Mao advocated that middle peasants should also attend meetings to determine class status and to deal with the landlords and rich peasants since by listening only to the views of the poor peasants the legitimate demands of the middle peasants could be ignored.

As he saw it, the primary role of the poor peasant leagues was not so much to press forward their separate interests and demands but to act as a key in mobilising all possible sections of the rural population in developing soviet democratic power. Indeed, the point of the agrarian revolution was not to satisfy the demands of the poor peasants but to eradicate the feudal relations of production, and the object of struggle was not all surplus land per se, but those surplus lands drawing a feudal rent.[25] By involving the middle peasants at an early stage, they would be able to act as a moderating influence over the egalitarian impulses of the poor peasants which tended to emerge at the point of land confiscation and redistribution within the village.

Mao called for the involvement of all mass organisations to develop the land investigation drive into a widespread cultural and educational programme. Women's and Youth Associations and other mass organisations were to take part in a variety of wider campaigns from literacy and public hygiene to army recruitment and production drives as well as mobilisations to set up co-operatives.[26] In this way mass mobilisation would pave the way for democratic elections, with wide participation enabling the establishment of representative, not executive, committees to replace the formalist feudal ceremonial practices and the underlying arbitrary dictation.[27]

The problems of soviet power were not to be resolved simply by purging alien class elements within the organs of local government. Past experiences of leadership reform had also shown how an overemphasis on class background had meant that too many in the leadership had been attacked.[28] Mao himself had not been innocent here: in 1930 he had had thousands of officers in the Red Army arrested as suspected Nationalist infiltrators in the AB League and Futian incidents; some were killed; others were executed.[29] But purges again played into the hands of the traditional village elite who were experts at factional intrigue. After this experience, Mao began to warn against bureaucratism in covering up for others and exaggerating small mistakes. He favoured a constant review of leadership, and, in order to prevent unjustified treatment of cadres, he proposed that the problem of leadership should be handled by criticism and self-criticism with judgement based upon work rather than class origin.[30] Distinguishing between serious cases of corruption where cadres had acted in effect as landlords' agents, and lesser mistakes arising from confusion in analysing classes, Mao's view was that the reorganisation of unsound soviet agencies was a matter which involved educating people to understand their mistakes.[31] This was the method to be applied when dealing with cadres who had allowed their lineage loyalties to influence them and had been afraid to stand up to the gentry.

Mao's approach of building democratic mass power through education at the same time created relations of reciprocity between the leadership and the people. The traditional closed, segmented and factionalised communities organised around the defence of territory and resources were held together through social hierarchies under authoritarian leadership; the development of soviet power by Mao's methods was in contrast to form a different kind of centralised system based on mass democratic power with the involvement of women and youth, and with popular education, open mass meetings, and the election of leaders.

As land reforms saw the establishment of an individual peasant economy, policies to develop production in the base areas ended attacks on the petty-bourgeoisie, serving to transform the economic rationale of village communities from a traditional defence of resources by unleashing capacities within the rural areas for economic growth. The new socio-economic environment of independent peasant production brought about through the exercises of mass power in turn provided the underpinning for a new type of village political structure, guarding against the revival of traditionalism and bureaucratism through the development of new forms of leadership and institutions of democratic peasant mass power.

Where Li Lisan's rich peasant line and the '28 Bolsheviks' anti-rich peasant line had equally disorganised the peasant movement, Mao was able to guide the anti-feudal agrarian revolution on a principled basis: the application of Marxist class analysis to distinguish between different forms of exploitation and wealth as the basis of different classes made possible the handling of contradictions among the peasants to unite them as a force of democratic power. Raising their class consciousness through mass participatory methods, the peasants were able to move beyond the confines of traditional loyalties and divisions.

Taking the attitude of the middle peasants as central in determining the success or failure of the agrarian revolution, and taking into account the dual characteristics of the rich peasants as the basis for a policy of economic, though not political, leniency to secure their neutrality in the anti-feudal struggle, were the two key steps in the organisation of mass peasant power. In the eyes of the Trotskyists, the entire CPC had by now become a peasant Party under the influence of the rural capitalists; in fact, these shifts were the significant advances made by Mao in the sinification of Marxism.[32]

NOTES AND REFERENCES

1. Hsiao T-L, 1969, pp.243–8.
2. Lotveit, 1978, p.171–2.
3. Lotveit, 1978, p.171.
4. Mao, *Selected Works*, Vol. I, pp.138–40; see also Guo Dehong, 1981, p.43. The document was based in part at least on important research carried out in May 1930 by Mao into conditions in Xunwu County, Jiangxi province. The Xunwu Report provided a detailed record of commerce and land relations, and the land struggle in the locality. It not only covered the lives and conditions of the peasants but also included lengthy notes on the different types of landlords – large, medium and small – their attitudes towards ownership and their political affiliations. (Thompson, 1990).
5. Guo Dehong, 1981, p.49.
6. See Jin Dequn, 1981, p.65.
7. See Du Jing, 1982, pp.119–20.
8. Chayanov, 1966, e.g. p.64; p.195.
9. For further discussion, see Cox, 1984.
10. Mao, *Selected Works*, Vol. I, p.139; Du Jing, 1982, p.120.
11. Guo Dehong, 1981, *Ibid.*, p.50.
12. Mao, *Selected Works*, Vol. I, p.95.
13. See Guo Dehong, 1981, p.23.

14. cited in Guo Dehong, 1981, p.38; see also Hsiao T-L, 1961, pp.7–8; Rue, 1966, p.196.
15. See Guo Dehong, 1981, p.23; Mao, *Selected Works*, Vol. I, pp.99–100.
16. See Jin Dequn, 1981, p.59. See also Lotveit, 1978, p.283.
17. As previously noted Mao first began to criticise 'absolute egalitarianism' in December 1929. See *Selected Works*, Vol. I, p.111.
18. Marks, 1984, p.253; and pp.267–275, for his account of the internal problems underlying the downfall of the Haifeng Soviet.
19. Hsiao T-L, 1969, p.259.
20. *Ibid.*, pp.252–3; Mao, *Selected Works*, Vol. I, pp.94–96, on the problem of localism.
21. Hsiao T-L, 1969, p.259.
22. Hsiao T-L, 1969, p.214
23. *Ibid.*, p.246; p.252.
24. Lotveit, 1978, p.161; p.164.
25. Guo Dehong, 1981, p.46. In May 1935, the *Decision About the Change in Policy Towards the Rich Peasants* stipulated: 'We should only abolish the feudalist exploitation of the rich peasants, that is, confiscate their leased land and abolish usury. The land, property and trade managed by the rich peasants themselves (or their hired hands) are not to be confiscated. The Soviet government should ensure the freedom of the rich peasants to expand production…and to develop industry and commerce….'
26. Lotveit, 1978, pp.158–60; Huang, 1978, p.25.
27. Mao, *Selected Works*, Vol. I, p.92; see also Averill, 1987, pp.296–8.
28. Huang, 1978, p.23.
29. See Rue, 1966, p.193.
30. Hsiao T-L, 1969, p.250.
31. *Ibid.*, p.224.
32. See See Isaacs, 1962, p.342; also Gillin, 1961, who argues that the CPC was 'captured' by the peasantry.

17

From agrarian to national revolution

Realising the peasants' revolutionary alliance

The 6th CPC Congress *Resolution on the Land Question* had grasped the revolutionary nature of the Chinese peasants against feudalism as shaped not by the emergence of capitalism in agriculture but rather by their conditions of land hunger which pitted the vast majority against the feudal land monopoly and feudal power as they struggled to secure their land rights and livelihood. Whilst land hunger provided the objective basis for unity between poor and middle peasants, tenants and owner-cultivators, as potentially a huge force opposing feudal power and relations of production, in practice the peasant movement was caught up again and again in the rebarbative dynamics of traditional forms of conflict, of territorial defence versus bandit raids. To realise the general line of relying on the poor peasants and uniting with the middle peasants whilst neutralising the role of the rich peasants in the struggle against the landlords presented an enormous challenge.

Traditions of bureaucratic styles of leadership and secret brotherhood ways of organising with the corresponding patterns of peasant passivity or extremism, all exerted influence within the CPC and were reproduced in its practices, playing into the hands of the former power-holders and obstructing the emergence of democratic power. As it tended to link up first with outcast groups to capitalise on predatory traditions to overcome parochial closure of the settled communities, the CPC was easily embroiled in these traditionalist patterns of peasant protest and factional disputes. These problems, which were rooted in divisions among the peasants, were only resolvable through broader recruitment into mass campaigns, especially land reform, with participatory organisations strengthening the democratic power of the soviet government.[1]

At the centre here were the middle peasants who, as Mao came to recognise, were not vacillating at all but were a major force in the agrarian revolution, wavering only as struggles went to extremes. The dynamics of the peasant movement had shown that the feudal power of the village landlords could not be eradicated without their support: in isolation from the middle peasants, the poor peasants were exposed to landlord influence, but united with the middle peasants, the poor peasants were in a stronger position, with the majority in the villages forming a force capable of controlling the former powerholders.

Mao's agrarian programme focused on the confiscation of all the landlords' land and public lands, and the rich peasants' rented land, leaving surplus land farmed by middle as well as rich peasants untouched, with distribution on a *per capita* basis among the poor and middle peasants. This was the most suitable policy for a small peasant economy where class differences among the peasants were not advanced. It focused on land, not capital, restraining egalitarianism: it did not attack the rich peasants excessively but took into account their aspirations to 'get rich', and did not encroach on the interests of the middle peasants but rather protected them. Whilst thereby allaying the fears of the better-off peasants, it nevertheless gave the impoverished peasants an immediate, if partial, solution to their problems and some hope for the future. At the same time, the break-up of the economic basis of lineage organisation together with the development of the economy would encourage the rich peasants to abandon their traditional roles and concentrate on their private interests as capitalist farmers, whilst the needs of the impoverished for a livelihood were met not through dependence on patronage but through *per capita* land redistribution to establish their individual independence.

The agrarian programmes of both Li Lisan and the '28 Bolsheviks' failed to unite the peasants and activate the revolutionary force of their land hunger against the feudal land monopoly; nor did these succeed in weakening the feudal forces by driving a wedge between the landlords and rich peasants. By distributing land according to labour power, Li had instead strengthened the better-off peasants more than was necessary whilst creating difficulties for the labour-poor households and reinforcing their reliance on those more wealthy for support. The '28 Bolsheviks', whilst identifying Li as a Rightist nevertheless themselves fell into 'Leftist' errors of judgement in underestimating the importance of the middle peasant alliance and intensifying the struggle against the rich peasants, failing to take into account their demands concerning their capital in the process of land confiscation.

Against the tenacity of landlord and clan-patriarchal influences, Mao's methods of organising the mass of peasants as a democratic and independent force capable of maintaining a firm hold over the intermediate classes, transformed village power structures. The new controls were to be exercised not from above by the Party but from below by the unified mass of peasantry. 'Leftist' methods of Party purification and the organisation of the rural proletarian and semi-proletarian elements had on the contrary led to the substitution of the real struggles of the peasants by Party organisation. Such methods essentially expressed a mistrust of the peasants and an exaggeration of their traditional ties and loyalties, leading to arbitrarily and bureaucratically imposed efforts on the part of small groups of self-styled leaders to solve the problems of rural organisation, only to exacerbate the 'Leftist' errors. Mao on the other hand was less concerned with purging the leadership than with creating the conditions to prevent bureaucratic degeneration by activating the mass of the peasants to control their leaders and run village affairs democratically. Methods of criticism and self-criticism aimed to strengthen leadership in a democratic way, and the open-door methods of the mass line restricted the behind-the-scenes intrigue used by the local gentry and village elders to manipulate reforms to their own advantage.

Rather than imposing organisational solutions from the above, Mao sought to counter traditional influences within the peasantry from below by encouraging their self-education, relying on the peasants to transform their parochial and egalitarian tendencies themselves as they took part in the process of struggle against feudal relations of production and power. Without the creation of mass participatory organisations to support democratic government, power at the local and village levels would fall back into patterns of traditional intrigue and bureaucratic and patriarchal methods.

Up to 1927, the Rightist view of the peasants as essentially passive traditionalists underestimated their revolutionary potential and failed to take advantage of opportunities to advance the revolution by unleashing mass power in the countryside. In the subsequent years to 1935, 'Leftist' views which identified the rich peasants along with the landlords as targets of struggle whilst dismissing the role of the middle peasants as a conservative force, caused confusion in the organisation of peasants in land confiscation. Mao on the other hand saw through traditional patterns of political behaviour to analyse the peasants' underlying material interests, emphasising the key importance of the middle peasant alliance: the real strength of the agrarian movement lay not in the separate organisation of the rural proletariat and poor pitted against the village rich but in their ability to unite with the middle peasants.

As this understanding of the dynamics of the agrarian revolution began to crystallise within the CPC, it also corresponded with the beginnings of a reassessment of the class situation in China as a whole. 'Leftist' policies, which had stoked divisions among the peasants and driven the intermediate classes to the side of the counter-revolution, had uncritically assessed rich peasant 'defection' and middle peasant 'vacillation' as owing to the adverse influence of the national bourgeoisie seen to have betrayed the revolution. But as Mao came to understand the difficulties in the soviet bases in relation to the limitations of the CPC's own policies, he at the same time began to question this assessment of the national bourgeoisie.

On the revolutionary nature of the national bourgeoisie

Whilst the 6th CPC Congress had consolidated an understanding of the stage of the Chinese revolution as a democratic revolution, nevertheless limitations in the analysis of classes within both the national and agrarian movements opened the way to 'Leftist' errors in the subsequent period of the second revolutionary civil war from 1927 to 1935.

The prevailing view amongst the CPC leadership of the national situation after 1927 was that, whilst the entire camp of the landlords and bourgeoisie were united, the government under Chiang Kai-shek was in fact very unstable with constant splits between a Right wing faction representing class interests opposed to agrarian reform, and a left-wing faction of workers, peasants and petty bourgeoisie, whilst substantial sections of the national bourgeoisie vacillated between the two. This made an important distinction between the national industrialist bourgeoisie and the compradore bourgeoisie engaged in foreign trade, however Mao further came to recognise that within the national bourgeoisie itself there were also sections with more affiliations with foreign capital and Chinese landed interests, whilst other sections had little or no affiliations of this kind, and these in fact vacillated in their attitude towards the revolution: they disliked imperialism on the one hand, but they also feared the 'thoroughness' of the revolution.[2]

As suggested earlier, Stalin's advice to the CPC leadership in 1927 had underestimated the connection of the Right wing of the KMT with feudalism and compradore capitalism. During the Northern Expedition, the Nationalists had sought support from the traditional rural elites to provide taxes for the army rather than relying on mass mobilisation. This tended to reinforce the role of the landlords and militarists within the KMT which, as it advanced North, did not defeat but rather absorbed the warlords who then, in alliance with the compradore bankers and bureaucrat capitalists, took over the Party under Chiang's leadership.

When the KMT split after Chiang's White Terror, the 'Left' KMT government was affected similarly by the tensions between the national and social revolutions. The Wuhan leadership, seen by Stalin at the time as representing the revolutionary petty bourgeoisie in a three class bloc with the workers and peasants, in fact reflected the vacillating nature of the national bourgeoisie: some sections opposed agrarian revolution and leaned towards the compradore capitalists, however other less influential figures reflected the opinion of the more radical sections of the national bourgeoisie in their support of rent and interest rate reductions, and of the workers' struggles against foreign capitalism.

It was because Chiang Kai-shek was seen to represent the interests of the national bourgeoisie, and the Wuhan government those of the petty bourgeoisie, that Stalin and the Comintern understood Chiang's defection, followed by that of the Wuhan government, as the betrayal of the revolution by the national bourgeoisie, followed by the vacillating petty bourgeoisie. But on the contrary, it was the right wing of the KMT, with its connections with feudalism and compradore capital that first gave in to the counter-revolutionary forces in the face of the rising peasant movement.[3] As Zhou Enlai was to point out, radical sections amongst the national bourgeoisie and urban petty bourgeoisie remained on the side of the revolution and would have supported the Party had it seized leadership from the 'Left' KMT at Wuhan and organised agrarian reform and armed struggle.[4] It was not until June 1927, when this faction of the KMT caved in, that the middle bourgeoisie and petty bourgeoisie deserted the revolution.

The three uprisings which followed similarly overrode the interests of the urban petty bourgeoisie: they failed not simply as a result of the lack of response from the workers in the cities, rather, the excesses of land nationalisation and the two-class bloc policies which aimed to expropriate the merchants and take over the factories, alienated the small businessmen. In fact, when opposition was rallied against the warlords' taxes, the merchants and small businessmen joined in.[5]

Stalin's mistake was to assume that the Chinese national bourgeoisie was like the European bourgeoisie and would support agrarian reform: he had not grasped its peculiarity, that is, its vacillating nature. The deterioration in the revolutionary situation throughout 1927 was to expose the weakness of the national bourgeoisie in its inability to act as an independent force and lead the democratic revolution for, although they were in conflict with imperialism and feudalism, they had a tendency to compromise because of their ties with landed and compradore interests. Stalin then failed to recognise the necessity for the CPC to seize the leadership of the KMT from its right wing at the points of betrayal, firstly by Chiang and then the 'Left' KMT government in Wuhan.

After 1927, the underestimation of the Right KMT's connections with feudalism and compradore capitalism led to difficulties in identifying who would still support the revolution and who opposed it. For the Comintern and the CPC leadership, an alliance between the bourgeoisie and the landlords was now seen to have consolidated and, in Stalin's view, since the national bourgeoisie had betrayed the revolution before feudalism had been completely eradicated, it was now necessary to look to the proletariat to lead the democratic forces based on a two-class worker-peasant alliance. For Zhou Enlai, this failed to grasp that sections of the national bourgeoisie and urban petty bourgeoisie remained on the side of the revolution. The error was of dogmatically transposing the situation of Russia in 1905 to China: where the Chinese revolution differed, as Zhou saw it, was that it was not the petty bourgeoisie but the national bourgeoisie that was vacillating between radical agrarian reform and compromise.[6]

Mao had begun to recognise this distinct character of the national bourgeoisie already in 1928, in his assessment that the KMT had inflicted defeat not only on the workers, peasants and petty bourgeoisie, but also on the national bourgeoisie, since the feudal classes remained the most powerful within the KMT dictating policies which preserved their own interests.[7] The KMT government then, rather than incorporating the national bourgeoisie, essentially represented only the interests of landlords and the compradore bourgeoisie. The dominant 'Leftist' tendencies within the CPC however, now focused on the workers' movement in the cities to build the base for proletarian leadership, not only underestimated the rural revolution and the middle peasant alliance, but also generally neglected the democratic struggles in the cities rallying the urban petty bourgeoisie.

When the Japanese armies launched attacks on China in the early 1930s, the CPC's adherence to the policies of the two-class bloc effectively ignored the impact of this event on the national bourgeoisie. The domestic business class had essentially supported Chiang for the sake of national unification but now had begun to realise that they were gaining nothing. The KMT at this stage was failing to realise their demands to modernise China, stabilise finance, build a modern infrastructure, develop industry and the home market, resolve the peasant question, and get rid of foreign jurisdiction. Other than building railways with foreign loans, which increased taxes rather than promoting growth, the Nationalist government had done very little to develop the economy and domestic industry: it was chiefly the bankers and land speculators who had benefitted under their administration.[8] Now above all, the KMT stood in the way of national unification: its leadership, more focused on preparing to engage in, or actively carrying out, civil war against the CPC's Red Armies, had created a situation in which the Japanese had been able to step in and exploit the dissension.[9]

Towards New Democracy

The CPC leadership's assessment of the national situation, based on the estimation that the national bourgeoisie had betrayed the revolution leaving the petty bourgeoisie vacillating, was overly negative, exaggerating the strength of the counter-revolution organised by the KMT which in fact split when the national situation, under the growing encroachments of Japan, reached a crisis with the attack on Shanghai in 1931. Whilst the CPC leadership remained opposed to co-operation with bourgeois parties, Mao was in favour of taking advantage of the growing nationalist agitation from this time.[10] A shift in CPC economic policy began in January 1934 when Mao endorsed the promotion and encouragement of private enterprise within legal limits.[11] This anticipated the changes that were to come in 1935 with Mao gaining leadership of the CPC at the Zunyi conference held in January during the Long March. Immediately following the Comintern's shift to a new policy of popular front against fascism and war, Mao was ready to call for the establishment of a nationwide united front to resist Japan's mounting encroachment.[12]

The last weeks of 1935 saw the Long March end in success with the establishment of a new base at Yan'an. The CPC was now able to sum up the previous years' experiences and to begin to implement a more independent strategy for China's revolution, avoiding both Rightist tendencies of compromise and 'Leftist' tendencies of extremism. Mao opened criticism of the closed-door sectarianism of the 'Leftist' two-class bloc, foreseeing a turnaround in the position of the national bourgeoisie in the light of Japanese expansion.[13] Arguing that the principal focus of struggle in China had shifted from feudalism to imperialism, he began developing the basic tenets of New Democracy, that whilst the Chinese revolution was to be led by the proletariat, the national bourgeoisie were not counter-revolutionary; and that, although the workers and peasants were the main forces to be relied upon, the revolution involved not only the urban petty bourgeoisie but also the national bourgeoisie as allies.

The CPC also began to develop its land reform policies into a more coherent programme. One of the main lessons to be drawn from the past mistakes was that the purpose of the agrarian revolution was not to satisfy the demands of the poor but to eradicate the feudal relations of production, and that the object of struggle was not all surplus land per se, but those surplus lands drawing a feudal rent.[14] In this Mao managed to gain support for a more liberal policy towards the rich peasants as a force which could join in, or at least be neutralised in, the struggle against imperialist aggression and warlord feudalism.[15] New guidelines took account of their dual characteristics, on the one hand engaging in feudal exploitation, and on the other a part of the peasant economy involved in production. These stipulated that only the leased land of the rich peasants should be confiscated and that usury should be abolished, but that the land, property and trade managed by the rich peasants themselves (or their hired hands) were not to be confiscated, and that the rich peasants should have the freedom to expand production and to develop industry and commerce. Advocating unity 'with all potential anti-Japanese forces' and the establishment of 'the broadest Anti-Japanese National United Front', the adoption of this policy of promoting and encouraging private enterprise was of critical importance in paving the way towards realising, under favourable circumstances, a long-term alliance with the national bourgeoisie within the framework of New Democracy.

The shift in rural policy from confronting bourgeois influence among the peasants through the anti-rich peasant line, then went together with the shift in national policy to winning over the national bourgeoisie based on the understanding that their position was one of vacillation. 'Leftist' errors which mistook vacillation for betrayal, and had wrongly attacked potential allies, had tended to exacerbate the difficulties arising in the soviet areas under enemy blockade.

As Mao was to clarify later, the 'Leftist' line tended to exaggerate capitalism in the Chinese economy and as a result overemphasised the significance of fighting the capitalists and the rich peasants and exaggerated the existence of 'factors of the socialist revolution' in the democratic stage of the Chinese revolution.[15] In its semi-feudal and semi-colonial conditions, China differed in its class structure from Europe at the stage of the bourgeois democratic revolution: the restrictions on the development of capitalism by feudalism and imperialism created a weak and vacillating national bourgeoisie, with a semi-feudal, semi-capitalist rich peasantry, and an increasingly marginalised owner-peasantry opposed to the system of land monopoly.

Since it was economically and politically weak, unable to compete with and easily bullied by imperialist forces as well as linked in with the landlord-gentry on whose protection the accumulation of wealth from commerce and usury relied, the national bourgeoisie in China, unlike a European bourgeoisie, was incapable of promoting a thorough land reform and fulfilling the democratic revolution. Nevertheless, given their industrial interests in economic development, there was potential for winning their support for a democratic programme under CPC leadership aimed at releasing the nation from the economic and political constraints of imperialism and feudalism.

Mao summed up the experience of defeat in 1927 and near defeat again in the face of Chiang Kai-shek's encirclement and annihilation campaigns up to 1935 in terms of the dangers of Rightism in alliance with the national bourgeoisie and 'Leftism' when split from them.[16] If Rightism essentially relied on the national bourgeoisie as a force opposed to imperialism and feudalism overlooking its weakness, and 'Leftism' disregarded their potential as allies in the democratic revolution, the real problem for both was the failure to understand not only their vacillating nature as a class but the conditions and circumstances of their vacillation.

Much of the debate on the 1927 revolutionary failure, both at the time and subsequently, has focused on the question of the national bourgeoisie, however differing assessments as to the revolutionary potential of the peasants were also of critical importance. Stalin, in advocating the KMT-CPC alliance, saw the peasants as anti-feudal petty proprietors who would follow the national bourgeoisie as part of the four-class bloc; Chen Duxiu on the other hand prioritised national politics over social mobilisation, seeing both peasants and workers as too weak to take the revolution forward; meanwhile Trotsky, opposing the nationalist alliance, considered the poor peasants to be the main revolutionary force against capitalism as well as feudalism, calling on the proletariat to lead the poor peasant movement in a struggle against the rich peasant agents of the merchants and usurers as well as landlords. It was Mao who came to understand the peasants as the main force of China's revolution: the peasant alliance and peasant mobilisation against the feudal fetters were to provide the main foundation on which to influence and contain the vacillations of the national bourgeoisie.

The experience of the revolution up to 1935 had demonstrated that the national revolution could only succeed on the basis of social revolution with the mobilisation of the masses of workers and peasants. If the social revolution was not sufficiently organised, the national bourgeoisie would lead the revolution into a compromise with feudalism and imperialism; but on the other hand, if the mass power of the workers and peasants were organised, giving the revolutionary forces a chance of success in realising the democratic aims of national independence and economic recovery against the combined power of the opposing forces, the national bourgeoisie would follow.

Claudin has argued that up to 1927, Stalin in effect ruled the social revolution out of the national revolution in the United Front with the KMT by subordinating the CPC to KMT organisation and discipline thereby abandoning mass revolutionary organisation to bourgeois democratic organisation.[17] On the other hand, Swarup has argued that after the defeat of 1927, the 'Leftist' policies of the CPC under Stalin's influence abandoned the anti-imperialist aims of national revolution which were subordinated to the needs of social revolution.[18] However the real weakness of the CPC both before and after 1927 lay in its inability to fully grasp that the decisive role of mass revolutionary organisation in China existed in the armed struggle of the peasants to carry out land reform. To understand the interrelationship between the national and the social revolution, and the conditions influencing the vacillation of the national bourgeoisie, required an appreciation that the social revolution was essentially a matter of organising the peasants' struggle.

With the rise of the peasant movement in the first few months of 1927, as Zhou Enlai saw it, the conflicts that arose between the demands of the peasants and the KMT officers, who pressed for restrictions on land confiscation, indicated the persisting influence of small landlords and rich peasants in the nationalist movement which served as a brake on revolutionary mobilisation. Under these conditions, the CPC should have dealt with Chiang's betrayal by arming the peasantry, not relying on the KMT officers, 'pushing the KMT to the left' through organising the mass struggle.[19]

However, the leaders of the CPC did not understand at the time how a proletarian Party could lead the democratic revolution in China given the small working class base, and so resorted to Right Opportunism in seeking to help the KMT to power. After 1927, 'Leftist' policies, which, following the Russian 1905 model of city-based, nationwide revolution and looking to the organisation of the workers' movement to secure proletarian leadership, misconstrued the subjective conditions of the revolution which was actually taking place in the countryside. The focus on simultaneous uprisings in town and countryside essentially underestimated the forces of the peasant movement and the Red Army in a protracted revolutionary process.

Formulaic approaches placing the peasant movement in a subordinate role to the workers' movement and relying on the poor peasants as the main ally, led in practice to bureaucratism. Placing more faith in organisation in the cities, 'Leftists' implicitly expressed a mistrust of the peasantry, elevating cadres of working-class origin and creating splits between workers, peasants and intellectuals. This, according to Zhou, had an impact on organisation within the CPC as criticism inside the Party tended to degenerate into personal attacks, making it difficult to learn from mistakes of policy.[20]

Under the influence of Stalin and the Comintern, the rigid application of the Russian model with its overemphasis on the role of the cities caused confusion in understanding capitalism and the class structure of China. This formalism not only mistook the vacillation of the national bourgeoisie for betrayal but also inhibited understanding of the peasant movement and the roles of rich, middle and poor peasants. It was only through practice in organising the struggles in the rural areas that the CPC came to understand the differences between the conditions in China and Europe and to develop a land programme addressed to the problem of land hunger. It was on this basis that it became possible to mobilise the peasant majority against the feudal land monopoly so creating conditions for the mass democratic transformation of the village order.

This issue of mass power in the countryside was only resolved once the specific characteristics of the Chinese peasant movement were understood through the application of Marxism enabling a distinction to be made between the different forms of wealth and exploitation. Analysis of the intertwining of capitalist and feudal relations then explained why a semi-feudal, semi-capitalist rich peasantry, far from conforming to the Russian model of small proprietors demanding bourgeois reforms, were prone to side with the counter-revolution. At the same time this classification revealed the revolutionary nature of the peasantry in the unity of poor and middle peasants as a force capable of controlling the intermediate class in the villages. Restraining peasant excesses by encouraging the participation of the middle peasants in land reform, as opposed to the 'Leftist' tendency to follow rural radicalism, was to prove a further condition in containing the vacillations of the national bourgeoisie.

Without a clear understanding of classes in China and their shifting responses to the changing circumstances, the CPC had no means of bridging the agrarian and the national revolution: leadership only came with the absorption of Marxism, the viewpoint of the proletariat, into practice.

NOTES AND REFERENCES

1. Huang, 1978, pp.18–20.
2. Mao, *Selected Works*, Vol. I, pp.155–7.
3. See Zhou Enlai, 1981, p.185.
4. *Ibid.*, pp.187–8.
5. Mao, *Selected Works*, Vol. I, p.100.
6. Zhou Enlai, 1981, p.188.
7. Swarup, 1966, pp.82–3, points out that in May 1928 Mao maintained that the KMT was not representing the interests of the national bourgeoisie since under the new warlords there was no freedom even for the bourgeoisie – no right of speech and no free assembly. The defeat of the revolution was thus a defeat for the bourgeoisie. Swarup argues that Mao's view at this time held the germ of New Democracy which was the logical culmination of the view that the industrialists, the national bourgeoisie, were not in power under Chiang.
8. This was Mao's argument in December 1935 as he sought a change in CPC policy towards the national bourgeoisie. See *Selected Works*, Vol. I, p.156. Here he suggests that the national bourgeoisie had gained no advantage under the last nine years of KMT government – what they had got instead was bankruptcy or semi-bankruptcy of native industry and commerce. See also discussion in Chapter 4.
9. See Swarup, 1966, pp.65–7; see also Chesneaux and others, 1977, pp.190–1.
10. See *Ibid.*, pp.188–91.
11. Mao, *Selected Works*, Vol. I, p.144.
12. See Guo Dehong, 1981, p.46.
13. Mao, *Selected Works*, Vol. I, pp.167–171.

14. Guo Dehong, 1981, p.46.
15. Mao, *Selected Works*, Vol. IV, p.181; p.191.
16. See for example, Mao, *Selected Works*, Vol. IV, 1967, pp.219–20.
17. Claudin, 1975, p.277.
18. Swarup, 1966, p169.
19. Zhou Enlai, 1981, p.197.
20. See *Ibid.*, p.203.

PART 4

China's revolutionary experience from the Second United Front to land revolution (1937–1949) and the implementation of Mao's strategy

Introduction

The United Front against Japanese aggression brought the CPC for the second time into an accommodation with the KMT but this time on the basis of its own independent army and government. Under the arrangement the CPC set about building a new type of state in the base areas under its command – a New Democracy representing a joint alliance of all the different patriotic classes.[1] Whilst committing to a more moderate land reform of rent and interest rate reduction and a broader democracy, the CPC remained consistent in building grassroots organisation.

The CPC's patriotic mobilisation was hugely successful as, on the basis of peasant support, it grew to become a significant political force. When the CPC forces reached northern Shaanxi after the Long March, and established its headquarters in Yan'an in 1935, there were only some 40,000 Party members with 30,000 troops in control of an area with a population of about one million; by the time of Japan's surrender in 1945, the CPC had expanded into a membership 1.2 million with 900,000 regular troops covering revolutionary base areas across the North of China and into the eastern and central regions with a combined population of 100 million people. It was on a surge in popularity among the peasants that the CPC swept to victory four years later in 1949.[2] The Party's success in the countryside in the years of the resistance war has been a central preoccupation of Western scholars. Debate was triggered by Chalmers Johnson's influential thesis of 'peasant nationalism'. In *Peasant Nationalism and Communist Power*, published in 1967, he claimed that the main motivation behind the support among the rural population for the CPC, rather than socio-economic considerations, was its war of resistance which met the priority of the rural people for an anti-Japanese leadership. The thrust of his argument was to suggest that the Party's success among the peasants had little to do with Marxist class politics and the radical alteration of land ownership patterns. The peasants' indifference to social revolution was in his view evident since it was only after the outbreak of the Sino-Japanese war when the CPC gave up unpopular policies of land confiscation and shifted to compromise with the elites, virtually ceasing to advocate revolution to take up the nationalist cause, that they became more effective in winning the support of the peasants.

Others have taken issue with Johnson's view to emphasise the importance of the CPC's social and economic policies in incentivising peasant support for the guerrilla war. Most notable is Mark Selden's discussion of the 'mass line' in his classic 1971 thesis *The Yenan Way in Revolutionary China*.

Selden recounts how, out of an extreme crisis situation precipitated by the Japanese offensive and intensified KMT blockade, as the CPC responded with the launch of a new attack on the problems of rural society, there emerged a constellation of policies which opened up a new development path in the impoverished countryside. These initiatives took the form of new types of democratic arrangements and village institutions, which were to provide the foundation for an entirely new form of state as the CPC set about transforming the bureaucratic statis of the traditional state-village relationship.

This point of crisis was critical for CPC-peasant relations: the shift in policy from land confiscation demanded that the peasant farmers compromise their goals, but their support was now absolutely essential to raise production and to fortify the resistance against capitulationism.

Leadership methods and the Party-mass relationship were put to the test as the CPC faced the challenge of managing the contradictions which arose with diverse classes drawn to support the anti-Japanese resistance. For Selden, Party rectification became the driving force for a new democratic transformation of state-village relations with the CPC revolutionising its own leadership style as it reaffirmed its commitment to peasant interests through the implementation of the mass line, encouraging a bottom-up peasant participation as it sought to tackle bureaucratism.

Against Selden's view of a bottom-up egalitarian and participative transformation of village institutions and the village economy, others, drawing on studies of different base areas, have argued on the contrary that the CPC employed top-down authoritarian methods to displace the existing elites and establish its own control.

The debates here raise the whole question of democracy: how did the CPC set about building a new democratic state in its base areas? Were its methods really transformative or did it rather absorb traditionalist commandist methods into its own practice to exercise authority over the peasants? And how did it seek to tackle problems of corruption and degeneration in its own organs and institutions of governance?

Party rectification brought to the fore differences on questions of leadership and the mass line, evidenced in the contrasting approaches of Mao and Liu Shaoqi as they sought to analyse the obstacles to Party building and the challenge of breaking the power and influence of the traditional rural elites. Differences over open- and closed-door methods were rooted in contradictory perspectives on the countryside – Liu's view of its 'backwardness' as against urban enlightenment, and Mao's conviction in its revolutionary potential. Their differences were also reflected in contrasting methods in the practice of democracy: one based on universal suffrage, the other a more proactive approach to class organisation through the practice of democratic centralism as a means of harmonising or balancing the contradictions among the patriotic classes, including sections of the landlords, industrialists as well as workers and peasants, to create a joint force against Japanese aggression.

With the Japanese defeat in 1945 and the breakdown of the United Front into civil war, the pivot of the CPC's political activism and mobilisation shifted from 'nation' back to 'class'. The resumption of policies of land revolution and land confiscation ran once again into problems of the tenacity of landlord influence and contradictions among the peasants, as well as of commandist styles of leadership as previously experienced between 1931 and 1934. Attention turned in particular to the problem of 'not-so-thorough' land reform as under the 'double reductions' policies – of interest and rent – land had remained unevenly distributed.

Dissatisfaction among the peasants saw a further wave of extremism erupt and the situation in many villages became quite chaotic. Village studies carried out by Hinton and the Crooks at the time allow a detailed engagement with the complex transformation of land relations as directives zig-zagged from the moderate adjustments of the United Front period to radical land confiscation. An examination of the problems of 'not-so-thorough' land reform as well as peasant excesses, their causes and remedies, uncovers the impact of different policies of land reform on the different types of peasants.

Not only does this shed further light on peasant dynamics and contradictions, it also reveals how, with their differing perceptions as to the root of the problems, the contrasting approaches of Mao and Liu Shaoqi in tackling the persistence of landlord influence and rectifying Party organisation by developing democracy played out in practice. Whilst Liu's voluntarist approach to democratisation led to confusion and disruption, exacerbating the problems it aimed to tackle, solutions were to be found only through methods refined by Mao of class organisation – handling the contradictions among the peasants – through self-education, and through a process of Party rectification guided by criticism and self-criticism as the CPC opened its doors.

What comes out clearly from the analysis is how the relationship between the poor and middle peasants formed the core of China's democratic transformation. As it negotiated the shifting circumstances of the national and the social movements to bring the two together, the CPC built both from the bottom up and top down. Whilst the key to China's revolutionary process as a whole was that of village transformation, the strength of the CPC was demonstrated in its flexibility as it adapted to changes in the wider political situation and the balance of class forces to keep the peasants united at the centre.

NOTES AND REFERENCES

1. Although Mao's pamphlet 'On New Democracy' was not published until January 1940, the term was in common use from the spring of 1937. See Selden, 1995, p.134, note 6.

2. Li Lifeng, 2015.

18
The Anti-Japanese War (1937–1945) and the United Front

Challenges of Party building

In 1937, with the Japanese invasion challenging China's national survival, the CPC shifted the basic thrust of its political work from land revolution to the mobilisation of the popular forces in a war of resistance. The growing tide of anti-Japanese sentiment put Chiang Kai-shek under pressure, and the CPC and KMT concluded a second United Front alliance. This involved a new programme for a democratic government and the development of the economy in which all classes opposed to the Japanese invasion had a role. The arrangement was to hold more or less throughout the eight-year war until 1945 although tensions persisted between the two parties, at times to the point of breaking.

Under the arrangement, the CPC set aside its land confiscation programme, adopting instead a moderate agrarian programme of rent and interest reductions – the 'double reductions' policy – along with the guarantee of democratic rights. The new alliance was, however, a fundamentally different arrangement from the former CPC-KMT United Front since it was reached from a position of CPC independence. Under Mao's leadership, the CPC had by 1935 already begun to implement a more self-reliant strategy for China's revolution and with the new agreement, rather than being subordinated to KMT leadership as before, the Party now gained legitimate status within the United Front framework.

The CPC now set itself the task of forging a broad-based movement of national unity. Its aim was to create a completely different type of state, a democratic republic under the joint dictatorship of all anti-imperialist and anti-feudal people led by the proletariat. This path-breaking conception was made possible by the changes in class relations under the threat of national extinction. As Mao saw it, the national bourgeoisie, having followed the big bourgeoisie in 1927, was now swinging back towards the revolutionary camp, a shift that he had already anticipated in 1932. The new-type government would now include not only the national bourgeoisie but also patriots from the landlord class and from the big bourgeoisie in the interests of national solidarity.[1]

In the spring of 1937, the revolutionary base areas under CPC control began to transition from the system of soviet – worker-peasant – power based on land revolution, to a national unity government with democracy based on universal suffrage and the restoration to a degree of political and economic rights to landlords. This built upon the more moderate rural policies adopted by the CPC in 1935 as it abandoned the anti-rich peasant line to allow not only rich peasants but also small landlords to join in, or at least be neutralised in, a struggle directed against imperialist aggression and feudal landlordism.[2] In parallel with this shift, policies promoting and encouraging private enterprise had helped to prepare the way, given favourable conditions, for the longer-term alliance with the national bourgeoisie.[3]

Nevertheless, the CPC recognised that whilst the national bourgeoisie had a revolutionary aspect, it was prone to vacillation. It was, as Mao was to put it, 'extremely flabby economically and politically' and under pressure from Japan was liable to capitulate.[4] Despite the move away from agrarian revolution the CPC still adhered to policies of mass mobilisation in the national war in order to restrict the influence of the right-wing in the KMT and its tendencies to conciliate with imperialism. Whilst placing the emphasis on resistance to Japan and accepting that class struggle must be subordinated to the overall national interest, the CPC nevertheless continued to maintain a class perspective: the point was not to deny that class struggle existed but to ensure that the pursuit of class interests should not conflict with the national interest.[5]

Working within the moderate framework of United Front policies, the CPC's aim was to establish an independent government in the base areas through popular participation. Commitment to democracy was part of the agreement with the KMT, but for Mao, whilst the New Democracy was to be a system of universal and equal suffrage, it should not become one in which the government and army were 'privately owned by the few'. Political organisation aimed to ensure:

> a proper representation for each revolutionary class according to its status in the state, a proper expression of the people's will, a proper direction for revolutionary struggles to fight the enemies effectively.[6]

Democracy then also required a harmonising of the different class interests involved in the resistance to fully express 'the will of all the revolutionary people' in accomplishing the tasks before them.

The Party rectification campaign (1942)

The CPC bases already established from 1935 in North China began to see a great influx of patriotic intellectuals and students from the cities wanting to join the anti-Japanese struggle after 1937. At the same time, as its guerrilla armies expanded rapidly, the CPC was gaining control over vast areas of new territories as it extended behind Japanese lines.

To meet the needs of its growing administration, the CPC had to draw on the literacy skills not only of its urban supporters but also those of the local landlords, rich peasants and former officials in both its established bases and new territories. The fledging New Democracy, comprising a diverse mix of classes and social groups, was crisscrossed by conflicting loyalties and motivations – students and intellectuals committed to the nationalist cause; landlords and officials who often joined the United Front to preserve the remnants of their power at regional and county level; and the poor peasant activists at the lower levels of administration in townships and villages motivated primarily to fight for a better life. Particularly in areas liberated between 1935 and 1937, where the CPC had carried out land reform removing the landlord elite, many of local cadres who had risen from the ranks of the poor peasants and were committed to social change were concerned that the restoration of the landlords' rights would lead to a resurgence of landlord power.[7]

As CPC influence outgrew that of the KMT, relations within the United Front started to deteriorate with Chiang Kai-shek imposing an economic blockade on the CPC's base areas. Meanwhile, the danger of capitulationism was becoming acute. The change from land confiscation had put CPC-peasant relations in a certain jeopardy, however, facing the danger of a weakening resistance, the CPC looked to strengthen support amongst the peasants, not least its firmest allies, the poor peasants. It had to find ways to do so, however, without driving the patriotic elites to the opposition side. Managing the tensions arising from the social cleavages in the base areas was to put CPC leadership to the test.

To build up the peasant base, the CPC endeavoured to link its organisation of the anti-Japanese resistance with the ongoing struggles of the peasants against the landlords. In the last months of 1939, the 'double reduction' campaign was made the centre of mass work in all localities.[8] At the same time, to keep the KMT and the patriotic landlords on side, the CPC sought to demonstrate its commitment to democratic reform and its ability to share power by introducing a new system of representative government based on universal suffrage with elections carried out across the base areas. This established a 'three thirds' government system in which the CPC formally restricted itself to one third of all positions, with equal representation of non-Party progressives and moderates, and of members of the traditional elite who were guaranteed seats in local assemblies so long as they supported the anti-Japanese resistance.

Despite these efforts, relations with the KMT continued to worsen, even to the point of clashes in 1940. By 1942, the CPC base areas were coming under extreme pressure, not only experiencing serious economic and financial difficulties since Chiang had now tightened the blockade, but also since the CPC's armed forces were now bearing the brunt of the Japanese offensive. The Party responded on multiple fronts, building up mass associations to intensify the implementation of the 'double reductions' and to prepare for the organisation of village elections, at the same time unleashing a production drive to achieve self-sufficiency for the government and army so as to withstand the impact of the blockade.

The Party's response centred on a rectification campaign launched in 1941 which was to develop out of a study programme initiated in 1939. With the rapid growth of the Party drawing in a mix of members from different social backgrounds and different regions of China, many lacking both theoretical understanding and practical experience of revolution, the study programme had set out to familiarise cadres with Marxism and Leninism and the application of these approaches to China.[9] Texts included some Soviet documents but most were works from leading Chinese communists, Liu Shaoqi as well as Mao. Once settled in Yan'an, Mao had commenced writing a series of essays in which he summed up China's revolutionary experience: reflecting critically on China's historical legacy from a Marxist perspective to reassess the past experiences of the CPC, he set out in these essays the main issues confronting the Party, formulating ideas of class and nation under the New Democracy in a qualitative advance of his own theorising.

The Party rectification campaign has been seen as a move to impose uniformity over the CPC in a unified ideology moulded under Mao's dictatorial style; indeed for some it is held to be the origin of the cult of Mao.[10] The campaign certainly marked the turning point in the establishment of Mao's authority as both Party and national leader in a final break with the dominance of Soviet thinking.[11] But to understand this authoritarian turn, context is all-important as the Party rose to respond to the challenges it faced at this time of crisis. As Japanese attacks increased, with the KMT wavering towards capitulation, the United Front came under strain whilst at the same time CPC-peasant relations were at a turning point.

As Selden has argued, Party rectification was to serve the wider purpose of strengthening commitment to the Party and the revolution by broadening cadres' perspectives from an anti-Japanese fervour to the revolutionary transformation of Chinese society. Consolidating its own diverse membership into a unified Party was in turn key to developing a solid foundation for multi-class New Democracy.[12]

With some in the Party leaning towards accommodation with the propertied classes in order to strengthen the support of the KMT for the resistance, the rectification campaign turned instead to reaffirm the Party's commitment to peasant interests as it sought ways to drive up production to support the war effort. In doing so it was forced to confront the long-term stasis between the traditional bureaucracy and the village as it sought to build close cooperation between government and people. Particularly in the established pre-1937 revolutionary base areas, whilst the upper tier of government remained the stronghold of the literate classes – urban intellectuals, outsiders from other regions and the traditional elites skilled in the warlord administrations – the lower tiers of the local township and village administration had been transformed as cadres who had been involved in the struggle for land and who were often illiterate or poorly educated local partisans took up positions. The task before the Party was to close the gap between these two tiers, between state and village, to create a new-style government with quite different types of democratic institutions. To meet this task, Party leadership style and Party-mass relations were then placed at the centre of Party rectification.

Mao and Liu Shaoqi, whose writings on the Party formed key texts in the rectification campaign, were both committed to mass mobilisation. Nevertheless a comparison of their speeches and writings in this period reveals certain differences in their views on the obstacles facing Party work and therefore their approaches to Party-building.[13]

A question of method: Mao and Liu Shaoqi on Party-building

Mao and Liu both sought to address the problems of the lack of democratic life in the Party and local government, of Rightist and 'Leftist' errors and such malpractices as commandism and patriarchal despotism, authoritarianism and adventurism, self-seeking individualism and anarchism, and other anti-democratic behaviours. A comparison of their writings here however reveals differences in their views on the root cause of these errors and the ways to address them.[14]

Liu defined Rightism as 'unprincipled peace' – the unwillingness to criticise but rather cover up others' mistakes, and 'Leftism' as 'unprincipled struggle' – excessive and personalised attacks and the exaggeration of small errors.[15] These incorrect forms of inner-Party struggle were problematic since:

> First, they have given encouragement to the patriarchy inside the Party. Under such forms of inner-Party struggle, individual leaders and leading bodies oppress many Party members to such an extent that the latter dare not speak up or criticise

> thus leading to the arbitrary manner of an individual or a few persons inside the Party.
>
> Second, on the other hand, they have given encouragement to the tendency of ultra-democracy and the development of liberalism inside the Party. Many Party members in ordinary times dare not speak up or criticise and superficially peace and unity reign inside the Party. But when the contradictions can no longer be concealed, and when the situation has become serious and mistakes are exposed, they begin to engage in wild criticism and struggle, resulting in antagonism, splits and organisational chaos inside the Party which are almost beyond remedy. This is the opposite of patriarchy inside the Party.[16]

For Liu, 'Left' opportunism was the main danger in the Party since, as he argued, the CPC had never been influenced by the Second International ideologically or organisationally, and because the majority of Party members were petty bourgeois elements or peasants.[17] 'Left' opportunists ruled the Party like patriarchs, encouraged blind obedience and carried on merciless inner-Party struggles and penalisation creating a feudalistic order inside the Party.[18] Some comrades:

> ...command and control the Party, lording it over Party organisations, instead of acting within the organisation of the Party and obeying and submitting to the control of the Party. They want to act independently of the upper Party organisations in the name of inner-Party democracy, but they suppress the democratic rights of the Party membership and the lower Party organisations in the name of inner-Party centralism. In fact they observe neither democracy towards their subordinates nor centralism towards their superiors.[19]

Liu viewed these anti-democratic and autocratic tendencies as the reflection inside the Party of the privileged classes, that is, alien and hostile elements who had wormed their way into the organisation to exert their influence on the petty bourgeois and peasant members: ultra-democracy had appeared as a retaliation against absolutism, expressed as a petty bourgeois individualistic aversion to discipline.[20]

The source of wrong tendencies in the Party Liu saw to be the low theoretical level of its members, and the cultural 'backwardness' of the working people in general.[21] This was the basis on which 'Leftist' opportunists and dogmatists, who 'tore Marxist phrases out of context', then used these to assert their influence.

The emergence of patriarchal styles within the Party reflected the lack of democratic life in the country as a whole owing to the predominance of the patriarchal system of small-scale production.[22] Operating within this environment, the Party was exposed to the 'selfish intrigues and bureaucratic influence of the exploiting classes of the old society':

> …is it so strange that some members unavoidably bring some of the filth of the old society with them into the Party or reflect it there? Is it so strange that a person who has just crawled out of the mud is covered with slime? Of course not.[23]

The Party was infected with self-seeking individualism expressed in:

> …unprincipled quarrelling, factional struggle, sectarianism and departmentalism, [which] manifests itself in disrespect for and wilful violation of Party discipline. Most unprincipled struggles originate in personal interests. Those who go in for factional struggle and are given to sectarianism usually place their own individual interests, or the interests of a small minority, above those of the Party.[24]

The styles and habits of commandism and adventurism, which sacrificed the interests of the people for personal interests, Liu saw as alienating the people from the Party, and, as he stressed, everything is dependent upon and determined by the consciousness of the people and their voluntary action.[25]

Liu then counterposed self-seeking individualism with self-cultivation: Party members must overcome their desires to seek personal gain through self-cultivation and studying Marxism-Leninism to combat erroneous ideas and individualism.[26] Inner-Party struggles should be conducted on the basis of unselfishness: a cadre who serves the interests of the Party thereby wins the support of the masses, whilst those who seek self-interest isolate themselves from the masses. Against the corruption and backwardness of the old society, Party members should stand out as 'harbingers of enlightenment'.[27]

For Mao both Rightist and 'Leftist' errors undermined the Party's links with the people and made it difficult to create unity. The 'Left' organisational line expressed itself in various forms – bureaucratism, patriarchal despotism, authoritarianism, individualist heroism, semi-anarchism, liberalism, extreme democratisation, the assertion of independence; it violated democratic centralism, turned Party discipline into mechanical regulation and fostered blind obedience.[28] Mao too associated the errors with petty bourgeois democrats. With regard to the wider Left outside the Party, he saw these were to be accepted as a major revolutionary force in support of political and economic democracy. They were however susceptible to the influence of the ideology of the liberal or even big bourgeoisie and could swing to the Right or 'Left'. Inside the Party they could be re-educated and proletarianised in outlook to support the road to socialism.[29]

Mao conceived the key problems within the Party in terms of two mistaken approaches: doctrinairism and empiricism. Doctrinairism was the way of thinking of petty-bourgeois intellectuals detached from the practical processes of production, not starting from actual conditions but, as Liu also criticised, using phrases torn at random from Marxist-Leninist literature as dogmas regardless of their applicability under China's conditions.[30] Those associated with production on the other hand were liable to empiricism, suffering the narrow-mindedness, lack of discipline, isolation and conservatism characteristic of the small producer.[31]

Mao regarded doctrinairism as constituting the greater danger within the Party: his chief concern was that the intellectuals were isolated from the masses and divorced from reality.[32] It was the attitude of the educated members which constituted the biggest obstacle in the relationship between the Party and the people. This was itself partly an expression of a Confucian disdain for manual labour and partly a habit of urban sophistication looking down on the peasants:

> Generally speaking, if the cadres coming from the outside cannot get on with the native cadres, they should bear the principal blame...some people despise the native cadres and jeer at them, saying,...'What do the natives know? Clodhoppers all of them!'[33]

Liu, however, chiefly concerned with the low theoretical level of the Party members, considered that the main task of the Party was to overcome empiricism.[33] He criticised the anti-intellectualism of the 'Left'.[35] The problem as he saw it was that worker and peasant cadres:

> ...are often proud of their social origin and look down on the cadres from the ranks of the intellectuals.[36]

Empiricism, namely, the low cultural and theoretical level of these worker and peasant cadres, was for Liu the dominant aspect of 'Left' opportunism and was to be overcome by self-cultivation. But for Mao, whilst there were problems with the commandism and adventurism of the petty bourgeois and peasant cadres which alienated the masses and disrupted the Party, as well as the difficulties posed by the peasants' antipathy towards outsiders and intellectuals, the main problem lay in the attitude of the intellectuals themselves.

Rather than turning the cadres' attention inward in self-cultivation, Mao looked to create conditions for democracy both within the Party through resolving the contradictions between the intellectuals and worker and peasant cadres, and between Party and non-Party people. For Mao, the main problem was that Party members failed to apply Marxist-Leninist theory to the practice of the Chinese revolution.[37] The problem of the empiricism of the worker and peasant cadres in fact required that the outlook of the intellectuals be transformed. The theory guiding the Party had to be drawn from the practical experiences of the worker and peasant cadres; in some respects, Mao pointed out, they were more knowledgeable than the revolutionary intellectuals.[38]

The contrast of approach to Party rectification is clear in that whilst for Liu the problem was self-seeking individualism, which was to be addressed through self-cultivation, for Mao, the problem was that the intellectuals were divorced from reality and that had to be remedied by uniting theory and practice, drawing knowledge from practical experience. To overcome the alienation of the Party from the people and transform Party-mass relations, the focus for Mao had to be on remoulding the outlook of the intellectuals through practice.

In tackling the problems of 'unprincipled struggle' and 'unprincipled peace' to promote democracy in the Party, Mao favoured methods of criticism and self-criticism, dealing with cadres' mistakes by 'learning from past experience, in order to avoid similar mistakes in the future' and 'treating the illness in order to save the man.'[39] Confronting attitudes of exclusiveness towards non-Party people, which hindered the Party's work of uniting with the whole people, for Mao meant 'opening the door' of the Party to the broad masses.[40]

Liu on the other hand stressed that in the process of Party rectification a strict line should be drawn between struggles waged inside and outside the Party. He was concerned that some Party members would rely upon and make use of forces outside the Party to conduct inner-Party struggles and to blackmail and intimidate other Party members.[41] Liu was evidently concerned about the tendencies of Party organisations at local levels to degenerate into instruments of factional intrigue and personal gain, playing into the hands of the landlords. A strict demarcation of Party and society aimed on the other hand to preserve the Party as a disciplined, centralised organisation to be protected from the 'slime' of the old society so as to root out the traditional political practices of power-seeking, bureaucratism, and petty-bourgeois anarchism.

In this, Liu reflected the attitude of Lenin towards the petty-bourgeoisie:

> They surround the proletariat on every side with a petty-bourgeois atmosphere, which permeates and corrupts the proletariat, and constantly causes among the proletariat relapses into petty-bourgeois spinelessness, disunity, individualism, and alternating moods of exaltation and dejection. The strictest centralisation and discipline are required within the political party of the proletariat in order to counteract this, in order that the organisational role of the proletariat...may be exercised correctly, successfully and victoriously.[42]

Mao and Liu on the challenges of rural work

These differences in methodological approach to the problems in the Party were indicative of the contrasting attitudes Mao and Liu had towards the peasantry and the rural environment in which the CPC operated. To break through the patriarchal conditions of small-scale production and the low cultural levels that obstructed democracy, Liu looked to building a forward-thinking and enlightened Party uncorrupted by feudal political practices to carry the democratic revolution forward.

Mao too saw the lack of democratic life in China as rooted in the system of small-scale production dominated by the clan system.[43] However, his attitude towards the cultural challenge was more complex and nuanced. Rejecting 'wholesale Westernisation', he wrote:

> A splendid ancient culture was created during the long period of China's feudal society. To clarify the process of development of this ancient culture, to throw away the feudal dross, and to absorb its democratic essence is the pre-requisite for the development of our new national culture and for the increase of our national self-confidence; but we should not absorb anything and everything uncritically. We must separate all the rotten things of the ancient feudal ruling class from the fine ancient popular culture that is more or less democratic and revolutionary in character.[44]

From a Marxist viewpoint, Mao saw China's history as a history of class struggle – of peasant rebellion against the political and economic power of the landlords. Distinct from the dominant Confucian ethic, the peasants had their own culture, on the one hand narrowly parochial and traditional but also offering a source of revolutionary aspirations and practices which held the potential for the regeneration of Chinese society.

Liu's concern with self-cultivation in the making of a good cadre expressed something of the Confucian ideal of a 'clean' official opposing the corrupt rule of an autocratic Emperor. This deep-rooted traditional ideal was challenged by Mao, recalling his own transformation:

> I began as a student...I used to feel it undignified to do any manual labour...At that time it seemed to me that the intellectuals were the only clean persons in the world, and the workers and peasants seemed rather dirty beside them... Having become a revolutionary I found myself in the same ranks as the workers, peasants and soldiers of the revolutionary army...It was then and only then that a fundamental change occurred in the bourgeois and petty-bourgeois feelings implanted in me by the bourgeois schools. I came to feel that

it was those unremolded intellectuals who were unclean as compared with the workers and peasants, while the workers and peasants were after all the cleanest persons...[45]

Mao was to fundamentally break with Confucian notions of political legitimation as he sought to explain 'Left' and Right deviations in terms of class struggle and political line in the wider context of the overall revolutionary situation. Liu saw 'Left' and Right opportunism only in their manifestation as behavioural tendencies within the Party whilst for Mao these behaviours were linked into political lines influenced by objective conditions: 'Leftism' which ignored the possibility of participation by the national bourgeoisie in the revolution, was influential when the CPC and KMT forces were split; Rightism which tended to underestimate the efforts of the bourgeoisie to undermine the independence of the Party, was a threat in periods of alliance in the United Front.[46] Liu's main concern was with 'Leftism', however Mao saw that Right Opportunism also had to be addressed: although there was little basis for social reformism in China, the evident danger was that national and class capitulation might exercise some influence within the working class expressed in the tendency to accept limited reforms as the bourgeoisie endeavoured to bring the CPC under its control.[47]

In setting opportunistic tendencies in the Party within the objective class situation, Mao saw the problems not so much in the general terms of self-seeking individualism and cultural 'backwardness' but as arising under specific revolutionary conditions. Liu on the other hand did not look much beyond the boundaries of the Party itself, confining his methods of Party bolshevisation through individual study to strengthen loyalty within the frame of its own organisation. There is no conception in this of how the Party might itself be transformed through interaction with the outside world.

Beyond the issue of divided loyalties which Liu saw as obstructing inner-Party centralism and unity, Mao's concern was to address the divisions between town and countryside as these manifested in Party practice. His was not the view of the city as the sole source of enlightenment and democracy in opposition to the tyranny of feudal power and the narrow-mindedness of the small producers; on the contrary, he saw a certain Confucian disdain for manual labour as tending to reinforce urban disregard of the positive potential of the countryside.

In Mao's broader view, the problems in the United Front and the hierarchical divisions between the upper and the lower echelons of the administration were reinforced by contradictions between town and countryside, between people drawn from the cities into the base areas to fight the Japanese and the village cadres committed to rural change, that is, between the national and the agrarian revolutions. Rather than administrative solutions, Mao sought policies that would mobilise the masses and consolidate the two movements.

The path to China's modernisation for Mao lay not merely in reforming the state but in transforming village power. Party rectification was thus aimed at strengthening the ability of the cadres to activate and organise the peasants. Whilst Liu drew a strict demarcation between inside and outside the Party, between the backwardness of the countryside with its feudal traditions and the enlightened practices and attitudes cultivated inside the Party, Mao aimed to draw on revolutionary traditions outside the Party which were part of the peasants' own struggles against oppression and exploitation in order to challenge the feudal order. The peasants indeed had their own idea of what a good leader was, and in response to the peasants' antipathy to outsiders and bureaucratic interference, Mao appreciated that reforming leadership style and successfully linking with the peasant movement were two sides of the same process.

NOTES AND REFERENCES

1. For example, Mao, *Selected Works*, Vol. III, p.150.
2. See Guo Dehong, 1981, p.46.
3. See Mao, *Selected Works*, Vol. I, p.171.
4. Mao, *Selected Works*, Vol. III, p.117.
5. Mao, *Selected Works*, Vol. II, p.250.
6. Mao, *Selected Works*, Vol. III, p.121.
7. Selden, 1995, p.128.
8. Li Lifeng, 2015.
9. Selden, 1995, p.154.
10. Karl, 2010, pp.67–8; see also Selden, 1995, pp.155–7. For example, Wylie (1980) argues that the Party Rectification Campaign was aimed at consolidating Mao's leadership within the CPC against rivals at a time of intense rivalry between the KMT and the CPC, and that, by 1943, the campaign had developed into a cult of Mao. pp.190–2.
11. Dorris, 1976, pp.701–7.
12. Selden, 1995, pp.152–160.
13. Liu Shaoqi: 'How to be a Good Communist' (1939); 'On Inner-Party Struggle' (1941); and 'On the Party' (1945) in Liu Shaoqi (1980). Mao Zedong: 'Reform our Study' (1941); 'Rectify the Party's Style in Work' (1942); 'Oppose the Party 'Eight-Legged Essay"' (1942); 'Talks at the Yenan Forum on Art and Literature' (1942), in *Selected Works*, Vol. IV (1956).
14. Mao and Liu had quite different experiences in Party work with Liu's work in the cities contrasting with Mao's experience in peasant organisation.
15. Liu Shaoqi, 1980, p.61.
16. *Ibid.*, p.132.

17. *Ibid.*, pp.111–112.
18. *Ibid.*, p.186.
19. *Ibid.*, p.246.
20. *Ibid.*, pp.247–8.
21. *Ibid.*, p.145; p.212.
22. *Ibid.*, p.248.
23. *Ibid.*, p.75.
24. *Ibid.*, pp.60–1.
25. *Ibid.*, pp.210–1.
26. *Ibid.*, p.36.
27. *Ibid.*, p.220.
28. Mao, *Selected Works*, Vol. IV, 1956, p.206; also, Vol. II, p.258.
29. *Ibid.*, pp.211–2.
30. *Ibid.*, p.208
31. *Ibid.*, p.213–4.
32. *Ibid.*, p.36.
33. *Ibid.*, p.40.
34. Liu Shaoqi, 1980, p.268.
35. *Ibid.*, p.187.
36. *Ibid.*, p.271.
37. Mao, *Selected Works*, Vol. III, p.64.
38. Mao, *Selected Works*, Vol. IV, 1956, p.32.
39. *Ibid.*, pp.313–4.
40. See for example Mao's criticisms of sectarianism, *ibid.*, p.37.
41. Liu Shaoqi, 1980, p.155.
42. Lenin, *Collected Works*, Vol. 31, p.44.
43. Mao, *Selected Works*, Vol. II, p.255.
44. Mao, *Selected Works*, Vol. III, p.155.
45. Mao, *Selected Works*, Vol. IV, 1956, p.67.
46. Mao, *Selected Works*, Vol. III, pp.58–9; Vol. IV, 1956, p.214.
47. Mao, *Selected Works*, Vol. III, p.64.

19
Building the new democratic state

Selden on mass participation and the Yan'an Way

Selden's study of the Shen-Kan-Ning base area in the North West, where the CPC was headquartered at Yan'an, sets out his argument that, as Party rectification opened into a wider production drive, this led to a transformation of Party-mass and state-village relations through the development of new organisational forms, leadership styles and techniques of the mass line in what he called the Yan'an (Yenan) Way.

Taking issue with Johnson's claim that it was the nationalist cause rather than any Marxist notion of social revolution that drew the peasants to the side of the CPC, Selden sought to show how in fact the mass line strategy and socio-economic policies were vital in developing support for the anti-Japanese war among the wider rural population. The case presented in *The Yenan Way*, first published in 1971, is that through its participatory practices in village political and economic transformation, the CPC succeeded in raising peasant consciousness and so unleashing their revolutionary potential.[1]

Within the Party rectification campaign Selden highlights a tension between two leadership styles expressing two contrasting political impulses, one hierarchical and centralised, focussing on bureaucratic management; the other, egalitarian and participatory, a populist impulse towards the arousal of the peasant masses.[2] Whilst one placed emphasis on unity and stability underpinned by rational administration, the other stressed reliance on the revolutionary force of peasant mobilisation emphasising broad political participation and change through struggle.[3] These two impulses, Selden sees as joined in an 'uneasy co-existence' which manifested in tensions within the administration in the base areas between the upper level where bureaucratic methods flourished and the lower levels focussed on mass mobilisation.

The return of former officials to join the government apparatus of the base areas, Selden argues, left the CPC exposed, at least unintentionally, to the elitist impulse towards bureaucratism at the expense of popular demands. These personnel tended to run the administration along traditional lines with policies generally formulated at the upper level and passed down to the grassroots where local cadres acted as little more than tax collectors and recruiting officers. This then simply reproduced the pre-existing state-village pattern of a bureaucratism isolated from the villages.

However, pressure from the Japanese war drive and the KMT economic blockade forced the CPC to downsize the administration to reduce costs and to turn to methods of mass mobilisation to drive up production in support of the war effort. The only way to succeed, Selden highlights, was through organising the social revolution. This demanded the rectification of bureaucratism and the use of command by the upper-level administration which neglected the interests of the peasants whose participation was essential both in increasing production and in military recruitment.

As the revolutionary impulse in the Party was pushed to the fore, Party rectification and mass production campaigns took on an anti-bureaucratic and anti-elitist character with the emphasis on mass participation to transform Party practice and counter the continuing influence of the landlords and officials.[4] Higher government levels were transferred 'down to the village' to engage in economic work to be joined by students and other intellectuals; meanwhile peasants from the grass roots active in 'double reductions' campaigning with skills in rousing latent peasant energies, were promoted through Party rectification to positions of leadership at village level in place of the traditional village elite. As these new activist cadres took charge of the village production programmes they were to become the driving force in the new democratic transformation of state-village relations, redefining power and community from the base.

With people from urban and rural backgrounds mixing together the barriers between town and country, mental and manual labour, began to dissolve.[5] The influx of outsiders helped to break down the isolation of the rural communities, revolutionising village life: since they were lacking in personal ties in the localities, these new additions to the village populations tended to disrupt the pre-existing patterns of traditional elite influence. The shake-up was to facilitate the establishment of village self-government allowing local leaders to come to the fore, shifting conceptions of leadership as they took an active part in production and set about reorganising the village economy, generating community activity where previously village life had been left untouched by administrative reforms.

Selden's argument is then that the linkages between state and village were transformed as political initiative transferred downwards to promote local self-reliance with the production programmes penetrating the local communities. Administration was decentralised and debureaucratised: the departmental vertical top-down chain of command was broken by rerouting decisions through local committees which linked Party, Army and administration to better adapt to local conditions and integrate with practical work. In this way Party and government were brought closer to the people, away from bureaucratic management where decisions were in the hands of intellectuals and officials at higher levels.[6]

From this moment of crisis, as Selden argues, was to emerge an entirely new approach to social and economic change in poor rural areas, a labour-intensive development in conditions of capital shortage involving popular mobilisation at village level to break the centuries-long cycle of oppression and stagnation. In addition to private and individual enterprise, socialist-type elements also played a role with various forms of co-operative enterprise and with the development of traditional practices of mutual aid which brought peasant households with and without tools to work together, fostering participation, reciprocity and practices of shared benefit. The Yan'an Way of popular participation, decentralisation and community power, was, in Selden's words, 'a synthesis of the most significant and distinctive features of the Chinese contribution to the practice of peoples' war, revolution and the transformation of rural society'.[7]

Chen Yungfa on Party authoritarianism

Selden's view of the vital importance of social revolution in developing support for the anti-Japanese war among the peasants has been shared by others.[8] Pepper for example, also countering Johnson, highlights how the CPC, whilst shifting away from the issue of land ownership, continued to mobilise the peasants around rural tensions other than tenancy, including usury and corruption in local government, to build up the anti-Japanese resistance.

However Selden's viewpoint has also been challenged: Chen Yungfa, leading the counter argument, whilst also rejecting Johnson's notion of 'peasant nationalism', takes Selden to task for idealising the Yan'an Way as an effort at participatory community-building without showing how the CPC's populism was combined with authoritarianism as a means of state-building. His contention is that, rather than mass participation from below, the mass line essentially spearheaded the CPC's penetration of rural society from the top down, using existing peasant grievances to transplant the traditional elite only to substitute its own leadership controls.[9]

Based on a study of CPC organisation in East and Central China, Chen traces how the Party expanded into these new regions through military conquest and then set about establishing its own control over the territory. At first, the CPC met with political apathy on the part of the peasants, the result of ignorance, timidity and habitual acceptance of traditional values and power structures. Dedicated cadres with the necessary organisational and agitational skills and experience in united front work were sent to galvanise villagers into mass associations – of women, youth and militia. Using struggle meetings to unleash peasant activism against the landlords, cadres were able to rouse the villagers but having done so they then had to moderate the peasants' demands so as not to alienate the elites and drive them into opposition.[10]

In constructing a new village order, as Chen shows, the CPC sought firstly, through the rent reduction campaign, village elections and the creation of mass associations, to effectively dislocate the traditional elites from their peasant base. Then, once displaced from the village power structures, members of these elites would be co-opted into the three-thirds system on a new basis of universal suffrage and reabsorbed into the new administrative structures where their skills were put to use. In areas where spontaneous local mobilisation against the Japanese pre-existed the arrival of the Party's armed forces, the CPC sought to infiltrate these elite-led armed bands – landlord militia, lineage organisations, secret societies and bandits – to then recruit the leaders in a similar process of deconstructing the particularist and parochial bonds that underpinned their position, then reconstructing the power relations as the local fighters were reabsorbed into the CPC's army units.[11]

Chen finds that in fact the rural cadres were often not as committed to fighting oppression as Selden suggests, but were susceptible to the temptations of power and the rewards of office, remaining in the grip of old habits and the pull of non-Party bonds, of ties to factions, clans and brotherhoods.[12] Indeed, in his study of peasant organisation in the Taihang mountains, Thaxton also found that prior to the Party rectification many Party leaders entered peasant life as old-style benefactors developing a patron-client approach in handling services such as flood-relief grain, helping with rent reduction, and promoting village mutual aid. In this way they were to establish personal dependency ties with the peasants, recreating Party clienteles among the rural poor rather than fostering independent effort.[13] As Chen sees it, in these circumstances, the CPC turned to methods of internal discipline and rectification to impose control.

According to Chen then, Selden, in overemphasising the egalitarian and anti-bureaucratic aspect of the Yan'an Way, failed to recognise the Party's entirely opposing policies of restraining peasant demands, wooing the traditional rural elites into government and encouraging peasant capitalism. This saw power concentrate in the hands of Party cadres, themselves tending towards bureaucratism and elitism. Rather than acting as a transformative force, the CPC used its organisational networks to manipulate the rural population by meting out rewards, incentives and punishments to fulfil its state-building goals, turning traditions of localistic loyalties and obedience to authority to its own purposes in establishing its own authority on the basis of command.[14]

In the methods used by the Party to direct the mass movement, Chen then sees tendencies of authoritarianism, even totalitarianism. Since the rectification campaign did not challenge the authority of the Party, it served as a means of strengthening centralisation: rather than promoting peasant participation, the CPC denied the peasants any leadership other than its own. Once in control of the policy process, the Party was then able to use the mass organisations to penetrate the reach of the state into the village economy and production relations.[15]

Differing approaches to differing challenges?

CPC campaigning undoubtedly had to adapt to local circumstances according to the challenges it faced: to what extent then is it possible to account for the different approaches observed by Chen and Selden in terms of the varying conditions in their different case study areas?

For example, the North West borderlands between Shaanxi, Gansu and Ningxia, where the CPC was headquartered in Yan'an, lay beyond the reach of Japanese troops, far removed from any fighting, whereas the situation behind enemy lines in East and Central China was rather less stable and the CPC presence was more precarious as it sought to establish and consolidate territorial control. In the North West base areas, where widespread land reforms had been carried out between 1935 and 1937, the power of the traditional elites had largely been broken; however in the territories just being brought under CPC control, the struggle for leadership at village level was an ongoing process.[16]

Arguably the priority in Yan'an, as Selden maintains, was to tackle the problems of bureaucratic rigidity in the administration, staffed by urban intellectuals and the local literate elite who lacked knowledge and experience of village conditions. At the same time, the Yan'an headquarters was at the centre of the ongoing struggle between Mao and the doctrinaire Soviet-educated leaders who continued to challenge the rural-based strategy.[17] In the differing conditions of the East and Central China with the CPC expanding into new territories, the challenge was clearly to break through the barriers of landlord power and community closure in order to establish strong and effective organisational control.

With Mao based in Yan'an and Liu involved in Eastern and Central China, these different challenges of mass organisation may also provide a clue as to their different approaches to Party-building. Liu's efforts were evidently aimed at tackling the tenacity of the traditional elites as well as the parochial resistance to outsiders that obstructed grassroots mobilisation for the war effort. His reliance on internal Party organisation, discipline and the cultivation of loyalty evidently addressed the susceptibility of peasant cadres to the influence of non-Party traditional ties. Given the persistence of bonds of clan and brotherhood, the CPC, as Chen puts it, sought to immunise itself ideologically against assimilation.[18] At the same time, Liu sought to tackle careerism and opportunism amongst Party members who were more concerned with their own power rather than the development of the mass movement.

But this kind of approach could also play into the hands of the bureaucrats: as Selden reasons, a rationalised bureaucracy staffed with the most dedicated Party and technical elite was not enough to break the cycle of rural poverty and oppression in the villages.[19] Mao on the other hand saw bureaucratism as arising from the separation of the Party and administration from the peasant base. The problem was not the so-called backwardness of the peasants but rather the bureaucrats and the Soviet-educated Party leaders who lacked practical experience of the Chinese revolution.

At the same time, where Liu was preoccupied with 'Leftism' and the problem of unprincipled struggle which opened the Party ranks to landlord factionalising, Mao's concern, given the danger of capitulation on the part of the national bourgeoisie, was with Party Rightists who sought to restrain peasant activism which they saw as disrupting the policies of class accommodation within the United Front.[20] Focussing on the relations between intellectuals and worker and peasant cadres, and between Party and non-Party people, Mao considered it necessary to 'open the doors' of the Party so as to transform the very basis of leadership.

Although, the circumstances in the different base areas presented different challenges for Party building, the Selden-Chen debate nevertheless poses a general question about the top-down commandist nature of CPC methods versus the bottom-up participative impetus of the mass line. In fact, for Mao, the mass line was never anything other than both a bottom-up and a top-down process: authoritarianism was always present in the CPC's drive to establish power as it sought to balance peasant mobilisation with securing the support and contribution of the elites in order to contain Rightist capitulationism. The process of unity-criticism-unity within the Party encompassed both a democratic and an authoritarian aspect. Nevertheless, contrary to Chen's analysis, elitism and authoritarianism, as Keating has pointed out, are not the same: for the former, the wider population is problematic; for the latter, it can be a resource.[21]

Mao and Liu on democracy and the mass line

The question of democracy was central for the CPC in the United Front: how was this to be reconciled with the conception of its leading role in the four-class anti-Japanese alliance? Mao and Liu were both advocates of the mass line and both stressed the importance of voluntary action: they thought that emancipation could not be bestowed or granted, and that it was wrong to act on behalf of the masses. However, in their discussion of leadership errors – 'commandism' and 'tailism', Rightism and 'Leftism' – there were again particular differences in approach which held important implications for the practice of the mass line.[22]

Liu considered 'commandism' to be the major obstacle in Party leadership: 'tailism' or following behind the spontaneity of the mass movement had not in his view proved a major difficulty in the CPC.[23] 'Commandism' however overstepped consciousness and violated the principle of voluntary action. Against this he argued that, in applying the mass line, cadres should adopt the viewpoint of the masses: Party policies should incorporate the demands of the masses and if policies were correct, they would gain mass support, but if not, no support would be forthcoming. For Liu, the mass line was seen to turn on the question of whether a cadre served the interests of the Party, and thereby the people, or whether he acted according to personal interests. To counter commandist tendencies to dictate policy, Liu emphasised the importance of the formation of public opinion 'free from coercion from above' so as to protect peasant interests against abuses of Party power by cadres adopting feudal bureaucratic and patriarchal modes of behaviour.[24]

Democratic practice in the base areas was to draw on the earlier organisation of mass democratic power in the soviet bases with the involvement of women and youth, as well as popular education and open mass meetings, in preparation for the election of leaders in the three-thirds system. In 1940, Liu was to take on responsibility for setting up mass organisations at local levels to be developed in parallel with the Party rectification campaign and the production drive.[25] His particular approach was evident in the style of work which focused on government intervention and Party control as the main problem, seen as stifling mass participation and sapping the energy out of grassroots organising. The 'double reductions' campaign, for example, had revealed tendencies to resort to administrative fiat to enforce compliance.[26]

In order to preserve the autonomy of mass organisations against government-managed and -controlled mass mobilisation, Liu's emphasis was placed on promoting the values of voluntary membership, group independence and organisational work from the grassroots upward. He then called on Party organisers to clearly distinguish between the functions of mass groups and those of the military, government and Party, and to avoid control of the former by the latter. The introduction of a system of popular representation in village mass organisations was seen as effective in stimulating mass activism and developing a sense of autonomy.

Taken together with his closed-door approach to protect the Party against sectarianism and landlord intrigue, Liu's methods in effect separate mass struggles and Party organisation, with grassroots cadres working in the mass organisations serving as a conduit between the two, and all apparently depending on their loyalty and commitment to the Party. This approach to the Party-mass relationship is essentially a passive one with Party policies either gaining popular support or failing to do so. However, the problem with taking the principle of 'freedom of expression' as the guide to gauging the mass viewpoint is that it did not take into account the different sections of the peasants with their varying concerns and perspectives, nor did it consider the possibility of peasants' consciousness changing in the course of struggle and their confidence shifting as they experienced victories or defeats.

Mao criticised 'tailist' as well as 'commandist' errors in Party leadership: the mass line was not simply a matter of reflecting the opinion of the masses.[27] His previous experiences of revolution in the South had shown that the implementation of the mass line was not, given the traditional factional divisions and underlying conflicting viewpoints among the peasants, a simple matter of opening the doors to spontaneism. Rather it required organisation of the different demands around a concrete programme which united sectional interests into a common struggle, whether of radical land confiscation or for more moderate rent and interest reductions. This essentially involved a process of education and self-education: it was not something that could be accomplished overnight:

> ...mass meetings called on the spur of the moment can neither thrash out questions nor give political education to the masses; furthermore they are very apt to be manipulated by intellectuals and careerists.[28]

The mass line operated in different ways in different types of campaigns. The 'double reductions' campaign aimed to involve as many people as possible as quickly as possible. The production drive however was different. For example, in organising mutual aid teams, Mao was critical of voluntarism and advised that holding a mass meeting was not a good way to go about things: to build a durable organisation, rather than unleashing a widespread campaign what was required was propaganda and preparation to overcome the peasants' initial reservations. Demonstration by example, setting up a small number of teams to convince villagers of the efficacy of the practice provided a means of education, allaying the fears both of the rich peasants regarding of the misappropriation of their tools and animals, and of the poorer peasants for whom the traditional exchange of labour for tools and animals had been highly exploitative. [29]

For Mao, democratic centralism was not just a method for organising within the Party but was to be applied in its relations with the people.[30] Democratic practice was not simply a matter of substituting spontaneism and non-interference for commandism: the mass line involved a dynamic interaction between the masses and the Party which led, not by issuing directives, but by example and education, harnessing the impetus for change from below, respecting peasant traditions to guide their struggle to transform their communities in a process which allowed their consciousness to develop.

The politics and economics of the New Democracy

The politics of democracy practised by the new-style government in the base areas combined mass participation with CPC leadership of the four-class alliance. For Liu, this politics was framed in terms of voluntarism against commandism, but for Mao, it was the challenge of class organisation against capitulationism, a matter of reconciling or harmonising the conflicting interests towards the common goal of anti-Japanese resistance. This was not democracy in the Western sense of a directly elected representative government but one that reflected the national interests of China's people as a whole.

As Li Lifeng argues, whether the CPC's approach was top-down, consolidating military control first, co-opting local elites to secure its own leading position in the United Front then mobilising the peasants at the lower level, or bottom-up, arousing the peasants secretly or semi-openly first before seizing control of the upper level after the bottom was consolidated, the point was that either way the Party's emphasis was on 'the pervasive and active involvement of peasants'.[31]

Li suggests that the CPC's success lay in its ability to balance socio-economic reforms with the building of democratic government from local levels upwards, at the same time flying the nationalist banner through anti-Japanese mobilisation. This poses the question as to how this balancing was achieved: how did the CPC coordinate the national and social goals? How did it handle the class contradictions as it mobilised the peasants without splitting the patriotic front? Or as Li Lifeng puts it himself, how was the CPC able to win the support of the peasants but at the same time to pacify the rural elites?

The answer demands consideration of both the economic and political aspects of CPC's democratic programme, designed to work together to build cross-class cooperation, rallying the peasants through measures which effected a redistribution of wealth and power without a direct assault on the landlords and rich peasants involved in the administration of the United Front.

The political frame of the New Democracy, as has been seen, was not simply an electoral one but was structured through the three-thirds system to give a voice to all classes that supported the anti-Japanese resistance. Thus the three groups, the CPC, as representatives of the proletariat, the non-Party petty bourgeoisie, as well as the enlightened elites – the national bourgeoisie from the cities and the traditional local gentry – were all drawn together. At village level, elections based on universal suffrage went together with policies of mass involvement. By encouraging peasant involvement in elections, Li argues, their awareness of their own political participation was increased so 'giving them the sense of being their own masters'. At the same time the system convinced rural elites to believe that 'they still have political futures, and therefore nine out of ten of them won't choose to resist'.[32] In this way then mass mobilisation around village elections helped to break the political subservience of the peasants to the traditional elites.

These political changes saw the emergence of a new local leadership recruited from the poor and middle peasants, countering the influence of the traditional powerholders whilst transcending the limits of the peasant parochialism. For Li, the CPC's greatest success was in establishing by these means a complete, innovative political and institutional structure in the base areas which developed particularly at the grassroots, beneath the level of the county, through reliance both on the United Front and mass mobilisation.

National unity however required more than just giving all the different patriotic classes a say. Underpinning the multi-voice political structure were policies of economic democracy which initiated a particular dynamic of development starting from the village production programmes where a mixed economy system saw the private sector playing a major role in rehabilitating production and stimulating commerce, industry and finance.[33]

As discussed earlier, by 1935 the CPC, learning from the mistakes of the 'Leftist' two class bloc and the anti-rich peasant line, had come to recognise capitalism as a progressive force in the democratic stage with the national bourgeoisie representing comparatively progressive social elements against feudalism and imperialism, not to be attacked but to be encouraged to promote production. Although the shift to the 'double reductions' that followed under the new United Front stopped short of the complete elimination of feudal exploitation and did not give the poor peasants all that they wanted, it nevertheless meant placing restrictions on feudal relations and landlord power and, by lessening the feudal burden of rent, it helped mitigate the immediate hardships of poverty.[34] At the same time, it gave greater space for economic development so that, with the revival of trade compensating the landlords' loss of income from rent, they were encouraged to turn to their commercial and industrial interests.

A rich peasant economy was allowed to develop, growing in size as more well-to-do farming households were encouraged to 'get rich' through labour thereby increasing tax payments to support the army and securing rents paid to the landlords which also helped maintain the latter's support in the United Front. The increase in production for the market and raised consumption levels also stimulated the sidelines of the middle peasants lifting their enthusiasm to produce, and at the same time improved the conditions of the poor with more opportunities for employment. Facilities to borrow money at reasonable rates of interest provided the means to further self-reliance either by opening up new land or buying land which the landlords were more willing to sell.[35] Balancing the rich peasant economy and private enterprises, poor and middle peasants were encouraged to work together in mutual aid teams sharing the use of tools, and co-operative enterprises were also promoted.

The revival of the village economies, driven forward by the mix of private, co-operative and individual household enterprise as well as mutual aid, benefitted the base areas as a whole, providing government revenues, raising output and improving living standards and opportunities for all sections of the peasants whilst offering opportunities for enlightened elements among the rich peasants and landlords. As it helped to break down the isolation of village communities, economic revival afforded a way out from the vicious cycle of protection and predation, strategies to which both owner- and impoverished peasants clung for survival in conditions of economic stagnation and commercial decline.

In this way, the Yan'an-style village programmes, as set out by Selden and supported by Li Lifeng, offered something for everyone to foster the democratic United Front alliance and support the war effort. Social revolution was in these ways instrumental to the CPC's success in containing the Japanese aggression and, by effecting a radical change in the socio-economic structure of rural society, it opened up new directions not simply through outside intervention but by setting in motion within the villages an internal process of inclusive economic growth.

The key to the CPC's continuing commitment to the masses of the poorer peasants within the frame of the new democratic political economy lay in Mao's appreciation of New Democracy in the wider context of world revolution as a new type of revolution which, whilst clearing the way for capitalism, served to open up a still wider path for the development of socialism. Village co-operative enterprises were then seen as elements of socialism laying the basis for future development.[36]

Selden however, in the wake of the Tiananmen events of 1989, offered a corrective to his view in an epilogue to a new edition of his book. In this he gave way in part to the arguments put forward by Chen and others, to admit that he had originally paid too little attention to the 'dark side' of the Party.[37] Nevertheless, whilst indeed the Party was, and is, not immune from the 'slime of the old society', Selden's rethink might have considered further how an assertion of authority to tighten control was demanded by wartime conditions rather than reflecting some Communist idiosyncrasy.

If Selden's original conception of the Yan'an Way did tend to overemphasise mass participation and too easily conflated peasant and Party interests, CPC methods nevertheless involved a two-way process: as Li Lifeng puts it, participatory support through involvement in mass organisations and mass movements went along with acceptance of CPC leadership and a behavioural obedience based on support for its policies.[38]

Whilst CPC policies had seen improvements in the peasants' political and economic status, the Party had indeed subordinated their demands for social change to the overall national goal. Once the United Front broke down after 1945 and civil war ensued, pent-up frustrations amongst the poor peasants were released as Party policies shifted from class accommodation to land confiscation and the final elimination of feudal relations. In this difficult transition, the differences in approaches to democracy based on voluntarism or class organisation again came into play.

NOTES AND REFERENCES

1. Selden, 1995, pp.212–3.
2. Selden, 1971, p.188.
3. Selden, 1995, p.152.
4. *Ibid.*, pp.171–2.
5. *Ibid.*, p.182.
6. *ibid.*, pp.179–180.
7. *Ibid.*, p.144; p.170.
8. Pepper (1978); Dorris (1976); Li Lifeng (2015). Pepper sees the launch of the Party Rectification campaign as part of a leadership struggle which saw Mao and the policies of the mass line coming out on top, giving more priority to social revolution as a means of mobilising the masses to support the resistance, pp.233–44; pp.247–77.
9. Chen Yungfa, 1986, pp.4–6.
10. *Ibid.*, pp.12–3.
11. *Ibid.*, p.491.
12. *Ibid.*, p.15.
13. Thaxton, 1983, p.129.
14. Chen Yungfa, 1986, pp.16–7; p.517.

15. *Ibid.*, pp.14–5; p.503; p.508.; p.520.

16. On this question of the variation in conditions and challenges to state-building in the different base areas, Keating (1997) finds that the Yan'an Way in its most egalitarian and participatory aspect was a product of special circumstances as migrant populations settled in particularly inhospitable and marginal lands. Whilst it was indeed not replicable across China, she points out that this does not mean that it did not provide a model for other base areas to follow as they sought to adapt to their own specific environments and populations.

17. Dorris, 1976, pp.701–707.

18. Chen Yungfa, 1986, p.495.

19. Selden, 1995, p.171

20. See Pepper (1978), who, against Johnson, makes the point that the obstacles to mass mobilisation came not from the peasants but from Party Rightists, pp.233–44; pp.247–77.

21. See Keating (1986).

22. For Liu Shaoqi on the mass line see *Selected Works*, Vol. I, pp.388–9 and 1980, pp.206–226; for Mao on the mass line see *Selected Works*, Vol. IV, 1956, pp.111–5; p.226 and Vol. IV, 1967, pp.241–5.

23. Liu Shaoqi, 1980, pp.207–8.

24. Liu Shaoqi, *Selected Works*, Vol. I, p.392.

25. Dorris, 1976, p.711.

26. *Ibid.*, p.712.

27. Mao, *Selected Works*, Vol. IV, 1956, pp.312–3; Vol. IV, 1967, p.198.

28. Mao, *Selected Works*, Vol. I, p.91.

29. Dorris, 1976, pp.714–6; see also Perry, 1980, pp.240–4.

30. Schram, 1974, p.11.

31. Li Lifeng (2015).

32. *Ibid.*

33. Mao discusses the New Democratic economy in *Selected Works* Vol. III, pp.122–3. The New Democratic state, with a proper representation for each of the revolutionary classes, was to oversee a democratic system shared by all the common people. Feudal land ownership was ultimately to be ended in accordance with the principle 'land to the tiller; and big banks and big industrial and commercial enterprises were to be owned by the state and, under the leadership of the proletariat, would be socialist in nature and constitute the leading force in the economy as a whole which was to develop along the path of the 'control of capital', and never be 'monopolised by a few'.

34. Li Lifeng (2015); Selden, 1995, p.105.

35. Thaxton, 1983, pp.110–111; p.124.

36. Mao, *Selected Works*, Vol. III, pp.111–2; p.122.

37. see Selden, 1995, Epilogue, pp.222–252.

38. Li Lifeng, (2015).

20

The return to land revolution (1946-8)

From moderate to radical land policies

Following the defeat of the Japanese in 1945, the fragile truce between the CPC and the KMT broke down completely in the summer of 1946 as Chiang Kai-shek, with the full support of the US, aspired to wipe out the CPC base areas. A very bloody war ensued; at the same time the land revolution escalated throughout Northern China as the peasants, who had borne the brunt of the war, broke beyond the limits of the United Front's 'double reductions' policy in spontaneous land takeovers. As the CPC shifted once again from accommodative nationalism to a renewed emphasis on class struggle, transitioning from moderate to radical land policies, it confronted anew the problems of a lack of thoroughness in the land reform and an 'absolute egalitarian' reaction. There were considerable variations in conditions and levels of struggle from area to area but at the same time confusion was compounded by the different approaches taken by the CPC as, following the abandonment of Yan'an in February 1947, it separated into two groups, one led by Mao and Zhou Enlai in the North, another headed by Liu Shaoqi to the East.

What lay at the root of the problem of 'not-so-thorough' land reform? Had this arisen because the CPC, in pursuit of rather more mild and less effective land policies within the United Front, had abandoned social revolution and failed to challenge peasant apathy? Was it because of the Rightist influence of class accommodation which opposed mass mobilisation in land reform such that even the moderate reforms had not been fully implemented? Was it because the tenacity of feudal influence inhibited peasant activism so that landlords were better able to resist the implementation of policies? Or was it that the policies themselves had been inadequate such that the landlords had found loopholes?

'Not-so-thorough' land reform and the re-emergence of 'absolute egalitarianism'

In May 1946, the CPC issued an inner-Party directive to all liberated areas to oversee the transition from the 'double reductions' policy back to land confiscation.[1] The satisfaction of the peasants' demand for land was essential in providing the unity and support necessary during the coming civil war. The directive lent backing to the peasants' spontaneous seizure of landlords' land: 'land to the tiller' – the turnover of feudal lands to peasants with little or no land – was seen as a necessary step in the total destruction of the old pattern of Chinese society.

However to give some guidance to the peasants' direct actions, Liu Shaoqi, who bore the main responsibility for the directive, proposed not to abandon the 'double reductions' policy altogether but to spread and deepen it. Land confiscation was to be restricted to the properties of the big landlords, 'tyrants' and traitors, whilst the small and medium landlords, together with those who had co-operated in the anti-Japanese war, were to be treated with consideration and their cases handled by mediation. Rich peasants were to be subject to rent and interest rate reductions only, and middle peasants were to be drawn into the movement to participate fully in all decisions.[2] The tone of the directive was to encourage cadres not to exercise tight control over the direction of land reform but to allow this to be determined by the peasants' spontaneous actions, so as to experiment with different forms of land transfer. Nevertheless the emphasis was on the use of peaceful means in solving the land problem, pointing out that the methods adopted of confiscating only the land of major collaborators and encouraging the other landlords to sell their land voluntarily after rent reduction or as compensation to peasants, were methods that put the peasants in a legal and tenable position:

> ...having obtained a share of land on a fair and rational basis and having their ownership of land fixed, the peasants will gain enthusiasm for production and so will work diligently, practice economy and become rich and prosperous.[3]

By February 1947, in the continuing momentum of the peasant upsurge, there was some evident dissatisfaction in some villages due to the lack of thoroughness in land reform.[4] Some cadres complained of attacks on middle peasants, whilst in other areas there were criticisms of a 'rich peasant line' which had allowed the landlords to retain more than the average peasant holding.[5] The problems of persisting inequalities were noted by Mao, who, evidently going beyond Liu's *May 4th Directive*, favoured a process of 'evening up' to ensure that peasants with little or no land obtained some. At the same time he warned that it was 'absolutely impermissible' to encroach on the interests of the middle peasants, including those relatively well-to-do, recommending also that appropriate consideration be given to rich peasants and small and middle landlords.[6]

Following further investigations, Liu Shaoqi recommended the convening of a National Land Conference to review the lack of progress in land reform. The outcome of this conference, held in Hebei in September 1947, was an *Outline Land Law* aimed at remedying the shortcomings of the earlier *May 4th Directive* which had left the landlords with some land

and the rich peasants' land untouched.⁷ The Law confirmed 'land to the tiller' as the goal of thorough land reform and emphasised the injustice of the agrarian system. It aimed at the abolition of feudal and semi-feudal exploitation entirely, with the confiscation of all, not just the excess part, of the landlords' land together with all public and surplus land, and the cancelling of all debts. Land was then to be redistributed on an equal *per capita* basis. Article 6 stated:

> ...with regard to the quantity of land, surplus shall be taken to relieve dearth, and with regard to the quality of land, fertile land shall be taken to supplement infertile, so that all the village people shall obtain land equality...⁸

Faced with the limited success of land reform, it was generally agreed that the peasants had not been sufficiently mobilised and that the formation of poor peasant leagues was necessary to remedy the problem of 'not-so-thorough' land reform. The *Outline Land Law* called for these to be established throughout the Liberated Areas and for people's courts to punish those who resisted or violated the provisions of the Law.

There was no distinction made between different types of landlords, no special provisions for the rich peasants and no mention of protecting the interests of the middle peasants. In his speech concluding the conference, however, Liu filled in some of these gaps.⁹ He pointed out that it was imperative to unite with the middle peasants, the majority of whom had received land through redistribution, but whilst efforts should be made to unite with the well-to-do middle peasants and to compensate those who had been unfairly treated, Liu argued that it was advisable to appropriate a part of their land to 'prevent them from falling under the influence of the landlords and rich peasants'. However, those middle peasants who were unwilling to give up land should not be forced to do so:

> Of course if certain middle peasants are strongly opposed to equal distribution of land or even collaborate with the landlords and rich peasants, we must wage the necessary struggles against them. Still, the aim of doing so is to unite with them.¹⁰

Whilst the landlords must be 'brought to their knees' and those who opposed equal distribution 'rigorously suppressed', Liu advised that more leniency be shown towards the middle and small landlords who were willing to co-operate, and noted the need to distinguish between landlords and rich peasants, and old and 'new rich peasants' – those who had benefitted through CPC land policies – so that they would not join together to oppose the revolution. Such distinctions were to be made in accordance with the opinions of the masses in the peasants' associations of which the poor peasant leagues were to be the backbone. Liu pointed out:

> The worst thing that can happen is for a few cadres to distribute the land themselves, before the masses have been aroused or have fallen out with the landlords…experience shows that the policy of thorough and equal distribution is successful only when special contingents are formed by organising the poor peasants and farm labourers into peasant associations and only when the masses become politically conscious.[11]

The approach adopted by the Conference was influenced by the Party's experience when earlier in the spring of 1947 it had invited peasants to assess the performance of local cadres, and was shocked to learn of the intensity of the criticisms of the leaders' shortcomings.[12] Not only had landlords and rich peasants been allowed to retain some properties but it appeared that often village cadres had reaped the most benefits from land reform. Liu took this up in his Conference speech, attributing the problems of 'not-so-thorough' land reform not only to inadequacies in the policies guiding the movement but also to defects in Party organisation and bureaucratism.[13] Agrarian reform had, according to Liu, been obstructed by serious corruption in the Party and the *Outline Land Law* aimed to correct this. The defects in Party organisation – the spread of petty bourgeois spontaneism, liberalism, sectarianism and organisational confusion – were connected with landlords and rich peasants 'sneaking into our ranks' and Party members being unclear about the Party's class line. These defects aggravated the bureaucratism that existed inside the Party:

> The most serious and frustrating kind of bureaucratism for the masses is that which relies on coercion and commandism for the 'speedy and vigorous' execution of orders… Exponents… of bureaucratism stand above the masses and order them… Bureaucratism is a reflection within a proletarian Party of the thinking of the landlord and other exploiting classes, and some Party members have fallen under its influence.[14]

The necessary readjustments in land redistribution were then to be accomplished alongside Party consolidation. Liu called for landlords, rich peasants, alien class elements who had infiltrated the Party, and degenerate cadres to be 'combed out', and cadres of worker and peasant background, who practised bureaucratism under the influence of the feudal classes, to be educated, criticised and when necessary, subjected to disciplinary action. Leading bodies were to consolidate the Party through commendation and criticism – they should not turn a blind eye to, but should criticise Party members who acted 'arbitrarily and with impunity' and should take care not to give rewards where a task had been fulfilled through bureaucratic methods: 'those who reward bureaucratism are themselves bureaucrats'.[15]

Liu's view was that land reform had been obstructed in many areas because the landlords and rich peasants had managed to retain their influence:

> Many landlords and hooligans have infiltrated the Party and turned the Party's branches into small sectarian groups, doing evil deeds and suppressing the masses.[16]

Furthermore, the upper levels of the Party were seen to have often condoned or even colluded in this.[17] Corruption, commandism and coercion thus explained the failure of the masses to mobilise and carry out land reform thoroughly. This approach was consistent with Liu's previous writings, when he had earlier observed:

> In a backward country like China, the head of a village or the secretary of a county Party committee can lord his position over the people in his village or county. Some people are bound to become degenerate or bureaucratic.[18]

For this reason, the Party had to tighten up its organisation, step up education, enforce discipline and purge its ranks. Failure to do so would indicate collusion of the upper-level bureaucrats in malpractices at the lower levels. In tackling bureaucratism and alien class elements within the Party, Liu's focus was directed against those rural cadres who were like 'rocks' weighing down on the peasants: they were to be removed from their posts and expelled from the Party.[19]

As the readjustment programme under the *Outline Land Law* got underway, it appeared to Liu that the problem of cadre corruption was extremely serious. On the one hand, when the masses were mobilised to criticise the bad cadres, the landlords apparently took the opportunity to intrigue and incite the masses against all the cadres, without distinguishing between the good from the bad; on the other hand, the Party work teams sent to guide readjustment would try to protect the village cadres regardless of their errors.

The *Outline Land Law*, and the Party rectification which accompanied it, sparked off the most radical phase of land reform in the winter of 1947. Tendencies towards 'absolute egalitarianism' came to the fore as peasants in some areas demanded the thorough redivision of village land; there were instances not only of excesses in the treatment of rich peasants and encroachment on middle peasants' land as well as attacks on industrial and commercial properties, but also of the beating and killing of landlords. These developments had the effect of undermining the alliance against the landlords in the newly liberated areas whilst in the established liberated areas, where few landlords and rich peasants remained, demands for a second land reform targeted the village cadres as Party purges intensified.

As the movement developed to extremes, the CPC started to come to the realisation that successful land readjustment, as well as Party consolidation, could only be accomplished by reining in the radical trend towards 'absolute egalitarianism'. From his base in the North, Mao began to call for the correction of 'Leftist' errors from December 1947, warning again against infringements of middle peasant interests. Where Liu had in effect sanctioned struggles against middle peasants to give up land, Mao urged that in carrying out equal distribution it was necessary to listen to the opinions of the middle peasants and make concessions to them if they objected.[21]

In the following weeks, in order to deradicalise the movement, Mao issued various instructions to confirm that the targets of struggle were the feudal classes not peasants who had become rich as a result of land redistribution; to counter the wave of beatings and killings, stressing that the aim was to wipe out the landlords as a class not as individuals; to reaffirm the policy of encouraging landlords and rich peasants to invest in industrial and commercial undertakings; and for particular care to be taken not to classify middle peasants as rich peasants, to treat rich peasants differently from landlords, and to distinguish between different types of landlords.[22] Noting in particular the importance of the middle peasants in the old liberated areas where, as a result of previous land reform, they tended to form the majority, he called for their active incorporation into both the membership and leadership of the peasants' associations.[23] At the same time, a more detailed version of *How to Analyse the Classes in the Rural Areas* was issued.[24]

In February 1948, Mao marked out three different types of liberated areas where different tactics were to be taken: the old liberated areas, established before the Japanese surrender, where land was not to be redistributed a second time round; the semi-old liberated areas, which came under CPC control between 1945 and 1947, forming the largest part of the liberated areas, where thorough land reform was to be carried out, and where, if this was not well done, a second distribution should be considered; and the newly liberated areas where it was necessary to take a staged approach.[25]

Meanwhile Liu issued new instructions in February 1948 to tighten up Party rectification. These now abandoned the closed-door methods of dealing with the sectarian groups which were seen as giving landlords the opportunity to carry out their intrigues and isolate the Party from the masses.[20] Departing from his earlier adherence to internal methods of cadre discipline, Liu now favoured opening the doors first to small groups of poor, then middle, peasants, to give vent to their pent-up feelings against the cadres and to obtain redress for their grievances.

Mao's recommendations on the other hand were followed later that month by new instructions modifying the *Outline Land Law*. The *Directive on Land Reform and Party Rectification Work* drafted by Zhou Enlai prohibited those old or semi-old liberated areas that had already conducted relatively thorough land reform from pursuing 'absolute equalisation' and instead required the use of more moderate adjustment methods.[26] This was accompanied by advice to increase the number of middle peasant members of the peasant association also taking on leadership positions.[27]

Whilst Liu had blamed the problem of 'not-so-thorough' land reform on landlord obstruction, Zhou presented a somewhat more optimistic assessment of the successes of land policies in the old and semi-old liberated areas. Where land reform had been carried out thoroughly, class composition had altered with the numbers of landlords and old rich peasants greatly reduced and middle peasants forming the majority from 50 to 80 per cent of the rural population. Of these up to or over half were 'new middle peasants' while poor peasants and farm labourers constituted a minority of 10 to 40 per cent of the rural population. The landholdings of the middle and poor peasants differed but not by a great deal – the average amount of land owned by the middle peasants exceeded that of the poor peasants by about one half and whilst only a handful of landlords and rich peasants possessed more and better land and property, many cadres were also in this position. 'New rich peasants' had also appeared and in some areas outnumbered the old ones.

But in the areas where land reform had not been thorough, there were more landlords and rich peasants still owning more and better land, middle peasants remained a minority of about 20 to 40 per cent of the rural population, among whom 'new middle peasants' were a minority, whilst poor peasants and farm labourers still constituted the majority of 50 to 70 per cent of the population. In these areas, the average amount of land owned by the middle peasants was double that owned by the poor. Again cadres tended to own more and better land and property but 'new rich peasants' were few in number.[28]

Despite the additional instructions by Mao and Zhou, 'Leftist' errors persisted well into the spring of 1948.[29] Later in April 1948, Mao directly addressed the shortcomings of the Liu's National Land Conference which had not paid attention to the possible dangers of extremism. In particular he highlighted the limitation of the *Outline Land Law* in its failure to adopt different tactics and tailor policies according to the differing conditions in the newly liberated areas where land reform had to be initiated, and the old and semi-old liberated areas where only minor adjustments might be necessary if poor peasants remained dissatisfied with reforms already enacted.[30]

The middle peasant and the poor peasant lines

The complications that arose in tackling 'not-so-thorough' land reform and in the attempts to 'even-up' have been revealed in village studies carried out at the time by David and Isabel Crook (1959; 1979) and by William Hinton (1966). These allow a detailed engagement with the dynamics of peasant struggles and the challenges faced by the CPC in peasant organisation.

Ten Mile Inn, the focus of the Crooks' study, is situated in the borderlands adjoining Shanxi, Hebei, Shandong and Henan provinces, straddling the major trade route of the area. Before reforms in 1937 initiated by the CPC, although land ownership was not particularly concentrated and there were only 50 tenant families out of about 400, 70 per cent of the population had lived in the most dire circumstances. Landlords and rich peasants owned 30 per cent of the land and eight of these lived in the village. There were 40 or so families of upper-middle peasants who owned 40 per cent of the land, whilst the vast majority struggled to survive on uneconomic plots in the absence of alternative occupations. The lack of non-agricultural work stemmed from the failure of the village rich to invest in industries within the village, preferring to use their money for usury or in the textile trade in the neighbouring town. There was further inequality in the ownership of draught animals: the 20 richest families owned two each whilst the remaining families shared one between four.

However, over the years, Communist-led reforms had set in motion a process of gradual redistribution of wealth which changed the class composition of the village: by the time the Crooks arrived in early February 1948, the holdings of the former landlords and rich peasants had been reduced to one sixth, whilst roughly one third of the former poor peasants had become 'new middle peasants'. These 'new middle peasants' were mostly those militant poor peasants who had been courageous enough to take the first initiatives in the reforms introduced by the CPC. They had as a result risen from the ranks of the poor and become office holders in the new village power structure.[31]

In the spring of 1946, the peasants had stepped up the 'double reductions' movement, imposing fines on landlords and rich peasants who had evaded taxes during the anti-Japanese war. Whilst this was in itself a step forward in the peasants' struggle for greater equity in the village, the 'fruits' of this struggle, the confiscated properties of the tax evaders, were subsequently put on sale so that only those who could afford to buy, the middle peasants, gained from the struggle.[32] It was this fact that saw the middle peasants, including the 'new middle peasant' cadres, continue to gain as land reform progressed whilst one third of the village remained poor. This was then the cause of difficulties in the further implementation of reforms as well as disgruntlement with the new village leaders.[33]

The Crooks recount how the village cadres returned from a sub-county conference in September 1946 with the slogan 'For every man, land, a house and a horse' to commence the readjustment campaign in which the remaining poor peasants would be mobilised to express their demands and take actions to satisfy them.[33] In the following months, Ten Mile Inn was to witness acts of violence against the landlords and rich peasants in a struggle to 'cut off the feudal tails'. Also targeted in the campaign were the upper middle peasants, many of whom were, as the result of the practice of division of property between sons, downwardly mobile landlord families who had retained their cultural and educational advantages and their contacts as close kin of landlord families with connections with officials.

But the fact was that Ten Mile Inn had already undergone a certain degree of land reform with few landlords and rich peasants remaining. When this renewed campaign to 'cut off the feudal tails' failed to produce sufficient 'fruits' to satisfy the demands of the poor peasants, they turned in an increasingly angry and frustrated state on the 'new middle peasant' cadres. It became clear that the reason why the poor peasants' demands could not be met was because these activists and other middle peasants had managed to acquire the main benefits of the original struggles, and there was simply not enough land left over to go around. Instead of making orderly progress to thorough land reform, the readjustment campaign gave way to fierce attacks and personal criticisms leading to factionalism as personal grudges were acted out.[35] The campaign to 'cut off feudal tails' renewed class hatred in the village – everyone became suspicious of their neighbours as feudal 'tails' were traced back as much as three generations. All this made mutual aid and co-operation difficult, disrupting production, even more so as Party consolidation, linked with the readjustment process and aimed at purging alien class elements from leading posts, saw middle peasant cadres who led mutual aid teams also removed from their positions.[36]

As the Crooks observed:

> ...these defects were a consequence of the middle peasant line...when the 'fruits' had been put on sale instead of being distributed according to need. It was because this method of disposing of the 'fruits' had not solved the economic problems of the poorest that such desperate efforts were made to squeeze still more from the 'struggle objects'... Little was forthcoming, however, for the very good reason that little remained hidden. The best of the fruits had already been acquired by the middle

peasants. It was perhaps for this reason that the villagers, feeling frustrated and angry, resorted to violence.[37]

At this stage, fearing the worst, the county-level cadres called off the readjustment campaign but not before having gained the impression from the complaints of the peasants that the village cadres had, in fact, very grave defects.[38] In early 1948, a work team arrived in Ten Mile Inn prepared to encounter widespread cadre corruption. They encouraged the peasants to freely criticise the cadres only for the situation to verge on an outbreak of factionalism and anarchism which could have turned to the landlords' advantage.[39] But as the Crooks pointed out, the cadres were not seriously corrupt in the main: they were in fact courageous individuals from poor peasant families who had led, and gained, by the earlier CPC-initiated reforms. Their error had been that in taking control of Ten Mile Inn they had not organised the masses but had relied on a few individuals with whom they had shared the fruits of the struggle.[40]

What emerges so clearly from the Crooks' account of the events in Ten Mile Inn from the spring of 1946 to the summer of 1947 was the way in which the 'middle peasant line' gave way to the 'poor peasant line' as the village moved into a second phase of land redistribution. The main weakness in the land readjustment campaign was to lie in not maintaining unity with the middle peasants who now formed a considerable proportion of the village population. Instead of taking this into consideration, a one-sided 'poor peasant-farm labourer line' had been pursued. As Mao, in criticising 'Leftism', had observed:

> The slogan, 'the poor peasants and farm labourers conquer the country and should rule the country', is wrong. In the villages it is the farm labourers, poor peasants, middle peasants and other working people, united together under the leadership of the Communist Party, who conquer the country and should rule the country...not the poor peasants and farm labourers alone...[41]

Hinton's *Fanshen* shows similarly how Longbow village also suffered from excessive attacks on rich and middle peasants and exaggerated criticism of village cadres as the work team sent to investigate the situation set about to search out 'reliable' poor peasants to rectify the limitations of land reform.[42] The fact was that there was little landlords' land remaining for confiscation but the pressure from below, from the poor peasants, was to increase the numbers of families classified as rich peasants. Disagreements over class status in the campaign to 'cut off the feudal tails' and personalised criticism of the cadres created disunity among the villagers in a very confused situation. Hinton reports how eventually the 'ultra-poor peasant line' – 'base everything on the interests of the poor peasants; carry out the demands of the poor peasants' – was criticised with one county-level cadre saying:

> ...even to speak of such a 'line' is wrong, unreal. A Communist can have none but a proletarian line, the class line of the working class, and that class line is: depend on the poor peasants; unite with the middle peasants; and join up with all anti-feudal elements to eradicate the feudal system. That is the whole of it. No one part can be omitted.[43]

A cadre from the Party committee of the Taihang sub-region where Ten Mile Inn was located, described the error of excessive attacks on landlords, rich and middle peasants in the readjustment campaign:

> The mistake is basically a form of extreme equalitarianism. This is typical of the ideology of the peasantry and reflects the character of their production – small-scale agriculture. It is the same thing as Agrarian Socialism. This is revolutionary when it is applied against the feudal power of the landlords and rich peasants...The critical point comes when the peasants go on to distribute the property of the middle peasants. Equalitarianism then becomes reactionary.

> Many cadres of peasant origin did not clearly understand about the turning point, so they made mistakes. It is for this reason that the peasants must be under proletarian leadership. Without proletarian ideas to guide them they make just this kind of mistake and harm the revolution. It has been our experience that whenever the peasants are mobilised they push on toward extreme equalitarianism and the cadres are apt to be swept along with them. In this case, we senior cadres must take the blame for not having given the junior cadres full explanation and education of the point beforehand.[44]

The problem, at least in part, lay with the decisions that had been taken in 1947 at the National Land Conference which, in attempting to address the problem of 'not-so-thorough' land reform, had not done enough to prevent the emergence of extremism. In addition to the absence of clear guidelines to address the varying conditions in the different types of liberated areas, Mao, noting further weaknesses of the Conference, was to point out:

> ...on the question of identifying class status it adopted an ultra-left policy; that on the question of how to destroy the feudal system it laid too much stress on unearthing the landlords' hidden property; and that on the question of dealing with the demands of the masses, it failed to make a sober analysis and raised the sweeping slogan, 'Do everything as the masses want it done'.[45]

NOTES AND REFERENCES

1. Liu Shaoqi, 'Directive on the Land Question', May 4th, 1946, in *Selected Works*, Vol. V, pp.372–8.
2. See Crook and Crook, 1959, p.180.
3. Liu Shaoqi, *Selected Works*, Vol. I, p.376.
4. Mao, *Selected Works*, Vol. IV, 1967, p.124.
5. See Pepper, 1978, pp.284–9.
6. Mao, *Selected Works*, Vol. IV, 1967, p.124.
7. This is reproduced in Selden, 1979, pp.214–8.
8. *Ibid.*, p.216.
9. Liu Shaoqi, *Selected Works*, Vol. I, pp.379–92.
10. *Ibid.*, p.383.
11. *Ibid.*, p.385.
12. Moise, 1983, p.51.
13. Liu Shaoqi, *Selected Works*, Vol. I, p.380.
14. *Ibid.*, p.382.
15. *Ibid.*, p.382.
16. Liu Shaoqi, *Collected Works*, 1945–1957, p.120.
17. Liu Shaoqi, *Selected Works*, Vol. I, p.386.
18. *Ibid.*, p.410.
19. See Mao, *Selected Works*, Vol.V, p.49, note. 4.
20. Crook and Crook (1959) and (1979).
21. Mao, *Selected Works*, Vol. IV, pp.164–5. Writing in December 1947, Mao was supportive of the *May 4th Directive* and *Outline Land Law* but warned against repetition of the 'Left' line of 1931–34. At this time, the CPC was circulating the 1933 versions of *How to Differentiate the Classes in the Rural Areas* and *Decision Concerning Some Issues in the Land Struggle*. (Li Lifeng, 2015).
22. *Ibid.*, pp.182–6.
23. Mao, *Selected Works*, Vol. IV, 1967, pp.174–5; p.182; p.188.
24. The original version was annotated to include more detailed quantitative criteria for distinct classes. For instance, the difference between landlords and rich peasants was that rich peasants worked by themselves, while landlords did not do physical labour or did only auxiliary work, and the boundary between rich and middle was drawn at an amount of exploitation in excess of 15 per cent of total yearly output. See Li Lifeng (2015).
25. Mao, *Selected Works*, Vol. IV, 1967, p.194.
26. Zhou Enlai, 1981, pp.322–331.
27. Moise, 1983, p.67.
28. Zhou Enlai, 1981, pp.323–4.
29. Moise, 1983, p.68.

30. Mao, *Selected Works*, Vol. IV, 1967, pp.231–2.
31. Crook and Crook, 1959, p.127.
32. *Ibid.*, p.128.
33. Crook and Crook, 1979, p.11.
34. Crook and Crook, 1959, p.126. The house was strictly figurative: it stood for 'power'.
35. *Ibid.*, pp.150–1.
36. *Ibid.*, pp.131–3.
37. *Ibid.*, p.155.
38. *Ibid.*, p.159.
39. Crook and Crook, 1979, p.26.
40. Crook and Crook, 1959, p.156.
41. Mao, *Selected Works*, Vol. IV, 1967, p.182.
42. Hinton, 1966, pp.243–316.
43. *Ibid.*, p.491.
44. Crook and Crook, 1959, p.135.
45. Mao, *Selected Works*, Vol. IV, 1967, p.232; see also p.198.

21

Mao's methods refined (1946–8)

Rectifying policy errors

Whilst Liu had been focused on impurities in the CPC itself and the persistence of landlord influence to explain the limitations in land reform, the appearance of the 'middle peasant line' and the 'poor peasant line' demonstrated that weaknesses in peasant organisation were also an important factor. As one of the villagers said when asked why problems had arisen at Ten Mile Inn:

Well, it was partly the landlords' fault and partly the cadres'.
And it was partly that we ourselves weren't united.[1]

From his observations of the dynamics between the different types of peasants in the course of the agrarian struggles in the earlier period of land revolution and civil war in Southern China, Mao had reached a deeper understanding of how mass activism was inhibited by contradictions among the peasants. The persistence of landlord influence and the tenacity of patriarchal clan ties in a low ebb were obversely but integrally connected to the tendencies towards 'absolute egalitarianism' in an upsurge. The danger in an upsurge was not only of increasing the will of the landlords and rich peasants to resist, but also of alienating the middle peasants, so leaving the poor peasants isolated as the upsurge faded. To break the hold of the traditional elite powerholders it was necessary to unite the middle and poor peasants, overcoming not only the segmentation of traditional clan loyalties but also guarding against further damaging division from 'absolute egalitarian' demands.

As Party policy after 1946 transitioned from the moderate 'double reductions' to land confiscation aimed at the complete transformation of feudal exploitation and power within the village, success depended first and foremost on how the peasants were organised and on the institutions and policies geared to unleash mass activism. Unity between the poor and middle peasants had to be secured as the movement radicalised, winning over the masses step by step as land reform unfolded.

The directives set out in 1946 and 1947 had failed to anticipate the dynamics among the poor and middle peasants in the course of land reform as activism accelerated. The *May 4th Directive* had given no guidance on land transfers and no direction to the peasants' spontaneous land takeovers. Instead, its emphasis on legalistic means merely ratified the limited actions such as those taken at Ten Mile Inn, which moved only cautiously, for example, by fining tax evaders without involving the whole village. Its flexible provisions regarding methods of land takeover giving latitude to the local cadres not only provided loopholes for those from landlord and rich peasant background to protect the properties of their families but also, in lacking clarity on the question of confiscation of the rich peasants' land, had failed to identify the way forward to an orderly confiscation of feudal properties within the villages.

Mao was to observe how the middle peasants took a 'wait and see' attitude to the *May 4 Directive* in October 1946.[2] He was also to note that if there was no resolute struggle against the landlords, or if there was struggle but no victory, the middle peasants would vacillate.[3] It was therefore necessary from the outset to set up poor peasant leagues as the backbone of the struggle. In stressing non-disruptive and legal actions, the *May 4th Directive* had neglected this recommendation and had therefore failed to confront the passive attitude of the middle peasants so inhibiting mass mobilisation. Instead the directive tended to reflect their hesitancy, following the 'middle peasant line' which resulted in limited land reforms benefitting the few to the dissatisfaction of the poor peasants.

The *Outline Land Law* on the other hand, with its emphasis on satisfying the demands of the poor in campaigns to 'fill in the holes', had given virtually unlimited powers to the poor peasant leagues to do what they pleased. As the 'middle peasant line' of the *May 4th Directive*, whereby land had been distributed according to sale not need, gave way to the 'poor peasant line' which demanded confiscation of all lands surplus to subsistence, the *Outline Land Law* not only gave free expression to the spontaneous demands of the poor peasants for 'absolute egalitarianism' but also lent these the stamp of legitimacy.[4]

Placing responsibility for land confiscation as well as Party rectification with the poor peasant leagues without any guidance as to involving the middle peasants, the *Outline Land Law* implicitly accepted the taking of land from the middle peasants to 'fill in the holes' of the poor peasants' holdings. In failing to differentiate between the different types of liberated areas, the *Outline Land Law* generalised the targets of struggle and the policies of adjusting land ownership, at the same time universally adopting the poor peasant leagues to unleash the class struggle regardless of specific conditions.

The measures recommended by Mao and Zhou Enlai in early 1948 involved a finer tuning, narrowing the targets as appropriate and carefully calibrating the development of poor peasant leagues and peasant associations involving the middle peasants. In the newly liberated areas, Mao recommended that land reform should proceed in two stages. In these areas, the peasants had not yet been fully aroused and the middle peasants still maintained a 'wait and see' attitude. Meanwhile, the KMT, the landlords and rich peasants still had a great deal of influence. The first stage was to direct efforts exclusively against the landlords whilst neutralising the rich peasants:

> This stage should be further subdivided into several steps, namely, propaganda, preliminary organisation, distribution of movable property of the big landlords, distribution of the land of the big and middle landlords with some consideration being given to the small landlords, and finally the distribution of the land of the landlord class.[5]

He subsequently recommended even more caution in these initial stages, arguing that the stage of rent and interest rate reduction should not be skipped in any of the newly liberated areas.[6] One issue was that if land was redistributed too soon, it would place the entire military burden in the civil war on the peasants instead of the landlords and rich peasants, so undermining the possibility of uniting with all the social forces that could be drawn into the struggle and neutralising much of the opposition. Only when the situation was militarily secure and the peasants fully mobilised should land reform move to the second stage of distributing the surplus land and land rented out by the rich peasants.

In Mao's view, it was important not to attempt to wipe out the whole system of feudal exploitation overnight, but to do so in a discriminating way.[7] It was necessary to proceed carefully in the initial stage of land reform, and to concentrate on scoring victories against the obvious targets of tyrants, traitors and big landlords, in order to neutralise the rich peasants and secure the support of the middle peasants, most of whom would benefit from land redistribution. In this way it would be possible to mobilise the majority of the peasants. Once the larger landlords had been dealt with, the remaining feudal forces of the smaller landlords and rich peasants in the villages would themselves be isolated, without external support whilst facing a united majority of peasants. These then would be easier to deal with as the struggle advanced to the second stage of eradicating feudal exploitation within the villages and transforming the traditional village order. The 'Leftism' of the *Outline Land Law* was evident in its failure to narrow the scope of activity in the newly liberated areas in order to neutralise the rich peasants.[8]

To ensure that agrarian reform unfolded beyond its initial moderate stage, it was necessary from the outset, with the middle peasants still hesitant, to establish poor peasant leagues first. However, these were then to be developed into peasant associations which, whilst excluding landlord and rich peasant membership and maintaining poor peasant activists as leaders, were also to draw middle peasant activists into leadership positions.[9] The movement would then be able to progress to the setting up of representative conferences whilst land reform was taking place.[10]

In recommending the formation of the poor peasant leagues or peasant associations with the poor peasants as the main body, Mao saw these acting as a nucleus of leadership in the initial stages of land reform around which to rally mass support by concentrating firstly on propaganda against the obvious targets, then introducing reforms gradually when the masses were ready.[11] Whilst the formation of poor peasant leagues in the early stages would ensure that land reform would not stop halfway through the process by preventing the consolidation of the 'middle peasant line', the involvement of middle peasants in the peasants' associations and the formation of broader village institutions in the midst of land reform as the masses were mobilised aimed to guard against the emergence of the 'poor peasant line' as the struggle gathered momentum. Precisely at this point of division of properties within the village when 'absolute egalitarian' tendencies were liable to break out, drawing the middle peasants into the actual direction of the campaigns would ensure that their interests be protected.

The *Outline Land Law*, relying on the poor peasant leagues alone, had failed to chart the transition from the initial to the further stages of land reform in the newly liberated areas whilst also leading to confusion in the old and semi-old liberated areas. In the old liberated areas, where villages had been under the control of the CPC during the war, and the semi-old liberated areas which came under CPC control between 1945 and 1947, landlords and rich peasants had sold off land under the pressures of taxes and rent reductions, in accordance with United Front policies and their continuation under the *May 4th Directive*. Whilst they concentrated instead on their industrial undertakings, their land had been bought up mainly by the better-off middle peasants: the poor peasants could not afford to do so.[12]

As wealth began to shift from the rich, the poor had benefitted unevenly so that whilst there were still numbers of poor peasants who had insufficient land, few landlords or rich peasants still had any surplus lands. Meanwhile, as has been seen, 'new middle peasants' now held land often twice the average holdings of the poor peasants. The problems that arose in these areas were essentially contradictions among the peasants and it was here also that the *Outline Land Law* fell short. Omitting to identify the purpose of the poor peasant leagues to draw the middle peasants into peasant associations, free rein had been given to the egalitarian tendencies of the poor peasants.

Readjustment or 'evening up' for the sake of the remaining poor peasants potentially threatened the interests of the middle peasants, since, where the numbers of poor peasants remained large, their demands could not be satisfied by redistributing what was left of the lands of the landlords and rich peasants. Since the middle peasants were therefore reluctant to get involved in land readjustment, it was necessary to rely on the initiatives of the poor peasants.[13] However, for Mao, a key distinction was to be made between those areas where poor peasants still formed the majority and those where middle peasants had become the majority.

The latter in the main were the old liberated areas where Mao recommended there should be no second land distribution and no arbitrary organisation of poor peasant leagues: separate organisation would leave the poor peasants isolated since the middle peasants saw the leagues as a threat and feared that as land reform progressed they would themselves become targets for land confiscation. Instead the poor peasants were to be organised in groups within the peasant associations providing the backbone of the leadership but not to the exclusion of middle peasant activists.[14] Indeed Mao recommended that where middle peasants formed a majority in a village they should make up one-third of the committee membership of the peasant associations.[15]

In fact in Ten Mile Inn, where the old and 'new middle peasants' together made up two-thirds of the village population, successful readjustment and Party consolidation was completed only with the involvement of the middle peasants after the formation of a poor peasant league in which 'new middle peasants' made up one third of the members.[16]

Meanwhile in the semi-old liberated areas, where middle peasants remained a minority, the problem of 'not-so-thorough' land reform had arisen since the peasants had not been fully mobilised from the start. To counter the middle peasants' 'wait and see' attitude, poor peasant leagues were necessary to ensure thorough land reform but with the aim of winning the middle peasants.[17]

Dealing with the cadres' errors

As the results of the investigations in 1947 revealed that many peasants remained poor, Liu had drawn the conclusion that landlords and rich peasants had wormed their way into leadership positions at village levels and had sabotaged the implementation of policies with the collaboration of village cadres who resorted to commandist and coercive practices to oppress the masses. A pessimistic assessment of political conditions in the villages led him then into a general theory of Party impurity.

Mao, like Liu, was concerned that the presence of landlords and rich peasants in the primary organs of power in the countryside and in local Party branches was alienating the peasants and preventing land reform from being thorough as they 'tyrannically abuse their power, ride roughshod over the people and distort the Party's policies'.[18] However, his approach to the handling of cadres' errors was to show a certain leniency. Indeed, if the problem of 'not-so-thorough' land reform was seen in the context of contradictions among the peasants, this presented a less severe view of the defects in Party organisation. The difficulties in completing thorough land reform were not those of obstruction by the landlords alone but also those of effecting the transition from moderate to more radical policies of land transfer with the 'double reductions' policy benefitting only a portion of the peasants so as to create a problematic situation of considerable inequality between peasant holdings.

The continuing presence of landlords and rich peasants in the local organs of power and in the Party itself was at least in part of result of United Front policies when large numbers of patriotic gentry had in fact been encouraged to join the governments in the CPC base area. Mao however was to confirm in December 1947 that the 1942 rectification movement had been largely successful whilst noting that some problems still remained in the class composition of the ranks and in the style of work in the Party's primary organisations in the countryside.[19] Nevertheless as the situation shifted into the more radical stage of complete confiscation of all landlords' land, Mao still thought it necessary to abide by the principle of United Front government, as indeed did Liu, recommending that the patriotic landlord-gentry who had joined the anti-Japanese struggle should not be made a target of struggle but should be allowed to retain their positions in the new institutions of power on the condition that they gave up their feudal holdings.[20]

Landlords and rich peasants had gained leading positions during the United Front because they had managerial and literacy skills but, as Zhou Enlai pointed out, the problem was not whether in principle Party members recruited from among the landlords and rich peasants should or should not remain in the Party:

> First, although it is true that many opportunist alien elements may be found among such Party members, it cannot be said that there are none who have voluntarily given up exploitation or severed their relations with the exploiting classes. Second, since mistakes are made in class identification, some Party members of middle peasant status are inevitably treated as if they were rich peasants. Third, as the local Party organisations recruited so many landlords and rich peasants during the War of Resistance…the present sudden suspension of their membership is certain to have some impact on the Party branches at the township and village levels, and it may have even more widespread repercussions.[21]

If class background was to be taken as the sole criterion in Party consolidation this would have led to the indiscriminate suspension of tens of thousands of Party members who came from landlord and rich peasant families. This was a danger in applying Liu's methods of purge and discipline and was compounded by the manner of the 'open door' provisions of the *Outline Land Law* which encouraged the poor peasants to freely criticise and impeach the village cadres. Indeed, as in Longbow, Party work teams arriving in the villages would seek out poor peasants in their homes to elicit criticisms of the village leadership rather than holding a public meeting; on other occasions the whole process of investigating class status, land holdings and assessment of the cadres had been accomplished in a series of public meetings one after another in a single day.[22] Such methods were liable to heighten emotions rather than encourage considered assessment of cadre performance.

As the Crooks pointed out, in attempts to consolidate Party work through meetings including non-Party people which exposed the cadres to public criticism, it was important that care was taken to avoid indiscriminate attacks and purges otherwise:

> ...many of the most able, intelligent and forceful members of the newly emancipated classes might be swept out of office instead of being reformed. This would leave only inexperienced leadership in the villages. Such a danger could not well be risked at a time when the new political and economic gains had hardly been consolidated.[23]

To contain excesses in Party consolidation, Zhou Enlai stipulated two preconditions for the application of the open door methods:

> The first is that the leadership at the next higher level must be strong, the second that there must be several good Party members serving as the mainstay of the branch in question.[24]

He advised against the dissolution of Party branches: 'generally speaking there are always some good Party members in a Party branch'. Mao recommended the unfolding of criticism and self-criticism within the Party first, and further stressed that in order to resolve the problems of impurities in organisation it was necessary to involve the broadest masses, that is, rather than the house-to-house calls carried out by Party work teams.[25] This would reduce the danger of venting personal grievances against cadres.

Liu set high standards of Party loyalty and ideological purity, and whilst his methods had shifted from self-cultivation and internal Party discipline to external disciplining by the peasants, without unity in the mass movement it was difficult to correct the cadres' mistakes. The problem with Liu's methods, whether closed or open door, was that they focused on the organisation of the Party rather than the organisation of the masses. The new village leaders tended to resort to commandism when the peasants were divided; at the same time, if they could not rely on broad support among the peasants, they would become all the more isolated and vulnerable to the manoeuvrings of the landlords. Party rectification then could not be accomplished without addressing the problems in uniting the mass movement.[26]

Mao had specifically warned against using the same methods for dealing with cadres who had made mistakes as dealing with the enemy.[27] This was one of the main reasons in drawing the distinction between the old and semi-old liberated areas, where land redistribution had been carried out at least in part and where peasant cadres had taken control, from the newly liberated areas still to undergo land reform, where the landlords were still very influential and feudal land monopoly was still the main issue. Without this distinction being made, the danger in applying the *Outline Land Law* in the areas of 'not-so-thorough' land reform was that, whilst the attention of the peasants who remained poor focused on the cadres, the latter would receive the same treatment as the traditional powerholders had done.

In setting high standards, it was easy to find shortcomings in cadres' performance. At the same time, in the Party rectification that accompanied the *Outline Land Law*, the success in land reform was apparently measured in terms of the standard of cadres' behaviour rather than the actual changes in land ownership. Thus when the work team arrived in Longbow village, they had been so alarmed by the apparent abuse of power by local cadres that, without making a detailed investigation of conditions, they promptly arrested the four worst offenders on the assumption that they had been in collaboration with the local landlords.[28]

Mao's approach to dealing with the problems within the Party followed principles of 'learning from past mistakes to avoid their repetition', 'curing the sickness to save the patient', and 'clearing up wrong thinking while uniting with comrades'. Distinctions were to be made between major and minor mistakes.[29] Landlord obstruction and cadre corruption did not tell the whole story: the cadres' failure to mobilise the masses of peasants in thorough land reform was related rather to their inability to overcome the initial passivity of middle peasants and to handle the contradictions among the peasants, which as has been seen, had been exacerbated by reforms which had benefitted only a few whilst leaving many peasants poor.

In adopting this approach, Mao demonstrated a more optimistic view of the possibility that both the peasants and their leaders might change their behaviours. Even in cases of more serious abuse of power, Mao held a more lenient attitude, stressing education as the means to strengthen discipline. The problem with cadres at Ten Mile Inn and at Longbow was considered not so much due to the infiltration of alien class elements but rather that one or two of the 'new middle peasant' cadres started to abuse their powers once they had gained a position of authority.[30]

Recognising the problem of bad habits retained by poor peasant leaders of the peasant associations in Hunan in 1927, Mao had argued:

> They can only be regarded as 'the few undesirables', and we must not echo the local bullies and bad gentry in condemning indiscriminately everybody as 'riffraff'. To tackle this problem of 'the few undesirables', we can only, on the basis of the association's slogan of strengthening discipline, carry on propaganda among the masses and educate the undesirables themselves…but we must not wantonly send soldiers to make arrests, lest we should undermine the prestige of the poor peasantry and encourage the arrogance of the local bullies and bad gentry.[31]

In the areas of 'not-so-thorough' land reform, whilst some landlords and rich peasants had maintained influence in the new institutions of power, the problems and obstacles to land reform had been exaggerated. The extent of alien class infiltration had led to numbers of misclassifications whilst expectations of high standards of leadership had combined with pessimistic views of village conditions. The difficulties in land reform had been laid at the door of the cadres who were suspected because, as activists, they had gained the most. The problems, however, to a large extent lay in the application of the land policies themselves.

Liu's argument that the land reform had been unsuccessful, that landlords still had land, and that this showed the cadres to be ineffective and corrupt, protecting the landlords, had itself led to problems in the areas of 'not-so-thorough' land reform since in fact there was little feudal property remaining for distribution: most of it had been acquired through purchase by the more well-to-do peasants as a result of the limited methods of carrying out land reform.

A question of goals

How successful land reform was seen to be depended on the goals it was measured against. In assessing the extent of the problem of 'not-so-thorough' land reform, an important distinction had to be drawn between the 'absolute egalitarian' ideals of the peasants and the eradication of feudal exploitation. In the former, all the land in the village, including the surplus lands cultivated by the middle peasants, was taken into consideration in distribution on a *per capita* basis to establish equal landholdings; in the latter, it was only surplus lands rented out that were the object of confiscation.

Rural cadres had been found wanting in their efforts at land reform often as a result of a confusion over goals. As one Longbow cadre explained:

> It is because the cadres judge their work from an egalitarian point of view that they end up thinking that land reform has not been completed. As soon as this point of view is disregarded it is easy to see that the work of land division has not only been completed, but has been carried out too far.[32]

The extent of landlord subversion and cadre corruption had thus been exaggerated by the dissatisfaction of the poor peasants: it was only in the light of their egalitarian aspirations that land reform appeared less successful than it had been and that the cadres therefore seemed less reliable. It was rather the *Outline Land Law* that was wanting: in failing to warn against excesses as the peasants' direct actions outstripped the moderate constraints of the United Front period, relying instead on peasant spontaneism, it had tended to encourage the venting of personal grievances against the cadres whilst legitimising the peasants' egalitarian ideals in its provision of 'taking from those with a surplus to give to those with a shortage, and taking from those with better land to those with worse land'.

In Ten Mile Inn, the egalitarianism of the 'poor peasant line' had been expressed in the slogan: 'For every man, land, a house and a horse'. The vision presented was that of a small peasant economy. But given the situation of land shortage, this led to undue emphasis on the demands of the poor peasants, and the encroachment on the land of the middle peasants which threatened the condition of unity among the peasants vital to resisting the efforts of the landlords to preserve their influence and protect their property.

As a cadre at Ten Mile Inn argued:

> The idea of levelling everyone off and making everything even is not correct. In the past, inequality was due to exploitation. But whatever inequality exists now it is not a result of exploitation. It is only inequality in comparison with the middle peasants. If they have more land than others, this is a result of their own labour, and it is only right that they should have a higher yield than others. It would be wrong to take anything from them. The middle peasants don't hire long-term labourers; they belong to the same family of poor-and- hired.[33]

The confiscation of feudal properties only for redistribution on a *per capita* basis regardless of differences in peasant land ownership, on the one hand led to the establishment of a system of unequal holdings under cultivation; on the other hand the redistribution of all surplus lands would have seen instead the creation of an economy of more equalised family farms. From a Chayanovian viewpoint, family-based farms are seen as more productive, applying more labour per unit of land to achieve higher yields than the larger farms which hire labour to apply more capital per unit of land. So in conditions where, rather than the development of capitalist farming, parcellised small production persists and land is scarce, it might seem desirable to maximise output by redistributing land from the richer peasants hiring labour but with lower yields to the remaining poor peasants to create more viable and more efficient family labour-based units.

However in China, as has been argued previously, capitalist farming was not so much inhibited by the greater efficiency of peasant production but rather by the high concentration of land ownership in conditions where a massive demand for land on the part of the peasants inflated rent: it was this that was the barrier to investment in production since capitalism can only emerge from petty commodity production if the level of capitalist rent is at least as high as pre-capitalist rent. Under conditions of monopoly rent, peasants clung to small plots, applying labour-intensive methods not because these were more efficient, but because these were the only means of survival. Rich peasants meanwhile gained a higher income from renting their surplus lands than from investing in new techniques to increase labour productivity.

The rationale of preserving the surplus lands cultivated by the rich and well-to-do peasants, protecting their interests in land reform, was not only to allow for production to increase but also, as has been argued, to forge the broadest possible unity among the peasants to oppose the feudal interests. For Mao, 'absolute egalitarianism' was reactionary, backward and retrogressive in nature. The goal of land reform, the elimination of feudal exploitation, was to be achieved through the organisation of the democratic struggles of the peasants. Of paramount importance then was the unification of the poor and middle peasants and the neutralisation of the rich peasants.

With its provision of 'taking from those with a surplus to give to those with a shortage', the *Outline Land Law* had implicitly condoned the taking of land from the middle peasants. Liu's remarks at the September 1947 land conference, although emphasising unity with the upper middle peasants, also admitted circumstances in which it was permissible to confiscate some of their land. However, as far as Mao was concerned, the principle of equal distribution of land was to apply to the redistribution of feudal properties only: the confiscation of the surplus lands of the middle peasants cultivated by themselves was forbidden. So whilst he considered it was necessary to respond to the immediate demands of the poor peasants, this should not be done at the expense of the alliance with the middle peasants. The middle peasants in fact should be allowed to keep more land than the average holding of the poor peasants.[33] Mao thought that it was possible to persuade well-to-do middle peasants to voluntarily give up their surplus land to lighten their tax burden but stipulated that it was permissible to take such land for readjustment only with their consent, making concessions if necessary.[35]

On the question of the rich peasants, the *May 4th Directive* left their surplus lands untouched subject only to rent reduction, but made no mention of the need for a further stage to develop the struggle against them, for example, through the formation of poor peasant leagues. The *Outline Land Law* subsequently identified the rich peasants as a target of struggle along with the landlords but made no mention of treating them differently. Mao was also to make a further distinction between old rich peasants who had strong ties with the landlords, who could initially be neutralised but would later become a target in the final stages of eradicating the feudal order, and 'new rich peasants' whose interests were to be protected and who were in fact to be treated like well-to-do peasants in that their surplus lands should not be taken without consent.[36] The point was that unlike the old rich peasants, the 'new rich peasants' had gained not through feudal exploitation but rather through taking advantage of the opportunities of limited land reforms initiated by the CPC after 1937. These had seen many well-to-do tenants buy back their lands sold to the landlord as they benefitted also from the revival of agriculture, commerce and industry in the base areas. For Mao, it was important to protect these gains for the sake of the anti-feudal alliance since this also gave reassurance to the middle peasants.

Neither the *May 4th Directive* nor the *Outline Land Law* had clearly distinguished the targets at the different stages of land reform and as such both had tended to jeopardise the anti-feudal alliance. With the aim of uniting the broadest range of peasants in the anti-feudal struggle, subsequent corrections to the provisions of the *Outline Land Law* restricted confiscation to surplus lands rented out by the rich peasants whilst land farmed by them was to be retained. This gave recognition to their dual semi-feudal, semi-capitalist characteristics. Furthermore, the recommendation was made to raise the criterion demarcating middle and rich peasants from 15 to 25 per cent income from exploitation.[37] Although the provision was not adopted until 1950, it aimed to protect those who had gained from rent and interest rate reductions with the classification of many 'new rich peasants' as middle peasants.

Resolving the contradictions

As has been seen, 'not-so-thorough' land reform had arisen in the difficult transition from the initial stages of land reform to the later stages of dealing with feudal exploitation within the villages. Whilst the large landholdings of the landlords had generally been broken up, the small landlords and rich peasants still retained some properties and influence since the peasants had not been mobilised fully at the beginning. At the same time, divisions among the peasants had been exacerbated since, given the limited initial mobilisation, only a minority had benefitted from the reforms, provoking later an extremist reaction on the part of the remaining poor which threatened the Party and the new village institutions as well as the middle peasant alliance. To deal with the remnant feudal holdings of the small landlords and rich peasants in these areas, and to correct the unequal outcome of the 'middle peasant line', it was necessary in some areas to make some minor readjustments. But at the same time the pressures from the poor peasants for a second round of land reform had to be contained.

The most important factor in limiting excesses in the treatment of landlords, rich and well-to-do peasants was the involvement of the middle peasants in the process of agrarian reform: since they were permitted larger holdings than those of the poor peasants, their involvement moderated demands for 'absolute egalitarianism'.

Successful land reform required then the clarification of the goals of land reform with clear methods of class identification based on criteria of exploitation distinguishing between the different types of surplus lands. At the same time, it was only made possible by the creation of institutions and policies which enabled the gradual unleashing of mass activism as the dynamics between the poor and middle peasants unfolded.

Under the *Outline Land Law* the poor peasants had been allowed to give vent to their immediate grievances in outbursts of personal emotion. But as Hinton's *Fanshen* shows, it was only through a lengthy and convoluted process involving long discussions that the villagers of Longbow came to decisions concerning class status, the assessment of village landholdings, and the abilities of the cadres, correcting the previous hasty decisions such as the arrest of the four cadres. As these decisions were discussed firstly by the poor peasant league, then by the peasant association, and finally ratified in the village congress, this process of decision-making saw the reshaping of the economic order of the village integrally connecting with the creation of new village institutions of mass democratic power.[38]

Changes in the land and power relations of the community then came about not so much through external Party decree: it was the peasants themselves who transformed their traditional patterns of behaviour in a process of self-education. The work teams served only to guide the process in which the peasants, to resolve their material conflicts, had to confront and overcome the traditional and personal prejudices which kept them divided, inhibiting their activism and weakening their new institutions.[39]

In Ten Mile Inn, the work team sent to guide readjustment changed its direction once the Party began to criticise 'Leftist' errors. Following instructions not to get bogged down in the problem of cadre corruption, they shifted their focus onto the adjustment of land holdings rather than on punishment by the people's courts.[40] Since in fact there had only been a small number of landlords owning not a great deal of land, whilst the middle peasants did not own much more land than average, their investigations found that the poor peasants' need for land exceeded the land still available for redistribution, the problem being unequal distribution between the peasants. The situation was similar in Longbow where before readjustment about one-third of the 400 or so families had still been poor.[41]

The line of the *Outline Land Law* had seen intensifying rivalries between the peasants in areas of land shortage but it was in fact to prove possible in both Ten Mile Inn and Longbow to resolve the limitations in agrarian reform which had aroused the dissatisfaction of the poor peasants by correcting the 'poor peasant line' and carrying out land readjustment and Party consolidation with the involvement of the middle peasants in the process of thorough land reform and the transformation of village power.[42]

The villagers of Ten Mile Inn were finally able to reach a successful conclusion by emphasising not the equalisation of landholdings but the better distribution of resources to maximise production.[43] This made it possible to draw the middle peasants into the campaign and eventually, with a certain amount of social pressure some of the 'new middle peasants', who had formerly been poor peasants, were persuaded to return some of their surplus land for readjustment to those in most need. In this way over a hundred of the poor families received land and became 'new middle peasants' able to support themselves on an independent basis. The middle peasants who originally had larger holdings now had less land than before but their holdings still exceeded the average with a surplus above subsistence.[44]

As a result of the readjustment of the 'middle peasant line', the majority of peasants now had holdings of a sufficient size to guarantee subsistence and were able to support themselves outside of any dependency relations. This satisfied the immediate demands of the poor peasants to meet their needs of subsistence. However, readjustment also preserved a considerable number of farms with a potential for growth providing a dynamic for economic revival.

As distinct from the utopian small producer dream of egalitarianism, readjustment saw the establishment of a system of unequal holdings under cultivation with different capacities for expanding production. The limited availability of cultivable land in effect ruled out the possibility of a small peasant economy of equalised holdings being viable. Whilst egalitarianism divided the peasantry in their struggle to eradicate feudal exploitation, the removal of the constraints of the feudal land monopoly, by unleashing the productive potential of the countryside, opened up the possibility of managing the contradictions among the peasants and meeting the peasants' demands for a better life along a path of economic development.

NOTES AND REFERENCES

1. Crook and Crook, 1979, p.31.
2. Mao, *Selected Works*, Vol. IV, 1967, p.116.
3. *Ibid.*, p.188.
4. See Moise, 1983, pp.61–2.
5. Mao, *Selected Works*, Vol. IV, 1967, p.194.
6. *Ibid.*, pp.251–55.
7. *Ibid.*, pp.236–7.
8. *Ibid.*, p.219.
9. *Ibid.*, p.201; see also Zhou Enlai (1981), p.329.
10. Mao, *Selected Works*, Vol. IV 1967, p.165; p.193; p.230.
11. *Ibid.*, p.194; p.201.
12. Moise, 1983, pp.47–8. According to one estimate, 54 per cent of the land had been bought by middle peasants.
13. p.116; p.194.
14. *Ibid.*, pp.193–4.
15. *Ibid.*, p.188.
16. Crook and Crook, 1979, p.105.
17. Mao, *Selected Works*, Vol. IV, 1967, p.194.
18. *Ibid.*, p.166.
19. *Ibid.*, p.166.
20. *Ibid.*, p.184.
21. Zhou Enlai, 1981, p.335.
22. See for example Pepper, 1978, pp.312–6; Hinton, 1966, p.276; and Moise, 1983, p.60.
23. Crook and Crook, 1959, p.158.
24. Zhou Enlai, 1981, p.330.
25. Mao, *Selected Works*, Vol. IV, 1967, p.233.
26. Hinton, 1966, p.249, makes a similar suggestion when he points out that commandism and opportunism fed on the antagonisms among the peasants, and if these were not resolved, democracy could hardly expect to flourish.
27. Schram, 1969a, p.314.
28. Hinton, 1966, pp.256–8.

29. Mao, *Selected Works*, Vol. IV, 1967, p.175; Vol. II, p.253.
30. Crook and Crook, 1979, p.138.
31. Mao, *Selected Works*, Vol. I. p.33.
32. Hinton, 1966, p.492.
33. Crook and Crook, 1979, p.273.
34. Mao, *Selected Works*, Vol. IV, 1967, p.235; p.239.
35. See *Ibid.*, pp.164–5; p.175; pp.183–5.
36. *Ibid.*, pp.184–5.
37. *Ibid.*, p.183; see also Selden, 1979, p.219; and note 24 above.
38. See Hinton, 1966, p.411, for an outline of the steps in this process.
39. *Ibid.*, pp.307–8. Almost half of the poor peasants in Longbow were not invited at first to join the poor peasants' league for a variety of prejudices, including reasons of 'traditional purity'.
40. Crook and Crook, 1979, p.149.
41. Hinton, 1966, p.305.
42. Crook and Crook, 1979, p.217; Hinton, 1966, 350–7.
43. Crook and Crook, 1979, pp.206–7.
44. *Ibid.*, pp.230–1.

PART 5

Peasants, revolution and the
Communist Party of China

Introduction

In seeking to analyse the CPC's success in mobilising the peasants, Western scholars have explored various dimensions of Party leadership and peasant motivations and consciousness. Drawing variously on the wider academic theorising as to the nature of the peasant household economy and political behaviour, and the relationship between modern revolution and traditional peasant rebellion, they have developed their debate on the Chinese experience of agrarian revolution around questions of class and tradition.

Why was CPC leadership to succeed where past peasant rebellions failed to achieve a thorough social transformation? How did the CPC manage to penetrate the village order and integrate its organisation and programme with the peasants' struggles at grassroots levels? What was the nature of the peasants' collective actions and how did the CPC reconcile peasant motivations to reshape their local rural order with their own goals of national and social revolution? How did the Party gain legitimacy in the peasants' eyes? Were the seeds of a new order to be found in the peasants' own struggles and demands?

Western scholars have been divided as to the congruence of CPC and peasant goals, and the continuities or discontinuities between traditional forms of peasant protest and revolutionary action in China. Bianco for example pointed to a fundamental discontinuity in that, as he saw it, CPC strategy was deliberately offensive whereas peasant agitation resembled the 'defensive reaction of a beleaguered organism'. Seeing their spontaneous protests and uprisings characterised by localism and parochialism, he regarded peasant class consciousness as weakly developed.[1] Chesneaux, on the other hand, was to find in the secret societies, which united poor peasants with the urban proto-proletariat and the illegal bourgeoisie, a source of opposition to the well-to-do, to the state, and to the traditional Confucian order. Although he claimed these organisations were tied to the old society, especially given their superstitious ideology, Chesneaux argued that in schooling the Chinese people in clandestine political activity, they provided a precedent for the strategy of protracted armed struggle central to the modern Chinese revolution.[2] Alavi and Wolf however have countered this view of the role of the dispossessed in revolution, advancing the 'middle peasant thesis' to highlight the centrality of the role of owner-cultivators.

The works considered here, Marxist as well as non-Marxist, examine widely the revolutionary nature of peasants and the connections between the objective conditions of class exploitation and the peasants' subjective consciousness, as well as the role of traditions and the peasants' own political ideas, culture and behaviour. Scholars differ as to the peasants as market-oriented individual producers or simply survivalists; whether or not there was any correspondence between the goals of the peasants and the CPC; and the extent to which CPC organisation was able to build on the peasants' spontaneous collective actions and pre-existing forms of rural protest. There are also commonalities in the recognition that peasant awareness of class relations was obscured by non-class loyalties to kin and lineage, and a questioning then of whether peasant goals were determined directly by their material interests or mediated through their own political ideas and culture. There is the important issue here of how and to what extent CPC organisation was able to penetrate clan and patron-client ties and to undermine the influence of the Confucian ideology of benevolence that underwrote these social relations to unleash peasant class organisation against the landlord-elite.

Alavi, seeking to explain what the CPC did differently from other political parties, and Wolf, considering the distinctiveness of peasant rebellion, have taken a comparative approach, examining various experiences of peasant rebellion and revolution. Perry, Thaxton and Marks have used micro-studies to explore peasant collective actions and political organisation in China in-depth. The answers they provide clearly have implications for understanding not only the role of the CPC leadership but also the social outcomes of land reform and in particular the potential for future development. Undoubtedly their analyses and studies help to widen and deepen understanding of CPC-peasant relations in revolution if ultimately failing to grasp the issues of class power, the Marxist essence of analysis of China's agrarian revolution.

NOTES AND REFERENCES

1. Bianco, 1972, p.213, and 1986, pp.301–2.

2. Chesneaux, 1972, pp.17–21.

22

From traditional rebellion to modern revolution

Alavi's 'middle peasant thesis'

Alavi and Wolf have both advanced the argument that the CPC succeeded in organising the rural revolution because it was able to utilise the energies of the independent-owner-cultivator-middle peasants who, as that section of the peasants least under landlord domination, were initially the most militant. Both see the poor peasants as unlikely initiators of peasant rebellion and revolution being too closely tied to or dependent upon landlords.

Alavi's work spans the experiences of the peasant movement in Russia, China and India. His argument is that the major obstacle in unleashing peasant revolution is clientelism – the ties of patronage binding poor peasants to the landlords on whom they are dependent economically – which are seen to inhibit their active role as a class pressing the most revolutionary demands. Comparing the Russian and Chinese experiences, he contrasts the failure of the Bolsheviks with the success of the CPC in grasping the role of the middle peasants so as to help create the preconditions which would allow the poor peasants to emerge as the leading element in the agrarian struggles.

Alavi essentially follows the Leninist understanding that, whilst the peasants as a whole were allies in the democratic stage of revolution, the middle peasants' conservative regard for private property tended to limit the goals of land seizure, so that the poor peasants had to take the leading role in order to create the best conditions for the transition to the socialist stage of revolution. However in the case of the Bolshevik revolution, the traditionalism of the middle peasant tended to inhibit class consciousness among the poor peasants, creating difficulties in uniting the peasants into revolutionary committees such that leadership of the movement fell to the rich peasants.

Alavi points out that Lenin later explained the failure to organise the poor peasants in terms of their 'immaturity, backwardness and ignorance', envisaging that they would emerge as a revolutionary force only after the bourgeois democratic revolution was completed and the landlords had been defeated.[1] What Lenin neglected, according to Alavi, was the role of the middle peasants in a dynamic that ultimately would have unleashed the more revolutionary demands of the more subordinated poor peasants. This he argues was demonstrated by the experience of the Chinese revolution.

In analysing the 1926–7 peasant upsurge in China, Alavi sees a distinction between tackling the immediate problems caused by the excessive demands of the warlords and tax officials and the actual ending of the exploitation of the landlords to unleash the development of agriculture. He argues that since, according to Mao's Hunan report, the peasant associations' demands focused on merely preventing rent increases, the peasant movement was in fact at its weakest in 'dealing economic blows against the landlords'. This he suggests meant that the peasants had not yet begun to challenge the fundamental class position of the landlords. The demands put forward in his view were those that essentially affected the middle peasants most: had the poor peasants provided the main force of the movement, it is inconceivable in his view that such demands as the reduction or abolition of rent would not have been at the forefront of the struggle.[2]

Alavi explains the initial caution of the poor peasants along with the militancy of the middle peasants in terms of the landlords' patronage and hold over the poor:

> The landlords, while exploiting the poor peasants to the limit, adopted a paternal attitude toward them and even afforded them some protection against the extortions by such third parties as warlords and taxmen. On the other hand, the independent smallholders, the middle peasants, stood exposed and weak, and were the principal victims of the warlords and taxmen.[3]

Alavi's argument is then that the poor peasants, although potentially the most revolutionary force against the landlords, tend to be initially the least militant class among the peasantry, and that it is the more economically independent middle peasants, although their perspective is limited to one of conservative proprietorship, that first take the initiative as the most assertive element of the peasantry. This meant that the middle peasants could be a powerful ally of the proletarian movement in the countryside precisely because their initial militancy in dealing blows against the landlords and thereby weakening their patronage powers, contributed to the creation of conditions for the mobilisation of the poor peasants.

He goes on to argue that it was only once the Red Army was organised and the CPC's base in the Jinggang mountains was established that, with the landlords and rich peasants isolated, the revolutionary energies of the poor peasants were released. As the poor peasant leaders gained a new perspective and new confidence, stepping forward to displace the middle peasant leaders, preparing to take positive action against the local landlords, this opened a new phase of the Chinese revolution.

Alavi then sees the agrarian revolution in China as unfolding in two stages reflecting two distinct movements: the initial thrust of the middle peasants against the excessive demands of the warlords and tax officials, moving on to the more revolutionary demands and energies of the poor peasants which challenged the fundamental class position of the landlords through the confiscation and redistribution of their lands.[4]

In conclusion, Alavi considers that the Bolsheviks, seeing the middle peasants as a social force in disintegration, polarising under the development of capitalism, underestimated their role and ultimately failed in the face of the difficulties of organising the poor peasants. Comparing this with the Chinese experience, he argues:

> The success of Mao and the Chinese Communists in bringing about a revolutionary mobilisation of the peasantry lay in their subtle dialectical understanding of the respective roles of the middle peasants and the poor peasants. The task confronting them was to raise the revolutionary consciousness of the poor peasantry…precisely because the poor peasants were initially the more backward section, but were, at the same time, potentially the more revolutionary section of the peasantry. On the other hand, Mao and his comrades had to take full account of the fact that it was the middle peasant who was initially the more militant and his energies had to be mobilised fully in carrying forward the initial thrust of the agrarian revolution. Precisely because the middle peasants were not a revolutionary class, the revolutionary initiative had to be maintained independently of them by the revolutionary leadership, while fully utilising their energies, and without antagonising them. This initiative was then to be carried forward to a second stage of the agrarian revolution by the newly aroused poor peasants.[5]

Alavi's 'middle peasant thesis' has been influential not only within academia but also among political activists. The question he poses is not so much whether peasants were revolutionary or not, but rather under what circumstances do they become revolutionary. Following on from this is the consideration of what roles the different sections of the peasantry play in revolutionary situations. His intention was simply to set out some analytical pointers of relevance in understanding the nature of the worker-peasant alliance and in doing so, he grasps key points about the Chinese revolutionary experience – the importance of the middle peasants as well as the leadership role of the CPC in managing the dynamics of rural struggles so as to raise the peasants' revolutionary consciousness. As he notes, it was the proletarian perspective of the CPC and the establishment of the Red Army that essentially prevented the agrarian revolution from degenerating into an ineffective peasant uprising.[6]

However his key hypothesis, reversing the sequence of poor peasant-middle peasant anti-feudal activism suggested in Mao's texts, seems hard to sustain. As previously noted, others have argued rather that tax resistance movements saw owner-cultivators ally with landlords in defence against state impositions. Further evidence suggests that the CPC had little influence in the tax resistance movements finding the parochial, territorial peasant organisations unreceptive to its policies. As previously noted, writing in 1938 about the Red Spears movement which rose in opposition to warlords and tax collectors, Liu Shaoqi observed it to be made up essentially of self-defence organisations led by 'tyrants or gentry' making it difficult to mobilise into the anti-Japanese resistance.[7]

Alavi recognises that the revolution unfolded in stages but to suggest that these represented separate struggles, first of the middle peasants against warlords and tax officials, opening the way for poor peasant opposition to landlordism, is to draw too deep a dividing line among the peasants. In fact, as Mao noted, substantial numbers of the middle peasants were not only in deficit and dependent on the patronage of landlords and rich peasants for loans, but also experienced a degree of land hunger.

Alavi's account essentially treats the phases of the peasant movement in isolation from the context of the revolutionary situation in the nation as a whole. Land confiscation was simply not on the agenda of the first United Front led by the KMT and Mao's investigations over the winter of 1926–7 covered only the preliminary stages of peasant organisation. The peasants' spontaneous opposition to the rises in rents and interest rates, as well as an end to grain speculation, would at this time have come not only from the more vulnerable sections of the middle peasants but also from the poor peasants who were the hardest hit.

Mao's Hunan report shows the system of benevolent patronage in disintegration: if the peasants' class consciousness was at first limited in terms of their economic demands of remedialism, his account emphasises the political blows dealt against landlordism in general as the peasants rose to challenge the power of the 'bad gentry and local bullies'. Within weeks, as the KMT armies swept North against the warlords, the peasants' political actions developed more boldly into spontaneous and chaotic land takeovers well before the CPC's retreat to the remote mountain areas.[8]

Alavi accounts for the fact that Mao unequivocally emphasised the leadership of the poor peasants in the associations in Hunan in terms of a concern at the time to conform with Stalin's orthodoxy.[9] Yet Mao here clearly notes the 'wait and see' attitude of the middle peasants who only joined the newly formed associations once the authority of these organisations had been established.[10] This caution on the part of the middle peasants was to remain a central preoccupation of the CPC throughout the revolutionary period even after the influence of the Comintern was reduced as Mao assumed leadership of the CPC.

Whilst poor peasant consciousness remained within the frame of traditional remedialism, Mao saw that, uncertain of the outcome of the revolution, they were still susceptible to the conciliatory gestures of the village elites. Recognising how the dynamics of the revolution impacted on peasant attitudes, he understood that the peasants would only take action against the smaller landlords and rich peasants at village level at a time of revolutionary upsurge, and that then, to withstand the blandishments and manipulations of the local elites, the poor peasants had to rely on the support of the middle peasants.[11]

Wolf and the 'middle peasant thesis'

Wolf has also placed emphasis on the 'tactical power' of the more mobile middle – or peripheral – peasants as the decisive factor in peasant rebellion. Like Alavi, he considers that poor peasants, lacking control over their own resources and tied within the power domain of the landlords, will not rebel unless they can rely on strong external support to ensure success.[12] However, where Alavi from a Leninist starting point was interested in questions of class organisation, Wolf, drawing more on a neo-Narodnik viewpoint, emphasises the role of tradition in revolutions. Seeing peasant rebellions 'as parochial responses to major social dislocations, set in motion by overwhelming societal change' his particular concern is with the conditions under the impact of capitalist imperialism which bring the peasants to revolution.

Wolf treats poor peasant subservience and middle peasant militancy as inbuilt attributes, where for Alavi these conditions are not absolute: only when the landlords and rich peasants are challenged by the militancy of the middle peasants may the revolutionary energies of the poor peasants be set in motion; and when the peasant movement advances, the middle peasants may waver, to be drawn into the struggle for land only once their fears are allayed.[13] For Alavi, whilst the conservative demands of the middle peasant as petty proprietors point in the direction of capitalist development, the poor peasants are the most amenable to the socialist vision; for Wolf on the other hand the traditional subsistence struggles of the smallholders make them inherently revolutionary in their confrontation with world capitalism.

Wolf's argument is that the middle peasants or owner-cultivators, whilst the most bound up in traditional social arrangements for survival, are in fact most vulnerable to the economic changes wrought by commercialisation, poor market conditions and state taxes.[14] His starting point is the notion of traditional social equilibrium balancing the transfer of surplus to the rulers with guarantees of minimum security for the cultivators, who are also protected by patron-client relations of mutual obligation sought by the peasants to reduce risks and improve stability.[15] A crisis in this social equilibrium is what sets in motion the dynastic cycle of peasant rebellion aimed not to overthrow the state, but to uphold the 'mandate of heaven' by restoring the balance to subsistence.

Wolf then sees this traditional equilibrium thrown out of balance under the impact of the expanding capitalist markets with industrialisation and the emergence of new class forces heightening the contention for power. As traditional relations are weakened, the impact produces a major conflict centring on the issue of land. This he argues is not a commodity but an attribute of the peasant community encumbered with social ties and obligations which must be stripped away to transform it into a commodity so that capitalism may develop.[16] In the crisis of social equilibrium impacted by world economic crisis which unleashes the cycle of peasant protest, Wolf then sees a conjuncture that produces revolution with the traditionalist peasants brought into conflict with capitalism as they throw up protective barriers in response to the dissolution of their traditional economy by commerce.

For Wolf, it is the attempt by the peasants to remain traditional, resisting subordination to the market, that makes them revolutionary such that the middle peasants, as the bearers of traditions, become the pivotal group in peasant revolution.[17]

The CPC, he then maintains, managed to gain a firm foothold in the villages and succeeded in influencing the structure of village political and economic power because it gained the support of a particular type of tactically mobile land-holding peasantry in the marginal areas where landlord power was weak and there were fewer tenants.[18] In his view, the Chinese revolution reversed the structure of society to make the millenarian dreams of past peasant rebellions a reality as the CPC '… were able to harness peasant energies, but for ends never dreamed of by the peasantry'.[19]

Whilst for Alavi, CPC success rested on the ability to handle the peasant class dynamics, for Wolf, as a vanguard Party, the CPC operated as an external force imposing modernisation on the peasant movement.

Again, like Alavi, Wolf's intention was essentially to open up new areas for debate, and whilst his notion of peasants as inherently traditional and market-averse is to be queried, he, like Scott, brought questions of traditional ideologies and practices back to the centre of discussion, drawing other scholars to subsequently study collective action in peripheral peasant communities where the direct control of the landlords was weakest.

Perry and the peasants as traditionalist subsistence-producers

Asking the question: why peasants rebel, Perry examines patterns of peasant collective action in her study of a particularly harsh environment of Huaipei, in Central China on the borders of Anhui and Shandong, over the period of a century from 1845 to 1945. In this area, surplus production was low, tenancy low, commerce was relatively undeveloped and farming mostly concentrated on staple foods. It was here that the Red Spears peasant movement arose at the end of the 1920s.

Like Wolf, Perry puts traditions of survival at the centre of analysis of peasant behaviour to similarly find a fundamental discontinuity between pre-existing patterns of rural insurrection and the success of China's modern revolution. However where Wolf sees traditionalist peasants as revolutionary against capitalism, Perry sees them as localists trapped in a parochial dialectic of predation versus protectionism.

From the protectionist crop watching and local militia organisations and tax resistance mobilisations to the predatory smugglers, robbers and bandits, Perry finds these to be locally-bound responses to scarcity and insecurity, confined within the framework of competition over existing resources rather than intrinsic expressions of class interests or challenges to the state.[20] Where resources are unequally distributed, those without are prompted to seize the resources of the relatively affluent, however, Perry argues, this is not to suggest that one particular class of peasant was more or less revolutionary. In her view, peasants acted collectively on the basis of kin or territorialism rather than class, and whether predatory bandits or protectionist communities, the social composition of both groups was forged not along class lines but according to communal bonds embedded in the existing social order.[21]

Perry also makes a distinction between the survival strategies of the peasants and the ambitions of their leaders interested in expanding their own influence, arguing that rather than representing the interests of the poor peasants, the traditional forms of collective violence and anti-state organisation were essentially elite strategies used by dissident gentry as an alternative route to power.[22] As she sees it then, what determines whether peasant collective action becomes revolutionary or reactionary depends on the nature of the outside forces it fights or allies with.[23] In other words, it is the impact of the state and outside enemies or allies in changing historical circumstances that are crucial in determining the political implications of peasant actions.

The peasant strategies of survival based on communal organisation and the CPC's radical class policies are then seen by Perry to be essentially contradictory: it was not possible for the CPC to absorb these peasant modes of action; on the contrary, the persistence of these historical patterns of collective action presented CPC cadres with some of their thorniest problems. At first, finding the parochial bonds of the Red Spears an obstacle to the organisation of the peasants on a class basis against the traditional leadership elites, the CPC turned to look for support from the local predatory rivals, only to change tack again, attempting to involve the Red Spears as a local protection organisation in the resistance against the Japanese.[24] In other words, as Perry sees it, the CPC used the different traditions of peasant collective action according to its own circumstances, forming tactical alliances which did not fundamentally overcome the discontinuities between elite-led rebellions and modern revolution.

Perry's argument is then that modern revolution was not a continuum of earlier revolts, built neither on traditions of predatory bandits nor the protective strategies of the tight-knit communities. Rather it required a major breakthrough to transform the deep-rooted traditionalist cycle of rural collective violence into the positive articulation of new social arrangements.[25] What made it possible to transform peasant behaviour and alter the structure of collective action was in part because the new CPC policies produced new methods of survival.[26]

However, in assuming that all peasants' motives were simply those of non-interference, Perry draws too sharp a divide between their subsistence strategies and the CPC's goal of a new socio-political order. Against both Wolf's and Perry's conceptions of the traditionalist peasant, it is worth noting again Mao's refutation of the notion of Oriental culture in 1927. Taking up the question of the restrictions placed by the peasant associations on the export of grain from the villages, he argued that these were not against trade as such but directed against exploitation by the city merchants:

> …As the prices of industrial goods are extremely high and those of farm products extremely low, the peasants are impoverished by the ruthless exploitation of the merchants; thus they cultivate frugality as a means of self-protection. As to the peasants' ban on sending grain outside the area, this was imposed because the poor peasants, not having enough grain to feed themselves, had to buy grain on the market and consequently prevent the price from going up. All these are due to the impoverishment

of the peasants and the contradiction between town and country; the peasants are certainly not practising the so-called doctrine of Oriental Culture by rejecting industrial goods or trade between town and country.[27]

Food riots were not uncommon in times of scarcity and famine, increasing in frequency in the early twentieth century, as peasants took collective action – at once protectionist and predatory – to block roads to prevent scarce grain from leaving their localities, or to seize the hoards of the large landlords and merchants. The majority of peasants had become involved to differing degrees in marketing their produce.[28] However, as has been seen, commerce developed in China not independently but under conditions of, and in fact on the basis of, the land monopoly as the collection of rent in kind gave the landlords control over the grain markets, enabling them to accumulate vast fortunes through speculation.

Rather than an expression of opposition by traditionalist subsistence communities against the disruption of the village economy under market penetration, food riots, as Marks has argued, were focused on setting a fair price, with the confiscation of the grain hoards of those who refused to sell at the price popularly determined by the crowd.[29] The peasants then were not opposed to free trade but against the market monopoly of the large landlords and merchants, and their defence was not to be seen as an expression of cultural disposition, an inherent closure against outside imposition, but rather one conditioned by agrarian decline as the towns drained the villages of their resources through unequal exploitative trade.

Thaxton sees in the restrictions on grain trade a demonstration of peasant unity in collective action. Whilst speculative market practices were a matter of concern for those with a surplus to trade, they also affected those with insufficiency who were dependent on borrowing from the village granaries. Whilst the big landlords and merchants preferred to send the grain outside the villages to market towns where prices were higher, refusing to loan grain even at raised interest rates, these peasants had little choice other than to seize grain.[30]

Despite the considerable power of her analysis of the peasants' subsistence strategies and how the destructive patterns of predation and protectionism caused peasant protest to fall under elite leadership, Perry's arguments are overly pessimistic, tending to overstate the unchanging nature of the economic environment. This leads her to over-emphasise the competition among the peasants in conditions of scarcity and to underestimate the potential for those with and without resources to unite in struggle against the landlords and the conditions of feudal land and market monopolies.

Where Perry sees only the tenacity of traditional elites in exploiting the predatory-protectionist cycle of peasant behaviour, Thaxton finds potential in rural protests amassing large numbers of peasant followers to develop beyond the control of the local elites.[31] Perry's argument tends to obscure the tensions between rich and poor within the kin and settlement groups, as well as between the peasants and their elite leaders. In fact the Red Spears, for example, were not entirely united: splits occurred between the defensive tactics of the landlords and rich peasants in one grouping, and the more offensive actions of the poor and middle peasants in another.[32]

What led peasant struggles to an impasse was not simply the limited nature of their survival strategies in a particularly inhospitable environment but rather the ways in which differences in material interests between those with and without resources came into conflict at different phases in their struggle. It was by using these conflicts that local powerholders were able to turn peasant protest to their advantage.

Marks on peasant consciousness – a Marxist analysis

Marks' study of the Peng Pai cult and Haifeng Soviet, which lasted only a few short months from late 1927 to early 1928, takes a different approach to CPC-peasant relations in examining how the subjective consciousness of the peasants, as reflected in forms of protest, changed as their objective conditions of deprivation worsened. With this approach, Marks finds continuity between peasant agitation and revolutionary action, with spontaneous protests developing within the deteriorating situation into a movement organised around specific goals.

From a Marxist perspective, Marks situates the peasant movement within the context of agrarian class structure and the historical experience of the peasants. Rejecting the notion that rural protest is the creation of a revolutionary elite, he takes a bottom-up approach, placing emphasis on the mass politics of the peasants as they endeavoured to foster a new order based on land control.[33] Where for Perry, peasants were simply a product of their environment, Marks argues they were actors, not passive objects of someone else's history since, through collective action, they themselves had a hand in making the very structures that patterned subsequent action.[34]

Mark's area of study, Haifeng county in Guangdong province, was more commercially developed than the border regions of Perry's study. Nevertheless the patterns of rural collective action were similar, with factional conflict between lineages cutting across class lines, reinforced in this environment not by scarcity of resources but by control over rural marketing systems. Marks finds however, again in contrast with Perry, that these forms of social conflict had by the second half of the 19th century begun to give way to class antagonism as a result of China's integration into the world capitalist markets. It was changes in the rural social structure, as landlords altered the terms of tenancy to their advantage and as the destruction of handicrafts cut off peasant sidelines, that conditioned the emergence of class conflict, favouring greater unity among the peasants since, as structural class relations changed, so too did the forms of collective action.[35]

The process however was not straightforward: as Marks argues, structural change occasioned by imperialism did not immediately give rise to class conflict. Avoiding deterministic arguments, he points out that mediating between the objective changes and the forms of collective action was peasant experience and the consciousness whereby they interpreted their experience.[36]

Following Mao, Marks takes the peasants' conception of moral economy as demonstrated in food riots as a revolutionary rather than a conservative consciousness, not so much in contradiction with capitalism as in conflict with the restrictive market practices of the state and big landlord-merchants. However, seeing objective and subjective change as interactive processes, he recognises the possibility for peasant consciousness and understanding, and so their ability to adapt forms of collective action, to lag behind structural changes in class relations.

To explain the emergence of the personality cult around Peng Pai's leadership of the Haifeng Soviet, Marks notes that, because the changes in material circumstances were recent and the peasants had little experience of them, and because peasant unity remained weak with distrust of neighbours easily fuelled into factional conflict, the form that collective action took was that of unity around a charismatic figure. The 'cult' – the peasants' apparent desire for an Emperor – arose not from the leadership, from Peng Pai, but from the peasants themselves. From their popular folklore came the belief that change comes about through the magical powers of a leader. Nevertheless Marks notes, Peng Pai's emphasis on mass activism contrasted with the controlling approach of the reform-minded gentry in 1911 and subsequently the KMT in the 1920s. In this way the cult represented a new form of social organisation that gave rise to class-based forms of collective action by the peasants in their demands for rent reductions and the seizure of feudal lands. The point was however that peasant consciousness and experience still fell short of recognising the powers of their own collective mass action, inhibiting their capacity to oppose and transform the bureaucratism of the cult.[37]

Marks analyses this disjuncture between the peasants' subjective consciousness, and their objective circumstances by situating its emergence at a particular point of breakdown in relations between town and countryside, with neither the KMT nor the CPC capable of formulating an agrarian programme addressed to the needs of the peasants.[38] The leadership cult is essentially seen to have filled a vacuum in urban-rural relations, serving as a bridge between the objective reality and the peasants' subjective understanding of it, as Peng Pai articulated the peasants' interests in ways which resounded with the values of their moral economy whilst defining goals towards which the peasants' united actions could be directed.[39]

Marks then sees the cult as a transitional form of collective action, a route for peasant participation in modern revolution, passing from factional to class conflict with the organisation of the peasant unions or associations as the instrument of class struggle. Posing the question: 'do peasants need an Emperor?', he points out that whilst the French peasantry, who were passive, isolated and economically self-sufficient, sought in Napoleon their representative, the Haifeng peasants were capable of collective action. Seeing peasant consciousness as shifting in the objective conditions of intensifying exploitation and hardships, Marks notes the possibility that the cult be transcended as other forms of collective action, namely the peasant unions, took shape.[40]

Marks then captures a particular moment in the Chinese revolutionary process as class relations were shifting the balance between the national and agrarian struggles. However, focusing on peasant subjective consciousness, he tends to reduce factionalism to a matter of loyalties to different lineage alliances, when in fact the obstacles which kept peasants divided as a class also had an objective basis, as Perry revealed, between those with and without resources.

The challenges of leadership of the peasant movement arose not simply from a vacuum in the urban-rural link but, in the wider context, were rather a matter of the relative influence of the different urban classes on land policies, that is, whether reform measures relied on a passive peasantry using legalistic methods of land redistribution favoured by the national bourgeoisie, or took instead the activist approach of a proletarian programme. Different land programmes had differing impacts on peasant social classes. Reforms within the framework of bourgeois legality allowed the small landlords and rich peasants to maintain their properties and tended to benefit the well-to-do peasantry most, causing dissatisfaction among the poor only to exacerbate divisions among a partially differentiated peasantry, increasing factional strife and traditional rivalries. On the other hand, mobilising the poor peasantry in a direct challenge to the landlord authority enabled the peasants to take the lead in transforming the traditional village order, guarding against traditional rivalries so long as the unity of poor and middle peasants was maintained.

The real challenge then for leadership was to prevent the degeneration of peasants' struggles into sectarian rivalries by handling the contradictions among the peasants that emerged given their different conditions of production within the interactions between the national and agrarian revolution.

NOTES AND REFERENCES

1. Alavi, 1973, p.251.
2. *Ibid.*, p.257
3. *Ibid.*, p.257.
4. *Ibid.*, pp.261.
5. *Ibid.*, p.260.
6. *Ibid.*, p.260.
7. Cited in Huang, 1985, p.245.
8. Schram, 1969b, p.100.
9. Alavi, 1973, p.258.
10. Mao, *Selected Works*, Vol. I, pp.30–31.
11. In support of his argument, Alavi cites the works of the Crooks and C.Y. Yang: in both of these village studies, a middle peasant was found to be in a leadership position in the peasant association. However in the case of Ten Mile Inn, the leader was in fact a new middle peasant – originally a poor peasant who, stepping forward earlier as an activist, had gained benefit under the 'double reductions' policy. Yang, noting how a work team sent to the village to 'set the masses in motion' appointed a middle peasant as leader, accounts for this deviation from CPC policy as a matter of the team choosing the 'least troublesome' method. Rather than looking for revolutionary qualities, they chose those already active in affairs in the old village order (Yang, 1959, pp.134–136). In other instances where middle peasants assumed leadership positions in peasant associations, this was not necessarily as Alavi suggests because they were more independent of patron-client ties, more likely it was because of their special skills, such as literacy and accounting.
12. Wolf, 1969, pp.290–1.
13. Alavi, 1973, p.275.
14. Wolf, 1969, p.292; pp.294–5.
15. *Ibid.*, p.279.
16. *Ibid.*, pp.277–8.
17. *Ibid.*, p.292.
18. *Ibid.*, p.153.
19. *Ibid.*, p.154.
20. Perry, 1980, pp.58 –95.
21. *Ibid.*, p.252.
22. *Ibid.*, pp.148–51.
23. *Ibid.*, p.254.
24. *Ibid.*, pp.145–6; pp.205–6, as discussed in Chapter 13.

25. *Ibid.*, pp.243–6. Perry in particular mentions mutual aid.
26. *Ibid.*, pp.245–7.
27. Mao, *Selected Works*, Vol. I, p.54.
28. It has been estimated that in late Imperial China peasants marketed from 20 to 30 per cent of their crops, rising to between 30 and 40 per cent in the twentieth century. See Lippitt, 1980, p.22.
29. Marks, 1984, pp.81–6; see also R.B. Wong, 1982.
30. Thaxton, 1983, p.69.
31. See Thaxton, 1983, pp.71–2. Wakeman, 1966, pp.112–6, also suggests that whilst clan feuds were instigated by the gentry, these brought the poor peasants together en masse enabling them to develop links of class solidarity.
32. see Slawinski, 1972, p.207.
33. Marks, 1984, pp.191–3; see also Little, 1989, pp.161–3.
34. Marks, 1984, p.282.
35. *Ibid.*, p.119–20.
36. *Ibid.*, pp.284–5.
37. *Ibid.*, pp.185–7. Marks' use of the concept of charisma to describe the cult follows Peter Worsley's work on the 'cargo cults' of the South Pacific. See Worsley, 1968, pp. xiii–xiv.
38. *Ibid.*, pp.228–9.
39. *Ibid.*, p.286.
40. *Ibid.*, pp.287–8.

23
Peasants as free trade familialists – Thaxton's contribution

Peasant culture and the CPC

Thaxton's *China Turned Rightside Up* provides a detailed study of peasant life in the Taihang mountains in Northern China in the 1930s and 1940s. There he finds the peasants in retreat from landlord brutality, living in this rugged area in 'violent non-conformity'. Unlike Perry, for whom the horizons of the Huaipei peasants were bound by kin and community as they divided in competition over scarce resources, Thaxton sees the peasants of Taihang united together as free-market familialists striking out for independence against the landlord-dominated system.

Thaxton aims to demonstrate that it was not so much the vanguard CPC that brought the peasants to revolution, injecting leadership and ideology from the outside, rather it was the peasants that influenced the process of revolutionary transformation by their own independent acts.[1] Against the view of traditional peasant rebellions as millenarian, sporadic, localistic and egalitarian, incapable of realising the peasants' interests to overthrow the feudal bureaucratic state, Thaxton argues that within peasant revolt there were the seeds of a totally different socio-political order, a counter-society capable of its own development.[2] In his view, the CPC succeeded only because it was able to absorb the peasants' own revolutionary traditions, pursuing a goal of establishing independent rural communities which corresponded with the peasants' own vision of a society without wealth or bureaucracy.[3]

Whilst recognising that the development of peasant consciousness was restrained by clan affiliation and dependency on the local elite, who had the power to allow or deny the right to subsistence through reciprocal arrangements, Thaxton makes the key point that such reciprocity was not based on a shared conception of community.[4] The landlords on the one hand conceived their obligations in terms of Confucian benevolence, seeing themselves as patrons responsible for the welfare of the people, and dispensing justice accordingly, but on the other hand the peasants' own folklore had influences of Buddhism and Daoism which regarded wealth and power as the root of evil. Distinguishing then between the Confucian traditions of the gentry and bureaucratic state, and the revolutionary, pre-Confucian and democratic folklore of the peasants, Thaxton shows how peasant opposition to the inequalities between rich and poor was influenced by their own standards of equity and justice, and how their antagonism to unjust rulers and the excessive demands of the state was infused with a hatred of those who lived in luxury in the towns whilst everything they had came from the people.[5]

This fact then that the peasants were not totally converted to the value system of the elite demonstrates for Thaxton that their aspirations for social harmony were not merely functional to the system, as Wolf maintained: peasant power as expressed in folk culture directly challenged the state and landlord ethic, informing demands for independence and market freedom.

Thaxton traces the development of peasant protest from remedialism to oppositionist actions. With the spread of the world market and the rise of absentee landlordism and land speculation, landlords began to withdraw their customary services, instead making greater demands on their tenants and on village resources.[6] As these violations of traditional social crisis guarantees, in particular the reduction of rents in times of bad harvest, drove the peasants increasingly into debt and tenancy, they began to resist with demands for the return of shared risks and responsibilities, even taking the landlords to court to uphold custom.[7]

Since as Thaxton argues neither a restoration of social harmony with the elite upholding their contributions to village welfare nor a new option of capitalist agriculture were available to satisfy the peasants' traditional appeals, these remedialist actions met with brutal response from the landlords, driving the peasants further into oppositionist tactics with the organisation of rural self-defence and secret societies engaged in salt-smuggling.[8] It was this combination of peasant impoverishment and the violent reaction to their pleas that crystallised the class conflict between landlord and tenant.

Under the KMT, Thaxton notes, the conditions of peasant revolt intensified. The Nationalist government, as it gave backing to the landlords in the courts, effectively condoned the overturning of the accepted procedures of remedial conflict resolution; at the same time it accepted de facto the situation of flood and famine since it had no alternative to offer.[9] The arrival of the 8th Route Army in 1936 on the other hand gave encouragement to peasant resistance as the CPC, entering this process of transition in peasant protest from traditionalism to opposition, began to organise the customary forms of protest more effectively. Methods of assisting peasants to pursue their demands on the landlords collectively, introducing advocacy into the informal and personal patron-client dealings, brought out the peasants' common experiences. This Thaxton argues allowed the antagonism inherent in the landlord-tenant bond to become the main mode of the relationship, displacing its perceived mutuality. By harnessing the peasants' own concepts of social justice and encouraging their independent actions to compel the landlords to accept permanent tenancies and reduced rents in times of bad harvest, the CPC was able to build the collective consciousness of the peasants against the landlords and the courts of the feudal state which upheld their claims.

Thaxton's focus on this process of breaking down patron-client ties stands out in contrast with the 'middle peasant thesis' of Alavi and Wolf. Rather than seeing the CPC efforts to promote a revolutionary peasant movement as being restricted by the landlords' hold over their poor peasant tenants, he considers that the CPC cracked the problem of clientelism from the inside. Using the differences between the landlords' and peasants' conception of a just society to find the weak link in the dependency relationship, the CPC effectively coupled the peasants' efforts to restore traditional rights with the development of collective class actions which brought the contradictions within the patron-client relationship to breaking point.[10]

Thaxton finds the impetus for agrarian revolution coming from the combined forces of the semi-landless and semi-rooted sharecroppers as well as the hired hands and migrants. These different sectors of the rural population, he recognises, were all drawn together as victims of high taxes, low yields and the vagary of market prices, and of the landlord practices of usury and land usurpation. Thus he notes that the leaders of peasant protest were not the more secure landowning middle peasants but the landless peasants, together with the poor smallholders who had lost the land and business income necessary for family security.[11]

Whilst rooting their political movement in the remedialist and oppositionist traditions and methods of peasant protest, encouraging their independent actions to resist the landlords' demands, the CPC also assisted in the organisation of self-defence squads against the armed rent collectors, and helped arrange peasant self-help to tackle the problems of finding food, shelter and work.[12] In these ways, through support for traditional morality and the custom and practice of subsistence and security, Thaxton maintains, the CPC, unlike the KMT, was able to win legitimacy in the eyes of the peasants. Critical in this was the Party's rectification campaign.

For Thaxton, the de-bureaucratisation movement and the reform of the administration together with the regeneration of the village economy were decisive in preventing the re-creation of a harmful clientelist relationship between the CPC and the peasantry.[13] Bringing out the connection between the revival of dependency and the provision of protection, Thaxton here also highlights the role of the Red Army which, in organising its own self-sufficiency, worked alongside the peasants to grow its own food without encroaching on their production. The CPC was then able to arrange for the peasants to assist the army without radically altering their own self-sustaining routines.[14]

The rectification movement for Thaxton, rather than being initiated from above by the CPC seeking to improve its leadership style, was one driven from below as the peasants resisted the emergence of new forms of patronage. The problem of clientelism lay not in peasant mentality: on the contrary, this conflicted with their own desire for autonomy, and it was only by developing a political work-style which stressed peasant self-reliance over institutional dependency that the CPC was able to gain their support.

Thaxton lays particular emphasis on the cultural aspect of the rectification movement in which the CPC came to absorb the 'widely treasured folk values that stood in opposition to Confucian high culture …'[15] Peasant culture was to have a major impact on the revolutionary process as popular tales and legends provided the basis for a new revolutionary folk order. Rather than establishing the hegemony of its political thought over the peasantry, popular slogans such as 'all peasants under heaven are one family', served to harmonise the CPC's own organisational style with the peasants' struggles for self-rule.

It was through assimilating aspects of rural life into its own organisation and thinking that the CPC was able to link up with the struggles of the rural poor and so to succeed in encouraging their independent actions in order to realise their own demands for communities free from landlord power.[16] The Taihang peasants then for Thaxton were no mere pawns in a CPC-orchestrated campaign but were capable of knowing and acting in their own interests, effectively capturing the CPC as it adapted to their demands. It was not then that the CPC roused the peasants to unconsidered acts of revolution, rather as he sees it: 'The CPC derived legitimacy by dancing to the demanding tunes of the decentralised peasant movements.'[17]

Demonstrating that the politics of the village were not just shaped by patronage, Thaxton gives the peasants agency. For Perry, the link between the CPC and the peasants' collective actions was simply one of tactical manoeuvring but for Thaxton it was far more than that: where Perry sees peasant lives shaped by an unchanging environment caught in a vicious cycle of predation and protection, Thaxton traces the dynamic interactions between the CPC and peasant traditions to show how Party rectification succeeded in capturing the momentum from below. With the influence of the peasantry transforming the CPC, the Party in turn transformed the peasants by raising their class consciousness as their collective actions took on more organised transformative forms.[18] The peasants however were not able to develop methods of leadership which prevented the revival of patronage and dependency relations: it was here that the CPC stepped in to do what the peasants could not do for themselves, so allowing the agrarian revolution to succeed where past rebellions had failed.

The rationale of the Yan'an village economy

Thaxton regards the Taihang peasants as all sharing a common aspiration to create self-supporting and independent communities. He saw this to be demonstrated in their united effort to prevent the sale of village food supplies by the landlords and merchants: as discussed earlier, he notes that the export of grain from the villages was a matter of concern for both those with and without resources, affecting the survival of the entire community dependent for collective welfare on the maintenance of village granaries.

The determination of the Taihang peasants to cut themselves off from the larger polity and the national markets he argues lay not in the pursuit of subsistence goals but in the desire for democratic control over their own village economies and their local food supplies.[19] Whilst the subsistence ethic provided the moral basis of the peasant economy, with the good of the family depending on the good of the community, his view is that the peasants' real aim of a good life was for an economy centred on free competitive village markets. Far from a retreat from the market, Thaxton argues that the peasant struggle against the landlords' economic control was a struggle to make capitalism 'available and beneficial to all'.[20] It is in the goal of independent communities based on democratic markets that he finds congruence between peasant moral economy and modern revolution.

Thaxton then sees the CPC's Yan'an-style production movement as responding to the peasants' demands to re-establish trade and tilling on their own terms, addressing the problems of landlord dominance and their own survival in a concrete way.[21] Facing brutal treatment by the landlords, villagers had been thrown back on their own practices of self-help and mutual aid, surviving through collective effort and self-rule. Where the KMT had alienated these free-trading familialists by increasing taxes but doing nothing to revive their rural markets, the way that the CPC was able to mobilise these traditions of mutual support as it introduced a self-reliant path of development in the village communities was to prove critical to its success.

By ensuring the villagers' democratic participation in exchange, the CPC enabled market power to shift away from the merchant-landlords. In opposition to the debilitating terms of monopoly-based trade, Party policies supported the peasants' efforts to recreate their shattered economies through both independent effort and reciprocal exchange by reviving rural fairs, organising community grain borrowing and lending facilities as well as offering tax relief.[22] The CPC's village programmes then established new autonomous communities of tillers in control of their own resources and food supplies – their conditions of livelihood.

However, in his assumption of a shared notion of a moral economy, with all peasants holding the same aspiration for free and equal markets, Thaxton oversimplifies the peasants' perspectives. As Polachek has argued in his study of the Jiangxi Soviet in the early 1930s, there was no one universal conception of the moral economy; rather, peasants had different ideas about how a 'just redistribution' might be structured, organising around different practices of risk minimisation and measures of protection against disaster, depending on their own access to resources. To link modern revolution with any one of these as a means of getting support from a section of the rural population would only, he points out, create opposition from the others.[23] As has been seen, it was precisely in handling the contradictions between the different types of peasants with their differing perspectives on developing the rural economy, that the CPC faced its major challenge in organising the peasant revolution.

Thaxton's strength lies in his grasp of the agrarian revolution in terms of the aspirations of the peasants to escape landlord domination, recognising the impetus for social transformation as coming from their own initiatives. However he fails to register the contradictions within the peasant movement, assuming that all peasants were equal in their embrace of the goal of an independent peasant economy, with the same familial free-trading motives. The Yan'an village programmes were indeed inclusive, mobilising all members of the farming communities to pull together, contributing to village production according to their different capacities in order to benefit from the regeneration of the economy, welfare and social life of their communities as a whole. But there were tensions here in the midst of the harmony of effort.

The crux of Thaxton's argument lies in his assertion that the CPC's success lay in 'nurturing capitalism from below'.[24] However all peasants, whilst sharing in the democratic goals against feudalism including the freeing of markets, do not have the same aim of developing capitalism. The 'middle peasant owner-cultivator' society created by land reform contained inherent contradictions: whilst land had been redistributed more evenly and individual household farming formed a common basis for the rich, middle and poor peasants, inequalities remained between peasant households with differing productive capacities. These then provided a basis for future polarisation as new patterns of urban-rural interchange opened up alternative paths of development.

It is here that Alavi has the advantage in acknowledging the different economic interests among the peasants and recognising the implications of different methods in organising land reform for the continuation of the social transformation of the Chinese countryside.

Thaxton's version of democratic capitalism sees free and open markets operating at the centre of the new village economy to serve the needs of the community by matching production and consumption. This envisions a system of equal exchange between individual producers for mutual benefit and therein lies the flaw in his argument: equating capitalism with a system of simple commodity exchange rather than seeing it as a process of accumulation ultimately driving peasant differentiation.

It is this question of accumulation that is left out of both Thaxton's account and the peasants' utopian goal of a society of equal producers. In the traditional village economy, resources, whether owned or used on an individual or communal basis, were basically means of consumption, for survival or for extravagant living. In circumstances of stagnation and scarcity, these became objects of competition and plunder. The CPC's village programmes were to fundamentally transform the rationale of the rural economy: instead of resources serving as a source of corruption and factional strife, these were to be put to use to generate a surplus for investment.

The real question from a Marxist perspective is what type of process of generating surplus emerges as agriculture develops? Whilst the peasants' partial differentiation offered the social basis for alternative models of accumulation, the mixed economy of the Yan'an programmes was to be a combination, using resources to increase production through investment both from a capitalist process of private accumulation and from seeds of a socialist process through social or public accumulation.

Recognising the revolutionary role of capitalism in driving the expansion of the productive forces, the CPC's land reform process created a sector of private enterprise and initiative to kickstart the development process. However, from an economic basis of unequal peasant farms, the rural development programmes were to mobilise the production capacities of the mass of the peasants with the overall goal of raising consumption levels to the benefit of the village economy and society as a whole. In other words it was to operate as a collective system for the benefit of all, not simply a competitive system in which the majority would lose out in the long run. In this, the CPC never abandoned its aim of facilitating the organisation of the poor peasants, keeping in view the long-term goal of socialism.

More than just freeing the market to unleash the process of private accumulation, the CPC established the two key components within the village programmes – the public and co-operative sectors, and the mutual aid teams. Arguably both were rooted in traditional arrangements, respectively, the village granaries which were maintained for collective welfare, and the reciprocal exchanges between households matching tools with labour. However both were fundamentally transformed under CPC guidance and policies from mechanisms of survival to key components of a collectivist-oriented economic development.

Co-operative banks provided loans and kept interest rates down, restricting the usurious practices of the landlords and rich peasants. State-run trading companies controlled the circulation of grain, thereby containing speculation and hoarding, and by stabilising prices, stimulating the peasants' enthusiasm to produce. Joint state-private producer and consumer co-operatives were key to the revival of domestic handicrafts like spinning and weaving. These co-operatives differed fundamentally from those organised by the KMT. The latter had relied on government support, placing management in the hands of an official or village headman, and had lost popularity in showing little benefit for the members. In contrast, the Yan'an-type co-operatives involved peasant shareholders in management, and poor peasants in particular were encouraged to join through a system of shares paid in kind, thus preventing the merchants from dominating the enterprises.[25] Relying on peasant contributions, hiring underemployed labour, offering competitive loans and supplies at low prices, and absorbing unused rural capital to support scarce handicrafts, these co-operatives gained the support of their members and contributed to the economic revival.[26]

In addition, the stimulation of commerce through the revival of rural capitalism provided an incentive for the poor and middle peasants to develop their traditional practices of mutual exchange of labour for tools and animals to increase production. It is important to recognise with Thaxton how the CPC rooted its decentralised production movement in the revival of these joint family practices to activate and unite the poor and middle peasants in a process of economic growth. However, whilst as he notes, the mutual aid teams were not organs of the state but created from traditions of mutual support embedded in the life of the village, nevertheless the CPC should also be credited for developing and transforming these indigenous methods from irregular practices varying in form according to local conditions into permanent year-round arrangements infused with the purpose of a new production rationale.

Mutual aid was to be instrumental in setting in motion the path of participative self-reliant development since, through such arrangements using age-old labour-intensive techniques, the poor peasants were able to draw on their own traditional skills and production practices to make up for their lack of capital. The mutual aid teams were not however without problems given the different economic circumstances of the villagers: the well-to-do peasants were fearful that their tools and animals would suffer from communal use; poorer peasants were also wary since traditional exchanges had often been exploitative; whilst middle peasants saw the efforts to set up the teams as time-consuming. To overcome the problems of trust, the CPC relied on already existing kinship groups or loan societies as a basis for setting up initial teams, but these were to transcend their origins in traditional mutuality as production increased.

Out of traditions then which originally served the peasant economy on an individual basis, the CPC was able to create and develop a widespread practice, raising it to a new level by not only enabling the peasants to regain land, escape debt and establish their individual independence, but further demonstrating the benefit of collective over individual effort, so increasing the peasants' enthusiasm for further co-operation.[27]

The new democratic policies of the CPC practised in the village programmes then went beyond the 'nurturing of capitalism from below'. Promoting the peasants' goal of independent household farming, at the same time utilising their traditions of self-help and mutual exchange, the CPC began a process which would not stop short of establishing individual production. What their policies did differently was to set in motion a particular dynamic of development in a mixed economy, using the positive qualities of rural capitalism to stimulate growth for the benefit of all classes involved in the democratic alliance, at the same time relying on the initiatives of the mass of the peasants, the majority of whom were poor.

Since the contributions of the public and co-operative sectors together with the mutual aid teams were not sufficient to lead the economic revival, the private sector took on the main role in rehabilitating the rural economy across the sectors of commerce, industry and finance. Nevertheless the former were to play a major part in strengthening the role of the poor peasants. The two ownership forms then engaged in an evolutionary development as private sector-led economic revival helped to strengthen the public and co-operative sectors, which in turn supported the initiatives of the poorer peasants in their search for new solutions to their problems of livelihood through alliance with the middle peasants.

Not only encouraging private enterprise, the CPC then also sought to address the differences between the richer and the poorer peasants arising from the unequal results of land distribution. The village programmes brought into play alternatives other than those existing within the framework of private capitalism reliant on the development of a rich peasant economy. By promoting collectivism within the production process, CPC policies sought to moderate rather than increase peasant polarisation as capitalism developed, enabling peasants with varying productive capacities to resolve their differences by working together as the village economy expanded.

In these ways, economic development initiated new interactions within the rural communities amongst the peasants themselves, releasing a broad activism and collective enthusiasm for production which laid the cornerstones for further social and economic advance. It was in this way that the Party was able to introduce its own long-term goals of socialism, fostering conditions favourable to its future development.

NOTES AND REFERENCES

1. Thaxton, 1983, p.136. Thaxton's main argument is directed against Johnson (1962).
2. Ibid., p.158.
3. *Ibid.*, p.135.
4. Thaxton's argument here may be compared with that of Faure (1988) discussed in Chapter 3.
5. Thaxton, 1983, p.154.
6. Thaxton, 1975, p.334.
7. *Ibid.*, pp.338–41.
8. Thaxton, 1983, p.223.
9. Thaxton, 1975, pp.336–7.
10. *Ibid.*, pp.354–5.
11. Thaxton, 1983, p.95.
12. Thaxton, 1975, pp.347–8.
13. Thaxton, 1983, p.130; p.228. Thaxton's account of the Party rectification movement corresponds with Selden's work and with Mao's approach to leadership reform discussed in Chs 19 and 21.
14. *Ibid.*, pp.224–231.
15. *Ibid.*, pp.131–2.
16. *Ibid.*, p.135.
17. *Ibid.*, p.227.
18. *Ibid.*, p.195.
19. *Ibid.*, p.226.
20. *Ibid.*, p.225.
21. *Ibid.*, p.223.
22. *Ibid.*, p.226.
23. Polachek, 1983, pp.826–7.
24. Thaxton, 1983, p.123.
25. Watson, 1980, p.117.
26. For more on the co-operatives see Keating (1997). Her study based on northern Shaanxi finds a strong tendency in the Communist areas towards centralisation and bureaucratic management of co-operatives with enterprises in one way or another falling short of co-operative ideals. Nevertheless her assessment is that, whether completely genuine or not, they played a major role in rural reconstruction. pp.17–22
27. Perry , 1980, pp.243–5; Watson, 1980, pp.27–8; see also Dorris, 1976, pp.714–6, and Selden, 1995, pp.194–5.

24
What difference did CPC leadership make?

On the question of traditions

Some time in the 4th century BC, a follower of the Daoist-influenced Agriculturalist School, apparently expressed in a conversation with Mencius, the view that:

> ...real leaders cultivate the ground in common with the people and so eat ...They prepare their own morning and evening meals, carrying on government at the same time. (Other types of leader) has his own granaries, treasuries and arsenals, which is oppressing the people to nourish himself. How can he be deemed a leader?[1]

Followers of the Agriculturalist School evidently:

> ...could see no use for sage kings. Desiring both ruler and subject to plough together in the fields, they overthrew the order of the upper and lower classes.[2]

Thaxton notes how the CPC actively encouraged the practice of involving the leaders of the mutual aid teams in production, recognising this as an important contribution in the rectification of bureaucratic styles of work.[3] As the above example shows, this method indeed chimed with the peasants' age-long view that the division between mental and manual labour lay at the root of inequalities in wealth and power.

In gaining leadership of the peasant movement, the CPC, as has been seen, faced major obstacles from the tenacity of the local networks of feudal power which penetrated ties of kin and community to obscure class relations and militate against class consciousness, causing peasant activism to degenerate into factionalism and clientelism. Insofar as the CPC had conceived these difficulties simply in terms of the 'infiltration by alien class elements' and 'rich peasant leadership', they tended to discount issues of the peasants' own traditional beliefs and understandings – their own subjective consciousness.

Once the CPC established a foothold in the villages linking up with traditional organisations such as those of crop-watching, village defence, bandits and sworn brotherhoods, there was a tendency for the Party to reproduce within its own ranks the old styles of elitist leadership of peasant movements. As Thaxton has understood, the re-creation of harmful dependency relations from the Party alienated the peasants, and in turn the lack of a mass base further exacerbated bureaucratic tendencies within the Party.

The Orientalist perspective sees the tenacity of bureaucratism and patronage as rooted at the base of Chinese society in the self-enclosed corporate village communities, making leadership degeneration inevitable. Perry accounts for the persistence of elite leadership in terms of the destructive dynamics of subsistence survivalism. Thaxton on the other hand, regarding the peasants as free trading familialists, essentially sees them as anti-bureaucratic: it was only by drawing peasant culture and ways of life into its own organisation and thinking, taking up the grass roots demands for independence and markets free from state and landlord control, that as he argues the CPC was able to correct and democratise its leadership style to capture the momentum from below.[4]

In its adoption of the peasants' anti-Confucian egalitarian values and folk ways, Thaxton maintains that the CPC, rather than applying Marxism, quite to the contrary was only to succeed in practice by diverging from the views of Marx and Lenin who saw revolution as a negation of tradition.[5] But this is to overstate the influence of the peasantry on Party organisation and to underestimate the limitations of the peasants' subjectivity. His analysis then plays down the need to apply the proletarian standpoint to escape the divisive influence of the traditional village elites.

Mao's Hunan report shows the peasants' attitudes to tradition as presenting a complex subjectivity: on the one hand, they called for the restitution of the traditional moral economy of benevolence and reciprocity with reductions in rent and the maintenance of village granaries; at the same time, they challenged the four 'thick ropes' of traditional authority that bound them. Mao observed how the peasant associations confronted superstitious practices and traditional clan organisation, describing how the poor peasants, including women, had marched into the clan temples and sat down at the tables where the elders were feasting, to the latter's great dismay.[6] These initial challenges by the peasants to the political power of the landlords he saw as a step towards the revolutionary transformation of the feudal system, leading on to the economic confiscation of the land of those who did not cultivate it.[7]

As has been seen, Mao was to argue that the success or failure of the agrarian revolution depended on whether or not the landlords – the local powerholders and dissident gentry who sought only personal power – or the peasants, the agents of fundamental transformation of the feudal system, took the lead. Seeing how landlords and rich peasants sought to join the peasant association, he opposed this.

However he was to draw deeper insights into the problem of leadership as he learned not only from the upsurge but also the ebb of revolution, when the persistence of clan sentiment and patriarchalism enabled the rich peasants and small landlords to regain their former influence by asserting their status within the local networks. To do so the traditional power holders sought to exploit divisions among the peasants as the middle peasants were made wary by indiscriminate attacks launched at the height of an upsurge not only against feudal properties but also the surplus lands cultivated by the rich and well-to-do peasants.

Traditions then were a double-edged sword: if traditional remedialism was crucial to the initial mobilisation of the peasants on a mass scale against the injustices of the landlord system, the CPC's appeal to the peasants' deep-rooted sense of social justice and their antipathy to wealth and power as the root of evil was not as unproblematic as Thaxton suggests. Traditionalist visions of 'absolute egalitarianism' were to undermine peasant unity at the point of land confiscation and redistribution, subverting the fundamental transformation of the social order.

Changing relations between the leadership and the led

There was indeed far more to the role of the CPC than the absorption of traditional values as it sought to resolve the problems of peasant organisation and relations between the leaders and the peasant masses to construct a path forward to the future. With the rich peasants tied into the landlord system, upholding the hierarchies of traditional power, and poor and middle peasants divided by clannishness and predatory behaviours, forging peasant class power presented the CPC with particular challenges in transforming the traditional village organisations and elite styles of leadership.

Whilst patronage and clan influences worked against the development of class consciousness and class struggle against the landlords, limiting agrarian reform and leading peasant struggles to degenerate into sectarian rivalries, what kept the peasants divided as a class was not just a matter of lineage loyalties or territorialism: obstacles occurred as contradictions between the land owning and dispossessed peasants emerged in the upsurge and ebb of their movement. The CPC was only able to make strides in organising the peasants' struggle to remove the feudal constraints of landlord domination and establish independent communities with security of household production as it addressed not only the problem of 'alien class influences' but also the differences within the peasant class.

What is left out of account in much of Western scholarship on the Chinese peasants in revolution is a recognition of these differences among them

– differences in access to resources giving rise to differences in outlook and different forms of behaviour, sometimes even in conflict with each other's interests.

Perry, as one who does bring into focus the differences, identifies the destructive dynamic of the peasants' protectionist and predatory behaviours which as she argues supported the persistence of elite leadership. However, she sees this as an absolute condition, attributing these weaknesses in peasants' traditional collective actions to the limited nature of subsistence survivalism. But where for Perry, the scarcity of resources was an environmental limitation, a Marxist perspective reveals the condition as exacerbated by the drain of agricultural produce from the villages, the more so as the national demand for grain accelerated with the drain of agricultural goods into international markets.

Rural isolation then, at least for an essential part, was a relative condition: not so much a matter of traditional clannishness but a feature of village communities cut off from the towns by landlord control of the channels of communication. Patronage ties persisted as peasants depended not least on the mediation of the elites for links with the outside world; on the other hand with the market freed from feudal constraint opening the possibility of the renewal of the urban-rural linkage, there was potential for a revitalising transformation of the patriarchal order to end stagnation. Indeed, in their resistance to unequal exchange with the towns, an assertion of independence from the landlords' control over the village economy, the peasants were already beginning to search for a different kind of relationship with the towns.

Class struggle clearly was not a straightforward process – peasant consciousness did not immediately grasp the necessity of revolutionary opposition. From a Marxist perspective, Marks saw the problem of leadership in the Haifeng Soviet in terms of the disjuncture between the peasants' subjective consciousness and their objective circumstances, with the form of peasant power lagging behind an actual recognition of the material circumstances of their exploitation, making it difficult to develop appropriate forms of action. As has been seen, these problems arose at a particular point of breakdown in relations between town and countryside when the national and agrarian revolutions were moving in different directions.

Mao recognised that peasants were able to change and learn through experience amidst the unfolding circumstances of revolution. His analysis was to encompass both the materialist and the subjective aspects of the contradictions among the rural classes. Seeing the revolutionary phases of ebb and upsurge as reflecting the shifting strength of landlord and peasant power, he was able to develop a strategy for the agrarian revolution within the overall process of the national revolution.

For Mao what led peasant struggles to an impasse was not the limitations of survivalism but their lack of unity given their conflicting demands at different phases in the struggle. By adapting policies to the dynamics of the rural classes, it would be possible to transform the traditional cycle of protest from within. This became clear as analysis of the rural relations of production revealed the dual characteristics of the rich peasants whose interests in production were inhibited by the persistence of feudal relations, pointing the way to the possibility of dividing the traditional village elites. At the same time, a grasp of peasant dynamics highlighted the central role of the middle peasants in restraining poor peasant excesses so as to forge a firm foundation for the anti-feudal struggle.

From this perspective on rural classes and their behaviour, it then became apparent how contradictions within the national movement, with different urban classes promoting different approaches to land reform, exerted an influence on peasant consciousness and behaviours and the shifts then in landlord-peasant power.

The critical question in leading peasant struggles out of their traditional cycle of defeat was that of the direction of change of the urban-rural relationship in the national democratic movement. On the one hand, reliance on a passive peasantry and the use of legalistic methods of land redistribution favoured by the national bourgeoisie fostered division among a partially differentiated peasantry so creating conditions of leadership degeneration. The activist approach of a proletarian programme in contrast aimed, whilst mobilising the peasants, to promote unity drawing the middle peasants into a process of social and economic transformation initiated by poor peasant mobilisation, and thereby creating a mass force capable of breaking traditional patterns of elite leadership so as to achieve the complete elimination of feudal relations.

The challenge of leadership then was to maintain peasant unity and activism to prevent the rich peasant and the small landlord village elite from regaining control once a revolutionary upsurge subsided.

Reform of land ownership was to offer the rural communities the way of escape from the dead end of traditional competition as the status and inter-relations between the different types of peasants were transformed. In conditions of stagnation, isolation, resource scarcity and lack of alternatives, the peasants clung to survival strategies, landholders and the dispossessed dividing from each other in predatory or protectionist behaviours. Land reform on the other hand enabled the poor to realise independence: with land sufficient for basic subsistence, they were freed from the ties of patronage or the alternative – a life of vagabondage and banditry; for the middle peasants, the changes also brought stability and security; and for the rich peasants, whilst the break-up of village properties removed their traditional corporate status, at the same time new opportunities became available for them to develop their private enterprise, providing a motor for growth in the village economy.

By unleashing this potential for growth, CPC policies further created conditions favourable to resolving the material contradictions among the peasants, finding ways of organising reciprocities between rich, middle and poor so as to consolidate their gains and make further advances through production. It was here that the CPC introduced a new element into the peasant world with the use of resources not for the building of elite-led factions but for investment in production for the overall prosperity of the community.

In this way the new democratic village communities, with the changed relations among the peasants, also saw the basis of village leadership and institutions transformed. Traditional styles of leadership based on clientelism and plunder required resources as well as mediation skills to organise both protectionist and predatory operations. The CPC's village development programmes on the other hand called for leaders with practical skills to set an example in farming, as Thaxton noted. However, more was required to handle the complex demands of reorganising production relations to bring the different types of peasants together in the implementation of policies of growth for collective benefit.

Land reform not only established security for individual household farming: it set up a particular dynamic of future development. New patterns of urban-rural interchange offered contrasting paths into a capitalist process of private accumulation or into a socialist process involving social or public accumulation. As has been noted before, this inherent contradiction within the path of development, opened once the constraint of landlord control of the surplus and of commerce had been lifted, was one obscured in the peasants' traditional conceptions of an egalitarian 'moral economy'. From the perspective of the CPC, the objective of the new economic democracy was not only to clear the way for capitalism but to clear a still wider path for the development of socialism as new patterns of interaction between cities and countryside were unlocked.[8]

The development take-off was not the uncomplicated process of the unleashing of capitalism from below that Thaxton suggests: as a rich peasant economy was to take the lead in promoting growth, all the more the unity of the poor and middle peasants had to be sustained, carrying on the democratic process to prevent the new village institutions falling again under the influence of the traditional – or a new rich peasant – elite.

The policies and organisational methods of land reform shaped the outcome of the new rural economy in a very particular way with a private sector of growth amidst an activated mass of small producers.

In setting a new development path in motion, the Yan'an style village programmes were designed to continue to uphold the proletarian line of peasant activism so as to maintain democratic unity against the revival of elitist leadership patterns, consolidating the newly-won gains of peasant independence and security by securing peasant leadership over the ongoing process of growth and change.

Why CPC leadership mattered then was that, whilst encouraging the rich peasant economy in order to move beyond the dynamics of survivalism, it aimed to ensure that the villages did not fall under rich peasant domination as the capitalist path was unleashed. Alongside a flourishing private sector, the existence of co-operatives and public enterprises together with the mutual aid teams served as guarantees of livelihood for the mass of the peasants. These elements of collectivism and socialism helped to sustain poor and middle peasant unity against the re-emergence of a rich peasant leadership and the restoration of landlord power. Economic democracy then provided the basis for a new political reality of mass democracy.

Through policies and methods which released peasant activism and collective enthusiasm for production, the Party then initiated a new type of village leadership based on mass participation with the representation of poor and middle peasants on village committees. Certainly, breaking with traditional patterns of leadership and eradicating old modes of behaviour was not something to be accomplished overnight. Nevertheless, changes in village land ownership, production patterns and relationships between households together with the transformation of exchange relations between town and countryside, opened up possibilities to transcend the traditional dynamics of subsistence and survival through a shared growth process as well as to fashion new types of socio-economic relations and institutional arrangements demanding new styles of leadership.

CPC leadership as Marxism in practice

The **works of the Western scholars** considered here have raised important questions, developed interesting angles and illuminated many of the problems and practices of peasant revolution and CPC organisation in China. Clearly there were variations from area to area which may account for differences in emphasis and explanation. For Alavi and Wolf, the intention was never more than to open up debate, whilst case studies, limited in time and geographical space, can only provide a particular snapshot of particular conditions. But at the same time these studies have produced contradictory conclusions on CPC-peasant relations as a result of their differing views of the nature of the peasants themselves as subsistence- or market-oriented producers. To better understand the guiding role of the CPC in the peasant movement in fact requires an appreciation of its class-based policies, that is, the application of Marxism in analysing the situation in the countryside within the changing demands of the anti-imperialist struggle.

In critiquing Marxist class conflict theories, Little has pointed out that there is more to understanding peasant rebellion than the material circumstances of exploitation: beyond the expression of social tensions created by contradictions within the economic system are issues of the peasants' subjective consciousness.[9] The way that the bonds of patronage, kin and brotherhood cut across class lines to reproduce patterns of elite leadership was indeed the most difficult challenge faced by the CPC in organising the peasants in revolution.

From observation and through trial and error, Mao built up an understanding not only of the material conditions of exploitation that defined the basis of the different classes but also the changing conditions of the revolution and how these impacted on peasant class behaviour. Peasant consciousness could be seen to shift from traditional conceptions of remedialism to opposition as the rural upsurge took off, with peasant power prone to millenarian forms – the personality cult, 'mountain-topism', adventurism and radical egalitarian idealism – in the vacuum created as the national and agrarian movements diverged, then to revert to dependence on patronage, kin or community for protection as the struggle ebbed. Based on an analysis of the material circumstances of the differing sections of the peasants and of the dynamics between them as their struggles unfolded within the changing context of the wider national movement, the CPC was able to adapt to the circumstances and step by step unleash the revolutionary potential of the Chinese peasant movement.

At root, the problems of the tenacity of traditional bonds, the persistence of landlord influence and the degeneration of peasant struggles into clan factionalism, which hindered the development of class consciousness and complicated the landlord-peasant class struggle, were nevertheless about class relations. To overthrow the feudal system and end its monopoly conditions required a class-based strategy of land reform which fostered mass power, enabling the poor and middle peasants to set aside their differences and cement their alliance, whilst drawing the rich peasants down the path of expanded production away from feudal landlords. Following land confiscation and redistribution, peasant independence was firmly rooted in village production programmes which, whilst unleashing the productive power of the surplus-producing rich peasants, maintained collectivism and the mass power of the poor and middle peasants. In meeting these requirements the CPC provided guidelines which enabled the peasants, rather than any former or new village elites, to control the process of rural reform and transformation.

The CPC-peasant relationship which developed over time is best understood as a negotiated one, both top-down and bottom-up. From a Marxist perspective, the CPC addressed not only the objective contradictions between landlord and peasant but also those amongst the peasants which in turn were framed by the struggle between the national bourgeoisie and proletariat for leadership over the land reform process. At the same time, the CPC led by addressing the subjective limitations of the peasant world outlook whilst also appreciating the peasants' ability themselves to change and learn from experience, as Thaxton and Marks have shown.

The Marxist essence of CPC leadership of the peasant movement comprised a revolutionary strategy based on the analysis of classes in the countryside and adapted to peasant dynamics. Taking poor peasants as the active drivers, and middle peasants, whilst not the prime movers as Alavi thought, as serving at the centre, the strategy was further adjusted to the interactions between the agrarian and the national movements which turned on the question of reliance on peasant activism or passivity. The CPC then was able to promote rural development within the New Democratic economy in a way which opened the door not only to capitalism but also to socialism.

NOTES AND REFERENCES

1. Needham, 1956, pp.120–1.
2. *Ibid.*, p.121.
3. See also Watson, 1980, p.28.
4. Thaxton, 1983, pp.231–2.
5. *Ibid.*, pp.132.
6. Mao, *Selected Works*, Vol. I., pp.45–6.
7. see Schram, 1969b, p.100.
8. Mao, *Selected Works*, Vol. III, p.111–2.
9. Little, 1989, p.166.

CONCLUSION

China's pre-revolutionary political economy: the hidden foundation

Developments in Western peasant studies applied to China have provided insights to allow a more detailed appraisal of the achievements and limitations of the CPC's policies for rural transformation beyond rigid Marxist formulae. Nevertheless, whilst many Western scholars have aimed to transcend what they consider the inadequacies of the Marxist approach, class analysis remains the central ingredient in understanding the success of the CPC in unleashing the productive potential in the countryside and guiding the peasants' struggle for land to success.

Huang, for one, whilst recognising the harsh conditions of landlord exploitation, questions the centrality of the landlord-peasant class struggle in the revolutionary process. As has been seen, for Huang as for Perdue, the landlord-peasant relationship, though important, was only one among many of the diverse axes of exploitation and conflict in China, suggesting that the revolutionary process itself was more complex than that of a transition from a feudal land system with the emergence of a bourgeoisie and proletariat.

Huang and Perdue both take a variegated approach drawing from different theoretical models as they seek to assess the various dimensions of the pre-revolutionary crisis: the ecological crisis, the pressures of population growth on limited resources, the crisis in the political authority of the state as well as the increasing class conflict between landlord and peasant.[1] Seeking to adapt to regional variations, this flexible approach has the advantage of capturing the diversity of the peasantry – the potentially entrepreneurial but nevertheless non-capitalising village rich, the semi-proletarianised poor and the small owner-peasants – as well as the various issues that affected them in different ways – natural disasters, corrupt officialdom, increased taxes, the problems of debt and marketing as well as exorbitant rents. It also recognises the complexity of peasant responses, including banditry and village closure against bureaucratic intervention as well as opposition to the landlords, taking in the fact that peasant behaviour was not simply determined by class position but influenced by tradition and shared conceptions of community.

However, such eclecticism not only fudges what are after all fundamental theoretical differences but also tends towards a piecemeal approach. Huang suggests that further research on the revolutionary nature of the Chinese peasantry should differentiate sets of class relations according to how each of the two parties changed or did not change.[2] An investigation of the different axes of relations between landlord-tenant, employer-employee, state-village would also, he argues, reveal a clearer understanding of the differing capacities of the peasants to respond to revolutionary transformation.

Huang's own suggestion is that the combination of a non-capitalising elite with a semi-proletarianising peasantry created a particularly revolutionary situation.[3] In contrast, as has been seen, others have suggested that it was the smallholders in China who were the revolutionary subjects. This view mirrored that embraced by the populists in Russia who considered that capitalism impoverished the peasants rather than developing agriculture since merchant and usurer exploitation drained the owner-peasant communities of their resources, and it was this that created the conditions of peasant protest against the state and the market.

As the argument elucidated here has shown, the Chinese agrarian revolution was distinctive in both the activism of the poor peasants and the involvement of the middle peasants. It is clear that neither of these sections of the peasantry alone describes the revolutionary nature of the Chinese peasantry. Indeed peasant class struggle became confused under both the 'poor peasant line' and 'middle peasant line'. The strength of the poor peasants lay not in their separate organisation but rather in their alliance with the middle peasants, who, in turn became a revolutionary force on the basis of poor peasant activism.

Huang's argument falls short in separating out the different economic conditions of the peasantry which he sees as corresponding with different types of village organisation and power structure: the atomised communities of the semi-proletarianising poor, and the more closely knit owner-peasant communities. This is to suggest that not only were there separate peasant struggles around the different issues – rent, wages, taxes – but also different forms of collective action with greater or lesser potential for revolutionary organisation and peasant participation in transformative struggle. For Huang, whilst the capacity for collective action on the part of the semi-proletarianised peasantry is to be set in the context of the impersonal relations of their atomised communities dominated by local tyrants, this he sees as contrasting with the owner peasants whose collective action of village closure mobilised under endogenous leadership in defence of their property and communal organisation against outside intervention.

Tax resistance then is seen as a separate dimension of rural conflict from landlord-tenant tensions, with poor peasants more in conflict with the landlords than the state, since they did not pay much in tax, whilst the tax-paying owner-peasants conflicted more with the state.[4] However this emphasis on these sectoral divisions, separating the actions and demands of the owner and semi-proletarianised peasants, loses sight of the underlying conditions of their fundamental unity in realising the final, thorough, eradication of the feudal system.

In a discussion of Marx's concept of the mode of production, de Ste Croix argues that it is not in fact how the bulk of the labour of production is done that distinguishes each mode, but how the dominant propertied classes, controlling the conditions of production, ensure the extraction of the surplus. He demonstrates this with an illuminating quote from Marx from Volume III of *Capital*:

> The specific economic form in which unpaid surplus labour is pumped out of the direct producers determines the relationship between those who dominate and those who are in subjection, as it grows directly out of production itself and reacts upon it as a determining element in its turn. Upon this, however, is founded the entire organisation of the economic community which grows up out of the production relations themselves, and thereby at the same time its specific political form. It is always the direct relationship of the owners of the conditions of production to the immediate producers…which reveals the innermost secret, the hidden foundation of the entire social structure and therefore also of the political form of the relations of sovereignty and dependence, in short, the corresponding specific form of State. This does not prevent the same economic basis – the same as far as its main conditions are concerned – owing to innumerable different empirical circumstances, natural environment, racial prejudices, external historical influences, etc., from manifesting infinite variations and gradations of aspect, which can be grasped only by analysis of the empirically given circumstances.[5]

Discussion in preceding chapters has shown that in pre-revolutionary China, monopoly rent, as the main form of surplus labour, was the 'hidden foundation' beneath the distinctive characteristics of Chinese feudalism – the bureaucratic state, the patriarchal village, the pattern of parcellised cultivation – which non-Marxist analyses have struggled to penetrate. Its predominant form – rent in kind – and its rate at 50 per cent of the crop or more – indicated that the economic surplus was produced by a labour force subject to extra-economic compulsion.

The importance of landlordism was not then confined to one sector of agricultural production, namely that undertaken by tenant-farmers: it was the determining element in the economy and society, providing limits to the development of wage labour and usury. Nevertheless, these feudal relations took a form different from European manorial serfdom.

The persistence of small-scale cultivation as opposed to large landed estates expressed in fact the contradiction between the concentration of land ownership and its fragmented use, given the increasing demand for land to cultivate by the peasant with their under-utilised labour and unmet consumption needs. At the same time, state and landlord, apparently separated with their bases in tax and rent respectively, in fact rested together on the fusion of economic and political powers of the dominant class at the base of society.

The perpetuation of the Asiatic hierarchical structures of state and kinship upheld by Confucian ideals of benevolent patronage helped to preserve landlord prestige and privilege with the local rural elites mediating between the large landlords and the bureaucratic state on the one hand and the patriarchal village on the other. The patron-client arrangement combined political and economic power in a particularly flexible way which allowed the feudal system to adapt to the development of commerce, with landlords using the system of land purchase to grow at the expense of the state whilst keeping peasants tied to the land.

As has been seen, existing explanations of the processes of agrarian change within the Western literature have been found wanting in their analysis of the distinctive features of Chinese society where the development of commerce led not so much to capitalism in agriculture as to stagnation with the persistence of traditional customary practices and a particularly tenacious type of feudal power. The central difficulty here lies in grasping that the relations between landed property on the one hand and commerce and credit on the other, which from a European perspective are in contradiction, in China were intertwined.

The structure of landlordism based on land purchase and patronage created the conditions of land monopoly and peasant land insufficiency which formed the basis of monopoly rent as the major constraint on the development of capitalism. Whilst Huang's analysis shows how commercialisation led to a partial differentiation of the peasantry, he sees the reasons for the blocked transition lying within the peasant rather than the landlord economy. The argument that has been made here however is that the conditions of economic stagnation under monopoly rent saw the assimilation of the entrepreneurial rich peasant with landlordism, with an apparently homogenised mass of increasingly impoverished small producers clinging for survival to traditional, but increasingly weakening, bonds of patronage, kinship and community.

The limitation in Huang's analysis lies in its failure to situate the different economic conditions of the different types of peasants in their relation with the main determinant of the agrarian economy, monopoly rent. Insofar as this form of exploitation constrained growth, landlordism affected not just tenants but all types of peasants. At the same time, the development of commerce under landlord dominance meant that, in addition to their control over their tenants, landlords had economic power over both owner and entrepreneurial peasants, involving them in different ways in their power domain.

Rather than treating the axes of landlord-tenant, employer-employee, debtor-usurer, buyer-seller, state-village all separately, a focus on the constraint of monopoly rent reveals the connections in particular between the poor peasants' burden of exploitation and the stagnating village economies of the insular owner peasant communities. Despite local variations in the state-village-landlord balance as well as the different forms of exploitation and types of rural conflict, the common problem for owner, part-owner and tenant peasant alike was land insufficiency.

An analysis of Chinese society in terms of the main agrarian relation thus highlights the particular class polarisation and complex power dynamic between the landlords and rich peasants on one side, and the poor and middle, tenant and owner peasants on the other, with their common problem of land hunger and under-utilised labour providing the potential around which to develop a revolutionary unity against the conditions of land monopoly.

The Chinese revolution was not, however, simply the inevitable outcome of the intensifying contradictions of the objective structure of the economy. The hidden foundation, the main agrarian relation whereby surplus is appropriated, indeed provides the context not only for the interactions – political and economic – of the various classes, but also shaped the state-village dynamic of bureaucratic intervention and community closure. Although the objective potential for unity among the peasants was there, competition due to scarcity under economic stagnation created a divided and isolated peasantry separated in segmented hierarchical claims to resources or dependent on patronage and protection for survival.

The landlords' domination of the countryside made mass power the central issue in a rural transformation that was aimed to benefit owner and tenant peasants alike. With the seizure of state power the ultimate goal, as the Communist-led armies captured localities and territories, landlord power at the base of society crumbled bit by bit: by dealing with the big landlords first, depriving the local elites of back-up, relations of land and power at village level were reordered through the organised power of the peasants.

Imperialism, nation and rural reform

Whether from a traditionalist opposition to market intervention or as a resistance to capitalist exploitation, peasant discontent in China has been seen as linked to the impact of imperialism. With rural society exposed to the volatility of international markets and the disruptive effects of accelerated commercialisation, whilst Trotsky considered peasant impoverishment to be mainly caused by commercial exploitation and usury linking up with international capital, Tawney too, from a very different perspective, likened the Chinese peasantry to a 'propertied proletariat'.[6]

Was China impelled into a capitalist transformation through an increasing participation in the world capitalist system or was it to experience a blocked transition? Whether or not imperialism promotes or inhibits the development of capitalism in Third World countries has been the subject of much debate. Frank, in his work on Latin America, saw in the extension of commercialisation a chain of exploitation extracting and transmitting surpluses through a series of metropolis-satellite links.[7] Objecting to Frank's equating of commerce with capitalism, Laclau, pointing to the absence of free wage labour in agriculture, came to the conclusion that underdevelopment was generated as imperialism reinforced existing relations of extra-economic coercion so restricting internal processes of development and inhibiting capitalism.[8]

For Alavi, Laclau's analysis involves the problematic assumption of articulation between fundamentally contradictory capitalist and pre-capitalist modes of production.[9] Drawing from both sides of the debate to explain the persistence of small-scale cultivation in India, Alavi argues the case of peasant subsumption under capitalism within the changed context in which colonialism imparts a new meaning and significance to the unchanging form of production relations. With the dissolution of the structures of local power and generalised commodity production, Alavi considers that peasants were subordinated to capitalism since commodity circulation was completed only via the metropolitan power where surplus value was realised.

In China, the demands of semi-colonialism and the effects of commercial intensification also saw a certain corruption of clan and patron-client ties – persisting in form but changing in content and emptying of reciprocity. But despite these changing conditions, peasant subsumption under capitalism was not completed: the drain of the surplus through the channels of marketing and credit depended on feudal extraction and the power of the landlords who, as their traditional legitimacy weakened, resorted increasingly to brute force. The links of circulation remained conditioned by the internally-structured land monopoly.

In China, as has been seen, the adaptation of feudal relations to the spread of commercialisation, leading not so much to capitalist development as to the persistence of small-scale agricultural production and peasant impoverishment, preceded the advent of semi-colonial imposition.

Despite their very different perspectives, Tawney and Trotsky both made the same error in failing to recognise the connections between market and land monopoly such that the intensification of commerce under imperialism strengthened the economic position of the landlords, exacerbating the contradiction between land hunger and the monopoly control of land and grain so as to inhibit the development of the internal market.

It was this peculiarity of the feudal system in China, which saw commerce grow under landlord control, that accounted for the contradictory effects of imperialism, warranting the characterisation of China as a semi-feudal, semi-colonial society.

In these conditions, elements of a bourgeois class began to take shape. Was it essentially dependent on international markets and capitalism, as Frank's argument suggests, or was it rather, as Laclau points out, that imperialist restrictions on growth provided the basis for a revolution in which the domestic bourgeoisie played an important role? In a highly controversial claim, Warren argued that in fact imperialism, at least in the long term, should be seen as bringing progress to developing countries. He cites China as a case in point, seeing its nascent middle class challenging feudalism in direct response to outside interference and intervention. Far from frustrating an emerging capitalism already in existence, he argues, imperialism created one that would otherwise have been much slower to take shape, opening up the path to an independent industrialisation.[10]

But in fact China's twisted growth under imperialist domination saw the appearance of a fragmented, weak and dependent bourgeoisie. On the one hand, the colonial powers were able to promote a compradore and bureaucratic bourgeoisie closely bound up with the system of land monopoly through purchase. Through these contacts with state officials and merchants, international capital was able to rely on the feudal extraction of surpluses as it linked into the indigenous credit and marketing systems which had grown up in conformity with feudal landed property.

This further convergence of interest among the absentee landlords, merchants and officials was not to be confused with the landlord path of capitalist development of the Prussian or Meiji type since the wealth derived from rent, usury and commercial super-profits, where it was not siphoned off into international markets, was used for the purposes of speculation not productive investment.

At the same time, a national bourgeoisie began to emerge catering to a growing urban demand. However, needing agrarian reforms to release the constraint on the internal market in order to facilitate its independent development, it was ultimately too weak to see these through.

Peasant conditions and peasant behaviours presented particular problems for the urban-based reformers seeking to modernise China. As Chen Boda had demonstrated, whether in the areas given over to cash cropping and monoculture or the stagnating backwaters of the agrarian economy, the peasant farmers were the losers. Such conditions gave rise to mounting peasant protest. In opposition to their lack of rights within the feudal landlord system and the corruption of clan and lineage organisations, resisting the parasitism of the town-country relationship and the isolation imposed by the landlords' domination of commerce, the peasants' struggle for land represented the emergence of a movement for a democratic transformation of the countryside. Nevertheless, the particular conditions for such a transformation were complex with a partially-differentiating peasantry trapped within the feudal structures.

The rich peasants with their partial roots in feudal exploitation offered no base for an alliance upon which urban reformers could rely, whilst the increasingly impoverished masses on the margins of subsistence were liable to resort to indiscriminate attacks upon the wealthy, in the towns as well as the countryside, blocking trade and seizing the merchants' reserves of grain. This extremism was not however a resistance to modernisation: in the semi-feudal, semi-colonial conditions of China, the peasants were not just traditionalists, and far from seeking to cut themselves off from the cities in a retreat into rural isolation, their efforts to restrict trade represented their opposition, not to free markets, but as has been argued, to the debilitating effects of unequal trade under merchant-landlord and bureaucratic controls. In imposing their own controls over local markets, the peasants, on their part, were looking to rebalance and transform the existing unequal exchange between town and countryside.

The urban nationalists for their part, still with some roots in landed property in their home villages and fearful of unleashing peasant excesses, preferred a passive peasantry. However bourgeois reforms limited to the creation of conditions most favourable to the development of capitalism provided an inadequate response to the subsistence needs of the impoverished. Indeed, furthering the interests of the well-to-do only added to the frustration of those too poor to take advantage of improvements in marketing conditions, deepening their antagonism to all forms of wealth.

The problem for the reform programme of the KMT Nationalist government, as Crook and Gilmartin put it, lay in the failure to identify the power structures and vested interests that were hostile to the reform agenda or to develop allies to meet the challenge of the complex rural environment.[11] Alavi's observation is pertinent: the failure of a bourgeois perspective lies in its abstract view of society which tends to mask informal power influences especially in circumstances where the form of individual rights contains the content of personal dependencies.[12]

With the richer strata at local levels entangled with feudal power relations and closely linked with the landlord economy, the majority of impoverished peasantry clung on to traditional strategies of survival. Competing over scarce resources, peasants divided according to traditional loyalties, communal bonds, and hierarchical rights of access to land, such that the traditional elites were able to maintain their hold over the villages. As bourgeois reforms promoted further divisions among the peasants, these tended only to stoke factionalism, perpetuating landlord influence as existing powerholders took advantage of the room for manoeuvre.

What made the dynamics of the peasant movement so complicated was that underlying the subjective expressions of loyalties and rivalries were differing conditions of production and hence differing positions in relation to the release of market constraints. The failure of the nationalist-based reform movement lay ultimately in the inadequacy of its policies based on urban business needs to handle the contradictions among the peasants and the differing expectations that arose amongst them in the transformation of the town-countryside relations.

The national bourgeoisie then were not only weak, they had no solution to the problems of rural impoverishment and dependency and, with nothing to offer the poor, they were unable to establish stability in the countryside. In this way, they vacillated, caught between their need for reform to open up the domestic market for their own independent development and their need to rely on the small landlords to maintain social order in the face of their failures and inability to influence the poor peasants themselves.

With the traditional bonds of benevolent protection in the countryside crumbling, undermining the whole Confucian framework of legitimation which had held the system together, new social forces for change in the countryside were struggling to be unleashed. What was required to sufficiently resolve the demands of the majority, the land hungry, and prevent the revival of relations of dependency, was the radical redistribution of feudal properties including those of the village landlords and rich peasants. This was only to be achieved by uniting the mass of the peasants in action.

The CPC and peasant class struggle

The nature of the relationship between the CPC and the peasants has been much contested in the Western academic literature. Skocpol has suggested that scholars in the early years after the CPC victory in 1949 tended to focus on the intentions of the Party as if it had been able to mould society at will.[13] Warning against this type of approach, she argued that it is not possible to understand a revolution by following any one class or organisation, not least because intended actions have unintended outcomes.[14] But neither is a revolutionary process the inexorable working out of structural contradictions regardless of the will of its participants.

Later scholars, endeavouring to avoid both voluntarism and structural determinism, have sought to treat the peasants as revolutionary actors whose behaviour and demands are to be understood on the one hand in relation to how the rural structures shaped their lives, and on the other hand in relation to how they felt and expressed this experience in terms of their subjective consciousness and organisation.[15] These scholars then turned their focus on the village order as shaped by the informal bonds of patronage, kinship and community, and on pre-existing patterns of peasant protest.

Indeed, the contradiction between land monopoly and land hunger was not expressed so directly in a class struggle between landlord and peasant, and the peasants' attitude to revolution was not a simple or straightforward expression of class or economic interests. In seeking to mobilise the peasants within the frame of class struggle, the CPC's efforts were hindered by the influence of traditional values and pre-existing local networks.

Village organisational hierarchies based on kinship and community bonds which controlled settlement rights and access to property were instrumental in embedding landlord power within rural society. However they were not just a creation of the rural elites, serving only to maintain their positions of power and privilege: they were also used by the peasants as means of survival. In this way then, vertical ties tended to overlay horizontal solidarities with loyalties to lineage and local leaders dividing the peasants as a class.

The failure to tackle the informal structures of elite power at the grassroots level had been the downfall of the Nationalist reformers. How the CPC broke through these structures, unravelling the tangle of feudal and capitalist relations, and how it handled rural struggles complicated by factionalism and egalitarianism have been core questions in this discussion of peasants and revolution. Mass power was the means of rural revolutionary transformation but what conditions were then necessary for the realisation of the peasants' revolutionary potential? How did the peasants make the transition from the ties of tradition and patronage to revolution, and how did the CPC guide them through this process?

The peasant as traditionalist had more than one face: community closure; antipathy to wealth and power; and belief in reciprocity between rich and poor and in remedialism as a means to balance inequality. Customary practices and traditions were in fact double-edged, providing potential opposition but also prone to divisiveness and elite leadership. Whilst the system of clan, religious and patriarchal authority upheld feudal power, insofar as the peasants shared in these institutions, accepting landlord leadership for protection and survival, they did not share the same conceptions of social justice and equality. As Thaxton has convincingly shown, the peasants also held their own pre-Confucian beliefs about morality and social justice.

With traditional reciprocities and moral standards of benevolence crumbling, the peasants, as Mao discovered from his investigations in Hunan, were beginning to break the bonds of tradition as they took over control of their clan and community organisations. Here, he grasped, was a revolution in the making with feudal power, which over succeeding dynasties and under warlord rule had denied peasants' rights, now under challenge. This recognition marked a break with the reform agenda: social change required not just a readjustment in state-peasant relations nor simply a renewal at the top tier of bureaucracy nor even just the capture of state power but the transformation of the structure of village power. This, as he grasped, was a matter of which class led. Barring the landlords and rich peasants from membership of peasant organisations removed the backbone of feudal power as it were, making it possible for the peasants to take over power from within their communities. This then paved the way for a thorough land reform which did not exclude the land rented out by the village elites from confiscation.

Taking the peasant revolution as central, Mao came to lead the CPC, resolving the questions of the nature and character of the revolution and the matter of proletarian leadership. As it sought to adapt its policies to the distinctive conditions of the rural localities, the Party had to develop its own style in the face of the inherent dangers of its vanguard position assuming a traditional leadership role over the peasants. Itself the product of the circumstances of the revolution, the CPC had to overcome its own limitations of organisation and consciousness as it put the theories of Marx and Lenin to use as a guide in transforming its goals into effective action.

To understand revolution, the CPC initially looked to the example of the Russian experience. However the conditions that gave rise to revolution in China were quite different, not least since its main content was the agrarian movement. As has been seen, a rigid adherence to Leninism and the Russian model was to prove an obstacle in grasping the specific revolutionary nature of the peasantry, and in identifying the roles of the various rural classes, which led to errors as the CPC sought to unleash the full force of the peasants against landlord power.

The conditions of the rural revolution defied simple analysis. Drawing the line between the targets and proponents in the struggle over land was particularly taxing given the complexities of rural relations of exploitation through rent, usury and labour hiring. At the same time, in the absence of a clear polarisation among the peasants into distinct classes of rural bourgeoisie and proletariat, identified by Lenin as the revolutionary forces in the Russian countryside, the Chinese peasants had the superficial appearance – tenants and owner-cultivators alike – of a homogenised mass of small producers. But were they essentially conservative petty proprietors, predisposed to authoritarian leadership? Were they traditionalists taking up arms in defence of their own way of life against interventions by the state or by market forces? Or were they a social force in dissolution, their traditions of communalism and reciprocity breaking down to make way for an emerging rich peasantry at the cutting edge of capitalist development as well as for poor peasants whose activism would open up the path to socialism?

Both Trotsky and Stalin misjudged the situation. For Trotsky, the break-up of the rich peasantry was to be the first, not the second, step in an anti-capitalist struggle. But in this he failed to take account of the feudal form of surplus production. Stalin on the other hand, although he understood the democratic stage of the Chinese revolution, continued to apply class distinctions derived from the European pattern. How then to explain the rich peasants, who rather than supporting land reform policies, took the side of the elites? And with the lack of a rural proletariat, were the poor peasants in a strong enough position to take the lead?

Given the nature of China's rural economy in which capitalist relations were caught up within the feudal integument with a partially differentiated peasantry tangled in the hierarchies of patronage and privilege, peasant positions in the revolutionary process – the poor, the middle and the rich – took on particular characteristics which influenced the distinctive dynamics of their movement as a whole.

The CPC was to learn from trial and error as the policies of its Comintern-influenced leaders as well as the methods of Liu Shaoqi, proved inadequate in dealing with the subversive manoeuvrings of the local elites amidst divisions among the peasants, as well as in dealing with its own organisational shortcomings. Up to 1927, the CPC erred to the Right in failing to take full advantage of opportunities to advance the revolution through mass mobilisation. Subsequently 'Leftist' tendencies, which essentially underestimated the revolutionary role of the middle peasants and sought instead to rely exclusively on the organisation of the poor, gave way to excessive attacks on both rich and well-to-do middle peasants causing confusion in peasant organisation.

Through the zigs and zags of the revolutionary path, the Party had to come to terms not only with the dogmatic application of Leninism and the Russian model but also with simplistic attitudes to wealth and power. The Chayanovian effect of peasant homogeneity apparently challenged the relevance of the Leninist categorisation, but in fact an analysis of class relations based on the distinction between different types of property was necessary to see beneath the surface appearance of subjective divisions to the fundamental contradictions among the rural classes.

Marxist analysis, by identifying different ways in which the rural people got rich – by their own labour, by capitalist and by feudal exploitation – was to provide the means by which the CPC uncovered the conditions of peasant differentiation. Contrary to the Rightist view of peasant homogeneity, the CPC was able by this method to identify a lower middle peasant strata experiencing land hunger alongside the poor peasants. At the same time, as distinct from the 'Leftist' view which exaggerated class polarisation, it was able to draw a line between the upper middle peasants, who had grown rich through labour, and the rich peasants who lived by exploitation. Meanwhile, the rich peasants, with their productive potential inhibited within the existing rural system, remained semi-feudal, entwined within feudal relations of traditional power and contributing to the conditions of land monopoly.

Applying the Marxist perspective, the CPC came to understand that the force behind the peasant struggle for land in China was not that of a rising petty bourgeoisie but of completely impoverished peasants, less interested in the absolute preservation of private property than, given their land insufficiency, in the confiscation of landlords' land. With a large mass of the peasants likely to support policies of land confiscation and redistribution, the middle peasants from their lower to their upper ends, lay in fact at the centre of this revolution. No mere passive bastion of conservatism and neither a social force in dissolution nor rising in populist rebellion, this peasant sector formed part of the revolutionary base, serving in fact as the pivot of a movement motivated neither by profit nor a traditionalist community defence but by land hunger. As for the rich peasants, if they were not so much agents for the national bourgeoisie, neither were they entirely feudal patriarchs: their dual characteristics at least opened up the possibility of neutralising their position.

No matter which approach was adopted – whether policies of reform or the application of a strictly Leninist-styled classification which exaggerated peasant polarisation or the adoption of a neo-Narodnik small producer populist perspective against wealth in general – all spelled disaster for peasant class struggle in practice. Closely observing the roles of the different types of peasants in the revolutionary process and analysing their material basis in the rural relations of production, the CPC was able from this to develop a strategy for agrarian revolution adapted to the shifts in rural class dynamics, that is, to grasp the 'subtle dialectic', as Alavi puts it, between the different roles. This made it possible to identify the weak spots of landlord power so as to break down the existing ties of patronage and dependency in a staged approach.

As they sought to retain or regain their privileges and influence, the traditional powerholders used peasant divisions as a basis for manoeuvre. Past movements of rural protest and rebellion had then tended to disintegrate from within as a result of elite capture and factional struggles. CPC strategy to counter this was to avoid the dual pitfalls of middle peasant passivism and poor peasant radicalism which alienated one from the other leaving the poor peasants isolated, and to build their unity step by step to finally bring the village elites under peasant control.

At the same time, leadership problems of commandism and adventurism, bureaucratism and spontaneism, arose amidst peasant disunity. Party rectification was then an essential condition for establishing peasant independence as the foundation of the democratic process.

The CPC was no mere embodiment of revolutionary ideology: its members were also actors on the revolutionary scene who, together with the peasants, were to learn from their experiences amidst the changing objective environment.

Rather than treating the peasants as conservative, backward and superstitious, imposing change from above or using traditional mechanisms of influence to substitute its own authority as it broke up the old feudal networks, the CPC entered the dynamic processes of the rural politics at its fault lines to take forward the pre-existing forms of struggle and protest against the landlords, state imposition and unequal markets.

By linking into a process of change initiated by the peasants themselves, the Party was able to begin to build a new type of relationship with them, creating new forms of mass power to prevent capture by existing powerholders and factionalist corrosion, as well as the reproduction of traditional elitist styles within its ranks. Party rectification and the mass line went hand in hand in transforming peasant protest and rebellion into revolution as the CPC sought to overcome its own defects so as to enhance the ability of the poor and middle peasants to unite in their exercise of mass democratic power.

Revolution unfolded as both Party and peasants learned together through mutual exchange. Agrarian transformation in China was to involve a dialogue which enabled both participants to develop and change, as the peasants, drawing from their evolving experiences, outgrew their traditional forms of organisation and consciousness, whilst the Party gradually developed appropriate policies, institutions and leadership methods adapted to the dynamics of the peasant movement. Guided by the CPC, the peasants were finally able to find the way out of the trap of traditional survivalism and realise their objective potential to carry out land reform through independent mass organisation in such a way as to prepare for a socialist future.

The CPC between agrarian and national revolution

The **key to the success of the** CPC-led revolution, as Li Lifeng has pointed out, lay in the ability of the Party to mobilise people effectively. This transformation in the structures of power depended fundamentally on the Party's relations with the peasants who were to express their support politically, through participation in mass movements and in mass organisations and the Party itself, and materially, in the form of paying the land tax and the tax grain, and in the form of human resources, enlisting in the Red Armies and providing logistic support to the front. The peasants, Li argues, came to identify with the Party as they gained through the redistribution of resources: the efficacy of rural mobilisation was apparently proportional to the number of people who truly benefited from land reform. This, he endorses, was the essence of the CPC's programme.[16]

The CPC's success in mobilising peasant support has brought into focus its strategy and leadership in managing rural class contradictions: divisions among the peasants were to pose a particular obstacle in bringing their anti-feudal struggle to fulfilment. The ultimate challenge of revolutionary leadership, as has been argued, lay in fact in understanding the interconnections between the national and agrarian revolutions which unfolded independently but in interaction with each other's class dynamics.

The agrarian movement was the main content of the Chinese revolution but its class dynamics had to be understood in the national context. As has been seen, the status and power of the CPC varied from stage to stage of the revolution. The effectiveness of the rural mobilisation lay in the Party's ability to adapt to the changing circumstances with policies and approaches shifting over time from rent reduction to land confiscation and redistribution. Consistency in its commitment to peasant mobilisation meant flexibility in the way the CPC managed the calibrations of landlord-peasant power within the shifts in the overall revolutionary situation. But this depended critically on understanding how class contradictions in the national movement impacted on peasant class dynamics and vice versa, as the different urban classes, favouring different policy approaches to land reform with a differential impact on the peasants' various material circumstances, exerted an influence on peasant consciousness and behaviour.

The countryside indeed had its particular political patterns but whilst the peasants had their own beliefs and ways of doing things, town and countryside were not entirely separate worlds. The persistence of traditional behaviours as economic stagnation inhibited the emergence of democratic conditions in the countryside, was essentially perpetuated by the parasitism of the cities upon the villages. Peasant behaviours then, were also reactive, influenced by developments in the urban class dynamics.

The challenge faced by the urban political parties in leading rural transformation lay in the fact that different types of peasants responded to land policies in different, and even conflicting, ways. Whilst middle peasant passivity and clannishness persisted under the influence of the national bourgeoisie, poor peasant extremism arose in particular when the rural and national movement drew apart.

As the differing approaches of Mao and Liu Shaoqi have shown, the CPC struggled within its own ranks to understand the conditions of rural isolation, the tenacity of landlord influence and the patterns of peasant traditionalism. Once analysis of the objective conditions of production revealed on the one hand the peculiarities of the landlord system in which feudal and proto-capitalist relations intertwined, and on the other hand, the divisions among the peasants, the problems of rural work were seen not in absolute terms but as a particular feature of the urban-rural relationship under the landlord monopoly. The CPC was then able to come to terms with the subjective dimension of the revolutionary process – the dynamics between and within the elite and peasant classes – and how these were influenced at different junctures in the national revolution.

Whilst the traditional styles of the rural elite power prevailed as peasants competed over resources, the CPC was to offer a qualitatively different form of leadership since it was committed to the promotion of agrarian transformation through the worker-peasant alliance. To transcend patterns of dependency, protectionism and predation, egalitarianism and village closure, to break up the traditional hierarchies and bring the rural elites under control, required an agrarian programme which built unity by sufficiently benefitting the peasant majority in deficit but without sacrificing the interests of the more well-to-do cultivators. On this basis, the CPC's village programmes found a way to release the entrepreneurial energies of the rich peasant economy without unduly strengthening the forces of capitalism, maintaining peasant leadership over the rural transformation process and preventing degeneration by using resources for expanded reproduction rather than the mobilisation of factional power.

The land policies of the CPC were eventually to realise the aims of the democratic revolution, unleashing mass activism in an organised way, since they resolved the contradictory class and economic interests of the peasants in an agrarian programme which offered something for all. Only the CPC, by adopting the perspective of the working class in whose interests it was to promote the role of the poor peasants in the countryside, proved able to develop such a programme. *Per capita* land redistribution was to meet the poor peasants' need for minimum subsistence against the revival of dependency, and the further development of the alliance with the middle peasants through mutual aid offered hope for a future.

It was by demonstrating its ability to influence the poor peasants and moderate their extremes by setting out a path of sustainable rural economic growth for the benefit of the many, that the CPC was able to gain the confidence of the national bourgeoisie, so containing its vacillations and resolving the rift between town and countryside.

It may seem that in adopting the mass line, the CPC was essentially a populist Party which rose to power on the crest of a spontaneous peasant upsurge. However, as shown here, the way the Party eventually, learning from past mistakes, came to handle the contradictions among the peasants – the 'rich peasant question', middle peasant hesitancy and the question of egalitarianism – has proved this view to be purely superficial.

Posing voluntarism against commandism did not lead to democracy but to chaos. The mass line was not merely a mechanism for unleashing peasant spontaneism: it was rather a method of organising the peasants on a class basis, resolving their material differences. Nor was Mao merely a populist figurehead: rather than viewing the problems of the countryside in terms of wealth and poverty and exploitation in general, as the Narodniks had done, he followed Lenin, if not to the letter, in applying a class analysis.

Schram has seen Mao as a voluntarist, prioritising the consciousness of the masses in the process of social transformation in defiance of the limitations of objective conditions.[17] But on the contrary, the account here has shown that, whilst he was unafraid to strike while the iron was hot to take the mass movement forward, Mao did so from a materialist basis. He was equally capable at other times, to work against the grain of spontaneism, to balance the national and agrarian revolutions not least in pursuing moderate land policies in order to build the widest possible anti-Japanese resistance.

The CPC's understanding of the democratic revolution was to develop as it confronted problems within its own organisation of bureaucratism and commandism. Differing perceptions of the challenges of rural work gave rise to different views on democracy.

Liu Shaoqi raised concerns about the tendency of Party organs at grassroots level to degenerate in the environment of rural backwardness with the infiltration of alien class elements drawing local cadres into the informal networks of elite power.

However voluntarism was not the answer. As Womack has pointed out, a simple majoritarian approach to land policy, given the majority of poor peasants, would have been in favour of more radical confiscation policies which would have alienated the middle peasants. Mao's preference, he highlights, was for non-alienation as a decisive policy guideline.[18]

Mao's democracy, the method of the mass line, was developed as a form of class organisation through democratic centralism. Not simply a matter of the introduction of universal suffrage, democracy was about adapting policy flexibly to the dynamics of class behaviours to achieve unity around common goals according to the juncture of national and agrarian revolutions. As such it encompassed an economic as well as a political aspect to manage or harmonise inherent class contradictions within the revolutionary process together with an open-door method which brought the Party and peasants together in a constructive process of self- and mutual education.

Previous studies have sought to explain CPC success in peasant mobilisation in terms of nationalism or social revolution, however, the case that has been argued here is that it is the interaction between these two aspects, the anti-imperialist and the anti-feudal revolutions, that requires analysis. These interactions as has been seen involved a two-way process in the way the class dynamics of the national revolution impacted on the political and ideological contents of the peasants' struggles and in the urban reactions to peasant activism.

Not to assume that CPC policies were entirely responsible for the outcome of the revolution, nor that its own organisation and consciousness were not limited by both objective factors and processes as well as subjective errors, the point here is that the particular historical role of the Party, given the heterogeneous nature of the peasantry, is revealed at the point of articulation between the national and agrarian revolutionary processes.

The CPC failed in the 1927 revolution since, lacking an understanding of class positions and behaviours, it had no way to bring the national and agrarian revolutions together. The existing theories of Lenin, Stalin, as well as Trotsky, regarding the revolutionary role of a vanguard Party and the peasants in a democratic revolution to lead to socialism did not match well the conditions of the national and agrarian revolutions in China.

It was by bridging the town-country link, mobilising the broad peasant masses together with the working class in alliance with the national bourgeoisie, that the CPC came to lead a force capable of defeating feudalism and imperialism and beyond this, to open up a new interchange between peasants and urban classes, allowing both cities and countryside to find new ways forward together.

Entering the new post-1949 era

Following the establishment of the People's Republic of China in 1949 and the completion of land reform in 1952, rural development was to follow further twists and turns from mutual aid to collectivism to the commune movement only to turn to the revival in 1979 of individual household farming as communal farming arrangements were dismantled. Questions have been raised, with hindsight, as to whether the CPC really did understand the revolutionary nature of the Chinese peasants after all; whether in fact they overestimated the potential for socialism that existed within the peasantry, neglecting their aspirations as private producers.

The fact that the CPC was to make greater strides among the predominantly owner-cultivator communities in the North after 1937 than it had previously in organising the poor peasants of the South where landlord-tenant polarisation was more pronounced, appears to lend weight to this suggestion that the CPC gained its support from middle peasant owners than the rather than the disaffected poor. Chang Liu for example has argued that, in contrast with the spasmodic spontaneous uprisings that characterised peasant protest against the local tyrants and bullies in the South, which surged then equally rapidly fell away, the North China villages provided a more stable long-term organisational base of support for the CPC.[19]

The salient point in terms of a balance of forces however was that landlord power in the North was weaker than in the South. Chang, nevertheless, acknowledges that the class line always played a vital role as a powerful means to transform property relations and class structure within the village community.[20] Whether in the South or North, the question of class organisation to unite both poor and middle peasants, as has been seen in the works of the Crooks and Hinton, was fundamental.

In arguing that the North China village was key to understanding CPC success, Chang goes on to emphasise the importance of these types of communities in shaping the patterns of CPC organisation and mobilisation after 1949 with their efforts to restore household-based production revitalising egalitarianism and hence solidary bonds.[21] Marx, in later life, as his draft letters to Vera Zasulich reveal, had begun to consider the possibility of a peasant path to socialism. The Russian commune, the *mir*, a leftover from pre-class society, once freed from constraint under the despotic state and revived from inertia might, he thought, be capable of broader development in a socialist direction. Through its organisation, the peasants' familiarity with communal property and collective cultivation could pave the way for collectivism so long as industry supported agriculture, providing a market for its products, thus exerting a need for collective labour.[22]

However the point is that the CPC, with its methods of class organisation, was to succeed where the Taiping rebels in their efforts to reconstitute an owner-cultivator society around egalitarian ideals had failed. For the CPC, agrarian socialism was seen as double-edged: revolutionary against feudalism but also with a reactionary side.

In China, the removal of the backbone of the landlords' political authority and of monopoly rent as the major constraint on economic growth released the fetters on the closely bound village communities, overcoming parochialism to open up the potential for revitalising the rural economy that existed within the countryside in the context of a new more equal exchange between the towns and the countryside. But far from re-establishing the moral economy of the owner-cultivator society of the past, *per capita* land redistribution, carried out by mass power rather than elite leadership, whilst realising the subsistence needs of the poor peasants, fundamentally altered traditional hierarchies of social kinship. With the break-up in particular of village collective properties, owned by clan or lineage, the peasants were transformed from corporate to individual members of the community.

Within peasant studies, the subsistence producers of Scott's paradigm are juxtaposed with Popkin's peasant entrepreneur. Thaxton attempted to resolve the contradiction between these two conceptions – of the peasant motivated by the shared values and reciprocal bonds of a community and the peasant motivated by individual economic interest – with his own notion of 'moral economy'. But in doing so he essentially obscured the partial polarisation within a peasantry, held in check under economic stagnation.

Huang, in eclectic fashion, claims the peasants combined multiple characteristics as agricultural workers, exploited cultivators and would-be entrepreneurs, the different facets of CPC rural policy reflecting these different orientations.[23] Selden's suggestion is that both visions of a market and a moral economy were joined in peasant consciousness, each being equally relevant to peasant participation in the land revolution depending on conditions. In desperate times, peasants prioritised subsistence guarantees over cash income and placed a premium on familial, lineage and village groups and networks, rather than the striving of autonomous individuals. For him then, the CPC succeeded because it addressed both aspects of the peasants' visions as it promoted subsistence together with markets for survival and for growth.[24]

The essence of CPC leadership as has been argued is to be seen as lying in its flexibility according to circumstances, building alliances among the peasants as differing and contradictory demands came to the fore in different phases of struggle and as the national context changed. Land reform was a temporary resolution of the contradictions of a peasantry, trapped by feudal relations in a partial differentiation. Its outcome resulted neither in the restoration of the traditional small peasant economy nor, despite the changes in land-owning status, in simply unleashing the peasants' economic individualism.

After 1952, the new land system, whilst providing for a certain minimum subsistence guarantee, also saw the emergence of a substantial minority of small producers contributing to economic growth with the opening of new market opportunities. Ash, in a useful study of land reform in Jiangsu province, reveals that whatever the regional variations in terms of tenancy rates and person/land ratio between the commercialised and less developed areas, the most striking feature to emerge was that, whilst land redistribution had doubled the holdings and the grain production of the poorer peasants, sufficient for survival, it enabled the middle peasants to move from marginal subsistence to a surplus for substantial investment in growth for, although they received less land than the poor peasants, their holdings were larger to start with.[25] The poor peasants still faced difficulties given a shortage of tools and animals, whilst their farms were too small for growth, without surplus for investment. Mutual aid eased their situation but the lack of means of production remained a major constraint on production.

The outcome of the agrarian revolution was therefore a situation of inequality and potential tension between the substantial surplus-producing minority of roughly 20 to 30 per cent of peasant households with aspirations to 'get rich', and the remaining poor who, pressing for more change to solve their problems of insufficient means and underemployed labour, had high hopes for the future in the further development of collective practices.[26]

With the active involvement of the poor peasants, the democratic process in the countryside had its socialist aspect but this was to be measured not so much by the collectivist strength of the semi-proletarianised poor nor the solidary bonds and shared values of the pre-existing collective communal arrangements of the moral economy, but rather in the complementarities which continued to bring the poor and middle peasants together in the sharing of tools and labour. The middle peasant alliance remained vital in the transition to socialism.

To observe again, the situation in China was quite different from that in Russia: whereas after the revolution, the Bolsheviks still had to establish an alliance with the peasantry and win the support of the middle peasants in particular, the CPC had come to power with the help of middle as well as poor peasants. Li Lifeng notes an emotional gratitude on the part of the many peasants who had gained land under CPC leadership.[27] A psychological acceptance of the CPC which saw obedience in behaviour, together served as a base of support for the new state.

Nevertheless, the peasants had not just been passive recipients of a strategy to restructure the agrarian economy with new organisations foisted on them from the towns. Emerging from the constraints of tradition as a result of their experiences in revolution, the peasants were active participants in a democratic process, engaging with the CPC in mutual learning, developing and transforming the popular traditions and practices of the countryside. Their activism then created new opportunities for the CPC in rural restructuring not available to the Bolsheviks.[28]

China was to rely on peasant manual labour in the decades to come. Economic and cultural transformation could not be accomplished overnight but with the changed relations among the peasants and between individual and community, a process had been set in motion whereby the peasants themselves engaged in modernising their own ways of doing, developing new forms of individual and collective organisation and production relations, raising their consciousness step by step.[29]

For some analysts, the popularity of the agricultural reforms of the early 1980s demonstrated the resurgence of the peasant proprietorial system suppressed during the preceding period under the Great Leap Forward and Cultural Revolution.[30] Chinese Marxists have even argued that capitalism had been suppressed under the 'wind of communism' by 'feudal autocracy and the egalitarianism of the small producer'.[31] Notions of the revival of 'agrarian socialism' have been debated with others instead attributing the mistakes to 'Leftism' within the CPC leadership.[32]

Even as the redistribution of land opened the door to class polarisation in the countryside and a rural economic modernisation on the basis of a rich peasant economy, the CPC in the 1950s chose the path of 'cooperation before mechanisation'. In this, there was no example to follow: there was no blueprint, and serious mistakes were made. To find the balance between the demands of basic subsistence and the capitalist tendencies of the rich peasants was fraught with difficulties. Insofar as the middle peasants continued to hold this balance in the tensions between the poor and well-to-do, a better description for the general trend of development in rural China is perhaps that provided by Marx, who recognised in the situation in the French countryside, a continual struggle between the peasants' traditional consciousness and their modern, independent consciousness.

Counterposing their superstition with their judgement, their prejudice with their enlightenment, their past with their future, Marx distinguished between the conservative peasants who wanting to 'consolidate the condition of [their] social existence, the smallholding,' remained 'gloomily enclosed within this old order and want to see themselves and their smallholdings saved and given preferential treatment by the ghost of the Empire', and the revolutionary peasants who strikes out beyond it... who want to overthrow the old order by their own energies, in alliance with the towns.'[33] It was the latter face of the revolutionary peasant that carried China forward.

NOTES & REFERENCES

1. Huang, 1985, pp.3–32; Perdue, 1987, p.249.

2. Huang, 1985, p.309. Here Huang is referring to the work of Jeffrey Paige (1975) which systematises various sets of rural class relations and their potential for change.

3. Huang, 1985, p.309. Paige, 1975, p.63, argues that it was landless sharecroppers who were responsible for the Hunan peasant associations: according to his schema these peasants involved in decentralised sharecropping systems were capable of the most powerful political organisation.

4. For example, Pepper (1978), in her study of a CPC base area in Shandong, suggests that among the local grievances of the peasants, issues of taxation and corruption weighed more heavily than rent and interest rates, pp.260–274.

5. See de Ste Croix, 1983, pp.51–2.

6. Tawney, 1980, p.72.

7. Frank (1967).

8. Laclau (1986).

9. Alavi, 1982, pp.68–71. See also Bernstein (1977), who argues that whilst the form of the peasant household remains unchanged, its economic content is transformed as its output and consumption are commoditised.

10. Warren, 1980, p.152.

11. Crook and Gilmartin, 2013, p.269

12. Alavi, 1973, pp.58–9.

13. For example, Hofheinz, 1977, p.67 and p.304, sees the peasants as easily manipulable, and the peasant movement directed by outsiders for goals external to the peasantry.

14. Skocpol, 1978, p.18.

15. Marks (1984), Thaxton (1983). Marks uses E.P.Thompson's definition of human experience, 1978, p.164.

16. Li Lifeng, 2015.

17. Schram, 1969a, pp.135–6.

18. Womack, 1982, pp.134–5.

19. Chang Liu, 2007, pp.189–190.

20. *Ibid.*, pp.97–8; p.109.
21. *Ibid.*, p.98.
22. These drafts are to be found in Shanin, 1983, pp.99–124.
23. Huang, 1985, pp.306–7.
24. Selden, 1995, pp.240–1.
25. Ash, 1976b, pp.525–30.
26. See Mao, *Selected Works*, Vol. V, p.213.
27. Li Lifeng (2015).
28. See Harrison, M. (1981–2), for an interesting discussion of the options available to the Bolsheviks for primitive socialist accumulation, which draws on Marx's analysis of primitive capitalist accumulation.
29. After 1949, of the two key alliances – with the peasants and with the national bourgeoisie – the CPC was to take the former as fundamental. Once land reform was completed throughout the rural areas, the continuing mobilisation of the poor and middle peasants in mutual aid teams was accelerated into a co-operative upsurge which the rich peasants, now facing shortages of hired labour, were induced to join with offers of compensation for pooling their draught animals and farm tools.

    At the same time, with the remaining industrialists and entrepreneurs left without any potential international backing following the declaration of independence in 1949, the state, through its links with the rural supply and marketing co-operatives, was able to 'bring the bourgeoisie under control' since to get raw materials they had to sell manufactured goods to the state. With the national bourgeoisie engaged in state capitalism and the ending of land purchase – the basis of rural capitalism – China transitioned fully from New Democracy to socialism in 1956. see Mao, *Selected Works*, Vol. V, pp.213–214. For an account of the socialist upsurge in the countryside see Shue (1980).
30. Cannon (1982).
31. Ruan Ming (1980).
32. Xue Xin, 1982, p.90, and see preceding discussion from p.85.
33. Marx, 1981, p.240.

GLOSSARY

baojia local-level government unit organised by household, involved in tax collection and other administrative duties.

ganqing a rapport or bond between two people, groups, or business partners.

huang shang big merchants working for state companies.

kulak (Russian) a rich peasant owning land and hiring labour.

mir (Russian) a self-governing community of peasant households.

mu (mou) a unit of area equal to about one-sixth of an acre.

shengyuan a scholar who has passed the lowest rung of the Imperial civil service examination.

yamen the administrative office or headquarters of a local
government official.

zamindars were landowners in India who collected rent from peasants and paid revenue to the Mughal court and later to the British.

BIBLIOGRAPHY

Alavi, Hamza, 'Peasants and Revolution', *Socialist Register* (1965)

_____ 'Peasant Classes and Primordial Loyalties', *Journal of Peasant Studies*, Vol.1, Issue 1 (1973)

_____ 'India: The Transition to Colonial Capitalism' in Alavi, Hamza and others, *Capitalism and Colonial Production* (London: Croom Helm, 1982)

Anderson, Perry, *Lineages of the Absolutist State* (London: New Left Books, 1974)

Ash, Robert, *Land Tenure in Pre-Revolutionary China's Kiangsu Province in the 1920's and 1930's* (London: Contemporary China Institute, School of Oriental and African Studies, 1976a)

_____ 'Economic Aspects of Land Reform in Kiangsu 1949–1952', *China Quarterly*, Nos.66 & 67 (June–September 1976b)

Averill, Stephen C., 'Party, Society and Local Elite in the Jiangxi Communist Movement', *Journal of Asian Studies*, Vol.46, No.2 (May 1987)

Balzacs, Etienne, *Chinese Civilisation and Bureaucracy* (New Haven: Yale University Press, 1964)

Beattie, Hilary J., *Land and Lineage in China* (Cambridge: Cambridge University Press, 1979)

Beijing Review Commentator, 'Let Some Localities and Peasants Prosper First', *Beijing Review*, No.3 (1 January 1981)

Bernstein, Henry, 'Notes on Capital and Peasantry', *Review of African Political Economy*, No.10 (September–December 1977)

Bianco, Lucien, 'Secret Societies and Peasant Self-Defense, 1921–1933' in Chesneaux, Jean, *Popular Movements and Secret Societies in China, 1840–1950* (Stanford: Stanford University Press, 1972)

Brandt, Lauren, 'Reflections on China Late 19th and Early 20th-Century Economy', *The China Quarterly* 150, Special Issue (1997)

Bray, Francesca, 'Part II: Agriculture', in Needham, Joseph and Bray, Francesca, *Science and Civilisation in China, Volume 6, Biology and Biological Technology* (Cambridge: Cambridge University Press, 1984)

Buck John L., *Land Utilisation in China* (New York: Paragon Book Reprint Corporation, 1964)

Cannon, Terry, 'Why do Peasants Want to Get Rich?', *China Now*. No.103 (July–August 1982)

Chang, John K., 'Industrial Development of Mainland China, 1912–1949', *The Journal of Economic History*, 27(1) (1967)

Chang Liu, *Peasants and Revolution in Rural China: Rural Political Change in the North China Plain and the Yangzi Delta, 1850–1949* (London and New York: Routledge, 2007)

Chao Kuo-Chun, *The Agrarian Policy of the Chinese Communist Party, 1921–1959* (London: Asia Publishing House, 1960)

Chang Chung-LiI (Zhang Zhongli), *The Chinese Gentry: Studies on Their Role in Nineteenth Century Chinese Society* (Seattle: University of Washington Press, 1955)

Chayanov, Alexander V., *The Theory of Peasant Economy* (Homewood: Richard D. Irwin, Inc., 1966)

Chen Boda (Chen Po-Ta), *A Study of Land Rent in Pre-Liberation China* (Beijing: Foreign Languages Press, 1966a)

_____ *On the Ten-Year Civil War, 1927–1937* (Beijing: Foreign Languages Press, 1966b)

Chen Hanseng, *The Present Agrarian Problem in China* (Chicago: Institute of Pacific Relations, University of Chicago Press, 1933)

_____ *Landlord and Peasant in China: A Study of the Agrarian Crisis in South China* (New York: International Publishers, 1936)

Cheng Yungfa, *Making Revolution: The Communist Movement in Eastern and Central China 1937–1945* (Berkeley: University of California Press, 1986)

Chesneaux, Jean, 'Secret Societies in China's Historical Evolution', in Chesneaux, Jean (ed), *Popular Movements and Secret Societies in China 1840–1950* (Stanford: Stanford University Press, 1972)

_____ *Peasant Revolts in China, 1840–1949* (London: Thames and Hudson, 1973)

Chesneaux, Jean, Le Barbier, Françoise, and Bergere, Marie-Claire, *China from the 1911 Revolution to Liberation* (Hassocks: The Harvester Press, 1977)

Claudin, Fernando, *The Communist Movement: from Comintern to Cominform* (Harmondsworth: Penguin Books, 1975)

Cox, Terry, 'Commodity Production and Class Relations in Peasant Societies', unpublished paper (1984)

Croll, Elizabeth, *The Family Rice Bowl: Food and the Domestic Economy in China* (London: Zed Press, 1983)

Crook, David and Crook, Isabel, *Revolution in a Chinese Village: Ten Mile Inn* (London: Routledge & Kegan Paul, 1959)

_____ *Mass Movement in a Chinese Village: Ten Mile Inn* (London: Routledge & Kegan Paul, 1979)

Crook, Isabel Brown and Gilmartin, Christine Kelly, *Prosperity's Predicament: identity, reform and resistance in rural wartime China* (Plymouth: Rowman and Littlefield, 2015)

Dirlik, Arif, *Marxism in the Chinese Revolution* (Oxford: Rowman and Littlefield Publishers, Inc., 2005)

Dorris, Carl, Peasant Mobilisation in North China and the Origins of Yenan Communism', *China Quarterly*, No.68 (December 1976)

Du Jing, 'On the Question of Land Confiscation and Distribution in the Agrarian Reform', *Social Sciences in China*, Vol.III, No.3 (September 1982)

Editorial Departments of *Renmin Ribao*, *Hongqi* and *Jiefangjun*, *The Struggle Between Two Roads in China's Countryside* (Beijing: Foreign Languages Press, 1968)

Elvin, Mark, *The Pattern of the Chinese Past* (London: Eyre Methuen, 1973)

Ennew Judith, Hirst, Paul, and Tribe, Keith, 'Peasants as an Economic Category', *Journal of Peasant Studies*, Vol.4, No.4 (July 1977)

Engels, Friedrich, 'The Origin of the Family, Private Property and the State', in Marx, Karl and Engels, Friedrich, *Selected Works* Vol. II (London: Lawrence and Wishart, 1950)

Esherick, Joseph W., 'Number Games: A Note on Land Distribution in Revolutionary China', *Modern China*, Vol.7, No.4 (October 1981)

Fang Xing, 'The Economic Structure of Chinese Feudal Society and the Seeds of Capitalism', *Social Sciences in China*, Vol.II, No.4 (December 1981)

_____ 'Why the sprouts of capitalism were delayed in China', *Late Imperial China*, Vol.10, No. 2 (December 1989).

Faure, David, *The Structure of Chinese Rural Society: Lineage and Village in the Eastern New Territories, Hong Kong* (Oxford: Oxford University Press, 1988)

Fei Xiaotong (Fei Hsiao-Tung), *Peasant Life in China* (London: George Routledge & Sons, 1939)

_____ *China's Gentry* (Chicago: University of Chicago Press, 1953)

Feuerwerker, Albert, *The Chinese Economy, 1870–1911* (Ann Arbor: University of Michigan Centre for Chinese Studies, 1969)

_____ *The Chinese Economy, 1912–1949* (Ann Arbor: University of Michigan Centre for Chinese Studies, 1968)

———— 'Economic Trends, 1912–1949', in Fairbank, John King (ed.), *Cambridge History of China: Republican China, 1912–1949* (Cambridge: Cambridge University Press, 1983)

———— 'The Foreign Presence in China', in Fairbank, John King (ed.) *Cambridge History of China: Republican China, 1912–1949*. (Cambridge: Cambridge University Press, 1983)

Frank, Andre Gunder, *Capitalism and Underdevelopment in Latin America* (New York: Monthly Review Press, 1967)

Fried, Morton, *Fabric of Chinese Society* (London: Atlantic Press, 1956)

Fu Yling, 'Capitalism in Chinese Agriculture', *Modern China*, Vol.6, No.3 (July 1980)

Geertz, Clifford, *Agricultural Involution: The Process of Ecological Change in Indonesia* (Berkeley, California: University of California Press, 1963)

Gilllin, Donald G., 'Peasant and Communist in Modern China: Reflections on the Origins of the Communist-led Peasant Movement', *South Atlantic Quarterly*, Vol. LX, No.4 (Autumn 1961)

Grove, Linda, and Esherick, Joseph W., 'From Feudalism to Capitalism: Japanese Scholarship on the Transformation of Chinese Rural Society', *Modern China*, Vol.6, No.4 (October 1980)

Guo Dehong, 'The Development of the Land Policy of the Chinese Communist Party During the Second Revolutionary Civil War Period 1927–1937', *Social Studies in China*. Vol.2, No.1 (March 1981)

Guo Xuyin, 'A Reconsideration of Chen Duxiu's Attitude toward the Peasant Movement', *Chinese Law and Government* (1984, published online 7 December 2014)

Han Xiaorong, *Chinese Discourses on the Peasant, 1900–1940* (Albany: State University of New York Press, 2005)

Harrison, James, *The Communists and the Chinese Peasants* (London: Victor Gollancz, Ltd, 1970)

Harrison, Mark, 'Soviet Primary Accumulation Processes: Some Unresolved Problems', *Science and Society*, Vol. XIV, No.4 (Winter 1981–2)

Hinton, William, *Fanshen* (New York and London: Monthly Review Press, 1966)

Ho Kan-Chih, *A History of the Modern Chinese Revolution 1919–1956* (Calcutta: Manika Barua Books and Periodicals, 1977)

Ho Ping-Ti (He Bingdi), *The Ladder of Success in Imperial China* (New York: Columbia University Press, 1962)

Hobsbawm, Eric, 'Peasant and Politics', *Journal of Peasant Studies.* Vol.1, issue 1 (1973)

Hofheinz, Roy Jr., 'The Autumn Harvest Insurrection', *China Quarterly*, No.32 (October –December 1967)

_____ *The Broken Wave: The Chinese Communist Peasant Movement, 1922– 1928* (Cambridge: Harvard University Press, 1977)

Hou Chi-Ming, *Foreign Investment and Economic Development in China, 1840– 1937* (Cambridge: Harvard University Press, 1965)

Hsiao, Kung-Chuan, *Rural China: Imperial Control in the Nineteenth Century* (Seattle: University of Washington Press, 1960)

Hsiao, Tso-Liang, *Power Relations Within the Chinese Communist Movement*, 1930–1934 (Seattle and London: University of Washington Press, 1961)

_____ *The Land Revolution in China, 1930–1934: a Study of the Documents* (Seattle and London: University of Washington Press, 1969)

Huang, Philip C. C., 'Analysing the Twentieth Century Chinese Countryside: Revolutionaries versus Western Scholarship', *Modern China*, Vol.1, No.2 (April 1975a)

_____ 'Mao Zedong and the Middle Peasants', *Modern China*, Vol.1, No.3 (July 1975b)

_____ 'Intellectuals, Lumpen-Proletarians, Workers and Peasants in the Communist Movement: the Case of Xingguo County 1927–1934', in Huang, Philip, Bell, Lynda S. and Walker, Kathy L. (eds), *Chinese Communists and Rural Society in the Jiangxi Period* (Berkeley: University of California Press, 1978)

_____ *The Peasant Economy and Social Change in North China* (Stanford: Stanford University Press, 1985)

Hussain, Athar and Tribe, Keith, *Marxism and the Agrarian Question*, 2 Vols (London: The Macmillan Press, 1981)

Institute of Pacific Relations, *Agrarian China: Selected Source Materials From Chinese Authors* (London: George Allen & Unwin, 1939)

Isaacs, Harold, *The Tragedy of the Chinese Revolution* (Stanford: Stanford University Press, 1962)

Jacques, Martin, *When China Rules the World: the End of the Western World and the Birth of a New Global Order* (London: Penguin Books, 2nd Ed., 2012)

Jin Dequn, 'Criteria For Land Distribution During the Second Revolutionary Civil War Period, 1927–1937', *Social Sciences in China*, Vol. II, No.1 (March 1981)

Johnson, Chalmers, *Peasant Nationalism and Communist Power: the Emergence of Revolutionary China, 1937–1945* (Stanford: Stanford University Press, 1962)

Johnson, Kay Ann, *Women, the Family and Peasant Revolution in China* (Chicago: University of Chicago Press, 1983)

Karl, Rebecca E., *Mao Zedong and China in the Twentieth Century World* (Durham and London: Duke University Press, 2010)

Keating, Pauline, Review of 'Making Revolution: The Communist Movement in Eastern and Central China, 1937–1945' (Author: Chen Yungfa), *The Australian Journal of Chinese Affairs*, Vol.16 (July 1986)

_____ Review of 'The Peasant Economy and Social Change in North China' (Author: Philip Huang), *The Australian Journal of Chinese Affairs*, Vol.18 (July 1987)

_____ *Two revolutions: Village Reconstruction and the Co-operative Movement in Northern Shaanxi, 1934–1945* (Stanford: Stanford University Press, 1997a)

_____ 'Co-operative Visions versus Wartime Realities: Indusco and the Chinese Communists, 1938–1944', *New Zealand Journal of East Asian Studies*, Vol.5, No.1 (1997b)

Kim, Ilpyong J., 'Mass Mobilisation Policies and Techniques Developed in the Period of the Chinese Soviet Republic', in Barnett, Doak A. (ed.), *Chinese Communist Politics in Action* (Seattle and London: University of Washington Press, 1969)

Laclau, Ernesto, *Politics and Ideology in Marxist Theory* (London: Verso, 1977)

_____ 'Feudalism and capitalism in Latin America', in Klarén, Peter F. and Bossert, Thomas J. (eds), *Promise of Development, Theories of Change in Latin America* (New York: Routledge, 1986)

Lasek, Elizabeth, 'Imperialism in China: A Methodological Critique', *Bulletin of Concerned Asian Scholars*, Vol.15, No.1 (January–February 1983)

Lenin, Vladimir, *Collected Works*, Vols 1–41 (Moscow: Foreign Languages Publishing House, 1960–1969)

Li Kan, 'The Taiping Peasant War and the Tragedy at Nanjing', *Social Sciences in China*, Vol. I, No.I (March 1980)

Li Lifeng, 'Rural mobilisation in the Chinese Communist Revolution: From the Anti-Japanese War to the Chinese Civil War', *Journal of Modern Chinese History*, Vol.9, Issue 1 (2015)

Li Wenzhi, 'China's Landlord Economy and the Sprouts of Capitalism in Agriculture', *Social Sciences in China*. Vol. II, No.1, March 1981.

Lippit, Victor D., *Land Reform and Economic Development In China* (White Plains: International Arts and Sciences Press, 1974)

_____ 'The Development of Underdevelopment in China' in P. Huang (ed.), *The Development of Underdevelopment in China: A Symposium*, (White Plains: M.E. Sharpe, Inc.,1980)

Liu Yichou, 'The Peasant Question in the Democratic Revolution', *Peking Review*, No.13 (31 March 1961)

Liu Shaoqi, *Collected Works, 1945–1957* (Hong Kong: Union Research Institute, 1969)

_____ *Three Essays on Party Building* (Beijing: Foreign Languages Press, 1980)

_____ *Selected Works, Vol. I* (Beijing: Foreign Languages Press, 1984)

Lotveit Trygve, *Chinese Communism, 1931–1934: Experience in Civil Government* (London: Curzon Press, Ltd, 1978)

Mao Zedong (Mao Tse-Tung), *Selected Works*, Vols I–III (London: Lawrence and Wishart, Ltd., 1954)

_____ *Selected Works*, Vol. IV (London: Lawrence and Wishart, Ltd,1956)

_____ *Selected Works*, Vol. IV (Beijing: Foreign Languages Press, 1967)

_____ *Selected Works*, Vol. V (Beijing: Foreign Languages Press,1977)

Marks, Robert B., *Rural Revolution in South China: Peasants and the Making of History in Haifeng County, 1570–1930* (Madison: University of Wisconsin Press, 1984)

Marx, Karl, *On China: Articles from the New York Daily Tribune, 1853–1860* (London: Lawrence and Wishart, 1968)

_____ *Capital*, Vols I-III (London: Lawrence & Wishart, 1970)

_____ *Pre-Capitalist Economic Formations* (London: Lawrence and Wishart,1978)

_____ *Surveys from Exile: Political Writings, Vol.2* (Harmondsworth: Penguin Books 1981)

Mavrakis, Kostas, *On Trotskyism: Problems of Theory and History* (London: Routledge and Kegan Paul, 1976)

Meisner, Maurice, *Marxism, Maoism and Utopianism* (Madison: University of Wisconsin Press, 1982)

Michael, Franz H., *The Taiping Rebellion: History and Documents*, 2 Vols, (Seattle and London: University of Washington Press, 1966–1971)

Moise, Edwin E., 'Downward Mobility in Pre-Revolutionary China', *Modern China*, Vol.3, No.1 (January 1977)

_____ *Land reform in China and North Vietnam* (Chapel Hill, London: The University of North Carolina Press, 1983)

Myers, Ramon H., *The Chinese Peasant Economy: Agricultural Development in Hopei and Shantung, 1890–1949* (Cambridge: Harvard University Press, 1970)

Needham, Joseph, *Science and Civilisation in China, Vol.2: History of Scientific Thought* (Cambridge: Cambridge University Press, 1956)

_____ *The Grand Titration* (London: George Allen & Unwin, 1969)

Nurkse, Ragnar, *Problems of Capital Formation in Underdeveloped Countries* (New York: Oxford University Press, 1964)

Osinsky, Pavel, 'Modernisation Interrupted? Total War, State Breakdown and the Communist Conquest of China', *The Sociological Quarterly*, Vol.51, Issue 4 (2010)

Paige, Jeffrey M., *Agrarian Revolution: Social Movements and Export Agriculture in the Underdeveloped World* (London: Collier Macmillan, 1975)

Patnaik, Utsa, 'Neo-Populism and Marxism: The Chayanovian View of the Agrarian Question and its Fundamental Fallacy', *Journal of Peasant Studies*, Vol.6, No.4 (July 1979)

Pepper, Suzanne, *Civil War in China: the Political Struggle, 1945–1949* (Berkeley: University of California Press, 1978)

Perdue, Peter C., 'Insiders and Outsiders: the Xiangtan Riot of 1819 and Collective Action in Hunan', *Modern China*, Vol.12, No.2 (April 1986)

_____ *Exhausting the Earth: State and Peasant in Hunan, 1500–1850* (Cambridge, Mass.: Council on East Asian Studies, Harvard University, 1987)

Perry, Elizabeth, *Rebels and Revolutionaries in North China, 1845–1945* (Stanford: Stanford University Press, 1980)

Polachek, James M., 'The Moral Economy of the Jiangxi Soviet, 1928–1934', *Journal of Asian Studies*, Vol. XLII, No.4 (August 1983)

Popkin, Samuel, *The Rational Peasant: the Political Economy of Rural Society in Vietnam* (Berkeley: University of California Press, 1979)

Potter, Jack, *Capitalism and the Chinese Peasant* (Berkeley: University of California Press, 1968)

Praznaik, Roxann, 'Tax Protest in Laiyang, Shandong 1910', *Modern China*, Vol.6, No.1 (January 1980)

Rawski, Evelyn, *Agricultural Change and the Peasant Economy of South China* (Cambridge: Harvard University Press, 1972)

Riskin, Carl, 'The Symposium Papers: Discussion and Comments, in Huang, Philip (ed.), *The Development of Underdevelopment in China: A Symposium* (White Plains: M.E. Sharpe, Inc., 1980)

Roy, Manabendra Nath, *A Marxist Interpretation of Chinese History* (Boston: New England Free Press, 1970)

Ruan Ming, 'The Need to Eliminate Feudal Remnants', *Beijing Review*, No.45, (10 November 1980)

Rue, John, E., *Mao Zedong in Opposition, 1927–1935* (Stanford: Stanford University Press, 1966)

Saich, Anthony, 'The Chinese Communist Party during the era of the Comintern (1919–1943)', article prepared for Jürgen Rojahn, 'Comintern and National Communist Parties Project', *International Institute of Social History*, Amsterdam. academia.edu, accessed: 27/4/2020.

Schram, Stuart R., *The Political Thought of Mao Zedong*, Revised ed. (Harmondsworth: Penguin Books, 1969a)

_____ *Mao Zedong*, Revised ed. (Harmondsworth: Penguin Books, 1969b)

_____ *Mao Zedong Unrehearsed* (Harmondsworth: Penguin Books, 1974)

Schram, Stuart R., and Carrere d'Encausse, Hélène, *Marxism and Asia* (London: Allen Lane, The Penguin Press, 1969)

Schultz, Theodore, *Transforming Traditional Agriculture* (New Haven: Yale University Press, 1964)

Schwartz, Benjamin I., *Chinese Communism and the Rise of Mao* (Cambridge: Harvard University Press, 1968)

Scott, James C. *The Moral Economy of the Peasant: Rebellion and Subsistence in South East Asia* (New Haven: Yale University Press, 1976)

Selden Mark, *The Yenan Way in Revolutionary China* (Cambridge: Harvard University Press, 1971)

_____ (Ed.) *The People's Republic of China: A Documentary History of Revolutionary Change* (New York: Monthly Review Press, 1979)

_____ *China in Revolution: the Yenan Way revisited* (Armonk: M.E. Sharpe, Inc., 1995)

Shanin, Teodor, *The Awkward Class* (Oxford: Clarendon Press, 1972)

_____ (Ed.) *The Late Marx and the Russian Road: Marx and 'The Peripheries of Capitalism'* (London: Routledge & Kegan Paul PLC, 1983)

Shue, Viivienne, *Peasant China in Transition: the Dynamics of Development toward Socialism, 1949–1956* (Berkeley and Los Angeles: University of California Press, 1980)

_____ *The Reach of the State: Sketches of the Chinese Body Politic* (Stanford, California: Stanford University Press, 1988)

Skinner, G. William, 'Marketing and Social Structure in China', *Journal of Asian Studies*, Vol. XXIV, Nos 1–3 (1964–5)

_____ 'Regional Urbanisation in Nineteenth Century China', in Skinner, William (ed.), *The City in Late Imperial China* (Stanford: Stanford University Press, 1977a)

_____'Cities and the Hierarchy of Local Systems', in Skinner, William (ed.), *The City in Late Imperial China* (Stanford: Stanford University Press, 1977b)

Skocpol, Theda, *States and Social Revolutions: A Comparative Analysis of France, Russia and China* (Cambridge: Cambridge University Press, 1979)

Slawinski, Roman, 'The Red Spears in the Late 1920's', in Chesneaux, Jean (ed.), *Popular Movements and Secret Societies in China, 1840–1950* (Stanford: Stanford University Press, 1972)

Stalin, Joseph, *Marxism and the National Question* (Moscow: Foreign Languages Publishing House, 1940)

de Ste. Croix, Geoffrey, *The Class Struggles in the Ancient Greek World* (London: Duckworth, 1983)

Swarup, Shanti, *A Study of the Chinese Communist Movement* (Oxford: Clarendon Press, 1966)

Sweezy, Paul and Others, *The Transition from Feudalism to Capitalism* (London: Verso, 1978)

Tanaka, Kyoko, 'Mao and Liu in the 1947 Land Reform: Allies or Disputants?', *China Quarterly*, No.75, (September 1978)

Tawney, Richard Henry, *Land and Labour in China* (London: George Allan & Unwin, Ltd., 1932)

Thaxton Ralph, 'Tenants in Revolution: The Tenacity of Traditional Morality', *Modern China*, Vol. I, No.3 (July 1975)

_____ *China Turned Rightside Up: Revolutionary Legitimacy in the Peasant World* (New Haven and London: Yale University Press, 1983)

Tornquist, Olle, *Dilemmas of Third World Communism: The Destruction of the PKI in Indonesia* (London: Zed Books, Ltd., 1984)

Thompson, Edward Palmer, *The Poverty of Theory* (New York: Monthly Review Press, 1978).

Thompson, Roger R., *Mao Zedong, Report From Xunwu* (Stanford, Stanford University Press, 1990)

Trotsky, Leon, *Problems of the Chinese Revolution* (Ann Arbor, University of Michigan Press, 1967)

_____ 'Manifesto on China of the Left Opposition', in *Writings of Leon Trotsky, 1930–1931* (New York: Pathfinder Press, Inc., 1973)

Wakeman, Frederic Jr., *Strangers at the Gate: Social Disorder in South China* (Berkeley: University of California Press, 1966)

_____ *The Fall of Imperial China* (New York: Free Press, 1975)

Wang Guchen, Zhou Qiren and Others, *Smashing the Communal Pot: a Formulation and Development of China's Rural Responsibility System* (Beijing: New World Press, 1985)

Wang Gungwu, 'Pre-Modern History: Some Trends in the Writing of the History of the Song: 10th–13th Centuries', in Yahuda, Michael (ed.), *New Directions in the Social Sciences and Humanities in China* (London: Macmillan Press, 1987)

Wang Hongmo, 'Chen Duxiu: An Evaluation of His Life's Work', *Social Sciences in China*. Vol. VI, No.4 (December 1985)

Wang Qingcheng, 'Recent Developments in the Study of the Taiping Heavenly Kingdom', *Social Sciences in China*. Vol. I, No.1 (March 1980)

Warren, Bill, *Imperialism: Pioneer of Capitalism* (London: Verso, 1980).

Watson, Andrew, (ed.) *Mao Zedong and the Political Economy of the Border Region: A Translation of Mao's Economic and Financial Problems* (Cambridge: Cambridge University Press, 1980)

Watson, James, L., 'Chinese Kinship Reconsidered: Anthropological Perspectives on Historical Research', *China Quarterly*, No.92 (December 1982)

Wiens, Thomas B., 'Review of the Chinese Peasant Economy', *Modern Asian Studies*, Vol.9, No.2 (1975)

Wittfogel Karl, *Oriental Despotism: A Comparative Study of Total Power* (New Haven: Yale University Press, 1978)

Wolf, Eric, *Peasant Wars of the Twentieth Century* (New York: Harper & Row Publishers, 1969)

Womack, Brantly, *The Foundations of Mao Zedong's Political Thought, 1917–1935* (Honolulu: The University Press of Hawai'i, 1982)

Wong, R. Bin, 'Food Riots in the Qing Dynasty', *Journal of Asian Studies*, No.41 (August 1982)

Worsley, Peter, *The Trumpet Shall Sound: A Study of "Cargo" Cults in Melanesia* (New York: Schocken Books, 1968)

Wu Dakun, 'Karl A. Wittfogel's Oriental Despotism', *Social Sciences in China*, Vol. IV, No.2 (July 1983a)

_____ 'The Asiatic Mode of Production in History as Viewed by Political Economy in its Broad Sense', in Su Shaozhi and Others, *Marxism in China* (Nottingham: Spokesman Books, 1983b)

Wylie, Raymond F., *The Emergence of Maoism* (Stanford: Stanford University Press, 1980)

Xue Xin, 'Scientific Socialism or Agrarian Socialism', *Social Sciences in China*, Vol. III, Part 1 (1982)

Yang, Martin C., *A Chinese Village: Taitou, Shantung Province* (London: Kegan Paul, 1948)

_____ *A Chinese Village in Early Communist Transition* (Cambridge: Massachusetts Institute of Technology, 1959)

Yao Wenyuan, 'On the New Historical Drama 'The Dismissal of Hai Jiu'', in Gray, Jack and Cavendish, Patrick, *Chinese Communism in Crisis: Maoism and the Cultural Revolution* (London: Pall Mall, 1968)

_____ *On the Social Basis of the Lin Biao Anti-Party Clique* (Beijing: Foreign Languages Press, 1975)

Zhang Weiwei, *The China Wave: Rise of a Civilisational State* (Hackensack: World Century Publishing Corporation, 2012)

Zhou Enlai, *Selected Works, Vol. I* (Beijing: Foreign Languages Press, 1981)

INDEX

A

'absolute egalitarianism', agrarian socialism 11, 224, 274, 278–9, 284, 287–8, 297, 299, 332, 358, 360
agrarian crisis 19, 26, 44, 57, 94
  explanations of 36, 51–2, 55, 156–7
  and imperialism 17, 62, 91, 104, 149
  impact of 94, 150–1, 161, 178
agrarian economy
  capital formation in 4, 18, 115–6, 118, 161
  commodity and money relations 55, 56, 57, 89, 140, 162
  land purchase 48, 54, 61, 67, 82, 85, 88, 93, 104, 109, 133, 134–5, 137, 139, 163, 342
  landlord domination of 5, 9, 104–5, 150, 158, 306, 325, 332
  managerial farming 50, 51, 114–23
  market and technological constraints 103–6, 347
  monopoly rent as determinant of 101, 103–13, 122, 129, 130, 133, 139, 149, 155, 163, 297, 341–3, 358
  stagnation and decline 5, 11, 17–18, 22, 41, 49, 52, 86–98, 106, 110, 111, 113, 114, 116, 117–8, 122, 132, 149
  underutilised labour 39, 92, 118–9, 343
  village economy 118, 245, 262, 265, 314, 322, 324–9, 333, 335
agrarian revolution, agrarian revolutionary movement, *see* peasant revolution

Agriculturalist School (4th century BC) 330
agriculture
  capitalist 114, 174, 297, 321
  cash cropping 48, 49, 53, 55, 56, 79, 81–2, 83, 85, 88, 90, 114, 162, 346
  commercialisation 9, 16, 34, 47–51, 55–7, 80, 83, 88, 89, 91, 98, 99, 100, 104, 108, 114, 117, 122, 123, 141, 149, 154, 155, 163, 311, 342, 344, 345
  parcellised farming, reasons for 9, 65–6, 99, 104, 108–10, 122, 135, 297, 341
  stagnation of 5, 17–18, 41, 49, 52, 98, 106, 111, 116, 117–8, 132, 149
Alavi, Hamza, 12, 24, 26, 304–5, 306–12, 322, 326, 336, 338, 344, 347, 352
  see also middle peasant thesis
Anti-Japanese War (1937–45) 10, 21, 236, 224, 245, 248, 249–51, 255, 261, 263, 267, 269–70, 285, 281, 292, 309
Asiatic mode of production 100, 124
Autumn Harvest Uprising (1927) 197, 201

B

'Bare Egg Society' 200
Balazs, Etienne 124
banditry, bandits 7, 11, 71, 72, 91, 145, 146, 175, 192, 264, 312–3, 330, 334, 339
bourgeoisie 124, 171–4, 182, 183, 185, 187–8, 190, 193, 197, 237, 254, 304, 345
  bureaucrat 84–5, 345
  compradore 56, 84–85, 87, 193, 233–4, 235
  national 10, 13, 21, 86, 87,

89, 169, 181–2, 183, 185–8,
186–8, 193, 196, 197, 208,
213, 224, 227, 232, 233–5,
236–7, 238–40, 248–9, 258,
266, 270–1, 317, 334, 338,
346, 347, 351, 354, 355, 357
  petty 12, 21, 142, 146, 173–4,
177, 181–2, 183, 184, 197,
208, 213, 224, 227, 233–5,
236, 256, 270, 330, 339, 346,
351, 354, 355, 357
  rural 3, 11, 99, 171–2, 178,
196, 350
British American Tobacco
Company 49, 82
Buck, John L. 32, 34–5, 40, 42,
43–4, 103, 107, 112
bureaucratism 15, 352
  criticism of in CPC 22, 224–8,
239, 245, 254, 256, 261–2,
264, 266, 267, 277–8, 355–6
  traditional 11, 316, 331

C

cadres 200, 213, 220, 222, 225–6,
239, 250, 251–2, 258–9, 262,
263–4, 268, 275, 280, 281, 313
  criticism of 15, 23, 219, 227,
255–6, 261–2, 277–9, 281–3,
287, 291–4, 295
  corruption, problem of 264,
266, 267, 283–4, 288, 356
  indiscriminate attacks on 282,
283, 293, 294, 296, 299
Canton Uprising (1927) 187, 209
capitalism, capitalist 3, 4, 6, 8, 9,
10, 13, 14, 17, 24, 25, 26, 28, 34,
51, 52, 55, 56, 67, 84, 85, 86, 87,
117, 122, 124, 129, 133–8, 157,
178, 182–7, 188, 190, 194, 207,
215, 220, 221, 223, 228, 231, 233–
5, 237, 238, 239, 264, 270, 271,
297, 298, 308, 310, 311, 312, 316,
321, 324–8, 335, 336, 338, 340,
342–6, 348, 350, 351, 354, 360
  emergence of ('capitalist
sprouts') 18, 101, 120, 133,
194, 161–3, 233
  explanations of 99, 101, 103–
5, 105–6, 107–13, 115–7, 112,
133–41, 157, 161–5, 177, 212,
230
  failure to develop (blocked
transition) 17, 80, 161, 237,
242, 344
  policies towards 157, 196, 223,
236, 271, 324–5, 238, 335, 347
  revolutionary role of 4, 170–3,
326
  rural 114, 174, 297, 321,
244–5
cash crops *see* agriculture, cash
cropping
Chang Chung-li 61
Chayanov, Alexander V. 99, 107,
110–11, 114, 116, 122, 221, 297,
351
Chen Boda 14, 15–16, 36, 346
  analysis of rent and land
monopoly 51–7, 108, 118, 129,
133
  background 30n.
  extra-economic coercion 16,
52, 56, 61
  rate of exploitation 81–2
Chen Duxiu 20, 175, 182, 184–5,
189–91, 207, 238
Chen Hanseng 14, 15, 133
  agrarian crisis, explanation of
36, 55, 15–7
  classification of peasant
families 37–9
  persistence of small-scale
cultivation 39–44, 111
  village corporate land,
administration of 90–1
Chen Yungfa 263–5
Chesneaux, Jean 7, 304
Chiang Kai-shek, 20, 182, 183–5,

189, 193, 198, 233–5, 237, 239, 248, 250–1, 274
  see also KMT, White Terror
Chinese Marxism 5, 14, 15, 18, 26, 35, 101, 125, 131, 133, 155, 360
  see also Mao Zedong, sinification of Marxism
cities 20, 37, 82, 88, 105, 124, 138, 153, 169–70, 183, 191, 196, 197, 198–9, 200–1, 202, 203–5, 234–5, 239, 249, 258, 270, 335, 346, 354, 357
  see also, markets, urban; urban working class
Civil War between CPC and KMT 10, 19, 23, 37
  1927–37 168, 198, 233, 287
  1945–9 22, 246, 272, 275, 285
clan system (patriarchal kinship) 16, 60, 70, 90, 100, 135, 257
class polarisation 9, 94, 221, 343, 351, 360
Claudin, Fernando 238
clientelism 24, 65–66, 67, 101, 150, 163, 306, 322, 323, 330, 335
collective action 4, 8, 24, 71, 145–7, 148, 150, 304–5, 312–4, 315–7, 323–4, 333, 340
  see also peasant rebellion
Comintern (Communist International) 12, 21, 168, 174, 183, 185–8, 202–3, 203–5, 208, 216, 223, 234, 236, 310, 350
  advice to CPC 10, 14, 20, 169, 181–2, 189, 191–4, 196–8, 199–201, 213
commercialisation 6, 99
  agriculture 9, 16, 34, 47–51, 55–7, 80, 83, 88, 89, 91, 100, 104, 108, 114, 117, 122, 123, 141, 149, 154, 155, 163, 311, 344, 345
  commodity production 5, 112, 133, 297, 344–5

  imperialist impact on 9, 55, 117, 155, 344
  and land concentration 17, 51–2, 54, 62, 83–4, 85, 91
  market towns 53, 72, 105, 139, 314
  Ming-Qing transition 49–50, 57, 61, 66
  and peasant impoverishment 17, 19, 51, 83, 93, 98, 103, 140, 163, 344–5
communal bonds/relations 5, 93, 312, 347
  organisation 313, 340
Communist Party of China (CPC), 3
  6th Party Congress 20, 185, 189, 196–8, 204, 207–8, 209, 230, 233, 253
    Resolution on the Land Question (1928) 208, 209, 230
    Resolution on the Peasant Question (1928) 208–9
  '28 Bolsheviks' 21, 207, 208, 209, 212, 213–7, 222, 223, 225, 228, 231
  authoritarianism 23, 252, 254, 263–5, 266
  branches 209, 223, 278, 291, 292, 293
  bureaucratic tendencies 22, 224–8, 239, 245, 254, 256, 261–2, 264, 266, 267, 277–8, 330–1, 355–6
  cadres' errors 23, 291–5
  class-based organisation of peasants 10, 15, 148, 183, 159, 179, 183, 317, 330–8
  and clientelism 24, 322, 323, 330, 335
  'commandism' 11, 22, 225, 252, 254, 255, 267, 269, 277, 278, 293, 352, 355–6
  'consciousness raising' 23
  corruption 245, 254, 263, 277,

278, 283, 294, 296, 300, 326
democratic centralism 13, 23, 27, 246, 254, 269, 356
doctrinairism 255, 265
formation of 25, 181
grassroots members 244, 261, 265, 267–8, 270, 356
growth and expansion 200, 244, 251, 265, 279, 292
inner-party struggles 12, 197–8, 208, 230, 252–6, 258, 352
KMT, relations with 10, 19, 21, 22, 168, 181–94, 198, 238, 244, 246, 248–67, 309
land policies of 21, 23, 179, 354, 355, 356
    1927–37 169, 199, 210, 212, 214, 215, 216, 295, 317
    1937–45 246, 248, 250–1, 262, 267, 274–5, 281, 287, 292, 355
    1945–47 22, 23, 274–9 275–6, 277, 279–80, 287–91, 293–5
leadership styles 13, 225, 245, 252, 259, 261, 323, 331
Left Adventurism 14, 196, 198
Marxist study 251, 254, 255, 256
mass line 13, 14, 20, 21, 22, 27, 170, 219, 224–5, 232, 244, 245, 261, 263, 266, 267–9, 352, 355–6
national revolution 13, 15, 23, 182, 186, 189, 191, 194, 202, 238, 240, 333, 337, 353–7
New Democracy 21–2, 27, 235–7, 244, 249, 250, 251, 267, 269–72
Party building 14
    Liu Shaoqi's views on, 245, 252–9, 265
    Mao's views on 14, 20, 21, 170, 224, 245, 248, 252, 254–6
    problems of 248–52
Party-mass relations 13, 22, 27, 245, 252, 256, 261, 268
Party rectification 22, 23, 245–6, 248, 251–2, 256, 259, 261–2, 264–5, 267, 278, 279–80, 287, 288, 291–2, 294, 322–3, 330, 352
    open-door policies 23, 232, 293, 356
    and production drive 227, 251, 261, 267, 268
peasant relations 23, 24, 26, 245, 250, 251, 305, 315, 33, 336, 338
policy errors 287–91
poor and middle peasant unity 21, 179, 211, 212, 215, 219, 222–3, 226, 230, 240, 246, 230, 240, 246, 271, 287, 297, 299, 317, 327, 335, 336, 352, 357, 359
proletarian leadership 12, 20, 174, 192, 197, 201, 235, 239, 349
    of the peasants, 10, 168, 169, 173, 192, 198, 204, 213, 284
Right Opportunism 183, 196, 198, 213, 214, 239, 258
and urban working class 173, 182, 186, 196, 198, 202, 203–4, 209, 216, 258, 357
'tailism' 267
United Front approach 10, 20, 21, 23, 168, 169, 181, 193, 197, 236, 244, 249, 267, 269, 270–2, 292
as vanguard Party 7, 10, 311, 320, 349, 356
village programmes 25, 325, 326–7, 328, 336, 354
workerist tendencies 216, 225
Zunyi Conference (1935) 236

see also Mao Zedong
community organisation 68–71, 72–3, 130, 145, 147, 154, 349
Confucianism, Confucian, 2, 16, 22, 63, 120,145, 146, 147, 323, 331, 349
    benevolent paternalism 67,136, 305, 320, 342
    disdain for manual labour 255, 258
    examination and education system 60, 61, 135, 162
    ideology 121, 135–6, 139, 143, 150, 257, 258
    and state 27, 64, 101, 125, 163, 164, 304, 347
co-operatives 105, 156, 227, 327
    see also Yan'an village programmes
Crook, David 23, 246, 281–4, 293, 357
    see also Ten Mile Inn
Crook, Isabel 23, 158, 246, 281–4, 293, 346, 357
    see also Ten Mile Inn
Cultural Revolution (1966–76) 28, 360

D

Daoism 320, 330
debt 38, 40, 43, 50, 51, 52, 54, 56, 67, 81, 82, 88, 92, 93, 112, 140, 156, 185, 276, 321, 328, 339, 343
democracy
    'doing everything the masses want' 23, 27, 246, 269–70
        see also voluntarism
    economic democracy 23, 27, 254, 269–71, 335, 336
        see also New Democracy
    Liu Shaoqi on 23, 246, 252–6, 269–70
    Mao Zedong on 246, 252, 254–6, 258, 268–9, 355–6
    participatory methods 226, 228
    three-thirds election system 264, 267, 270
    see also CPC, democratic centralism; CPC, mass line; New Democracy; participatory methods
Deng Xiaoping 28
dissident gentry, as leaders of peasant rebellions 19, 101, 143, 144, 150, 159, 164, 176, 312, 331
dynastic cycle 18, 144, 153, 311

E

economic stagnation and decline 11, 22, 86, 98, 111, 113, 114, 133
egalitarianism 216, 231, 296, 301, 348, 354, 355, 357, 360
    see also 'absolute egalitarianism'
elites, 11, 12, 13, 15, 23, 43, 84, 89, 91, 112, 120, 121, 128, 130, 139, 145, 147, 148–54, 155, 157, 163, 169, 176, 179, 198, 207, 209–12, 213, 215, 216, 220, 223, 233, 244, 245, 250, 252, 264, 265–6, 269–70, 310, 313, 314, 315, 331, 333–34, 337, 338, 342, 343, 347–50, 352, 354
    see also landlords; landlord class
Elvin, Mark 17–8, 98–9, 105–113, 114, 117–8
see also 'high-level equilibrium trap'
Esherick, Joseph W. 35–7, 41–2

F

Factionalism 144, 147, 164, 170, 192, 215, 216, 223, 224, 226, 282, 283, 317, 330, 337, 347, 348
family farming, persistence of 49, 98–9, 116, 117
Fang Xing 134, 138

Fei Xiaotong 103–4
feudalism, feudal relations 3, 4, 6–7, 11, 13–4, 15, 16–7, 22–3, 27, 32–5, 71, 98, 125, 129, 147, 153, 157–8, 161–5, 168, 171–3, 178–9, 183, 186, 190, 192, 193–4, 196, 208, 211, 215–6, 219–22, 222–3, 226, 227, 228, 230–2, 233–40, 249, 270–71, 272, 275–6, 277, 279, 282–4, 288, 289, 292, 294, 295–6, 297–8, 299–301, 309, 314, 316, 325, 331–4, 337, 339, 341–2, 344–7, 348–9, 353, 353–7, 358–60
    Asiatic features of 9, 18, 60–1, 67, 100, 143
    Chinese and European compared 8, 34, 65, 74, 91–2, 100, 125, 134, 168, 178
    and commerce/commercialisation 54, 112, 123, 188
    direct and indirect controls 92, 120–2, 322
    extra-economic coercion 131, 138, 139, 148
    hierarchical relations 70, 135, 136–7, 177, 257–9, 287, 320
    links with imperialist exploitation 10, 87, 93, 189, 197
    mode of surplus expropriation 99, 112, 118, 131, 138, 149, 341
    political and economic power 26, 140, 147–8
    refeudalisation 19, 26, 101, 131, 133, 162
    tenacity of 101, 133–38, 149, 274, 330
    see also rent
Feuerwerker, Albert 105
food riots 145, 153, 314, 316
    see also peasants, protest
foreign trade, banking and investment 17, 37, 49, 57, 62, 78, 79, 81, 82–3, 84–7, 88, 93, 98–9, 104–5, 106–7, 108–13, 116, 122, 134, 148, 161, 165, 168, 188, 235, 297, 326, 335, 345, 326
    see also imperialism
'four class bloc' 21, 182, 186, 238
    see also New Democracy
Frank, Andre Gunder 344–5
Fried, Morton 66
Fu Yiling 133

G
Ganqing 66, 136, 137
    see also patron-client ties
Geertz, Clifford 115
Gilmartin, Christina 158, 346
Guangdong 24, 35, 39–40, 41, 43, 63, 315

H
Haifeng Soviet (1927) 24, 200, 224–5, 315–6, 333
    see also Marks, Robert B.
'high-level equilibrium trap' 18, 105–7, 112
    see also Elvin, Mark
Hinton, William 23, 62, 120–1, 246, 281, 283, 299, 357
hired labour 36, 37, 38, 40–1, 49, 57, 110, 118, 119–21, 133, 137, 139, 171, 215, 221
    see also wage labour
Hobsbawm, Eric 4
Ho Ping-ti 61
Huang, Philip C. C. 5, 18, 42, 125, 145, 162
    commercialisation and peasant differentiation 49–51, 53, 99, 114
    importance of wage labour 40, 49, 67, 114, 116
    landlord-state-village relations 100, 127–9, 147–8, 154–6

limitations of analysis (eclecticism) 117–23, 129–31, 158, 339–43, 358
rejects Marxist analysis 18, 128, 129
see also managerial farming, critique of

I

imperialism 4, 9, 33, 124, 157, 168, 175, 181–2, 189, 192, 194, 196, 202, 236–8, 248–9, 270, 357
  and class structure 10, 27, 310–2, 316
  foreign trade and investment 37, 78–9, 81, 84, 86–7, 106, 158, 273
  and intensification of feudal exploitation 10, 87, 93, 149, 154–5, 189, 197
  and militarisation 78, 85
  and national capitalist class 10, 87, 181, 186, 188, 197, 233–4
  and rural economy 5, 17, 51, 80–4, 93, 117
  and rural society 6, 7, 88–91
  and uneven development 78–80, 112, 344–5
  world crisis 36, 37, 81, 83
industry, industrial production 12, 36, 55, 62, 81, 86, 87, 105, 135, 187, 190, 235, 236, 270, 298, 328, 358
  cotton and textiles 78, 79, 81, 86, 87
  handicraft production 3, 42, 47, 78, 79–85, 88, 100, 104, 105, 109, 110, 114, 116, 135, 155, 162, 316, 327
  national industry 79–80, 82, 86
irrigation 7, 60, 64, 70, 72, 74, 80, 88, 125, 133, 141, 145

J

Jacques, Martin 27
Jiangxi Soviet (1931–4) 209, 212, 325
Jin Dequn 35
Jinggang Mountains 201, 204, 209, 307
Johnson, Chalmers 244, 261, 263

K

Keating, Pauline B. 155, 266
kinship relations 5, 11, 14, 16, 65, 68, 69–72, 88, 89, 92, 93, 101, 130, 133, 136, 137, 145, 146, 148, 149, 150, 162–3, 164, 165, 328, 342, 348, 358
Kuomintang (KMT) 10, 19, 20, 21, 22, 23, 36, 51, 87, 127, 153, 154, 157–8, 169, 170, 175, 176, 185–6, 189, 192–3, 197, 198, 207, 225, 233, 234–5, 238–9, 244, 245, 248, 249–51, 258, 262, 274, 288, 309, 316, 317, 321, 322, 324, 327, 346
  'Left' KMT, 'Left' KMT government 183–4, 146, 190–3, 283, 234
  massacres (White Terror) 20, 183, 185, 186, 189, 198, 209, 233
  national revolution 21, 181, 182, 186, 189, 191, 192, 238, 240, 334, 337, 354
  'Nanjing Decade' (1927–37) and economic development 86–7
  Northern Expedition 20, 181, 191, 197, 233
  revolutionary/reactionary leanings 183, 184, 193, 233
  village reform failures 156–8
  First United Front (1924–7) 10, 181–5, 186, 185–7, 189, 192, 193–4, 309

Second United Front (1937–45) 10, 21, 22, 244, 246, 248–51, 269–72
see also Chiang Kai-shek; Republican China

L

labour hiring 118, 134, 137, 140, 221, 350
  see also wage labour
labour, under-utilised 39, 92, 116, 118–9, 343
Laclau, Ernesto 344–5
land confiscation 21, 22, 23, 169, 170, 173, 176, 184, 189, 190, 192, 207, 209, 211, 213, 215, 226, 231, 232, 244, 245, 245, 248, 250, 268, 272, 274, 275, 287, 288, 291, 309, 332, 337, 351, 353
land hunger 9, 16, 39, 84, 93, 111, 112, 117, 151, 168, 178, 192, 209, 215, 230, 231, 239, 309, 343 345, 348, 351
land investigation drive 213, 215, 219–20, 224–26
land laws 32, 209, 210–12, 216, 224, 275, 276, 277, 278, 279, 280, 288–90, 293–4, 296, 297–8, 299, 300
land ownership
  clan land 43, 63, 68, 69, 70, 90, 120, 121, 136, 145–6, 210
  concentration of ownership 16, 41, 44, 52, 108, 122, 140–1, 178, 297, 342
  customary arrangements 66, 69, 71, 88, 94, 137–8, 162, 176, 321, 342
  idle land 37, 83, 112
  land monopoly 9, 16, 51–7, 65, 84, 90, 106, 111, 151, 208, 211, 230, 231, 237, 239, 294, 301, 314, 342, 343–5, 348, 351

parasitic system 39, 51, 54, 104, 118, 122
peasant-owners 34, 35, 41, 42–3, 44, 65, 104, 108, 109, 134, 155–6, 211, 237, 296, 339, 340
regional variations 5, 7, 9, 34–7, 40, 41, 43–4, 55, 60, 62, 82–3, 91, 207, 357
land purchase 48, 54, 57, 61, 67, 82, 85, 88, 93, 104, 109, 133, 134–5, 137, 139, 163, 342
land redistribution 21, 43, 207, 277, 279, 283, 289, 294, 371
  Li Lisan's policies 207–9
  Mao's policies 209–15
  per capita basis 211–2, 222, 223, 224, 231, 276, 295, 296, 355, 358, 359
land reform policies
  CPC policies 21, 22, 23, 168, 179, 199, 214, 215, 216, 274–9, 295, 317, 354, 355, 356
    Directive on Land Reform and Party Rectification Work (1948) 279–80
    February 1930 Land Law 210, 212
    May 4th Directive (1947) 275, 287–90, 298
    Outline Land Law (1947) 275–6, 277, 278, 279–80, 288–91, 293–5
  'double reduction' policy 246, 248, 250–1, 262, 267, 274–5, 281, 287, 292
  KMT policies 153, 154, 156–8, 348
  legal methods 67, 119, 136–8, 140
  moderate (limited) 21, 22, 23, 184, 192, 212, 248–9, 274, 280, 287, 289, 292, 296, 328, 355
  National Land Conference

383

(1947) 275, 276, 284
'not-so-thorough' land reform 23, 246, 274–80, 281, 284, 291, 292, 294, 295, 299
political mistakes 7, 170, 190, 198, 204, 236, 270
   'middle peasant line' 23, 281–4, 287–90, 299, 300, 340
   'poor peasant line' 23, 281–4, 287–9, 296, 300, 340
   see also 'absolute egalitarianism'
   'rich peasant line' 12, 21, 208–11, 213, 216, 222, 228, 237, 249, 270, 275
problems in
   bureaucratism 22, 224–8, 239, 245, 254, 256, 261–2, 264, 266, 267, 277–8, 255–6
   contradictions among peasants 13, 23, 26, 127, 161, 193–4, 222, 228, 246, 269, 292, 294, 299, 301, 325, 335, 347, 353, 355, 359
   elite obstruction 11, 23, 80, 292, 294
   factionalism 164, 192, 215, 216, 223, 224, 226, 283, 317, 337, 347, 348
   influence of kinship ties 11, 69, 101, 148
   Party corruption 245, 254, 263, 277, 278, 283, 294, 296, 300, 326
   tenacity of traditional elites 101, 133–41, 149, 207, 231, 246, 265, 314, 330, 354
and revolutionary transformation 7, 13, 320, 331, 340, 348

unequal results of 296, 299, 300, 328
see also land redistribution; land confiscation
land speculation 54, 83–84, 88, 140, 155, 321
landlord class 19, 32, 41, 92, 112, 120, 126, 131, 134, 141, 159, 171, 175, 210, 212, 248, 289
   obstacle to development 138, 164, 168
   parasitic nature of 36, 39, 51, 54, 104, 118, 122
   regeneration of 89, 139, 158
   see also landlords
landlords
   absentees 34, 47, 57, 62–3, 66, 83, 86, 88, 89, 93, 104, 105, 107, 112, 119, 134–5, 138, 163, 321
   anti-Japanese war and resistance 236–7, 245, 250, 275, 281, 292, 309
   CPC policies, treatment of by CPC 8, 219, 249–50, 262, 264, 270–2, 275–80, 280–4, 288–91, 291–5, 299, 307, 314, 322, 324, 249, 351
   and commercialisation 17, 51, 54, 62, 83–4, 85, 91
   credit control of 54, 57, 92, 107, 121, 123, 158, 344, 345
   different types of 61–3, 276, 279
   extra-economic coercion 16, 52, 56, 62, 131, 138, 139, 148
   factions 130, 131, 266
   infiltrating CPC branches 169, 208, 277, 278, 330, 356
   informal power 11, 63–4, 93, 154
   land monopoly 9, 16, 51–7, 65, 84, 90, 106, 111, 151, 208, 211, 230, 231, 237, 239, 294, 301, 314, 342, 343–5, 348, 351

land purchase 48, 57, 61, 67, 82, 85, 88, 93, 104, 109, 133, 134–5, 137, 139, 163, 342
landlord-tenant relationship 32, 47, 88, 89, 92, 125, 137, 154, 171, 179, 321–2, 340, 342, 342–3, 357
as lineage leaders, 121, 156, 223
local militia, 64, 72, 73, 74, 85, 89, 91, 131, 147, 176, 183–4, 264, 312
and magistrates 62, 64, 66, 68, 73–4, 89, 137–8
as mediators 68, 72–4, 91, 163
meeting points 72
as merchants and officials (landlord-merchant-official trinity) 18, 54, 84, 134–5, 138, 316
patronage, patron client ties 24, 65, 70, 73, 88, 93, 98, 150, 207, 216, 264, 305, 311, 321–2, 342, 344, 348–9, 350, 352
political power of 15, 16, 32, 60–4, 89, 92, 93, 145, 164, 176, 189, 331
political privileges 135, 139–40
regional variation 5, 34, 35, 36, 40, 41, 43, 62, 68, 72
relations with peasants 9, 16, 17, 18, 92, 100, 155, 339
rental patterns 9, 16, 36–7, 39, 41–4, 47–8, 48–51, 51–7, 65–7, 74, 83, 84, 89, 90, 92, 101, 103–13, 118, 119–20, 133, 137, 138–9, 161, 163, 188, 220, 297, 314, 341, 342
speculation and market control 16, 36, 41, 62, 72, 82, 83, 92, 93, 103, 145, 109, 155, 121, 139, 155, 316, 345, 352
and state power 7, 60–4, 74, 130, 144, 153, 154, 155
surplus appropriation 51, 75, 89, 92, 108, 113, 118–9, 129, 134, 161, 162
tax avoidance 126, 139–40, 288
tax privileges 73, 89, 135–6, 138
village-based 34, 61, 63, 65, 131, 207
see also elites; landlord class
'Leftism' 197, 210, 237, 252, 258, 266, 267, 283, 289, 360
see also CPC, Left Adventurism
Lenin, Vladimir 10, 11, 18, 20, 168, 177, 178, 179, 190, 208, 331, 349, 350, 355, 356
1905 Revolution 172, 173–4
advocates worker-peasant alliance 10, 12, 174–5
classification of peasantry 38–9, 121
critique of Narodniks 26, 99, 158, 172, 174
critique of petty bourgeoisie 256
The Development of Capitalism in Russia (1899) 38, 171
revolutionary role of different peasant classes 3, 17, 168, 170–5, 306
vanguard (Leninist) party 7, 15
Leninism 251, 254, 349, 351
Li Lifeng 10, 269, 271, 272, 353, 360
Li Lisan 20, 198–201, 203, 207–8, 209, 210–2, 228, 231
Li Wenzhi 119, 133, 136–137, 140, 163
Liberated Areas 274, 276, 278–80, 284, 288–91, 294
Liberation War (1945–9) 21
lineage 43, 63–4, 67, 73, 131, 135, 145–6, 150, 156, 162, 163, 219, 227, 264, 305, 315, 317, 332, 348
corporate properties (clan land)

43, 63, 68, 69, 70, 90, 120, 121, 136, 145–6, 210
organisation 68–71, 71–2, 90, 91, 92, 93, 136, 137, 147, 200, 207, 223, 225, 231, 346
see also kinship relations
literacy 61, 70, 135, 227, 250, 292
Liu Shaoqi 14, 148, 251, 274, 309, 350, 354, 356
   Confucian-influenced approach 22, 257
   on inner-party struggle 266–8
   on mass line 267–9
   on Party building 245, 252–9, 265
   Party rectification 18, 22, 245–6, 251–2, 256, 279, 287, 291–3
   role in land reform (1946–7) 275–80, 295, 297
   on rural work, 257–9, 279
   voluntarism ('doing everything the masses want') 23, 26, 27, 246, 269–70
local bullies and tyrants 154
local government (magistrates, courts and tax collection) 62, 63, 66, 68, 73–4, 88, 89, 131, 137–8, 140, 153, 154, 176, 225, 227, 252, 263, 300, 321–2
Long March (1934–5) 10, 236, 244
managerial farming, critique of 50, 51, 114–23
   see also Huang, Philip C. C.

M

Mao Zedong
   'absolute egalitarianism' 11, 224, 274, 278–9, 287–8, 297, 299, 332, 358, 360
   Analysis of the Classes in Chinese Society (1926) 42, 177
   cadres

education 190, 251–2, 255–6, 294
errors of, dealing with 291–5
class consciousness 210, 213, 224, 228
classification of peasantry 170, 177, 219–22, 226, 240
criticised for non-class approach 223–4
critiques of doctrinairism and empiricism 255–6
critiques of 'Leftism' and Rightism 210, 237, 258, 266, 267, 283, 289
democratic centralism 13, 23, 27, 246, 254, 269, 356
'four ropes' binding the Chinese peasants 70, 331
guerrilla struggle 201–2, 205
How to Analyse the Classes in the Rural Areas (1933) 220, 279
leadership methods 12, 225, 252, 259
Long March (1934–5) 10, 236, 244
Marxist method, see sinification of Marxism
mass line 13, 14, 20, 21, 22, 27, 170, 219, 224–5, 232, 244, 245, 261, 263, 266, 267–9, 352, 355–6
mass power 7, 20, 175–9, 225, 226–8, 232, 238, 239, 337, 343, 348, 352, 358
middle peasants analysis of, 12, 21, 23, 26, 170, 179, 211, 212, 214–5, 216, 220–22, 223, 224, 226, 228, 230–2, 235, 275, 279, 288, 289–91, 298, 308, 309–10, 356
national bourgeoisie, analysis of 21, 232, 235–7, 248, 249, 258, 266, 334
New Democracy 21–2, 27,

235–7, 244, 249, 250, 251, 269–72
on 'Oriental Culture' 177, 190, 313–4
on Party building, open-door methods 23, 232, 293, 356
Party-mass relationship 13, 22, 27, 236–7, 245, 252, 256, 261, 268
patriotic mobilisation 22, 244, 249, 269, 292
peasants as active force for change 159, 222
on peasants as compared with Lenin 169–170, 175, 177, 178–9
on peasant excesses 20, 190, 215, 334
poor and middle peasant unity, importance of 21, 179, 211, 215, 219, 222–3, 226, 230, 240, 246, 230, 240, 246, 271, 287, 297, 299, 317, 335, 337, 352, 357, 359
Report on an Investigation into the Peasant Movement in Hunan [Hunan Report] (1927) 2, 11, 175
revolutionary potential of peasants 13, 22, 28, 177, 178–9, 232, 238, 245, 261, 337, 348
rich peasants, analysis of 170, 177, 190, 209, 210, 211–2, 214–6, 219–24, 225, 226, 230–2, 236, 237, 275, 279, 291–2, 309, 310, 331
rural-based strategy 11, 12, 14, 21, 169–70, 178, 203, 228, 265
sinification of Marxism 13, 21, 179, 219–228
subjective consciousness, importance of 13, 203
traditional culture 177, 331, 349
markets 4, 5–6, 8, 16, 17–8, 28, 32, 47–51, 51, 54, 55–7, 65–6, 67, 72, 80–1, 87, 91, 93–4, 98–9, 103–5, 105–7, 107–113, 114–7, 119–120, 124–9, 129–30, 134, 153, 156–8, 161, 162–3, 165, 193, 202, 235, 311, 320–2, 324–7, 340, 346, 347, 359
grain 53, 84, 92, 133–4, 145, 177, 313–4
international 17, 18, 24, 78–87, 112, 188, 316, 333, 344, 345
labour 86, 118, 133–4, 161
market towns 53, 72, 105, 139, 314
rural 67, 68–9, 72, 92, 104, 121, 271, 311, 331, 358
speculation/market price manipulation 16, 83, 103, 109, 121, 139, 155, 316, 345, 352
urban 104, 123, 138, 346
see also CPC
Marks, Robert B. 24, 131, 200, 224–5, 305, 314, 315–7, 333, 338
Marx, Karl 4, 99, 331, 349
Asiatic mode of production 100, 124, 143
capitalist differential rent 52
China's traditional condition 2
draft letters to Vera Zasulich 257–8
on French peasantry 2, 360–1
predominant form of surplus appropriation 341
Marxism, 7, 10, 11, 13, 14, 15, 21, 106, 108, 125, 127, 129, 239–40, 244, 261, 304, 331, 351, 360
CPC leadership 228, 251, 253–5, 256, 336–38, 349
debates on peasantry 4–5, 24, 26, 35, 170, 179, 305, 315–8, 326, 333, 339
landlords 53, 60, 125, 130, 131, 155
state power 61, 100

transition from feudalism 14, 18, 26, 101, 131, 133–40
see also Chinese Marxism; Mao Zedong; sinification of Marxism
Mencius 143, 330
mental/manual labour division 63, 120, 135, 150, 255, 257, 258, 262, 330, 360
merchants 53–5, 62–3, 72, 74, 81, 82–3, 84–6, 88, 89, 93, 103, 105–7, 119, 121, 134–5, 138–9, 145, 155–8, 177, 186, 234, 238, 313–4, 316, 324, 327, 345–6
middle peasant thesis 9, 12, 24, 26, 304, 306–12, 322
  see also Alavi, Hamza; Wolf, Eric
Ming Dynasty (1368–1614) 64, 124, 133–134, 162
Ming-Qing transition 49–50, 57, 61, 66
moral economy, *see* peasants, moral economy
mortgage, pre-capitalist 50, 54, 67, 104, 137
mutual aid 145, 263, 264, 268, 271, 282, 324, 327, 328, 330, 336, 355, 357, 359
Myers, Ramon H. 6, 105, 107–9, 111, 114

N

Narodniks 3, 26, 99, 107, 158, 171–4, 221, 355
national bourgeoisie 10, 13, 21, 86, 87, 89, 169, 181–2, 183, 186–8, 193, 196, 197, 208, 213, 224, 227, 232, 233–5, 236, 258, 266, 270, 317, 334, 338, 346, 351, 354, 355, 357
  revolutionary/reactionary leanings 188, 233–5, 236, 248
  as vacillating 194, 197, 233–40, 249, 347, 355
national movement, national revolution 21, 181, 182, 186, 189, 191, 192, 238, 240, 334, 337, 354
  interrelationship with peasant revolution 13, 15, 23, 194, 202, 338, 353–7
nationalism 244, 263, 274, 356
  see also KMT; national bourgeoisie; national movement
natural disasters 80, 339
Needham, Joseph 124
neo-Narodniks 9, 13, 310, 351
New Democracy 21–2, 244, 271
  Anti-Japanese War (1937–45) 21, 235–7, 270
  basic tenets 21, 27, 236–7, 249, 250, 251
  economic democracy 27, 254, 269–71, 335
  Liberation War (1945–9) 27, 269–72
  political methods eg 'three-thirds system' 264, 267, 269–70
Northern Expedition 20, 181, 191, 197, 233
Nurkse, Ragnar 17–18, 105–7, 111

O

Opium Wars (1840–2, 1856–60) 78
Oriental Despotism 61, 124
  see also Wittfogel, Karl

P

participatory methods 226, 228
patriarchal clan system 60, 70, 73, 100, 135, 231, 287
  see also lineage, organisation
patron-client ties 16, 24, 65, 66–7, 70, 73, 88, 93, 98, 150,

207, 216, 264, 305, 311, 321–2, 342, 344
  see also ganqing,
peasant mass associations, 2, 251, 264
peasant movement, 2, 8, 10, 12, 13, 19, 23, 24, 26, 144, 148, 158, 159, 170, 172–4, 177, 183, 184, 188, 190–1, 192–3, 194, 197–9, 202, 203–4, 215, 220, 228, 267, 230, 234, 238–9, 259, 306–9, 310–11, 312, 315–7, 322, 325, 330, 337–8, 347, 353
  class leadership of 10, 148, 159, 183, 317, 330–8
peasant rebellion 6, 7, 15, 18, 98, 131, 133, 135, 143–51, 159, 162, 176, 200, 257, 304–5, 306, 310–11, 320, 337
  Boxer Rebellion (1899–1901) 175
  dissident gentry 19, 101, 143, 144, 150, 159, 164, 176, 312, 331
  leadership 147–8
  Nian Rebellion (1851–68) 146
  Taiping Rebellion (1850–64) 148, 157, 358
  traditional 'right to rebel' 143
peasant revolution, 26, 141, 189, 196, 200, 202, 306, 311, 325, 336, 349
  CPC role, 304–5, 330–2, 332–6, 336–8, 348–53
  class contradictions 19, 127, 131, 161, 162, 163, 193–4, 269, 353–4, 356
  eradication of feudal relations 22, 23, 113, 295, 341
  mass mobilisation 11, 168, 182, 183, 192–3, 194, 225, 227, 233, 249, 252, 261, 262, 267–8, 270, 274, 288, 350
  land confiscation 21, 22, 23, 169, 170, 176, 184, 189, 190,

192, 207, 209, 211, 213, 215, 226, 231, 232, 244, 245, 246, 248, 250, 268, 272, 274, 275, 287, 288, 291, 309, 332, 337, 351, 353
  peasant capacity for rebellion 4, 17, 91, 94, 143–51, 172, 340
  post-1949 developments 357–61
  state-village relations 9, 18, 19, 22, 100, 127, 128–9, 141, 154–6, 156–9, 245, 262, 340–43
  United Front policies 10, 20, 21, 23, 169, 181, 197, 236, 244, 249, 267, 269, 270–2, 292
  see also CPC, peasant relations
Peasant Studies 2, 4, 14, 24, 339, 358
peasants
  activism 26, 175, 192, 219, 250, 264, 266, 274, 289, 291, 330, 336, 338, 340, 356
  attitudes to markets 8, 53, 92, 153, 324–6, 331, 346, 352, 359
  classification of 4, 38, 39, 121, 170, 177, 221, 222, 226, 295, 351
  see also Lenin, Vladimir; Mao Zedong
  collective action 4, 8, 24, 71, 145, 148, 150–1, 304–5, 312–5, 315–8, 323, 333, 340
  contradictions among 13, 23, 26, 127, 161, 193–4, 222, 228, 246, 269, 292, 294, 299, 301, 325, 335, 347, 353, 355, 359
  culture 7, 24, 150, 257, 305, 320–4, 331
  debt burden 38, 40, 43, 50, 51, 52, 54, 56, 67, 81–2, 88, 92, 93, 112, 120, 140, 156, 185, 276, 321, 331, 328, 339
  differentiation of 3, 5, 49, 99, 108, 114, 117, 122–3, 171,

177, 221, 326, 342, 351, 359
disunity among 8, 11, 15, 19, 23, 24, 25, 101, 147–9, 154–5, 192, 207, 214, 222, 228, 230, 232, 299, 317, 332, 334, 347, 350, 352, 353–4
dynamics 12, 13–4, 15, 22, 23–5, 168, 179, 212, 215, 230, 246, 281, 287, 299, 308, 310–1, 331, 334, 336, 337–8, 347, 350, 352–3
economic and legal rights 3, 48, 50, 66, 67, 69, 119, 136–7, 138, 157, 162, 168, 181, 182, 208, 230, 248, 275, 322, 346, 347, 348, 349
excesses 20, 169, 175, 184, 187, 190–4, 197, 215, 240, 246, 278, 296, 299, 334, 346
exploitation 5, 6, 9, 11, 13, 16–7, 21, 32, 34, 36–7, 38, 40, 43–4, 52, 56–7, 63, 67, 70, 81–4, 86, 89, 90–1, 93, 103, 110, 112, 120, 121–2, 125, 130–1, 136–8, 138–40, 143, 145, 147, 149–50, 156–7, 162, 170, 171–2, 177, 179, 187, 189, 208, 211, 220–1, 222–4, 226, 236, 239, 259, 270, 276, 287, 289, 295, 296–8, 299–301, 304–5, 307, 317, 333, 337, 339–40, 342, 342, 344, 346, 350, 351, 355
goals 2–8, 8–9, 19, 24, 28, 150, 245, 304–5, 325
impoverishment, explanations of 11, 17, 19, 41, 51, 53, 55, 80–4, 86–7, 92–4, 98–9, 101, 103–5, 107–13, 121–3, 139–49, 147–8, 154–6, 157, 161, 163, 164, 175–9, 190, 208, 223, 231, 271, 313, 321, 340–3, 343–7, 351
involution 18, 114–23, 163
kinship ties 5, 11, 14, 16, 65, 68, 69–72, 88, 89, 90, 92, 93, 101, 130, 133, 136, 137, 145, 146, 148, 149, 150, 162–3, 165, 328, 342, 348, 358
land hunger 9, 16, 39, 84, 93, 111–2, 117, 150–1, 168, 178, 192, 209, 215, 230, 231, 239, 309, 343, 345, 348, 351
landlord relations 32, 47, 88, 89, 92, 125, 137, 154, 171, 179, 331–2, 340, 342, 357
living standards 42, 215, 271
moral economy 4, 6, 316, 317, 324–5, 331, 335, 358–9
oral history and folklore 150, 316, 320–1
owner-peasants 34, 35, 41, 42–3, 44, 65, 104, 108, 109, 134, 155–6, 211, 237, 296, 339, 340
patron-client relationships 16, 24, 65, 66, 67, 70, 73, 88, 93, 98, 150, 207, 216, 264, 305, 311, 321–2, 342, 344
production relations 15, 99, 108, 118, 119–20, 158, 161, 158, 161, 265, 335, 341, 344, 360
protest, eg food riots, 145, 153, 155, 305, 314, 315, 316, 352
relations with CPC 23, 24, 26, 245, 250, 251, 305, 315, 336, 338
rental patterns 9, 16, 36–7, 39, 41–4, 47–8, 48–51, 51–7, 65–7, 74, 83, 84, 89, 90, 92, 101, 103–13, 118, 119–20, 133, 137, 138–9, 161, 163, 188, 220, 297, 314, 341, 342
revolutionary potential 3, 9, 13, 14, 22, 28, 174, 177–8, 232, 237–8, 245, 261, 337, 348
rich peasants, dual characteristics of 211, 228, 236, 334, 351

semi-proletarianisation 114–7, 122, 127, 154
small-scale cultivation 8, 17, 34, 98, 111
spontaneous land takeovers 121, 173, 184, 190, 192, 274–5, 287, 309
tenant-peasants 5, 9, 85
traditional survival strategies (predation and protection) 110, 113, 148, 150, 312, 314, 315, 334
traditionalism 2, 24, 25, 153, 228, 306, 321, 354
under-utilised labour of 39, 92, 116–7, 342, 343
see also peasant movement; peasant rebellion; peasant revolution
Peng Pai 200, 225, 315, 316–7
People's Republic of China (PRC) 10, 357
Pepper, Suzanne 263
Perdue, Peter C. 18, 100, 124–30, 137, 145, 339
Perry, Elizabeth J. 24, 145, 146–9, 150
personalised power 16, 67, 75, 92, 136, 137, 147, 149, 162, 164–5
  see landlords, informal power
personality cults, 11, 200, 316, 337
Plekhanov, Georgi 171
Polachek, James M. 200, 325
Poor Peasant Leagues 209, 213–5, 224, 226, 276, 288–91, 298, 299
Popkin, Samuel L. 4, 358
proletarian leadership, *see* CPC, proletarian leadership
property relations, *see* land ownership

Q

Qing Dynasty (1644–1911/2) 19, 50, 64, 67, 73, 74, 78, 80, 84, 89, 101, 115, 124, 125, 126–9, 131, 133, 135–7, 140, 153, 154, 163

R

Rawski, Evelyn 60, 47–8, 49–51, 53, 55, 56–7
Red Army 170, 198, 201, 203, 205, 227, 239, 307, 308, 309, 322
Red Spears 145, 146, 148, 200, 309, 312, 313, 315
reforms, reformers/'reformists' 101, 131, 158, 164
  class basis of 157–8
  failure and abandonment of 153–9
  Qing era 67, 101, 103, 126–9, 131, 133, 135–7
  Nationalist governments 153, 154, 156–8, 348
  Urban 153, 346
  remedialism 309, 318, 321–2, 337, 349
rent 9, 16, 18, 37–40, 42, 44, 50–7, 85, 87, 89, 99, 100, 118–22, 129–30, 133, 139–40, 157, 161, 163, 211, 220, 222, 226, 236, 271, 322, 340, 342, 345, 350
  absolute and differential 52, 133, 188
  fixed rent 47–8, 50, 57
  land speculation 36, 41, 62, 82, 83, 93, 155
  money rent 83, 90
  monopoly rent 52, 57, 101, 103–113, 122, 130, 133, 139, 149, 155, 163, 297, 341–3, 356
  regional variations in 43, 47
  rent deposits 47, 48, 51, 56, 57, 86, 138
  rent in kind 42, 48, 53, 54, 55–6, 57, 65–6, 74, 83, 84, 89, 92, 119, 137, 138, 162, 188, 341

rent increases 50, 297, 307
rent reductions 88, 156–7, 175–6, 184, 233, 244, 248, 264, 275, 289, 290, 298, 307, 316, 331, 353
share rent, 47–8, 162
see also feudalism; land reform policies, 'double reduction' policy
Republican China (1912–1949) 86
revolutionary process (upsurge and ebb) 2, 5, 7, 10, 12, 14–5, 19, 21, 24, 26, 168, 170, 174, 197, 199, 202, 239, 246, 317, 323, 332, 333, 339, 348, 350, 352, 352, 354, 356
Rightism 210, 237, 252, 258, 267
see also CPC, Right Opportunism
rural proletariat 35, 43, 114, 172, 215, 225, 232
rural protest 145, 153, 155, 305, 315, 352
   dissident gentry 19, 101, 143, 144, 150, 159, 164, 176, 312, 331
   divisions among peasants 147–9
   leadership 147, 164, 315
   limitations 149–50
   peasant survival strategies 110, 113, 148, 312, 315, 334
   predation and protection 148, 150, 314
   traditional patterns of resistance 7, 11, 71, 72, 91, 145, 146, 148, 175, 192, 264, 312–3, 330, 334, 339
Russia, Russian 3, 10, 11, 19, 99, 168, 169, 171, 172, 174, 177, 179, 182, 183, 190, 197, 198, 202, 203, 235, 239, 240, 306, 349–50, 350, 353, 358, 306, 360
   1905 revolution 172, 173–4, 197
   Bolshevik revolution 10, 19, 174, 183, 203, 208, 306
   Narodniks/neo-Narodniks 3, 26, 27, 99, 107, 158, 171–4, 221, 310, 351, 355

S

Saich, Anthony 191, 193
Schram, Stuart R. 190, 355
Scott, James C. 4, 6, 312, 358
secret societies and brotherhoods 71, 146, 200, 230, 264, 266, 304, 321, 330, 337
Selden, Mark 22, 244–5, 251, 261–72, 358
semi-colonialism 88, 91–4, 344
see also imperialism
semi-feudalism 91–3
see also feudalism
serfdom 8, 9, 60, 67, 74, 98, 105, 134, 136, 137, 341
see also feudalism
Shanghai 25, 36, 55, 56, 67, 78, 183, 185, 186, 236
Shanin, Teodor 26
Shanxi 281
Shen-Kan-Ning 261
sinification of Marxism, see Mao Zedong, sinification of Marxism
Skinner, G. William 5–6
Skocpol, Theda 348
Smith, Adam 99
socialism 3, 25, 27, 173, 182, 187, 203, 207, 254, 272, 284, 326, 329, 335, 336, 338, 350, 356, 357, 358, 359, 360
   see also Yan'an village programmes
soviet, soviet bases 10, 12, 20, 169, 173, 185, 186–7, 197, 198, 200–1, 203, 205, 207–9, 211, 212, 213–17, 219, 223, 224–27, 230, 232, 237, 248–51, 267

Stalin, Joseph 169, 183, 169, 183, 184, 185–7, 191–4, 309, 350, 356
  advocates 1924–7 CPC-KMT alliance 238
  analysis of national bourgeoisie 182–7
  on Chinese revolution 198–201, 208
    as compared to Russian Revolution 10, 182, 203, 239
    mistaken assessment of failure of 1927 revolution 20, 193, 233–5
    on stages of 193, 196–7, 203, 238
  criticises CPC 'errors' 183, 185, 189–91, 197, 204
  debate with Trotsky on United Front 20, 185–9, 196, 204
state (traditional) 17, 100, 163, 245
  bureaucratic system 2, 6, 8–9, 11, 15, 16, 17, 18, 22, 32–3, 60–4, 65, 74, 79, 91–2, 98, 100–1, 103, 105, 119, 124–38, 139, 147, 150–1, 153, 154, 155, 162, 169, 217, 224, 225, 232, 245, 252, 265, 320, 331, 341–2, 343, 349
  civil service 60, 61, 64, 131
  dualism (two-tier structure) 63, 74, 100, 127, 158, 252
  loss of political authority 6, 61, 78, 100, 126, 155, 339
  reform initiatives 84, 98, 125–8, 130, 131, 133–7, 153–6, 163, 164–5
  state-landlord relations 5, 18, 36, 60–1, 72–5, 101, 126, 127, 128, 131, 135, 136–8, 154, 164, 321, 340–3
  state-village relations 9, 18, 19, 100, 127, 128–9, 141, 154–6, 156–9, 245, 343
  traditional 'right to rebel' 143
  see also Confucianism; Qing Dynasty
state, revolutionary *see* New Democracy
Sun Yat-sen 175, 181

T

Taihang Mountains 264, 284, 320, 323, 324
Tawney, R.H. 6, 17–8, 32, 98–9, 103–112
taxation 9, 52, 61, 68, 71, 84, 86, 100, 125, 128
  exorbitant nature of 36
  landlord privileges 64, 70, 73, 89, 91, 101, 121, 135–6, 138–9
  tax avoidance 126, 139–40, 288
  tax officials, and *baojia* system 73–4, 89, 105, 141, 156, 307, 308, 309
  tax resistance 145, 146, 148, 153, 309, 312, 340
Ten Mile Inn 281–4, 287–8, 291–4, 296–300
  see also Crook, David; Crook, Isabel
tenancy, extent of 5, 16, 32, 34, 40, 41, 43, 44, 47–51, 54, 57, 65, 68, 80, 83, 86, 88, 92, 93, 104, 108, 118, 134, 156, 161, 177, 211, 263, 312, 316, 321, 359
Thaxton, Ralph 24, 150, 264, 305, 314, 315, 320–3, 324, 325, 326, 327, 330, 331, 332, 335, 338, 349, 358
towns, townships 7, 47, 53–4, 64, 72, 73, 83, 89, 104, 105, 127, 130, 133, 138–9, 141, 146, 149, 157, 158, 163, 171, 173, 177, 184, 185, 190, 191, 197, 198, 199, 200–1, 204, 207, 239, 250, 252, 258, 262, 281, 292, 314,

317, 321, 333, 336, 346, 347, 354, 355, 357, 358, 360, 361
Treaty Ports 55, 78, 79, 81, 83, 86, 106, 153
  see also imperialism
Trotsky, Leon 10, 12, 14, 169, 182, 197, 199, 212, 208, 218, 228, 238, 345, 350, 356
  on Chinese Revolution 196, 202–3, 338
  debate with Stalin on United Front 20, 185–8, 344
  on impact of foreign capital and class structure 186, 187–8, 344
  on national bourgeoisie 185–8
  rules out independent peasant movement 188
  on rural capitalism 244–5
  views on Canton Uprising 187

U

unequal exchange
  between town and countryside 190, 333, 346, 352
United Front 20, 21, 23, 64, 169, 181, 189, 192, 193, 197, 198, 236, 238, 244, 249, 258, 264, 266, 267, 269, 270–2, 274, 292
  international 78–9, 112
  First United Front (1924–7) 10, 181–5, 186, 185–7, 190, 193–4, 309
  Second United Front (1937–45) 10, 21, 22, 244, 246, 248–51, 269–72
urban working class 173, 181
usury 16, 37, 40, 41, 51, 56, 62, 65–6, 82, 92, 109, 110, 119–22, 135, 157, 161, 220, 222, 236, 237, 263, 281, 322, 341, 344, 345, 350

V

villages
  administration of (*baojia*) 73–4, 89, 105, 141, 156, 307, 308, 309
  economy, transformation of 245, 262, 265, 322, 324, 326, 333, 335, 339
  elections 27, 264, 270
  elites 15, 71, 91, 112, 128–9, 128–9, 139, 141, 154, 209, 211, 216, 220, 223, 234, 262, 310, 351, 331, 334, 338, 349, 352
  organisation of 5, 7, 68, 70, 71, 89, 127, 148, 176, 332, 340, 348
  power structure of 60, 68, 70, 71–2, 130, 147, 175, 176, 228, 231, 264, 281, 340, 349
  regional variation 5, 68–70
  self-government 156, 262
voluntarism 190, 268, 269, 272, 348, 355, 356

W

wage labour 4, 16, 40, 49, 66, 67, 88, 92, 116–22, 137, 220, 341, 344
  see also labour hiring
Wakeman, Frederic 63–4, 131
warlords 56, 78, 83, 84, 87, 91, 93, 175, 176, 181, 184, 188, 189, 191–2, 202, 233, 234, 236, 252, 307–9, 349
Warren, Bill 345
'White Terror' 20, 198, 209, 233
  see also Chiang Kai-shek; KMT
Wittfogel, Karl 61, 100, 124
  see also Oriental Despotism
Wolf, Eric 6, 24, 304, 305, 306, 310–11, 312, 313, 321, 322, 336
  see also middle peasant thesis
Womack, Brantly 356
Women's and Youth Associations

227, 264
worker-peasant alliance, 13, 20, 169, 172, 173, 174, 186, 187, 190, 200, 203, 234, 248, 308, 354
Wu Dakun 124, 135, 140, 141
Wuhan, *see* KMT, 'Left' KMT

Y
Yan'an 25, 236, 244, 251, 261, 271, 274, 324, 325, 326, 327, 336
Yan'an Way 263, 264, 265, 272
Yan'an village programmes 25, 263, 264, 271, 272, 336
    co-operatives, co-operative banks 272, 327
    production drive 261
    role of private sector 324–5, 326, 327
    socialist elements 326
    transformation of state-village relations 262–3
    see also mutual aid

Z
Zasulich, Vera 357
Zhang Weiwei 27
Zhou Enlai 14, 184, 192, 193, 196, 197, 204, 234, 235, 238, 239, 274, 280, 288, 292, 293
Zhu De 202
Zunyi Conference, *see* CPC, Zunyi Conference (1935)

www.ingramcontent.com/pod-product-compliance
Lightning Source LLC
Chambersburg PA
CBHW040746020526
44116CB00036B/2966